REVENGE

Also by Jonathan L. Bowen

Anticipation: The Real Life Story of Star Wars: Episode I—The Phantom Menace (iUniverse 2005)

The Categorical Imperative of a Confucian Evil Demon in America (iUniverse 2005)

"'Hokey Religions and Ancient Weapons': The Force of Spirituality" in *Finding the Force of the Star Wars Franchise: Fans, Merchandise, & Critics* (Peter Lang 2006)

REVENGE

The Real Life Story of Star Wars: Episode III—Revenge of the Sith

JONATHAN L. BOWEN
AUTHOR OF *ANTICIPATION:*
THE REAL LIFE STORY OF STAR WARS:
EPISODE I—THE PHANTOM MENACE

iUniverse, Inc.
New York Lincoln Shanghai

Revenge
The Real Life Story of Star Wars: Episode III—Revenge of the Sith

iUniverse books may be ordered through booksellers or by contacting:

iUniverse
2021 Pine Lake Road, Suite 100
Lincoln, NE 68512
www.iuniverse.com
1-800-Authors (1-800-288-4677)

Because of the dynamic nature of the Internet, any Web addresses or links contained in this book may have changed since publication and may no longer be valid.

The views expressed in this work are solely those of the author and do not necessarily reflect the views of the publisher, and the publisher hereby disclaims any responsibility for them.

ISBN: 978-0-595-42923-3 (pbk)
ISBN: 978-0-595-87533-7 (cloth)
ISBN: 978-0-595-87262-6 (ebk)

Printed in the United States of America

For my mom, Janet Elaine Bowen, who attended the first three Celebrations with me and always supported my *Star Wars* collecting habit. She gave me support with everything I have done in life, and I would never have become the person I am today without her. My mom lost her battle with breast cancer on October 15, 2006.

Contents

Preface

When I first thought of writing a *Star Wars* history book, *The Phantom Menace* was more than six months from reaching theater screens and Lucas had only told half the *Star Wars* story to audiences. In the intervening years, much has happened in the *Star Wars* universe and in the fan base. The divide between fans who favored the *Special Edition* changes to the Original Trilogy and those who did not, the "purists" as many have called them, hardly seems significant compared to the rift between fans that has occurred with the prequels. One group appreciates and enjoys the prequels while the other has blasted Lucas personally and professionally for his return to the galaxy far, far away. Most fans fall somewhere between hatred and adoration, though even fans with moderate opinions feud with one another over perceived shortcomings in the films.

On message boards around the Internet, I found myself embroiled in the battle between prequel enthusiasts and prequel detractors. While at times the war of words is a simple matter of expressing opinions over the films and their various details, the rift in fandom has created a professional problem for me as well. I received one rejection letter from a major publisher for my first book because the editor did not feel I represented the voice of the fans and was not "objective" in my account of the release of *The Phantom Menace* in my first book, *Anticipation*.

I could not have provided more facts, figures, and statistics in support of the information I gave in *Anticipation*, yet media perception remains that despite all of the incredible proof otherwise, most fans strongly disliked or hated the first prequel. One publishing company informed me that it saw my book appealing to a "small audience of die-hard fans," though the small audience to which the editorial staff referred is the same massive group that has made *Star Wars* the most profitable movie franchise in history.

The challenge of trying to write *Star Wars* history books, as has become a niche of mine that I wish to continue into the future, is giving voice to all types of fans, not just the supporters and not just the detractors. I make no apologies for being a supporter of the prequels, and a lover of the entire saga, yet I also believe in objectively recording the areas in which *Star Wars* faltered either commercially or with fans. Nonetheless, when I set out to write *Anticipation*, my goal was to write a positive book that put the film's incredible accomplishments into perspective for current and future generations of film enthusiasts. I still believe *The Phantom Menace* is one of the most significant film events in motion picture history.

Another challenge I faced with both *Anticipation* and *Revenge* was the level of detail to include in the books to satisfy hardcore *Star Wars* fans but not bore casual readers. Although I strive to make my books readable to a wide audience, using terminology that casual readers can understand, I am ultimately writing for serious *Star Wars* fans. I have included extensive detail about the box office success of *Revenge of the Sith*, for instance, not all of which will interest many readers. Having posted to message boards online with hundreds of box office enthusiasts, however, I felt inclined to give readers as much information as possible about the final prequel's success both in North America and internationally. I would rather include too much information than not enough. Readers are free to skim sections that do not interest them, but if the information is absent entirely, the book would be incomplete and my fellow box office enthusiasts would be disappointed.

While writing *Anticipation*, I began to consider that I could write a trilogy of books, one for each *Star Wars* prequel. I have included a preface to this book partially because of my decision not to write a book about *Star Wars: Episode II—Attack of the Clones*. While I enjoyed the film immensely and watched it repeatedly in theaters, it did not change the way movies were made and marketed as much as *A New Hope* had done in 1977 and *The Phantom Menace* had done in 1999. It still was a huge film event, and like all *Star Wars* movies it pioneered new technology and became a massive commercial success. Unfortunately, though, its box office grosses were not indicative of the global popularity of the *Star Wars* franchise, nor was the hype surrounding the film particularly impressive. I did not believe I could write a significantly long and in-depth book about the film that was different enough from my first book to appeal to readers.

I was even skeptical about whether *Revenge of the Sith* would warrant a book because I had become convinced that *The Phantom Menace* was such a rare event in the movie industry that it could not be duplicated or even approximated any time soon, let alone by the same franchise. The immense anticipation, marketing, hype, enthusiasm, and expectations for *Revenge of the Sith* proved me completely wrong. *Revenge of the Sith* is a defining film because it bridges the gap between the first two prequels and the Original Trilogy in such a successful way, for most fans, that it forces a re-evaluation of both the earlier prequels and the classic films. Aside from its merits artistically, *Revenge of the Sith* was a phenomenon of its own, with a massive marketing campaign and promotional tie-in bonanza rarely seen even by other huge blockbusters. It also generated impressive box office grosses and licensing revenue records to match its hype.

When I first envisioned becoming a non-fiction *Star Wars* author, I wanted to tell the history of the *Star Wars* franchise from where Garry Jenkins's *Empire Building* (Carol Publishing Group 1997) ended. To that end, I started my first book with a brief history of *Star Wars* in the early 1990s and its resurgence through the *Special Edition* releases. Similarly, though this book's title suggests it focuses merely on *Revenge of the Sith*, I will bring readers up to date on the events between *The Phantom Menace*'s release to DVD and the start of production on *Revenge of the Sith*, before focusing on the events and records that made the final prequel a landmark film. Thus, the first several chapters focus on *Attack of the Clones*, the *Star Wars: Clone Wars* cartoon series, and the Original Trilogy's long-awaited release to DVD.

I hope readers will find the story of *Star Wars* from 2001 through 2005 as exciting and amazing as I have. For long-time fans, perhaps this book will serve as both a nostalgic reminder of an exciting period of fandom and an illuminating analysis of a major cultural event. For film enthusiasts in general, I hope to place *Revenge of the Sith* in context of early twenty-first century filmmaking and mar-keting, demonstrating how it both represented and redefined the power and influence of blockbuster movies. For *Star Wars* fans fatigued and annoyed by all of the critics, skeptics, naysayers, and cynics who thought *Star Wars* was dead or that the franchise had lost its luster, 2005 was nothing short of sweet revenge.

Attack of the Media

A Certain Point of View

After numerous popular "Expanded Universe" novels such as *Heir to the Empire* and its sequels by Timothy Zahn had broadened the franchise's story in book form, *The Phantom Menace* successfully restarted the *Star Wars* franchise in the film medium. Fans had three years to wait between the first prequel and its sequel, *Attack of the Clones*. Despite a massive worldwide box office gross of $924.3 million, with $431.1 million from just North America, *The Phantom Menace* suffered from a strong backlash by a large minority of disheartened fans, mostly in their late twenties and thirties. The critical and fan reaction to *Attack of the Clones*, to say nothing of the media's continuing bias against the prequels, is even more confusing to examine than that of its predecessor. While fans embraced the second prequel upon release, the media continued to spread the message that it was bitterly detested or disappointing, though critics gave it generally positive reviews.

Attack of the Clones brought out a minority crowd of detractors in the media who wished to make themselves the majority, voicing opinions as definitely as facts and proclaiming that *The Phantom Menace* had been a huge disappointment and that everyone hated it. None of the facts supported such sweeping statements, nor were most people displeased with the first prequel. *The Phantom Menace* was a divisive film in many respects when it came to theaters because it was unlike any *Star Wars* movie at the time insofar as it showed viewers mostly new locations and a murkier, more subtle plot with less clearly defined heroes and villains.

Upon its release to theaters, *The Phantom Menace* required patience from viewers to see how the entire story transpired over the course of the prequels. Like all of the entries, the first prequel relies on the complete saga for much of its richness. Instead of taking a patient approach to judging the movie, many people felt compelled to measure it against the entire Original Trilogy and thus proclaimed it a massive disappointment for reasons ranging from Anakin being too young to Lucas focusing too much on politics and trying too hard to add comic relief.

By the time *Attack of the Clones* opened in theaters, the vast majority of reviews and media articles mentioned the overwhelming disappointment that fans supposedly had over *The Phantom Menace* because of its lousy quality, but the writers were quick to mention that everyone hoped for more with the second prequel. Many critics and journalists mentioned how the second prequel was a big improvement from its predecessor, even while they noted that *The Phantom Menace* had lowered everyone's expectations. Whatever the reality, most fans were eager to see Lucas's next installment, either hoping it would vindicate the first prequel or that it would continue its success.

Regardless of its apparent triumph over its predecessor, *Attack of the Clones* suffered the same criticisms from media writers as had the first prequel by the time three years had passed. By 2005, the media proclaimed that everyone hated both prequels, that they were huge disappointments, and that they were boring, incoherent movies loaded with political dialogue and complexity, yet were ultimately plotless kids' movies with poor dialogue. One wonders how a movie can at once be political and overly complicated, but also too childish with simplistic dialogue and too many special effects, though writers making such comments usually offered little argumentative support for their views.

Before any discussion of *Revenge of the Sith* and its success can commence, the lies and misinformation as well as the poor reporting and disgusting bias that surrounded the first two *Star Wars* prequels deserve a thorough examination with facts and data that, unlike opinions, cannot be refuted. Below is a sample of media comments that suggest widespread or at least disproportionate disappointment with the first two prequels:

- "But even [Lucas's] most ardent acolytes must have found themselves losing faith as 1999's *The Phantom Menace* (pure gibberish) begat 2002's *Attack of the Clones* (a slight improvement) …"—Charlotte O'Sullivan, *The Evening Standard* (London)

- "After 16 years away from the saga, Lucas returned in 1999 with 'The Phantom Menace,' a movie that managed to make nearly a billion dollars in spite of the fact that nobody seemed to like it very much."—Bruce Newman, *San Jose Mercury News*

- "*The Phantom Menace* … was *not* the second coming *Star Wars* fans had been pining for."—Jeff Jensen, *Entertainment Weekly*

- "Unlike the last two 'Star Wars' movies, which many fans considered a disappointment, 'Sith' has a strong positive buzz on the Internet."—Phil Kloer, *Atlanta Journal and Constitution*

- "… with episodes *I* and *II*, [Lucas] disappointed [fans] again, by going heavy on the exposition and goofiness."—Tom Roston, *Premiere* magazine

- "… there is a disturbance in the Force, and it's called *The prequels have stunk like bantha poodoo*. Excitement for *Sith* is palpable here at Celebration [III], but in the wake of *Episode I—The Phantom Menace* and *Episode II—Attack of the Clones*, it is tempered by a wariness that has resulted from unmet expectations, mostly among adults for whom the original trilogy is something of a sacred experience."—Jeff Labrecque, *Entertainment Weekly*

- "… no one was hurt more by the 'Menace' than Lucas's tireless legion of fans. Forget about money. They lost their faith."—John Horn, *Newsweek*

The media claimed fans were hugely disappointed with the two prequels Lucas had released before 2005, the first of which already enjoyed a proper defense in *Anticipation*, my first book. The facts show that *Attack of the Clones* is in similar need of an objective defense, however. TheForce.net, the largest *Star Wars* fan site, asked its visitors in a poll that started in November 2002, "Did AOTC [*Attack of the Clones*] meet your expectations?" Of more than fifty-five thousand responses, 69 percent said the film was "Better than I expected," 21 percent said it was "Just what I expected," and only 7 percent said it was "Worse than I expected" ("Did …").

Maybe fans had low expectations after a disappointing first prequel, the media might reason, but the results of another poll confirm fan approval. When asked in another poll on TheForce.net, "What did you think of AOTC?" 53 percent of fans responded that it was "Excellent," another 28 percent "Very Good," and 9 percent "Good," while just over 7 percent called it "Ok," "Mediocre," "Poor," or "Terrible," which by any measurement is a tiny minority ("What did …"). Because the poll began two months after the movie's release, the results were unlikely to be influenced too much by emotional reactions from fans returning from midnight showings or long line waits. Additionally, moviegoers polled by CinemaScore, which tracks audience sentiment toward new releases, gave the second prequel an "A–," with people under twenty-one giving it an "A" (Pandya "… May 17–19").

As for the myth that fans consider both prequels well below the stellar originals, only a little research also reveals the media has not reported fans' opinions

correctly on the order of rank of the films, either. In another poll on
TheForce.net that started in April 2003, allowing enough time for fans to have
more analytical, less emotional reactions, the site asked fans, "Now that you've
seen AOTC, where does it rate in the saga?" With more than forty-two thousand
votes, an astonishing 21 percent of fans called it the best, 30 percent the second
best, 27 percent third, 15 percent fourth, and only 3 percent said it was the worst
of the films ("Now …").

In a comparable poll relating to the rank of *Attack of the Clones* conducted on
the Official *Star Wars* Web Site (starwars.com) in mid-May 2002, 36 percent of
fans ranked the movie first, 30 percent second, 20 percent third, 11 percent
fourth, and only 3 percent last ("Where …"). The starwars.com poll probably
skewed more positively toward *Attack of the Clones* because of the enthusiasm fans
had over the newly released entry in the saga, but TheForce.net's poll took place
nearly a year after the release of the film. Because of TheForce.net's later polling
date, the results are more convincing with fans having had plenty of time to form
rational opinions about the movie.

Many readers might believe that perhaps the media was wrong about the fans'
opinions, but maybe journalists and writers are right to say that critics hated the
first two prequels, as Lesley Stahl said to Lucas during her *60 Minutes* interview
with him in March 2005. Checking RottenTomatoes.com gives the best general
idea of critical opinions about a film because the site displays dozens and sometimes hundreds of reviews from professional critics nationwide in magazines and
newspapers alongside amateur critics running review sites online. A quick glance
of *Rotten Tomatoes* at the time of release for *Revenge of the Sith* revealed that 62
percent of critics gave *The Phantom Menace* a positive review while 65 percent of
critics approved of *Attack of the Clones*. Neither percentage is high enough to say
that critics loved the first two prequels, but neither are they low enough to indicate critical disdain for the films.

The most frustrating criticism of *Attack of the Clones*, which most critics and a
fair number of fans voiced, was the love story dialogue, especially Hayden Christensen's acting in the scenes in question and his romantic dialogue. In one notable line, Anakin tells Padmé, "I don't like sand. It's coarse and rough and
irritating, and it gets everywhere. Not like you. You're everything soft, and
smooth." It is a terrible pickup line, but what is most incredible is not the silliness
of the line; it is the silliness of people who think Lucas was trying to write a great
romantic line and just failed miserably. They never seem to consider that maybe
Lucas wanted Anakin to come across as awkward, clumsy, and unskilled with
women.

In science and philosophy, Occam's Razor is a simple guideline, a commandment never to multiply explanations or make them more complicated than necessary. Applied to film criticism, assuming that in a major feature film each significant element of every scene is intentional is the most logical, most intuitive explanation. To assume instead that Lucas unwittingly wrote a terrible line of dialogue that stands out like an ignited lightsaber in a dark room, then nobody noticed it was bad, nobody spoke of it on the set, and Jonathan Hales, who Lucas summoned to help with the screenplay, never made changes is to assume a ridiculously absurd, illogical set of events. Instead, assume the obvious: Anakin, who has sworn as a Jedi not to have romantic relationships, lacks experience with women and, like most teenagers around beautiful girls, is tongue-tied and uncomfortable.

If instead of his awkward line about sand, Anakin started speaking Shakespearian dialogue about love, the effect would be jolting and unrealistic. How could someone with no experience in love have just the right line to deliver? A number of screenwriters come up with great dialogue throughout a script, but because each line sounds carefully considered and crafted, the general effect is unrealistic conversation between characters who never could have conceived of such witty remarks and insight in casual conversation. In other words, the dialogue is contrived.

Many people might argue that film dialogue need not mirror reality because film is fictional and idealized, which is a valid viewpoint, but not one that Lucas shares,[1] nor one that he should adopt just to suit critics or fans. Instead, Lucas aims for more realistic dialogue that tries to capture characters' natural reactions within the context of the scene. Contrary to prevailing critical opinion, when most people speak, they do not deliver elegant, beautiful lines, nor do Lucas's characters much of the time.

Sometimes, even the best critics make mistakes and misjudge films based on biased viewpoints and improper criteria. *Star Wars* has often suffered from such oversights because it is not a conventional film series. The opening crawls are reminiscent of serials from ages past, the symphony scores are more traditional than modern, and the acting emphasizes realism of character over idealization. For instance, in the first prequel, critics complained about Anakin shouting, "Yippee!" One innocent word, from a nine-year-old character, elicited the wrath

---

1.   As an example, consider his idea of a "lived in" universe with partially damaged spacecraft and elements of each location that suggest a history before the film's events.

of film critics and many fans who apparently forgot that kids often utter silly sayings and words. Likewise, critics blasted Natalie Portman for acting stiff, though her performance was supposed to be regal and unemotional, which one could call "stiff," because she was portraying royalty as Queen Amidala.

With *Attack of the Clones*, critics continued to show an inability to understand different types of acting, insisting instead that if performances did not match their preconceived expectations of how characters should be, the performers must be at fault. Christensen took a great deal of criticism for his acting style, which prompted a poignant response from the young actor three years later before the final prequel. He said, "I recall reading the script and saying to George, 'If I play Anakin as on the page—the whiny teenage quality—there's going to be a backlash.' And there was. But the critics got it wrong. Sometimes they were blasting me for Anakin's flaws" (Lyttle). Lucas agreed, saying, "Hayden is an extremely talented actor, but I had him play the whiny teenager. He really hated it, but I think he did a good job" (Koltnow).

Christensen ultimately did not harbor any frustration with Lucas for his decisions, though. He said, "George hired me to do a job, and if George is happy with the performance, then I'm happy with the performance" (Koltnow). He indicated that he much preferred playing the older, darker Anakin in *Revenge of the Sith*, but added, "Still, I defend the character I played in the last one because it was necessary to inform the decisions that Anakin would make later." With a trilogy of films to show the maturation of Anakin's character from a young boy to a mature but power-hungry adult, Lucas had the creative freedom to demonstrate character growth across a greater stretch of time than most filmmakers have on a single project.

As a result of most critics' lack of insight into the characters and their attributes, many of the "improvements" that they saw in the acting over the course of the prequels[2] were examples of character development, not improved acting. Judging acting and the ability of a director to work with actors without any concern for the filmmaker's intent regarding the characters' attributes is a huge mistake that will inevitably lead to unwarranted criticisms. Fans and critics have every right as moviegoers to feel that Lucas improperly portrayed Anakin in *Attack of the Clones*, or that Lucas should have written the love scenes to resemble *Romeo and Juliet*, but the important point is to be able to differentiate poor acting and bad writing from creative decisions and stylistic preferences.

---

2.   Such as Portman from the first to the second prequel and Christensen from the second to third.

To accuse Lucas of not being able to write and Christensen of not being able to act is to confuse conscious creative decisions with inept filmmaking, which is uninformed and ultimately wrong. The task of screenwriters when dealing with characters is to portray them in the script as intended in the mind and write dialogue to show a character's individuality and personality within the context of a specific situation. Subsequently, good acting is the ability of a performer to convey the writer's intent for the character and deliver the dialogue in a way the director desires to bring the script to life for audiences.

Lucas, as both writer and director for the prequels, told Christensen to act like a whiny, petulant teenager, so any criticism of Christensen's acting in the film using such terminology is invalid because the actor's job is only to play the role as the director instructs. Any criticisms of Christensen's acting must be based on his inability to meet Lucas's demands and criteria, *not* the critical or fan ideal for how the character should act, which is irrelevant to such qualitative judgments. Similarly, from a writing perspective, for Lucas to be deemed an incompetent writer, one would have to know that Lucas intended Anakin to be a confident, mature young man with great wisdom in romance and extreme patience, yet the script and dialogue make him look just the opposite. If one disagrees with Lucas's character decisions, he should be called a poor storyteller and not a poor writer.

If Lucas intended Anakin to be confident and mature, the resulting writing would demonstrate a poor effort because the intent of the screenwriter would be incongruent with the finished script. Instead, though, Lucas intended Anakin to be awkward romantically, impatient, and whiny, all of which many critics agreed he embodied in the prequel. So, unknowingly, most of the critics praised the execution of Lucas's writing and directing, they merely disagreed with the creative choices he made. "I have to make the movie that I see.... I tell a story my way, and hopefully, people like it. But if they don't, they don't have to listen to it," Lucas told the media (Pols). Although many criticisms of the first two prequels sounded similar, the scale of the hype for the two movies differed greatly.

Limited Merchandising *Attack*

One element of *The Phantom Menace*'s release that Lucasfilm tried to remedy with *Attack of the Clones* was the massive marketing and tie-in campaigns that surrounded the first prequel. With such an important and anticipated event as the first *Star Wars* movie in sixteen years, dozens of licensees wanted to promote their brands alongside the saga's newest entry, but problems arose when many of the companies overproduced merchandise. The licensees had signed such lucrative deals that they had no choice but to produce huge numbers of products, which in the end was too much for the marketplace to bear. Even with its record-setting $2 billion in revenue from merchandise, *The Phantom Menace* disappointed many licensees involved because not everyone wanted ten different beach towels or eight new *Star Wars* T-shirts (Nesbitt).

The retailers suffered the worst from the flood of merchandise, however, as they were often stuck with mass amounts of inventory that they had to discount after the hype subsided. "Last time, they just shipped too much. After a few months, retailers had to put a deep discount on [the products] and still couldn't move them," said Dave Gerardi, senior editor of *Playthings*, a toy industry magazine (ibid.). The massive quantity of items thrown onto the market gave many media writers the impression that *The Phantom Menace* had generated disappointing interest among consumers, or that fan backlash led to poor sales.

In reality, sales of products relating to *The Phantom Menace* and *Star Wars* in general for 1999 were extraordinary, which is to say sales bested any other film in history for such a short period in the number of dollars generated. Unfortunately, the unrealistic expectations that many of the companies had, created by the unprecedented hype, left many products unsold. "A lot of people got carried away with the hype before the film came out. It was overproliferated, and we've tried to learn a lot of lessons from that," said Howard Roffman, president of Lucas Licensing (Dedrick). According to *Newsweek*, which claimed to have obtained a confidential marketing pitch to Hasbro dealers about the second prequel, Lucasfilm considered the biggest blunder on the first prequel to be its excessive merchandising tie-ins.

The promotional tie-ins and licensee-generated hype, when combined with fan anticipation and rampant media hype, led to excessive exposure for *The Phantom Menace*, at least for many casual onlookers. "Licensing and merchandising is a very important part of the process. The companies involved often spend millions of dollars to promote their products, which adds to the event status of the film and becomes another layer of the marketing," said John Scott, director of marketing for Fox Film Distributors (Groves). With all of the prequels, Lucasfilm faced a challenge balancing the level of hype from numerous sources, including the media, licensees' ads and products, fan excitement and consequent word of mouth, and paid studio advertising.

For *Attack of the Clones*, Lucasfilm wanted to keep a lower profile, as much as is possible with a *Star Wars* film, not only by slashing the number of promotional partners but keeping a firmer grasp on the number of products released to the public. "We've scaled it back a lot. We're going to stick to the basics, toys, video games ... the things our fans prefer, rather than some of the fringe items," said

Roffman (Nesbitt). The company reduced the number of promotional partners from around eighty-five to about fifty. In Australia, *The Phantom Menace* had fifty companies producing goods for the prequel, but in 2002, Lucasfilm cut the number to just twenty for the middle film in the trilogy (Groves).

Lucasfilm, retailers, and even cast members agreed that marketing went overboard for the first prequel. John Reilly, a spokesman for KB Toys in Pittsfield, Massachusetts, said, "The licensing just exploded the last time. It was on everything, and I think there was a feeling that they overdid it. I like the way they're doing it this time. It's a lot cleaner" (Ascenzi). Portman agreed, telling *Entertainment Weekly* just before the release of the second prequel, "Personally, I'm glad not to be promoting Kentucky Fried Chicken anymore. That *really* wasn't the highlight of my moral life" (Jensen "Plan ...").

Despite a reduced product line, fans could buy numerous *Star Wars*–related items, like bandages from Curad, trading cards from Topps, *Episode II* cereal from General Mills, and snacks from Frito-Lay. Nokia also offered mobile phone customers content from a galaxy far, far away, with special graphics, ringtones, and games. Among the most popular toy products were Jango Fett and Yoda action figures. "The one that is hugely in demand that we may have underestimated a little bit is Yoda. Some of it has to do with not realizing what widespread awareness there would be. Clearly the fans seem to know that Yoda does some unusual things in this film," Roffman said (Dedrick). Jango Fett was the early best-selling action figure, despite Yoda's popularity.

The scaled-back marketing efforts from Lucasfilm combined with the reduced hype because of the shorter wait period between *Star Wars* movies, sixteen years with *The Phantom Menace* but only three for *Attack of the Clones*, led to reduced media coverage. Still, to say that the second prequel arrived under the radar would be silly, though it admittedly seemed much more like just a major blockbuster than a phenomenon. Despite many magazines that had placed the first prequel on their covers not doing so with the second, *Time* put Yoda on the cover of its April 29 issue with the headline, "Yoda Strikes Back!" Hayden Christensen also made numerous covers, including *Teen Vogue*'s Spring 2002 issue with actress James (Jamie) King and *Tiger Beat* magazine in May 2002.

Christensen shared many covers with Natalie Portman, like *Entertainment Weekly*'s April 12 issue and again for one of two May 17 covers of the publication, in addition to a cover appearance for *Teen People*'s June/July 2002 issue with both stars featured in "The 25 Hottest Stars Under 25." Portman appeared on the cover of *Allure*'s June 2002 issue as well. Christensen and Portman made numerous covers worldwide, like the Norwegian teen magazine *Topp*, Singapore's *Lime* magazine, *Premiere*'s Czech version, and *Vanity Fair*'s March issue. Although the prequel did not dominate every magazine cover as its predecessor had in 1999, it still managed to generate significant attention.

Purely Digital

Attack of the Clones was not a threat to steal *The Phantom Menace*'s title as the most anticipated movie ever, but it did offer several noteworthy technological innovations. The most significant technical achievement for *Attack of the Clones* was Lucas's use of the HDW-F900 from Sony and Panavision, a high-definition (HD) digital camera capable of providing crystal clear images rivaling 35mm film. The prequel was the first major movie ever shot entirely with HD digital cameras, a move that industry observers considered a landmark in the technological progression of the movie industry toward the digital age; *The Phantom Menace* had taken the first step, with digital projection. Lucas had initiated the development of an HD digital camera for filming applications in 1996, before filming started on the first prequel.

In the partnership with Sony, Lucas worked closely with Sony Engineering in Japan to perfect HD cameras capable of shooting at twenty-four frames per second. Previously, digital video cameras ran at broadcast standards of more like thirty frames per second or higher, which does not duplicate the look of typical films projected in theaters (Duncan, "Love ..." 62). Panavision entered into the partnership by developing two zoom lenses to work with the new cameras, which also provided a sense of familiarity for the camera operators using the new digital equipment. Fred Meyers, high-definition supervisor working for ILM as a technical liaison with Sony and Panavision, said of the Panavision contributions, "If we were going to take a film camera away from the DP [director of photography] and the camera operator and replace it with this digital camera, it was essential that we give them accessories they were familiar with" (62).

In all, six prototype HD digital cameras served Lucasfilm well on the set of *Attack of the Clones*, working better than anyone had expected and reducing shoot times significantly by eliminating the need to reload the camera. "We had absolutely not a single problem with the cameras at all," said Producer Rick McCallum (McGorry). The crew did not even include a camera mechanic for the desert shoots, which is rare for a major film in harsh conditions. The stored digital footage eventually used up 3.5 terabytes of data storage space. Lucas could quickly view any dailies, though, at a moment's notice. "The ILM engineers came up with a video server system and a way of viewing dailies where, on a computer, they would call up any shot George wanted to see for dailies in the morning," said McCallum (ibid.).

In *Attack of the Clones*, the most famous sequence of the movie quickly became Yoda's fight with Count Dooku, where moviegoers finally had the opportunity to see why Yoda is truly the greatest Jedi Master. For the second prequel, Lucasfilm made the tough decision to animate Yoda, in other words making him a digital character, for the first time ever; Lucas had chosen to use a puppet in *The Phantom Menace*. Ironically, the digital Yoda of the second prequel looks far more like the character seen in the Original Trilogy than *The Phantom Menace* puppet ever did.[3] Animator Rob Coleman faced a daunting task in trying to convince fans that Yoda could maintain his classic appeal as a digital character, though.

The toughest part about animating Yoda was making sure his movements, including eyes, facial expressions, and lips, matched the puppet from the Original Trilogy. "Early on, Frank Oz [the puppeteer behind Yoda] had warned me, 'You guys have too *much* potential'—meaning we could do things with a digital Yoda that Frank could never do," said Coleman (Duncan, "Love ..." 68). Hair and clothing movements also further complicated the ILM animators' jobs. Despite the challenges, ILM enjoyed such success with digital Yoda that Frank Oz felt moved to write Coleman a letter of praise after seeing the final character in the movie (ibid.).

Rob Coleman spent a year imagining and planning the fight choreography for Yoda's duel, though the battle is shorter than other duels in the saga. "I remember being worried when I first read about the fight in the script. It took over a year of constantly thinking about it and talking to George about it before I could get my head around the idea of an eight-hundred-year-old Yoda engaging in this very physical fight," said Coleman (Duncan, "Love ..." 117). Many of the animators agreed, initially unsure of how well the fight would fit with the character, but they envisioned Yoda pulling together enough strength to mount an impressive battle. Fans often laughed in theaters at Yoda moving around like a rabid animal, then reaching for his cane soon after combat, a nice touch from the animation team.

After struggling with how to use and apply many new technologies on *The Phantom Menace*, a movie that advanced special effects technology drastically, Lucas enjoyed a smoother process for the second prequel. With full command of

---

3. A few fans have affectionately called Yoda from *The Phantom Menace* "Stoned Yoda" because of his strange eyes and facial expressions that do not match up with the Original Trilogy puppet.

his new digital tools, Lucas commanded a team of talented artists able to help him put his vision on screen and tackle new challenges with *Attack of the Clones*, especially with increasingly complicated character animation. Lucas said, *"Attack of the Clones* was like a smooth-running car. I didn't have to think about the engine; all I had to do was get the story from Point A to Point B" (Duncan, "Love …" 119). Once he completed his story, fans lined up at theaters to see the results.

No Clone of *Phantom*

In the three years since *The Phantom Menace* premiered in theaters, much had changed in the industry in little time. Instead of the traditional slower rollouts of movies across many months throughout the world, studios increasingly desired to open their films worldwide simultaneously, or at least in as many countries as possible as quickly as possible. Studios figure that they can cut into piracy by releasing a film worldwide at roughly the same time, but also the sooner studios can make back their investments, the sooner they can put the money to use for future projects. Additionally, worldwide marketing is often easier to coordinate, though not always. One challenge for studios is to make enough prints available at the same time with all of the proper dubbing and subtitling, which is difficult because it requires coordination between the creative team making the movie and the studio's marketing branches worldwide.

Attack of the Clones enjoyed the largest worldwide release in history at the time, opening in seventy-four territories globally, including almost all of Europe, Australia, New Zealand, and most of Southeast Asia. A number of countries like Japan, South Korea, Mexico, Argentina, and Brazil still had to wait a few weeks, though. In all, the movie grossed $66.7 million overseas from various three-day and four-day opening frames. The simultaneous worldwide release made Lucasfilm's job a bit tougher because ILM had to create twenty-two versions of the opening crawl for international prints and prepare subtitles and dubbing in numerous languages by the time the film was ready for its North American release (Blake).

To complete the process, ILM had to lock reels starting in January, or in other words the visual footage had to be declared finished for at least the first few reels to start a dialogue list (Blake). From the dialogue list, each individual territory could create initial dubs to take advantage of the skills of native speakers, with various tweaks to the language to fit cultural understandings of terminology and phrases. Mixing took place back at Skywalker Ranch in California, where Skywalker Sound had to finish eighteen dubbed versions by May 2, necessitating the simultaneous running of five stages (Blake).

In North America, the prequel grossed a three-day total of $80,027,814 and a four-day total of $110,169,231. Its biggest day was Saturday, with $31,253,618, a higher total than its opening day, which was unusual for a *Star Wars* movie, given the huge national audience of die-hard fans who saw the movies at midnight upon their openings. The strong Saturday gross indicated it had nice crossover appeal to families and mainstream moviegoers. The second prequel's $30,141,417 total for opening day bested *The Phantom Menace* by only a small margin, though its four-day opening was bigger than the first prequel's gross from its five-day opening ($105.7 million).

With its three-day opening figure, *Attack of the Clones* ranked third on the all-time list of best weekend openings, well behind *Spider-Man*'s $114.8 million just weeks earlier and a bit behind *Harry Potter and the Sorcerer's Stone* (2001) with $90.3 million. Both films premiered on a Friday, though, and *Attack of the Clones* spread its audience over four days, not three, making the opening record tougher to obtain. Additionally, the prequel played on an estimated 6,000 screens, compared to 7,500 for *Spider-Man* and 8,100 for *Harry Potter*, so theaters were much busier for the prequel than for *Harry Potter*, though *Spider-Man*'s amazing numbers could not be toppled.

Because of the monstrous opening of *Spider-Man*, which was the first film ever to gross more than $100 million in just three days, a feat it accomplished easily, *Attack of the Clones* had the unfortunate position of competing with another phenomenon that had just opened three weeks earlier. Expectations, as a result, were much higher than the prequel could manage to meet, despite strong fan presence and positive buzz among moviegoers. Aside from its massive opening, *Spider-Man* showed staying power unlike most movies of its type, exhibiting remarkable crossover appeal to moviegoers of all ages and both genders. The opening of Lucas's middle prequel only dropped *Spider-Man*'s third-weekend gross by 36.9 percent compared to the prior weekend, to a still-strong $45.0 million. *The Phantom Menace* had faced stiff competition throughout a robust summer in 1999, but not until several weeks after its opening; it played almost unopposed for its first few weekends. *Attack of the Clones* did not enjoy such a luxury.

Attack of the Clones held fairly strong during its second weekend, which was Memorial Day Weekend. Falling 40.2 percent, the prequel grossed $47.9 million for the three-day portion of the weekend and $60.0 million for all four days, Friday through Monday. In the process, the prequel became the second-fastest film to gross $200 million, behind *Spider-Man*. Despite a much stronger first four days than *The Phantom Menace, Attack of the Clones* already fell behind pace after Memorial Day Weekend, grossing less during the four-day frame than its predecessor. The prequel suffered worse falls in the weeks ahead, failing to meet the high standards that analysts and fans expected of *Star Wars* movies, though it achieved a massive gross by normal blockbuster standards.

With *The Sum of All Fears* opening strong on the third weekend for *Attack of the Clones*, and without the benefit of a holiday, the prequel took a rough hit, falling 56.1 percent to $21.0 million, below the total *The Phantom Menace* made on its *fourth* weekend. Fortunately, the second prequel stabilized a bit afterwards, with only a 33.3 percent decline on its fourth weekend to $14.0 million. It fell about the same percentage in its fifth weekend, to $9.4 million. Eventually, the prequel ended its primary release on November 3 with $302,191,252, making it the eleventh highest grossing movie ever, though it broke several *Star Wars* traditions. Every previous film in the franchise had become one of the three highest grossing movies of all time upon first release and each had also won its respective year at the box office; *Attack of the Clones* finished third behind both *Spider-Man* ($403.7 million) and *The Lord of the Rings: The Two Towers* ($339.8 million).

For fans fortunate enough to have access to a digital theater, *Attack of the Clones* showed on ninety-four screens worldwide, courtesy of Texas Instruments' DLP Cinema projection technology. The digital versions never touched film at all. Lucas shot the movie digitally and Lucasfilm edited the footage digitally, so fans seeing the movie digitally projected were seeing the movie in its purest form. "If you actually want to see the film we made and see it in the way in which we want you to see it then the only way you can do that is digitally," said Rick McCallum ("Texas Instruments ..."). Hollywood trade paper *Variety* reported that theaters showing the movie digitally also enjoyed better box office results.

In all, sixty-one theaters in North America showed the prequel both digitally and conventionally, using film. On conventional screens, the prequel fell 47 percent from its first to second weekend in the locations tracked, 64 percent the next weekend, and 38 percent for the fourth weekend (DiOrio "'Clones' ..."). On the digital screens, however, the declines were much more modest at 28 percent, 45 percent, and 30 percent, respectively (ibid.). "It's become rather dramatic as the weeks have gone on. This is the wave of the future for this company and for the industry," said Fox Domestic Distribution President Bruce Snyder (ibid.). *Variety* estimated that the digital performance of *Attack of the Clones* "exceeded any industry norm." *Star Wars* fans are likely a more aware group of moviegoers than average, though, and knowing the improved quality of digital projection, many fans made an effort to see the movie in its purest format.

After the prequel had spent months in traditional theaters and digital cinemas, Lucasfilm announced a partnership with IMAX to bring the movie to the *really* big screen. On November 1, a few weeks before its DVD release, *Attack of the Clones* came to more than fifty IMAX screens in North America, where it enjoyed a long release of 181 days, playing through April 30, 2003. "You couldn't find a movie better suited for the IMAX format," said Bruce Snyder ("Star Wars: Episode II …"). The IMAX release gave fans an extra opportunity to see the movie, and on huge screens that further emphasized the awesome visual effects and action sequences.

Using a process called DMR, or Digital Re-Mastering, IMAX started converting regular feature films shot with 35mm cameras to IMAX format starting with *Apollo 13* (1995), released to IMAX just prior to the second prequel. *Attack of the Clones* was the first major blockbuster to arrive in IMAX form during its release year, a trend that continued with films like *The Matrix Reloaded* (2003), *The Matrix Revolutions* (2003), *Spider-Man 2* (2004), *The Polar Express* (2004), *Batman Begins* (2005), and *Harry Potter and the Goblet of Fire* (2005), among others (Hopkins "… Imax Screens"). *The Phantom Menace* was the perfect film to be the first-ever digitally projected mainstream movie, so *Attack of the Clones* had to continue the tradition of advancing movie presentation technology with its IMAX release.

Nobody at Lucasfilm or IMAX knew what to expect from *Attack of the Clones* as far as revenue in its large-screen release, but Lucasfilm launched a grassroots marketing campaign to promote the release. The company contacted local representatives of Fan Force chapters[4] throughout the country, enlisting the help of Chapter Representatives to spread the word about IMAX showings in their cities. Lucasfilm also made a nice poster with Yoda on it reading, "Size Matters Not. Except on an IMAX Screen." The film's title became, *"Attack of the Clones:* The IMAX Experience."

With its outreach to fans and the small number of theaters playing the IMAX version, Lucasfilm looked at the release more as an opportunity to give fans another chance to see the movie than as a cash cow. Lucasfilm Senior Vice President of Marketing and Distribution Jim Ward said, "Yes, it's out there again, and people will pay to see it, but that's not the main idea. We've got so many fans out there, this is a way to reward them in a different way" (Hopkins "… Imax Screens"). IMAX, though, was happy to see the movie converted and hoped for

---

4.   Fan Force chapters are groups of fans united on TheForce.net message boards who meet commonly to discuss *Star Wars* and plan community-related activities.

success commercially. "We know the *Star Wars* franchise is eminently commercial, and it will play very well," said Bradley Wechsler, co-chief executive officer of IMAX (ibid.).

Fans, though, had to tolerate numerous cuts if they wanted to see *Attack of the Clones* in IMAX. Because of the limitations of the projection-booth systems, the movie had to be cut to just two hours, which caused a jarring change to the movie for anyone who had seen it numerous times. A small group of fans argued that the cuts improved the pacing and made it play better, but the cuts made the film way too confusing for first-time viewers and, frankly, distracting to long-time viewers. Furthermore, Lucas did not supervise the cuts; instead, Lucasfilm editors were in charge. "You don't lose the continuity of the story by the scenes that have been taken away or shortened," insisted Bruce Snyder (DiOrio "Imax ..."). At the least, the shortened version that played on the massive IMAX screens provided a nice novelty for fans.

Attack of the Clones added nearly $8.5 million to its box office tally with the re-release, leading to a North American total of $310,676,740. The release, along with *Apollo 13*, helped IMAX to its first profitable year since 1999 (Hernandez "IMAX ..."). "Simply put, it is our goal that when it is time to see event Hollywood films such as *Harry Potter, Lord of the Rings*, or *Star Wars*, consumers will say, 'Let's go see it at the IMAX' and will be willing to pay a premium price for the experience," said Bradley Wechsler (ibid.). The company's revenues totaled $130.7 million, so the added income from *Attack of the Clones* made a modest but significant difference.

With an eventual worldwide gross of $649.4 million, *Attack of the Clones* was a massive blockbuster, but not a legitimate phenomenon as the first prequel had become. *Attack of the Clones* performed much more like *The Empire Strikes Back*, dipping from the highs of the first movie in the trilogy but still reaching a commendable level of success. Many fans, as with all of the films in the franchise, saw it countless times in theaters. "People will not go see a film over and over if they don't love it. I'll tell you that for sure," said Lucas (Pols). The film also helped establish the trend of releasing major blockbusters simultaneously worldwide, a strategy that further gained momentum in the years between the second and third prequels.

Because *The Phantom Menace* suffered from a bit too much hype, Lucasfilm overcompensated with *Attack of the Clones* and let the media promote the film too much, often negatively. More paid television advertising and promotional campaigns targeted at fans and the public would have given the movie a bit more of a presence after its opening weekend. The company should have pushed the prequel harder when it was suffering steeper declines in the subsequent weekends after its launch, but Lucasfilm learned from its mistakes on the second prequel and did not repeat them for the last film in the saga.

Regardless of any possible missteps from Lucasfilm's marketing department, *Attack of the Clones* was a worthy installment of the saga both artistically and financially, advancing the film industry technologically as well. It was not a popular culture benchmark like *The Phantom Menace*, nor was it the financial behemoth and surprise success that was *Spider-Man*, but it still provided a vehicle to push the boundaries of special effects and filmmaking technology. Its use of HD digital cameras and the strategy of releasing the movie almost worldwide simultaneously still made the second prequel an important film in history.

Despite the massive appeal and success of the first two parts in Lucas's new trilogy, Lucasfilm continued to learn from its experiences with promoting the franchise to fans and general audiences. In many ways, the first two prequels served as valuable experiments and case studies for planning the success of *Revenge of the Sith*, which seemed to combine the best elements from both films' marketing campaigns and struck the perfect balance of genuine fan-generated enthusiasm and company-driven hype. Unlike with the first two prequels, *Revenge of the Sith* also had the critics, and the media as a whole, on its side.

The Holy Trilogy in Digital

Since the introduction of the DVD format, fans had pleaded with Lucasfilm to release the *Star Wars Trilogy* (the official title for *Episodes IV–VI*) on DVD, but to no avail for many years. Lucas had initially indicated that he would not release any of the *Star Wars* movies on DVD until he had finished the entire saga (Gaudiosi "… DVD"). He later decided to release *The Phantom Menace* on DVD in 2001, but still had no plans to release the classic films on the format, saying he had no time to make proper versions of them with the necessary polish and bonus features. Fans circulated petitions online, practically begging for Lucas to take more of their hard-earned money to add to his empire, but the creator insisted he could not release the films yet.

For years, the *Star Wars Trilogy* had sat atop every list of the most requested DVDs on fan sites for the format, with its absence on DVD even more unusual after many classic films finally enjoyed digital releases. In May 2003, an *E! Online* report called the Original Trilogy the "most requested title never released on the format" ("The Most-Requested …"). On Amazon.com, the three films also held the top three spots on the "most-requested DVDs" list. In 2004, Lucas finally relented, announcing the first-ever DVD release of the Original Trilogy, marking not only a major event for *Star Wars* fans but for the DVD industry and its fans.

Announced in February 2004, the *Star Wars Trilogy* catapulted to #1 on Amazon.com's sales chart in April, just after becoming available for pre-order and nearly six months before its September 21, 2004, release date. The boxed set climbed to #1 on Amazon.com in just twenty-four hours after the site began taking pre-orders. The online store experienced such high demand, the company said the product had already exceeded expectations. "Based on an undisclosed number of sales, the *Star Wars* DVD set is so far the most requested DVD by our customers of all time," said a spokeswoman for the company in April (Kaplan). By the time of release, the set had broken United Kingdom sales records for Amazon with eighty-five thousand pre-orders, compared to fifty thousand for *The Lord of the Rings: The Two Towers* (2002), the previous record holder ("Star Wars DVD Rockets …").

At the time the set became available for pre-order, Lucasfilm had not finished revealing all of the bonus materials, but everyone trusted that the boxed set would be a superior product based on the incredible DVDs the company had released for the first two prequels. "Knowing how excited *Star Wars* fans are about this release, we're working very hard to make the films look and sound spectacular and to deliver a DVD collection that will be truly memorable," said Jim Ward, senior vice president of marketing and distribution at Lucasfilm ("On DVD ..."). The boxed set, with a suggested retail price of $69.98, was available in both pan & scan and widescreen formats, the latter for discerning fans and the former for people who have no problems with large portions of each film being hacked off the sides just to make the image fit on a television screen.

Lucasfilm wanted to release the DVD set in fall 2004 to begin building interest for *Revenge of the Sith*, reminding casual fans of the Original Trilogy story before offering trailers and marketing for the last prequel. The release also made sense from a sales perspective as the fall season before the holidays is the prime time for studios to release major blockbusters. "The timing is right since there is tremendous pent-up demand and DVD is now in more than 50 million households," said Fox President Mike Dunn (Hettrick "The force ..."). The *Star Wars Trilogy* was already the best-selling trilogy of movies in history on VHS, so analysts expected it to enjoy great success on DVD after such a long wait. "I think it will be a huge success and I'm sure it will be among the bestsellers of boxed sets," said Bo Andersen, president of the Video Software Dealers Association, which represents the industry (Maynard).

Lucasfilm confirmed that the versions fans would see on DVD would be the 1997 *Special Edition* re-releases, which bothered many purists who at least wanted to have both versions available, the original theatrical releases and the 1997 versions. Lucasfilm insisted that George Lucas had revised the films in 1997 because they were unsatisfactory to him at the time of their theatrical releases, so the *Special Editions* brought them closer to his original vision. "The official definitive versions are the 1997 *Special Editions*. That's the version the artist, in this case George Lucas, intended to be seen," Jim Ward said (Breznican "'Star Wars' DVD ..."). Fans did not know at the time that the DVD releases would contain new versions of the movies with slight modifications, proving to many fans that the final versions of the *Star Wars* movies may not be complete until Lucas is no longer alive to modify them.

In an interview with the Associated Press in September, Lucas addressed a few questions fans had often asked about the DVDs and about the films. Lucas claimed that he brought the *Star Wars Trilogy* out on DVD earlier than he anticipated because of piracy worries. He said, "Just because the market has shifted so dramatically.... there may not be a market when I wanted to bring it out, which was like, three years from now" (Germain "'Star Wars' Trilogy ..."). Perhaps his assessment was a bit dramatic, but in 2006 Apple's iTunes began offering movies to its customers, providing another alternative to DVD.

Lucas was no less dramatic about his decision not to include the original theatrical releases on the DVD set. Lucas said of the unaltered trilogy, "It doesn't really exist anymore," at least as far as he cared (ibid.).[1] He continued, "I'm the one who has to have everybody throw rocks at me all the time, so at least if they're going to throw rocks at me, they're going to throw rocks at me for something I love rather than something I think is not very good, or at least something I think is not finished," referring to the original theatrical versions. Many fans, though, were not clamoring for the original releases because they perceived them to be better, but to have the versions they saw as children or for historical perspective.

Lucasfilm announced that between the *Star Wars Trilogy* boxed set and the *Star Wars: Battlefront* video game, both released on September 21, consumers spent $115 million on the products on just their first day of availability. Lucasfilm claimed the boxed set had achieved record first-day sales for any film collection. Additionally, many of the licensees released products to celebrate the DVD release, like new toys from Hasbro. With popularity of the saga increasing again as the newest film release neared, companies with *Star Wars* products capitalized. "Everything we're getting in for *Star Wars* is just hot. And it's not just [popular with] the collectors. It's the kids, too," said Don Shepherd, a toy department manager for an Ohio Wal-Mart (Giovis).

The release of the *Star Wars Trilogy* on DVD received widespread praise, not just for its final appearance on the format but for the quality of the set and its extra features. *The Boston Herald* gave it 3.5 stars out of 4, calling the set "a joy that will transport you to a galaxy far, far away" and writing, "Lucas' model for the commentaries is outstanding" ("The force ..."). *USA Today* magazine also gave the set a glowing review, calling the bonus disc "an absolute gem" and writing of the enhanced films, "The special effects have been fine-tuned or, in some cases, redone to perfection" ("Obi-Wan ..."). The review concluded, "Without a

---

1.   Lucasfilm, because of intense fan demand, released the unaltered, original theatrical versions of the films in September 2006, though the 2004 DVD release versions were also included.

doubt, this DVD set is a valuable addition to any film buff's library." Lucasfilm completed a thorough package of extras to accompany the DVD release, too.

Lucas, Carrie Fisher, Sound Designer Ben Burtt, and Visual Effects Supervisor Dennis Muren recorded separate audio commentaries for each film, which were then edited into one audio commentary track. For *The Empire Strikes Back*, director Irvin Kershner also gave his commentary, focusing mainly on the characters and plot, in contrast with the more technical details Burtt and Muren discussed. In the years since the introduction of the DVD format, audio commentary tracks have become an essential element for format enthusiasts for any classic films because the commentary tracks provide an efficient way for filmmakers to discuss the specifics of each scene as it plays.

The biggest special feature of the DVD release was Kevin Burns's *Empire of Dreams* documentary, a two-and-a-half-hour look at the *Star Wars Trilogy* from all of the difficulties and triumphs of the first film through the subsequent sequels and the risks Lucas took for *The Empire Strikes Back*. "I wanted to bring people back to 1977, because this movie changed everything," said Burns (Szymanski "'Star Wars' ..."). A&E Television Networks funded a substantial amount of the documentary, in exchange for being able to air a shorter, edited version on its network.

The surprisingly candid comments from many involved, including former Fox Chairman Alan Ladd Jr. and George Lucas, is one of the greatest strengths of *Empire of Dreams*. In all, the documentary contains interviews with forty people involved with the movies. Many of the interviewees worried that they had already said everything they could recall about their experiences with the films over the past several decades, making the creation of the documentary more challenging from an originality perspective. "The standard that we had was to go out and provide fresh information on *Star Wars* to fans who had been consuming *Star Wars* for twenty-eight years," said Jim Ward (Wolf).

Aside from the primary documentary, the DVD extra features also included three smaller featurettes: *The Birth of the Lightsaber*, *The Characters of Star Wars*, and *The Force is With Them: The Legacy of Star Wars*. The final featurette, *The Force is With Them*, has commentary from directors like James Cameron, Peter Jackson, and Ridley Scott talking about the impact the films had on their lives and careers. Extensive photo galleries with promotional materials and posters also accompanied the other extra features, along with television spots and original trailers from the trilogy. "We went back into our archives and have for the very first time assembled the complete distillation of all the TV components of the promotion of the first three movies," Ward said (Wolf). He continued, "We knew people thought they'd seen everything there was to see about *Star Wars*, but no, they haven't."

The *Star Wars Trilogy* set provided advertising for other key Lucasfilm projects, including a behind-the-scenes preview of *Revenge of the Sith*. The preview focused on Anakin's journey to becoming Vader, with Lucas discussing the character's descent to the Dark Side. The footage showed a first look at the new costume for Vader created for the final prequel. Fans also could see a sneak preview of the epic battle between Obi-Wan and Anakin. Additionally, LucasArts offered a playable demo of *Star Wars: Battlefront* for Xbox users, a nice tie-in for the game as it arrived on store shelves the same day.

Perhaps most importantly for classic films making their debuts on DVD, the visual and auditory quality gave fans the best possible home experience for the saga. John Lowry of Lowry Digital, a leader in the field, used six hundred Apple G5 Macintosh computers to clean up the print quality of the movies, which had an estimated 60 million imperfections such as spots, scratches, and various blemishes (Szymanski "'Star Wars' …"). "It was one of the dirtiest, grimiest films I've ever had the pleasure of working on," Lowry said (ibid.). The detail work that Lowry and his company put into the films made them appear new and crisp for their DVD release, looking even better than they had during their respective theatrical releases. Lowry joked about working with Lucas, "I thought we were fussy, but boy, is this guy fussy. Working with a living director is a pain in the ass" (ibid.).

For the *Special Edition* re-releases of the *Star Wars* movies, Lucas made many changes, most of which were cosmetic, but a few alterations concerned many fans because of their perceived significance to the story. The most infamous change took place in the Mos Eisley Cantina, where in the original theatrical version of *A New Hope*, Han Solo shoots Greedo before the bounty hunter can shoot him. In the *Special Edition* version, Greedo shoots first (and misses, thankfully), which many fans thought softened Han's character and made him less of a rogue. In the DVD release, Lucas managed a compromise, having both characters shoot at almost the same moment. The uproar over the scene's changes is a bit absurd because whether Han shoots first or not should not define his character. In other words, Lucas should have left the scene as it was, but the fan uproar over the change is silly because either way, Han is more than just the sum of his actions in a single scene.

Another major change in the *Special Edition* release of *A New Hope* was the addition of a scene with Han Solo and Jabba the Hutt in Docking Bay 94, before Obi-Wan Kenobi and Luke Skywalker arrive. The scene is a nice addition to the saga as a whole because fans see Jabba in *The Phantom Menace* and heard about him in the *Star Wars Trilogy* before they saw him in *Return of the Jedi*, prior to his addition to *A New Hope*. Many fans complained that the computer graphics Jabba in the 1997 *Special Edition* did not look big enough or realistic enough, despite his size being the same as in *Return of the Jedi* based on exact measurements of the puppet.[2] Lucas had Jabba redone for the DVD release, to make him look more like the Jabba from *The Phantom Menace*.

In *The Empire Strikes Back*, despite changes to Cloud City that far improved the quality of the film visually, one *Special Edition* change that did not make many die-hard fans too happy was the addition of a digital scream for Luke as he lets go of the railing after dueling Vader and falls down the reactor shaft. The addition of the scream seems to make the fall an involuntary, frightening moment for Luke, instead of without a scream where he seems more in control of his destiny and sure of placing his trust in the Force to guide him to safety. Neither with nor without the scream is detrimental to the film nor to the character, but it influences what audiences are to think of Luke's action and development as a Jedi at the time. As such, the change seemed to indicate a lack of certainty on Lucas's part whether Luke felt scared and vulnerable or calm and in control. For the DVD release, Lucas removed the digital scream, restoring the scene to its original version.

The most noteworthy change to *The Empire Strikes Back*, however, caused little controversy and should not have angered any fans. Instead of Clive Revill voicing Emperor Palpatine, as with the original version, Ian McDiarmid replaced the character entirely and added consistency to the saga as he played the character in all five films in which he appears. In the previous versions, an uncredited female actress played the holographic character. Lucas had McDiarmid film the new footage during principal photography for *Revenge of the Sith* in 2003. The dialogue changed slightly, too, with Palpatine explaining to Vader that he has "no doubt" that "the young Rebel who destroyed the Death Star" is "the offspring of Anakin Skywalker."

The visual quality of the 2004 DVD scene with the Emperor is far superior to any previous incarnations. Not only is it clearer, but it is consistent with the rest of the saga. It also adds a small element of corroboration to Vader's statement in *Return of the Jedi* that his own name no longer has any meaning to him. In the

---

2.   As with much of film, size perception is based greatly on lighting and camera angles. In *Return of the Jedi*, Jabba is not tall nor is he as massive as he looks. Rather, he is shot on a throne and almost always from a low angle, which makes him look towering and even more grotesque.

new version of the scene in *Empire*, Palpatine speaks of Anakin as though he is a separate person entirely, almost the same way that Obi-Wan spoke of Anakin to Luke in *A New Hope*. In other changes to the middle film of the classic trilogy, Lucas removed Boba Fett's voice and replaced it with Temuera Morrison's to match with Jango Fett's voice, a change that annoyed a number of fans who preferred the familiarity of the previous voice.

Return of the Jedi, which to most fans had the least controversial story changes for its *Special Edition*, had the most controversial change for its DVD release. In the *Special Edition* version of the film, the most notable changes Lucas made included adding a band and a musical number to the scenes in Jabba's Palace, which many fans enjoyed and others did not, and a larger celebration at the end of the film, replacing the Ewok song. Most people not moved too much by sentimentality agree that the Ewok song was a bit lacking in quality, especially compared to the beautiful piece John Williams composed for the expanded celebration.

The added scenes of citizens celebrating across the galaxy helped make the Rebel Alliance's victory appear more universal and less personal, which is a necessary element for a successful myth. The hero of a myth must not only conquer, but his victory must benefit the community of which he is a part, which in *Star Wars* is the entire galaxy. For the DVD release of the film, Lucas added more celebration footage from Naboo, joining the brief scenes from Tatooine, Cloud City, and Coruscant. The addition is minor but seems appropriate given the large role Naboo plays in the prequels. Additionally, Lucas changed the Coruscant footage slightly, adding the Galactic Senate and the Jedi Temple, which was not destroyed when Palpatine ordered the slaughter of the Jedi Order.

The most controversial change on the entire DVD set, however, was the replacement of Sebastian Shaw as Anakin Skywalker in translucent ghost form with Hayden Christensen. Fans have discussed the change in detail, with many protesting it but others believing it makes sense for the story because, having rejoined the Light Side of the Force, Anakin should appear in his Jedi form, before he turned to evil. The new footage is a nice touch that helps connect the prequel trilogy to the Original Trilogy and serves effectively because Christensen's image recalls brighter days, when Anakin was a "good friend" to Obi-Wan and a "good man."

By the end of 2004, *Star Wars* fans had access to five of the six *Star Wars* movies on DVD, all but the as-yet-unseen *Revenge of the Sith*. The *Star Wars Trilogy* boxed set enjoyed great commercial and critical success. According to *Variety*, consumers spent a total of $215 million on the set just through 2004 (Hettrick

"'Revenge' ..."). The set eventually became the best-selling boxed set in DVD history, to befit its title as the most requested DVD boxed set ever prior to its release. No doubt, many future incarnations of the Original Trilogy will be available, but at last fans had their first digital copies of the films.

Critically, the set received praise and numerous awards, including three DVD Exclusive Awards, presented by monthly magazine *DVD Exclusive*, a publication of *Video Business*.[3] The set won Best Overall DVD in the Classic Film category while the documentary, *Empire of Dreams*, won Best Behind-the-Scenes Program, and Van Ling's menu design won him and the set an award for Best Menu Design. Fans had to rely on the *Star Wars Trilogy* release to hold them over until the final film arrived in theaters, or at least until they could see the first teaser trailer later in 2004. Fans also had a series of *Clone Wars* animated cartoons to help ease their impatience for new stories in the galaxy far, far away.

---

3.   *Video Business* is the sister publication of *Variety* and features similarly high-quality, in-depth industry news and commentary.

Bridging the Gap: The Clone Wars

Ever since Obi-Wan Kenobi told Luke Skywalker early in *A New Hope* that he fought in the Clone Wars, audiences had the same curiosity and sense of wonder about what happened as Luke expressed in the 1977 film. Because of the limited number of hours that George Lucas could devote to the prequel story in three films, the battles of the Clone Wars are not shown much at all in the prequel trilogy. The various clone wars do not start until the end of *Attack of the Clones*, where the Republic has massed its clone army to protect itself and its membership from the ongoing threat of the Separatists' droid army. Yoda declares, "Begun, the Clone Wars have." Three years later in the *Star Wars* galaxy, the Clone Wars are concluding, which *Revenge of the Sith* shows.

The battle above Coruscant to begin the final prequel is the boldest move yet by the Separatist forces, led by Count Dooku and General Grievous, who kidnaps Republic Supreme Chancellor Palpatine. Soon after, Obi-Wan and Anakin rescue the Chancellor, Anakin kills Dooku, and some of the remaining Separatist forces flee to Utapau. Obi-Wan goes on a mission to Utapau to kill Grievous, which he does, while Yoda takes a force to Kashyyyk to protect the Wookies. Spread throughout the galaxy in an attempt to end the Clone Wars, most of the Jedi perish when Palpatine gives Order 66 and the clone troopers turn on and kill their Jedi commanders. Once Anakin has turned to the Dark Side, Palpatine instructs him to slaughter the remaining Separatist leaders, who are gathered on the Mustafar system. Anakin's successful completion of his first mission as a Sith Lord ends the Clone Wars as the Separatist forces are leaderless.

From the perspective of a casual filmgoer, the Clone Wars seem to be a fairly quick engagement. The clone army masses on Coruscant at the end of *Attack of the Clones*, then in the next film the two armies, droids and clones, clash on various planets and the Separatist forces are subdued. In fact, though, the scope of the Clone Wars was far too large to show over the course of the prequel trilogy. Instead, George Lucas left most of the battles and events within the Clone Wars to novels, video games, comic books, and most significantly the *Clone Wars* cartoon series that aired on the Cartoon Network. The animated show gave fans a bit more backstory to flesh out the *Star Wars* galaxy.

Lucasfilm gave permission to cartoon director Genndy Tartakovsky (*Samurai Jack, Dexter's Laboratory*) to produce a set of twenty three-minute cartoon segments for Cartoon Network, each of which tells a small story, but combines with the other segments to fill the gap between *Attack of the Clones* and *Revenge of the Sith*. "Because this universe is so old and we've grown up with it, it feels legitimate," Tartakovsky said ("'Star Wars' cartoons ..."). Lucasfilm and Cartoon Network announced plans for the *Clone Wars* cartoons on February 20, 2003. "We are incredibly excited to be working with Lucasfilm in creating an animated story that extends one of the world's most beloved entertainment properties," said Sam Register, senior vice president of development for Cartoon Network ("Cartoon ..."). Likewise, Lucasfilm felt it had picked the right partner for the series. "Genndy Tartakovsky and the team at Cartoon Network are tops in their field," said Howard Roffman, president of Lucas Licensing (ibid.).

Tartakovsky, just a young boy when *A New Hope* came to theaters, did not see the film until 1978 at a second-run theater, after his family had immigrated from Moscow to Chicago. "I loved it. But we didn't have a lot of money so I couldn't buy ... a lot of the toys," he said (Gross). He became interested in superheroes and science fiction, soon finding himself watching hours of television, which led to an interest in cartoon work. He learned and refined his craft at the California Institute of the Arts, just outside of Los Angeles. Having entered the industry at twenty-four, Tartakovsky made a quick ascent with *Dexter's Laboratory*, which "is what I'm most proud of," he said of the Dexter character he created for the show. With Tartakovsky at the company, having also produced *The Powerpuff Girls* and *Samurai Jack*, Cartoon Network's viewership skyrocketed from 12 million to 85 million (Gross).

The first set of *Clone Wars* cartoons started airing Friday, November 7, 2003, at 8:00 p.m. Eastern on Cartoon Network with the next nine episodes appearing each weekday thereafter. All ten of the first batch of episodes then ran in order on November 21, from 7:30 p.m. to midnight, encompassing the prime time schedule. The second set of ten episodes aired starting Friday, March 26, with a similar arrangement of episodes so that fans could see them all within a few weeks.

Besides Anthony Daniels, who voiced C-3PO for the cartoon series, all of the other voice actors were different from their film counterparts, although they sound similar, so the difference is never jarring or distracting. Also, the series uses John Williams's music to give it a sense of familiarity to viewers. The series introduced Durge, a bounty hunter, and Asajj Ventress, a female assassin able to wield lightsabers and duel with the Jedi. It also gave fans more footage of the clone troopers, like the elite ARC Troopers, distinguished by their red and white armor coloration. Additionally, the twentieth *Clone Wars* chapter, at the end of the first series, had the first appearance of General Grievous, notable because he is one of the central villains of the final prequel.

Because of the short length of each *Clone Wars* episode in the first season, the focus had to be mainly on action. "Every shot had to be like a money shot," Tartakovsky said ("'Star Wars' cartoons …"). Initially, Lucas envisioned just one-minute episodes, but Tartakovsky said it was not enough time to develop any meaningful story. Lucas, being a fan of *Samurai Jack*, agreed to allow for three-minute episodes. "At first I was like, 'Wow, George Lucas watched my cartoon.' Then I was like, 'Oh, God, I'm actually going to make a *Star Wars* cartoon,'" Tartakovsky said (Finney). To test whether he could fit a story into three-minute shorts, Tartakovsky tried taking a twenty-two-minute episode of *Samurai Jack* and condensing it to three minutes, which proved successful and convinced the director to undertake the *Clone Wars* project.

The story centers around Obi-Wan leading Republic clone forces on the planet Muunilinst while Anakin leads a clone army in a space battle, disobeying Kenobi's orders, which demonstrates some of Anakin's impetuousness and cockiness. Tartakovsky's team had a fair amount of freedom on the show, though Lucas told the director to steer away from Anakin and Padmé's relationship and Lucas renamed several of the planets. Explaining the story, Tartakovsky said, "Basically, it's like D-Day and we get to see Clone Wars from all these different fronts" (Finney). Lucasfilm had to check each detail of the cartoon series to make sure they fit into the complete mythology. The studio also set strict guidelines as to which characters could be used and what the story could contain. "I think from watching the films, being such giant nerds and knowing so much about the films, it didn't turn out to be too much of a problem," said Paul Rudish, an art director on the project (Bentley "Toon …").

Although many American audiences equate cartoons or any animated work with kids' programs,[1] Tartakovsky and his team made the *Clone Wars* cartoon series to appeal to fans of all ages. It is engaging enough to appeal to adult viewers because of the extra plot and character elements it adds to the *Star Wars* story, but it is also fun for kids. "You have to get it right for both groups," said Tartakovsky, "that's one of the most amazing things about *Star Wars*—it works for all

---

1.   Exceptions are almost always animated comedy programs, like *American Dad, Family Guy, Futurama, South Park*, and *The Simpsons*.

age groups" ("Attack ..."). The *Clone Wars* cartoons do not pander to younger viewers as many American cartoons do, which is refreshing because it makes them enjoyable to older fans of the series as well.

The first *Clone Wars* cartoon series was immensely successful, both with fans and commercially. *USA Today* praised its "fast and furious action" while the *San Jose Mercury News* called it a "thrill ride through the world of *Star Wars*" ("Emmy ..."). More than 23 million people saw at least one episode when it aired on Cartoon Network, making it the #1 rated show on basic cable among boys 9–17 and teenagers 12–17. The first *Clone Wars* series also succeeded critically, earning an Emmy Award for Outstanding Animated Program (For Programming One Hour Or More).

The Official *Star Wars* Web Site interviewed Tartakovsky after the first ten episodes ran on Cartoon Network, asking the director about the reactions to his work and his opinions on the first twenty chapters of the series. He cited episodes twelve and thirteen as his favorites, because of Mace Windu's presence and a huge seismic tank that was "one of the first ideas" that he had on the project ("*Clone Wars* Q & A ..."). Speaking of fan reaction to the episodes, Tartakovsky said, "Overall, everyone has been happy with all the action and the way that we portrayed the characters ... Of course, there are always going to be people who don't like something. But it seems like about 90 percent of the people really liked it" (ibid.). The series was successful enough to warrant additional entries from Lucasfilm the following year.

The second *Clone Wars* series, chapters 21–25, started airing Monday, March 21, 2005, at 6:00 p.m. and continued throughout the week with minimal commercial interruption. Instead of short, three-minute episodes, *Clone Wars Volume II* had only five total episodes, or chapters, but each ran twelve minutes, which allowed for more story and character development while not lengthening the total running time for the series. Tartakovsky returned to direct the episodes, which are particularly relevant to *Star Wars* fans because they lead directly into the start of *Revenge of the Sith*. The final episode ends with Anakin and Obi-Wan being summoned to Coruscant, which is under siege after Separatist forces capture Palpatine.

The story for *Clone Wars Volume II* focuses on the growing crisis in the Republic and in the Jedi Council from the Clone Wars as well as the continuing threats of the Separatist forces. The Jedi Council votes, with reservations, to allow Anakin to become a Jedi Knight without undergoing the normal trials. Yoda and several other council members discuss how he has already endured much tougher trials, though psychologically he must undergo a trial of sorts on the planet Nelvaan. While on the planet, he sees into the future and into his own dark side in a way similar to Luke Skywalker's experience in a cave on Dagobah, where as fans know he slices open Darth Vader's mask only to reveal his own face.

Also in *Clone Wars Volume II*, many small plot points surface that fill some of the holes between the two prequels, *Attack of the Clones* and *Revenge of the Sith*. For instance, fans see C-3PO with gold plating for the first time, befitting a droid that is property of a senator. Perhaps most significantly, Mace Windu crushes General Grievous's lungs using the Force just as the villainous character is escaping, which is why in *Revenge of the Sith* Grievous frequently wheezes and coughs. Fans also see the villain train with Count Dooku in the skills of lightsaber fighting, which explains Grievous's abilities and his assertion to Obi-Wan in *Revenge of the Sith* that he has been trained in the Jedi arts. The series effectively establishes Anakin's relationship with Obi-Wan in more detail, as the two have grown from an unease master-apprentice relationship in the second prequel to being like brothers by the third. A few minor scenes in *Volume II* aim to establish the relationships the Jedi developed with the clone troopers during the Clone Wars, as with Obi-Wan and Commander Cody.

Lucasfilm obliged fan requests for more *Clone Wars* cartoon footage, which worked well because of the longer episode lengths and greater focus on story rather than just short action sequences. "We were really impressed with the quality of the animation and the storytelling abilities that Cartoon Network and Genndy [Tartakovsky] brought to the first *Star Wars: Clone Wars* episodes, and clearly viewers were, too, because the feedback we received ... was fantastic," said Howard Roffman ("The *Clone Wars* ... "). As with the first volume, *Clone Wars Volume II* received rave reviews from fans and critics. It also won an Emmy for Outstanding Animated Program (For Programming One Hour Or More), giving the animated cartoons a sweep of the category. The series won a second Emmy in the juried category of Individual Achievement in Animation[2] for Justin Thompson, a background key designer.

Lucasfilm had earlier ventured into animation with the *Droids* and *Ewoks* shows in the 1980s, though neither were too impressive or useful to the *Star Wars* mythology. Tartakovsky, who watched the episodes before doing his own cartoon directing work, called the shows "kind of lackluster" ("'Star Wars' cartoons ..."). By contrast, the *Clone Wars* episodes added such an immense amount of detail relative to the short running time of all the footage that *Star Wars* fans are compelled to take them as at least semi-canon, especially given that Lucas made sug-

---

2.   The juried awards do not have nominations; a panel of judges selects them.

gestions and gave direction throughout the process. Because of their close connections with the films themselves, the *Clone Wars* cartoons demanded more input from Lucas so as not to contradict anything from the final prequel.

Usually fans consider all material outside of the films "Expanded Universe," or EU, which means plot points and character development in which Lucas is not involved. Lucas has almost no input on the creative decisions with the novels, not because he is unable to give advice but because Lucasfilm has employees who keep a close watch over the continuity and storylines from the novels, which Lucas does not have time to read himself. Lucas gave much more input for the *Clone Wars* cartoons than he had any of the post–*Return of the Jedi* novels. Lucas had instructed Tartakovsky to add a quick scene where Jedi Master Mace Windu crushes Grievous's lungs to explain his strange breathing difficulties in the last prequel, for instance.

Fans who missed the *Clone Wars* episodes on Cartoon Network eventually had numerous other ways to see them. Any paid subscribers to Hyperspace, the Official *Star Wars* Fan Club section of starwars.com, could see the episodes online soon after they aired. Additionally, Lucasfilm released both volumes on DVD in two great products, each with exclusive bonus features, surround sound, and the episodes combined into a cohesive story for easy viewing. By 2006, well after the two DVD releases, the episodes became downloadable on Apple's iTunes music and video service. "As animated shorts, *Clone Wars* is the perfect content to watch on an iPod," said Tom Warner, senior director of marketing for Lucasfilm ("Emmy …").

No matter how fans chose to see the episodes, most viewers of all ages appreciated Tartakovsky's addition to the *Star Wars* mythology, which dovetails with the final prequel with remarkable ease and bravado. The episodes form one coherent story that fits between the second and third prequels much like Steve Perry's *Shadows of the Empire* (Bantam Books 1996) filled a gap between *The Empire Strikes Back* and *Return of the Jedi*, though it came to print long after the final film in the Original Trilogy arrived in theaters. While fans enjoyed the *Clone Wars* cartoons, Lucas and his cast and crew worked to bring the final prequel to moviegoers worldwide.

Completing the Saga

Preparing for *Revenge*

The total process for creating any *Star Wars* movie was a monstrous undertaking, requiring hundreds of talented individuals across numerous departments with skills ranging from sketching, costume design, and construction to computer animating, sound creation, and editing. Every major blockbuster requires great effort to complete, but none as much as a *Star Wars* film, where work started more than three years in advance for each prequel. Pre-production for the films lasted many months and included thousands of artist sketches, animatics work, location scouting, budgeting concerns, production scheduling, and cast signings, among other duties. The beginning of construction work on sets started the production process and continued through filming. The filming was the shortest section of work on each prequel, lasting only a few months, after which work began on the rigorous and lengthy post-production process that was the domain of Industrial Light & Magic (ILM).[1]

Work on *Revenge of the Sith* unofficially started on September 7, 2000, during the filming of *Attack of the Clones*, when Lucas opted to shoot a scene from the final prequel, set on Tatooine, where Obi-Wan delivers Luke to Beru and Owen Lars at their homestead (Rinzler 13). Because Lucas had first outlined the entire saga in the 1970s, and had ideas already for what needed to happen in *Revenge of the Sith*, he knew he could film the scene along with others set on Tatooine and save the production time and money on the final prequel, where Tatooine is not a central location. In April 2002, before the second prequel had arrived in theaters, the *Episode III* art department convened for the first time (13).

As with the other prequels, the vast majority of artwork and concept sketches for the spacecraft, planets, droids, weapons, and aliens had to be completed

---

1. This book provides a brief look at the filmmaking process for *Revenge of the Sith*. For a much more complete look with pictures included, refer to the official source, *The Making of Star Wars: Revenge of the Sith* by J. W. Rinzler.

before Lucas started the scriptwriting (13). With no script, the art department faced a more daunting challenge than for a standard feature film. Each artist had to work with Lucas in putting his vision on paper, before Lucas was sure how the plot would proceed and what would be needed, which is why the art department created much more artwork than was necessary for the final film. Usually Lucas reviewed the artwork and either rejected it completely if it did not meet his vision, or often gave an "OK" stamp to it, which meant it was fine but needed a few changes that he suggested. If the work was stellar, he stamped it with "Fabulouso" [*sic*], meaning it needed no further revisions, though he rarely bestowed such an honor (21).

The huge amount of work the various departments completed without having a single script page with which to work was perhaps the most surprising aspect of production. Producer Rick McCallum kept sending department heads to meet with Lucas to encourage the creative process and discuss key design issues, like costumes, construction, and possible locations where the film would take viewers (Rinzler 24). McCallum said, "I'm a man without a script. Usually you get a script a year before production begins, and it's broken down, and storyboarded, and costumes and sets are broken out; the actors are locked in to dates—but we don't have that" (47). Instead, Lucas oversaw much of the work by referring not to a physical script but to the vision he had for the movie in his head. "So everybody's taking the leap and focusing on what little information we get each week, which happens to be enough for us right now," McCallum said (47).

Even with more than three years to work on the prequel, the process was hectic for everyone involved because of the massive scale of the production. The costume department had to reserve Building 37 at Fox Studios Australia for fifty-one weeks (Rinzler 27), eventually completing more than five hundred costumes, according to Head Costume Designer Trisha Biggar (Biggar). The art department had frequent deadlines requiring artists to work overtime to keep pre-production on schedule. With such a long filmmaking process, delays at the start of the project could have been disastrous for Lucasfilm's planned summer 2005 release.

Because Lucas is a non-linear filmmaker, he takes advantage of opportunities as they arise. For instance, he sent Director of Photography Ron Fricke to Italy when Mt. Etna was erupting in 2002 to capture footage to be used later in the Mustafar scenes where Obi-Wan and Anakin have their climactic duel (31). The planet was known as "Mustafa" at the time, though later renamed. "Mount Etna started to blow up one weekend, so I called up Ron Fricke to get over there and shoot it—and we were literally a quarter of a mile from the volcano twenty-four hours later," Rick McCallum said (Duncan, "Toward ..." 91).

After Christmas 2002, production started full-scale operation, though Lucas still did not have a finished script. One of the biggest challenges for Lucas and his crew for *Revenge of the Sith* was connecting it both to *Attack of the Clones* and the Original Trilogy, specifically *A New Hope*, not only from a plot and character perspective but also from an aesthetics and design angle. When Lucas sat down to write the script, he tried to work from 8:30 a.m. to 6:00 p.m. each day, but found the process often agonizing, writing about five pages per day (Rinzler 48). "If I do four pages and I get onto the fifth page, I rationalize it: I've done my five pages," Lucas said (48). He finished a rough draft by March 21, 2003, and a first draft only a few weeks later, by April 10 (51).

Lucas put much thought into General Grievous, the film's primary action villain. He had long imagined the character would be at least part droid, but also able to speak and have a distinct personality. "I wanted it to be an alien who is mostly a droid, which is an echo of what Anakin is going to become. That was his job in the movie, and he needed to be designed in a way that was very compelling and very interesting to watch," Lucas said (52). Later in the production, when Lucas had to find a voice for the character, his own Supervising Sound Editor Matthew Wood submitted a recording anonymously and landed the role in an odd twist to the character's story. Wood had to explain to Lucas that he was the anonymous voice actor. Wood studied acting at the American Conservatory Theater in San Francisco and mixed Romanian and Eastern European accents to arrive at Grievous's voice ("The Voice ...").

Wood described the casting process for the primary new villain's voice as being much more difficult than expected. "We went down to L.A. to cast. We got a lot of people from Sydney, Australia," he said, noting that even Lucas and Burtt had tried to do the voice ("starwars.com at Celebration III; General ..."). Wood submitted a recording under the pseudonym "A. Smithee," a common name (Alan Smithee) used for directors who do not want their names attached to a project that turned out poorly. "I was kind of nervous when I did it. Ben was out of town that day. Rick called me three days later. I hadn't heard anything," Wood said (ibid.). "[Rick] said, 'George really likes A. Smithee, so if you could call Ardees [Rabang, Rick's assistant] and let her know who that is, we'll contact their agent and get them out here.' I remember I broke into an instant sweat when I heard that," he continued. Fortunately, Lucas was not bothered once he learned that Wood was A. Smithee.

Though screenwriting includes writing large segments of dialogue, it is more than just writing lines as it also encompasses describing how action sequences are arranged, how the plot comes together, and where characters are located at various key moments. Dialogue is not Lucas's favorite part to write, he acknowledges. "I think of it as a sound effect, a rhythm, a vocal chorus in the overall soundtrack. Mostly, everything is visual," he said (Rinzler 53). The writing process also had other unexpected difficulties. "Now they have a *Star Wars* Encyclopedia, and when I come up with a name or something, I look it up to see if it's already been used," Lucas said. He finished a second draft of the screenplay by June 13, 2003, that ran 135 pages long (60). He finished a fourth draft by late June, trimming it to 129 pages (62). With the script completed, the animatics department could start to prepare its previsualization work for the filming process that would eventually be useful for post-production as well.

Previsualization, or "previz," helps establish the flow of a scene from an early point in a film's creation, in the process saving the production money. "George can look at a sequence on our computer and fuss and play with it as much as he wants to without ever having to worry about ending up with a million dollar shot that has to go through expensive revisions," said Previsualization Supervisor Dan Gregoire (Szadkowski "Desktops …"). With most past productions, previsualization involved a series of still storyboards used to convey action, which is still an effective means of communicating ideas, but lacks the complexity necessary to map a variety of elements in a planned sequence. Lucas claimed the previsualization process for *Episode III* saved $10 million in production and post-production expenses (ibid.).

With a film as complicated visually as *Revenge of the Sith*, Lucasfilm's team worked on animatics sequences both before and after the shooting process. Gregoire's team of eleven computer artists created many rough shots before Lucas filmed any of the movie, but even after filming wrapped, Lucas used the animatics department for making ILM's job easier in post-production ("Episode III Animatics …"). During the spring before filming, early in the production of *Revenge of the Sith*, the animatics department worked long days to meet strict deadlines. Gregoire said, "We're in a rushed state from the word go. Last week was pretty intense. I think Wednesday, Thursday, [and] Friday some people got a total of five hours of sleep" (ibid.). Working with animatics is almost always a demanding, tense job, with work accelerating before important deadlines.

"Before I started here almost four years ago," said Senior Animatics Visual Effects Artist Bradley Alexander, "I thought previsualization was an extremely simple means of filmmaking where one would animate a box or cube to represent a character, and a simple move to represent a camera; then voila—you have an animatic" ("Caught …"). After working with the team for *Revenge of the Sith*, however, he soon changed his mind. "We have gone so far beyond the quality of traditional animatics. I think the quality of some shots we have is so high you could mistake them for a final shot in the film," he said (ibid.). Lucas reviewed animatics work on a daily basis to make sure the production proceeded on schedule.

Revenge of the Sith has eleven planets,[2] more than any other *Star Wars* film. A twelfth planet, Dagobah, was cut from the final film but appears in the deleted scenes on the DVD. One planet that was new to the film series, but not to the mythology, was Kashyyyk. Much like Coruscant, the planet had become part of Expanded Universe material; Lucas had written extensive descriptions of its environment previously. To gain more inspiration for the planet's look, the art department watched the 1978 *Star Wars* Holiday Special that played on television and featured the planet prominently. The show has since become a frequent joke in the fan community for its lousy quality.[3] Concept Design Supervisor Ryan Church joked, "We watched that on a loop about four or five times, avoided suicide, and went back to work" ("Kashyyyk …"). After an intense period of pre-production, Lucas and his cast and crew prepared for the filming process.

The Sith Steal the Show

Filming for *Attack of the Clones* finished at Shepperton Studios, but Lucas knew he would return to Australia for the final prequel. He even placed a full-page ad in *Variety* thanking Fox Studios Australia and vowing to return. With *Revenge of the Sith*, Lucas again had a pleasant experience filming Down Under. "Sydney has some of the most wonderful film crews in the world, and I've worked all over the world," Lucas said ("Star Wars director …"). He praised their professionalism and hard work, mentioning that he would return to Australia to visit soon. Besides a few brief shots elsewhere, almost the entire filming for the last prequel occurred in Australia at Fox Studios.

---

2.   Alderaan, Cato Neimodia, Coruscant, Felucia, Kashyyyk, Mustafar, Mygeeto, Naboo, Saleucami, Tatooine, and Utapau. Polis Massa, where Padmé dies, is not a planet; it is an asteroid group.

3.   Fox owned the rights to *Star Wars* and made the television special to capitalize on the first film's success, though Lucas and nearly all of the fans despise the show.

Revenge of the Sith had no location shoots, which is unusual for any high budget movie, though Lucas had a number of plates photographed in countries like Thailand, China, New Zealand, Switzerland, and Italy. For Kashyyyk, ILM used a composite of digital elements and real environments, combining footage from Phucket, Thailand, and Guilen, China, with digital trees and a painted lagoon and beach. "George had a particular liking for this mountain range near the Yangtze River," said Special Effects Supervisor Roger Guyett, so "I spent about three weeks in China, shooting those plates" (Duncan, "Toward …" 84). The Thailand footage, consisting of "a tracking shot across the ocean, which then came around an interesting rock formation to reveal a bay," was almost entirely replaced by other elements, according to Guyett (84). The beautiful mountain views seen at the end of the film on Alderaan were from Grindelwald, Switzerland.

With the screenplay finished and the art department having contributed thousands of concept sketches and images, Lucas was ready for production at Fox Studios Australia. Lucas set aside sixty-three days for filming with a planned finish on September 24, after starting June 30, 2003 (Rinzler 69). Several of the actors only had final contracts completed a few days before shooting started, according to McCallum (67). Pre-production involved many people and thousands of hours of work, but during the production phase the movie's creation became even more intense with construction crews building sets frantically before and during shooting along with the costume department working long days. Each day of shooting for the crew ran 14–15 hours, starting with breakfast at 6:00 a.m. (69).

For filming, Lucas used two HDC-F950 Sony digital cameras with custom-built Fujinon lenses. The camera footage displayed in real time on two Panasonic TH-42PHDS high-definition plasma screens in a mobile command unit called the "video village" that the crew could quickly assemble and disassemble on each of the soundstages (73). Additional equipment logged the exact iris, zoom, and focus information from the camera for every frame of footage shot so that ILM could use the information later if necessary for adding digital elements into the film (Hidalgo "… Lights, Camera, Testing").

Visual Effects Supervisor John Knoll was present for shooting, too, not only to advise Lucas on effects matters but to make note of various scenes and shots and how he planned to tackle their completion in post-production (Rinzler 73). "The shoot for this show was remarkably similar to the shoot for *Episode II* in that we were shooting in the same studio, with the same crew," Knoll said (Duncan, "Toward …" 68). He also praised the new 950 camera series, saying, "The new cameras are better in every way," mainly because of "less compression," "better signal-to-noise ratio," and a "better image—sharper, with better color resolution" (68).

Besides the sophisticated camera logging, Matchmove Supervisor Jason Snell had the task of digitally reconstructing the sets as filming occurred. Between takes, he placed digital tracking markers in the frame and took digital pictures of the set (Hidalgo "... Matching"). During filming, either on the filming set or on another set not yet being shot, he used ILM software designed to process the digital photographs for mapping the set in 3-D on the computer for later use. The tracking markers on the set identified the way in which the camera moved during shooting so that effects artists could add digital elements into the scene seamlessly.

In some cases, ILM had to move actors' positions on set if several takes were combined and the actors did not follow the same line of movement in each take, creating continuity issues (Hidalgo "... Quick"). Although the process requires time-consuming and expensive rotoscoping, because no blue screen is behind the actors many times, the cost of having ILM artists fix a scene is still cheaper than the time of everyone on set to redo the entire performance many more times. Although not always successful, Lucas and the visual effects supervisors always attempted to find the technique that would maximize the quality of the shot and minimize the cost, which often meant delegating tasks to post-production if they proved too time-consuming on set. The entire crew, from makeup to construction, was extremely conscious of continuity issues, always trying to match details from shot to shot and from movie to movie, knowing how much attention fans pay to the smallest aspects of each scene.

One common film industry joke is for a director to say, "We'll fix it in post," another way of heaping more work onto the special effects companies that deal with fixing problems after the filming ends. Lucas often said instead, "We'll let John fix it," which John Knoll knew meant more work for his department later in the process (Hidalgo "... Bring"). Most of the instances where Lucas needed ILM's expertise involved creating settings or characters that were either impossible to film realistically during production or too expensive to create outside of the digital realm. In other cases, though, Lucas delegated work to Knoll that the production could have done on set, but would have thrown the shooting schedule off target and likely cost more money in the end.

The construction department for the final prequel boasted 345 crew members total from its various departments, which included carpenters (the biggest portion), set finishers, plasterers, stagehands, riggers, steelworkers, and sculptors

(Rinzler 126). The construction department spent about $1 million on timber, plywood, and other board product. For *Episode III*, Lucas had about seventy sets constructed, rotating through seven soundstages (78). "Most films are road movies: They're on location, they're contemporary. Or if they're period films, they use period locations. But everything in the *Star Wars* universe has to be built," Rick McCallum said (78).

At the end of shooting on any given set, the construction crew had to destroy the set entirely and discard the materials, unless any elements could be re-used on a later set. *Revenge of the Sith* Construction Manager Greg Hajdu said, "Whether it's timber, plywood, MDF ... whether it's painted or not, it all ends up in thirty cubic meter skip bins and goes off to get burnt to run power stations instead of coal, basically" ("The Life ..."). The sets often took weeks to build, but only a day to demolish. "It's a shame, but it doesn't matter because it's been created. The set has already been captured on film or on tape. It exists forever," Hajdu said (ibid.).

As with the construction department, the costume department also had an immense amount of work and used up materials at a rapid pace. One person in the costume department required a week of ten-hour days to add the black hair to just one Wookie suit (Rinzler 84). Each suit, eight in all, took about twelve weeks. ILM later faced a similar ordeal in the digital world, initially rendering Wookies with 800,000 hairs, but the artists later decided on 150,000 digital hairs as the standard number (Duncan, "Toward ..." 87). Wookies close to the camera were to be live-action men-in-suits, so 150,000 digital hairs looked realistic enough given the virtual camera distance for any of the digital Wookies. For *Revenge of the Sith*, the costume department required two tons of liquid silicone for taking molds (Rinzler 126). Senator Amidala had twelve of the roughly five hundred costumes in the movie, which was more than what Biggar had expected initially for Natalie Portman's character.

With many of the background characters, where costumes had to be produced in larger quantities like with various guards, recasting the extras was easier than reproducing perfectly fitting costumes for the extras selected. For instance, a group of rather tall extras, around 6'1" or 6'2", came in to fill the Neimoidian costumes, but they still were not tall enough for the costumes, so finding taller extras was easier and less expensive than making entirely new costumes (Hidalgo "... Blue"). For the Wookie extras, Lucasfilm cast several professional basketball players from Australia, figuring their heights would be most likely to match with the tall, furry warriors (Hidalgo "... Return").

As with much of the design work on *Revenge of the Sith*, Trisha Biggar wanted to make sure that the look of many of the costumes transitioned smoothly between the first and second *Star Wars* trilogies. "There's a link of characters between *Episodes III* and *IV*. In terms of quality, there will always be a difference between how things look in *Episode III* and *Episode IV*, just because we have a great deal more time to achieve things," she said ("Heroic …"). Even so, Biggar continued, "There's always a mind to keep the flow from *III* into *IV*, and that's been achieved in color and feel." Obi-Wan's costume changed slightly, with a few color modifications to match the outfit he wore in *A New Hope*. Anakin, meanwhile, wore a darker Jedi costume. "This time, we've really taken shades of dark brown to give him a dark outline even though he's still a Jedi," Biggar said (ibid.).

As with all of the prequels, and in some respects every *Star Wars* movie but *The Empire Strikes Back*,[4] Lucas oversaw every aspect of production from the earliest stages through the final cut. "I guess I've been accused of being a micromanager, but as far as I'm concerned, that's what making a movie is all about. I'm really responsible for every single detail on the picture," Lucas said (Rinzler 78). He also had a great crew to help him manage the incredible number of details and issues that arose on and off the set. Aside from Rick McCallum's expertise, Lucas had a team of capable and experienced assistant directors.

Episode III's team of assistant directors, led by First Assistant Director Colin Fletcher, kept production moving smoothly and on schedule. The assistant directors helped extras find their places, made sure actors and actresses arrived on set at the proper times, helped arrange hair and makeup sessions, and directed smaller pickup scenes where major actors did not need to be present. Fletcher said, "Often when I was going through the script with George and Rick to see which scenes were coming up, we could try to work out where the scenes fit in and how to film them more efficiently," Fletcher said ("Direct …"). He continued, "We'd also use that time to deal with continuity concerns, characters, costume changes, and other day-to-day issues." Fletcher served directly under Lucas as a high-level personal assistant, almost like another on-set producer, making Lucas's job easier and more efficient.

Although Lucas maintained control over every element of production, he still had to yield to his own empire's products at times. Lucas had to take into account more Expanded Universe material than he had on the other films. At times, what

---

4.   Lucas directed *A New Hope* and, though he did not direct it, was on set almost constantly with *Return of the Jedi*.

Lucas included in the prequels has challenged Expanded Universe facts, but with *Revenge of the Sith*, a number of Expanded Universe elements found inclusion in the movie. The *Clone Wars* cartoon series also led directly into the opening events of the film. Aayla Secura (played by Amy Allen), a Jedi that John Ostrander and Jan Duursema of Dark Horse Comics created, gained a small role in both *Attack of the Clones* and *Revenge of the Sith*.

Fans should notice early in the final prequel that Anakin does not have the same fresh face he did three years earlier in the story's chronology; the Clone Wars have left him a bit weary and battle-worn. When John Knoll asked Lucas, "So how did Anakin get that scar, George?" Lucas responded half-seriously, "I don't know. Ask Howard [Roffman, president of Lucas Licensing]. That's one of those things that happens in the novels between the movies. I just put it there. He has to explain how it got there" (Hidalgo "… The Best"). Lucas had his own theory, though. "I think Anakin got it slipping in the bathtub, but of course he's not going to tell anybody that," he said. In fact, Count Dooku's apprentice, Asajj Ventress, gives Anakin the scar during the *Clone Wars* cartoon series.

With such a large, talented cast and crew surrounding him, Lucas handled the complexities of production gracefully, passionately, and with a good sense of humor. Hayden Christensen said in an interview around the film's release date, "[Lucas] was definitely more excited by the story he was telling. You could tell by the way he came to the set every day with a passion to get the scene right" (Lowman). People often have a tendency to read into a situation more or less excitement depending on their views of the final product. Christensen offered an opinion to explain Lucas's change of demeanor for the last prequel. "I guess there was maybe an ease or confidence that he hadn't had on the last film because he was very sure in the story, as we all were," he said. At least technologically, Lucas had many advantages with *Revenge of the Sith*, having already used digital cameras for *Attack of the Clones* and having already successfully turned Yoda digital.

Although *Revenge of the Sith* is a serious and tragic film, and its production was chaotic and fast-paced, Lucas and the cast and crew tried to remain good-humored about the scenes and any potential difficulties. Script Supervisor Jayne-Ann Tenggren said, "I always feel that no matter what happens, George will always take the problem on board and come up with a solution" (Rinzler 74). Between takes of their climactic saber duel, Christensen and McGregor joked with one another and faked death scenes, lightening the mood on set despite the serious mood of the scene (119). Because of the physical intensity of the fighting and its masterful choreography, McGregor said the fight "looks extraordinary" (119).

In May 2003, Lucas had brought in his friend and fellow filmmaker Steven Spielberg to help think of ideas for the Anakin-Obi-Wan fight at the end of the movie (56). "Ewan has always been a great swordfighter. He and Ray Park were very good. Christensen is very athletic, and he's also very good at it," Lucas said of the actors' fighting skills (133). "The difference in this particular film," he continued, "is they have to fight each other. As actors there's a little bit of competitiveness about who's going to be the better swordfighter." Stunt Coordinator and Sword Master Nick Gillard also praised Christensen's skills. "Hayden Christensen is one of the best there is. I've seen hundreds of sword fighters, people who do it for a living, and he leaves them all in his wake," Gillard said ("On the Level …"). Christensen trained for six hours per day doing saber drills, then spent two more hours each day working out to add mass for his role.

The fight sequence between Obi-Wan and Anakin, which took a significant portion of the filming process given its complexity and importance, not to mention high fan expectations and anticipation, required not only intense focus from both actors, but also lots of training and choreography from Nick Gillard. "It's like a game of chess played at one thousand miles per hour—and every move is check," Gillard said (Waugh "Charge …"). The speed and complexity of the moves for the fight sequence are impressive, but even more so its length. "The climactic fight scene is, at twelve minutes, the longest fight scene in cinema history," he said. In all, Christensen spent two months learning his moves while McGregor spent six weeks on his one thousand moves (ibid.). ILM later worked for months on the sequence, completing more than three hundred special effects shots for the legendary duel (Duncan, "Toward …" 90).

Long before a rough cut was assembled, Lucas knew his film might break the Star Wars tradition of PG-rated movies. During shooting, Lucas said, "We're somewhere between an extremely hard PG and a PG-13" (Rinzler 171). Dave and Lou Elsey, who worked on the Episode III Creature Shop and crafted much of the makeup for Episode III, had no clue how to honor the tradition of PG-rated Star Wars movies and do justice to Anakin's horrific scars. "I asked George in one of our very first meetings, 'How much can we burn him?' He said, 'It's going to be a bad burn, but for PG,'" Dave Elsey said (Mallory 58). After working on designs, though, he returned to Lucas and said, "I don't know what a PG burn is. I really think we should try and push it as far as we can" (58). Nervous of Lucas's response, Dave Elsey had no need to worry. "George said, 'Okay, then we'll make it a PG-13.' And I thought, 'Wow, that was unbelievably easy.'" Lucas had no desire to compromise the integrity or darkness of the story for a PG rating (58).

Besides the physical aspects of filming the final *Star Wars* movie with its extensive focus on lightsaber duels, serious dramatic performances were required, too. According to *Revenge of the Sith* Dialogue Coach Chris Neil, who worked with the major actors as well as coaching the minor ones, Christensen did not just excel on the physical side of acting but also as a deeper emotional actor. "Hayden's an incredibly soulful, deep-reaching actor. It's not easy to find the right times to be deep or to just play a young, hotshot pilot. Hayden has the tendency to go really deep," Neil said ("Chris Neil ..." 3). The most accolades from everyone on set went to Ian McDiarmid, though.

McDiarmid provided such a captivating performance, especially while speaking to Anakin during the opera house scene, that Christensen said, "I was so in awe of what he was doing in each scene, I'd find myself at times almost breaking out of character" (Rinzler 94). Lucas called his performance on the scene "absolutely amazing" (94). Many people on set watched McDiarmid's takes, "which could have been a distraction," the actor said, but "on that day, it was a help; I found it was rather like playing to an audience" (96). From on-set accounts, McDiarmid rarely flubbed his scenes' dialogue.

Although many people watched McDiarmid on some of his scenes, at other times, like the landing platform scene on Mustafar with Anakin and Padmé, nobody was allowed to watch except essential personnel (117). A black curtain also hid the video village from the actors' sight. Lucasfilm secrecy never kept the crew from watching any of the more important scenes in the movie, though. In fact, during all of the filming, nobody in charge asked the crew to leave the set unless their presence was distracting to the actors involved in production (Hidalgo "... Concentrated Action"). The infamous Lucasfilm veil of secrecy that sometimes came to the forefront of the other films' productions did not surface much with *Revenge of the Sith*, at least during production, especially given that fans had webcam access to large portions of the shooting process. The final *Star Wars* movie was also perhaps the least secretive during its filming.

The 12–16 hour days on set tired the crew, leading to roughly one hundred people visiting on-set nurse Marguerite O'Sullivan, usually with neck and shoulder pain (Rinzler 128). Though crew members often suffered from fatigue and homesickness, going weeks or months without seeing their families, one stuntman suffered a worse fate on set. "Rob [Coleman, animation supervisor] and I ended up doing second unit and there was a pretty complicated shot [during the

Windu-Palpatine fight]. The stuntman had rehearsed it for days and the first take was fine," said McCallum (128). "But when we did a second, safety take, he hit his leg on the stairs and broke it," he continued. The stuntman assured McCallum not to feel guilty about making him do a second take. McCallum said, "I turned to Nick [Gillard], and, without missing a beat, he said, 'Bring in the next stuntman.' That's the business they're in; those are the additional sacrifices they make."

The fight sequences between Christensen and McGregor provided solid amusement for the crew, but the most symbolic moment came when a familiar villain finally returned. "The most special day of the shoot was when Hayden got into the Darth Vader suit," McCallum said (138). "Every single person in the studio was waiting outside the stage doors—I'd told them they could get a glimpse of Hayden as Darth Vader. After he walked by, we had champagne and the party lasted for hours," he continued. Anthony Daniels's last day on set also provided a chance for reflection, as the actor had worked with Lucas on the entire saga from the beginning. On his last day on set for *Episode III*, Anthony Daniels said jokingly, "I guess this is show business. An empty stage and already I've turned to drink," as he sipped champagne from a styrofoam cup (125).

Many of the numerical facts of the filming process are mind-boggling to an outside observer. For instance, *Revenge of the Sith* cost about $333 a minute to make. "So if it takes three minutes to move a cable, it's one thousand dollars," said Chris Neil (Rinzler 141). In all, the cast and crew spent 709 hours and 25 minutes from the first shot until production completed, with an average of 4.9 hours spent per script-minute filmed. The crew completed 2,883 setups for 144 scenes (145).

Filming completed early, in only fifty-eight days instead of the planned sixty-three. Rick McCallum said of day fifty-eight, "The last day was very moving. It was a special, wacky day, because we shot on seven different sets—we were running constantly" (148). Lucas and the crew completed one hundred setups on the last day (149). Filming wrapped on September 17, 2003, at 6:42 p.m. ("Episode III: It's a Wrap"). While Lucas and McCallum were pleased to finish principal photography, they knew much work remained. McCallum said, "For George and I, this is only the mid-way point." Lucas re-iterated the point, saying, "I've been working on it for eighteen months and I have exactly eighteen months to go" (Rinzler 149). Post-production work began immediately back at Skywalker Ranch in Marin County, California.

Animating A Galaxy

After shooting, the post-production phase began. Lucas said of the filmmaking process for the prequels, "It is all about telling a story, but translating that story onto film, physically getting that stuff to be real has always been the challenge. In that way, filming this second series of *Star Wars* movies is following the same pattern as the first" (Duncan, "Love ..." 119). Lucas had to deal with three major areas: editorial (cutting the movie together), animatics (having a rough idea where elements are located in the scenes and how they move), and ILM effects work. Once Lucas had footage assembled or edited, and the animatics department had done its previsualization work, ILM started animating.

For creating the many digital characters featured in the movie, ILM relied heavily on Maya software from Alias, the world's most popular professional 3-D modeling, animation, and rendering software. "One of ILM's big breakthroughs with this movie is the level to which the digital characters engage the audience. The way they emote and interact with the live-action actors, often in epic battle scenes, is completely convincing," said ILM Chief Technology Officer Cliff Plumer ("Alias-Maya ..."). Rob Coleman said, "In our films, the animated characters have to hold their own with the live action characters. What I learned over the last couple of years, while working on Yoda, was that we animators are actually actors" (ibid.). The facial expressions for non-human characters like Yoda still needed to convey human emotions so that audiences could empathize with their performances.

Hollywood trade paper *Variety* ran an article in September 2005 discussing the rising cost of special effects in major movies, not because of the costs per shot increasing, but because of the rising number of shots per blockbuster (Cohen and Fritz). In the early 1990s, a big blockbuster had a few hundred special effects shots. Even the much-celebrated sci-fi film *The Matrix* (1999) only has about five hundred special effects shots, compared to several thousand for each prequel. Audiences expect more than just great effects; they expect effects they have never seen before and that trump previous work.

Variety mentioned in its article that almost all special effects professionals complain about studios being wasteful because of poor coordination with the effects companies and lousy planning, which is a problem Lucas entirely avoided with *Revenge of the Sith*. Combine his ownership of the premiere visual effects company in the industry with his eye for detail and veteran planning and the result was an effects budget that, while massive, still seemed marvelously reasonable. Considering the trend of summer blockbusters costing $150 million or more, largely because of their effects budgets, like *Superman Returns* (2006), the final prequel was a bargain.

McCallum said that all of the sets built for production cost $4.5 million, but all of the digital sets created later cost $10 million (Rinzler 156). Lucas said of the breakdown of virtual sets versus constructed sets, "On the first film we had maybe 25 percent digital sets; the second movie, we had maybe 50 percent digital sets and in *Episode III*, I'd say there's 85 percent digital sets" ("The Grand ..."). With a greater percentage of the sets created with computers, ILM's task became more complicated and demanding. Editor Roger Barton said, "Of all the movies I've worked on—and some have been big visual effects movies—they just don't come close to the amount of reinvention that goes on in post-production here" (Rinzler 179).

With the first two prequels, ILM used three visual effects supervisors, but with *Revenge of the Sith* the setup changed slightly, with two supervisors joining the production at different times. John Knoll was on set for filming and involved from the start, but Roger Guyett joined later. "Roger will have huge sequences. John Knoll's unit will end up having about one thousand shots, and I can easily see Roger having one thousand as well," McCallum said ("Episode III: Picking ..."). Not only did the special effects supervisors have huge numbers of shots to enhance, but the complexity of each shot was often substantial. McCallum said, "There are some shots with fifty or sixty different elements, most of which most people will never even realize are effects" ("An Introduction ..." 6).

When John Knoll asked Lucas about duplicating digital statues to use in several scenes, Lucas rejected the idea. Knoll said, "Well, I'm trying to save you money" (Rinzler 161). Lucas replied, "But this is art. Art!" Shooting and its related expenditures cost $59 million, but the remaining total of the $113 million budget went to effects (161). The visual effects department handled tasks as complicated as creating an entire space battle using computer graphics[5] and as relatively mundane as taking away Natalie Portman's pulse in the funeral scene for Padmé (119). Besides major effects work, ILM can change minor details like the color of a character's eyes if the makeup and costume departments lack the time to deal with the details on set.

Although many fans, and most casual moviegoers, assume the prequels relied almost entirely on computer graphics and sometimes bemoan the passing of

---

5.   ILM used practical elements from footage the effects artists shot, however, for 98 percent of the explosions, fire, smoke, and spark hits, rather than relying on computer graphics (Duncan, "Toward..." 74).

models and man-in-a-suit aliens, the prequels have used more models than the Original Trilogy and many costumed aliens alongside their digital counterparts, too. In fact, *The Phantom Menace* had more models and miniatures than all of the movies in the Original Trilogy *combined* (Gernand 1). Ideally implemented, ILM uses computer effects only when the cost of other techniques is too prohibitive or the realism is not sufficient for the film.

Utapau, the sinkhole city in *Revenge of the Sith* that serves as a Separatist stronghold, features an impressive miniature that introduced the sinkhole where the action on the planet occurs. The largest miniature for the entire Utapau sink-hole had a six-foot diameter and an eighteen-foot depth (Gernand 2).[6] Additionally, Practical Model Supervisor Brian Gernand and his crew constructed a 1:90 scale wall from the inside the sinkhole that stood sixteen feet tall and twenty-four feet wide (2).[7] Different parts of the wall could represent different areas of the sinkhole and individual elements could be reconfigured to form new looks. Gernand said, "We have some sections that are landing platform-intensive. Other areas are sort of residential. We have some that are commercial, some are financial district, and some are more industrial" (2). Gernand and his crew made other impressive miniatures for shooting, too.

Many of the shots on Mustafar showcased a large miniature that ILM had constructed for the film's finale. Gernand said of the twenty-foot wide, thirty-six-foot long set, "It was a rock-like environment with a four-foot wide and approximately forty-foot long path of lava coming down. Included with that were tributaries, waterfalls, [and] all kinds of other inlets and glowing hot spots around this environment" ("Hotter ..."). Because of the fifteen thousand gallons of methyl-cel, or methyl cellulose (used primarily for thickening foods, drugs, and cosmetics), that the crew had to penetrate with a light source from the bottom of the river beds, which were translucent, the set reached 110 degrees Fahrenheit with the 250,000 watts of light used (ibid.). Gernand called his work on Mustafar "the most challenging set for me" (Gernand 3). It was also the longest single miniature shoot in ILM's history, according to Roger Guyett, at eight months (Duncan, "Toward ..." 93). "There was every sort of setup, and they were all immensely complicated," he said (93).

---

6.   Duncan's article for *Cinefex* indicates a twelve-foot diameter and a height of seventeen feet, though from pictures given on starwars.com, the model appears six feet in diameter (80).

7.   Again, Duncan's article for *Cinefex* disagrees with starwars.com, citing a 1:36 scale wall measuring thirty-five feet wide by sixteen feet tall (80). Brian Gernand, however, told starwars.com that the model's scale was 1:90.

Sound effects are as important to Lucas as the visual quality of his films. As with the previous *Star Wars* films, Ben Burtt served as sound designer on *Revenge of the Sith*, along with being a co-editor. Burtt recorded a number of new sound effects for R2-D2, marking the first time since the Original Trilogy that he had added to the droid's repertoire. "We pulled out an old ARP synthesizer from under my house, and it was all moldy. Howie Hammerman, our engineer, got it working again so we did lots of new Artoo for this," he said ("Layers ..."). The sound crew of nine people had to tackle about a thousand different sound projects for the movie, including using their own voices for many of the minor characters.

The rough cut of the film took longer than Lucas had expected, but he finished it in May 2004 (Rinzler 185). Many of the scenes with Padmé and various senators became deleted scenes with the rough cut because Lucas had to focus the story around Anakin to prevent it from becoming unwieldy and overly long (176). Lucas said, "And when most of those scenes were cut out, suddenly all sorts of weird things started to happen that weren't intended in the script—but in some cases it actually worked much better" (176). In other words, more Anakin scenes dove-tailed one another and "one theme is infinitely stronger than it was before," Lucas explained. With a new focus, and a significant portion of the post-production work at least underway, Lucas had a number of scenes that needed more filming work.

Starting on August 23, 2004, Lucas and a much-reduced cast and crew assembled at Shepperton Studios in England for pickup shots, or additional footage that Lucas had decided he wanted to integrate into the film (199). For the pickup shooting, not everyone returned to their previous duties. Sometimes, old Lucas and McCallum friends and industry contacts helped replace crew members not able to return for the additional shooting (199–200). Lucas set aside eleven days for the additional filming. Because the shooting took place a year after principal photography, continuity was a big concern for Lucas and his crew, who had to make sure hair styles, lighting, scale, and wardrobe, among other areas, matched previous footage (200).

Going into the reshoots, the cast did not know what Lucas would ask of them, but understood from past experience that most of the work would be minor with maybe a few significant additions. "I haven't been told anything, so for all I know, it could be like walking or an insert shot of my hands, or it could be a whole new storyline. So I will be as surprised as you are," Natalie Portman told reporters (Szymanski "Portman ..."). Unlike with the previous two prequels, the first round of additional filming did not take place in the spring the year after principal photography, but in August because of "actor scheduling unavailability," McCallum said ("All Eyes ...").

The arrival scene at the opera house, where Lucas and Anthony Daniels appear briefly as patrons as Anakin runs past various attendees, was on the list of additional scenes to film. "There is a scene, a large crowd scene, which my daughters are in, and they sort of insisted that I be in it, and so I did it," Lucas told the Associated Press ("Lucas Makes ..."). McGregor and Christensen both had to be present for a few new shots taking place during the climactic final duel. Between the end of principal photography and the start of the additional filming, McGregor had travelled 18,500 miles on his motorcycle, constantly making Lucas nervous about any potential accidents (Rinzler 202). Ian McDiarmid and Samuel L. Jackson also returned for a few shots as part of the Palpatine-Windu lightsaber duel, where Christensen intervenes on the behalf of Palpatine (204–205). Lucas said of McDiarmid's gleeful victory over Windu, "I tell you, this is as good a villain as we've ever had. Darth Sidious emerges in this one" (206).

The duel between Palpatine and Windu changed significantly from its original version. Initially, Anakin was in the Chancellor's Office at the time Windu and the other Jedi came to arrest Palpatine (205). Anakin stood and watched much of the action unfold, without moving to help the Jedi or Palpatine, though Palpatine used the Force to take Anakin's lightsaber and use it against the other Jedi (Hidalgo "Did Palpatine ..."). Lucas decided, after watching the movie with a few close colleagues, that the sequence as originally filmed did not work. "The story was there, but it wasn't clear. It was too abstract. We opened up that part and looked at what we could do," he said (ibid.). Although most of the duel remained unchanged, Lucas reshot the start of the scene in late August alongside other pickup work on the movie.

Lucas and his crew on the previous two prequels had pioneered a new age in digital effects and digital filmmaking. Lucas said of the animation work on the prequels, "We were able to develop digital characters that could act—whether people liked them or not[8]—which paved the way for digital characters such as Gollum [in *The Lord of the Rings*]" (Waugh "The Billion ..."). Speaking of filmmaking technology, he said, "We developed all-digital cameras for *Episode I*, and we were able to shoot the entire film on them in *Episode II*. We jumped over all those barriers, and now we're pretty much there" (ibid.). McCallum said that

---

8.   After expressing frustration and surprise at the Jar Jar backlash from 1999, Lucas managed to joke about the character by the time *Revenge of the Sith* was nearing completion. "There was a time when I was going to have Jar Jar walk through every scene, like Hitchcock," he said (Rinzler 196).

with *Revenge of the Sith*, there are "no major technological achievements. There was nothing where we didn't know how we were going to actually accomplish it" (Roston 58). The level of familiarity with the equipment and with the special effects process, by all accounts, allowed for a smoother, less stressful process on the final prequel, even though everyone still worked long days to keep the movie on schedule.

The third rough cut of the film, completed October 1, 2004, ran two hours and twenty-five minutes, still too long to satisfy Lucas (Rinzler 217). Eventually, he trimmed the movie enough to fit his vision, allowing for a quickly paced final theatrical cut of the movie that delighted the vast majority of fans and critics everywhere. In all, ILM completed 2,151 effects shots for *Revenge of the Sith*, spread over 375,040 frames of work, taking ILM computers a total of 6,598,928 hours (trying to render the entire movie on one system would require more than 750 years).[9] ILM also constructed and shot forty-seven practical miniature setups and completed nearly 13 million renders and composites (Duncan, "Toward ..." 68). Coleman said, "In terms of animation, we had 1,269 shots that we animated. To put that into perspective, for *Episode I* we did sixty minutes of animation. For *Episode II*, we did seventy minutes. In this one we did ninety minutes" ("Big ...").

After working on the *Star Wars* saga for almost thirty years, Ben Burtt, sound designer on all of the films and a huge part of the technical success of the saga, decided to switch companies, joining Pixar Animation.[10] Burtt said of his move, "The last few years have been frustrating, so I was at a point of change" (Vadeboncoeur). Before he left, though, Burtt helped complete the *Star Wars* saga in glorious fashion, serving two roles on the final film by working on the editing and the sound design. Burtt was one of the few people to work on every *Star Wars* movie.

Using the most advanced digital filming equipment available, and the most sophisticated post-production techniques, Lucas again pushed the boundaries of film technology with *Revenge of the Sith*. Michael Rubin, author of *Droidmaker: George Lucas and the Digital Revolution* (Triad Publishing Company 2005), said, "*Star Wars* overshadows what Lucas has done for the industry. If it weren't for those movies, Lucas instead would be known as being one of the greatest innovators in film technology" (Modine). In all, roughly 1,650 people worked on

---

9.   "Big..."
10.   Lucas founded Pixar before selling it to Steve Jobs in 1986 for $5 million. Disney later acquired Pixar in 2006 for $7.4 billion in stock.

Revenge of the Sith from pre-production through post-production, leading to the movie's final cost of $113 million, almost exactly on budget (Windolf 111). Between the hard work, the cast and crew also managed to have a bit of fun on set. In the past, though, the stars working on *Star Wars* movies have not always had nice commentary about the films, the fans, or the shooting process.

The Light and Dark Sides of Acting

Because the story of *Revenge of the Sith* takes place shortly after the events in *Attack of the Clones*, all of the major roles were already filled before pre-production started. Among the villains, Ian McDiarmid returned as Supreme Chancellor–turned–Emperor Palpatine and Christopher Lee reprised his role as Count Dooku. On the other side, Natalie Portman had already signed a three-movie deal to play Senator Amidala, Ewan McGregor was also signed for all three prequels as Obi-Wan Kenobi, and Samuel L. Jackson returned for his third film as Jedi Master Wace Windu. Hayden Christensen returned for his second try as Anakin Skywalker, hero for most of the film and villain by the end, naturally. Most new actors and actresses filled minor roles. The primary cast members had plenty to say about their final performances in the saga and how they felt about the *Star Wars* experience.

One new major character was General Grievous, voiced by Supervising Sound Editor Matthew Wood. The story for how Wood won the voice role has quickly endeared him with the fans. For part of his sound work on the prequel, Wood, along with colleague Chris Scarabosio, was supposed to create the process to alter each Grievous candidate's voice using pitch and ring modulation. Scarabosio encouraged Wood to submit his own voice for consideration, which he did, anonymously. Wood said, "It wouldn't have worked out if I just asked George, 'Hey can I audition' ... In fact, if I did submit it under my name, he probably wouldn't have even listened to it to begin with" (Wood).

Against the odds, Lucas picked Wood to voice Grievous, which created a bit of a funny situation when he had to explain to Rick McCallum, the film's producer, that he was the winning candidate. Many rumors had previously cited Gary Oldman as having the best shot at the voice role. He did in fact read for the part, but quit the production once he realized it was outside of union rules. His manager, Douglas Urbanski, said, "He would like to be doing the movie but he would not step outside the union for it" (C. Robertson "Oldman ..."). Ultimately, Wood had an advantage anyway. "There had been so many auditions coming through our office and I had heard what he was asking for over and over, and I pretty much know George's language by now ... so it was like, 'Ok, I'm going to try this,'" Wood said (Wood). Having worked with Lucas for fifteen years, he was more familiar with the director's preferences and desires for the sound of the character.

Hayden Christensen remembers becoming a *Star Wars* fan in high school with the *Special Edition* releases, though he was aware of the saga as a child and often played with his brother's *Star Wars* toys, even imitating Darth Vader (P. Martin). He never thought he would be playing the iconic villain on screen, though. "I remember going and seeing *Episode I* when I was still in high school and thinking, 'Man, the guy who gets to play Darth as an older man is one lucky guy,'" Christensen recalled (P. Martin). When Lucas picked him to be the next actor to portray Anakin Skywalker, out of 442 candidates, consequently guaranteeing he would be the one to show the transformation to Darth Vader, Christensen was just out of high school (Christensen *Evening Standard*).

For his role in *Revenge of the Sith*, Christensen had to add muscle and train rigorously for five to six hours per day. To gain the necessary weight, as any body builder knows, requires the consumption of a huge number of calories per day. "I was on a strict diet, eating six meals a day and on every protein and weight gain supplement man has created," he said (Millar). Christensen spent months building the necessary mass and gaining the physical skills for his demanding lightsaber work in the film. "I put on 25 pounds, going from 160 to 185 pounds," he said (Millar). Christensen said he lost all of the progress he had made in the gym after the movie's filming ended, though, "all without any effort."

Although tens of millions of *Star Wars* fans worldwide looked forward to seeing his performance in the final prequel, and counted on him being convincing in showing Anakin's turn toward the Dark Side, Christensen had another focus. "As much as I felt I wanted to keep the fans happy, I was so indebted to George [Lucas] when he offered me the role that my biggest concern was making sure that he was happy with the work" (Millar). Since the beginning of the project, he had most looked forward to donning the Darth Vader suit and becoming everyone's favorite villain. "It was a good fifteen minutes to put on the whole costume—layer by layer and having everything fit," he said (Schaefer "Darth ...").

Wearing the legendary costume, however, was worth the agony of having to put on the heavy suit. Christensen said, "Walking onto the set and having a huge crowd of people there and getting to watch their faces as they sort of took in Darth Vader was very cool. It was an event—an event for myself and for everyone working on the film, finally getting to see Darth" (ibid.). More than fifteen hundred people tried to squeeze into a relatively small soundstage to see the event (C. Thomas). After the scene, the people in attendance applauded. "It's very empowering, very beastly," Christensen said of playing such a menacing character (P. Martin). "What I enjoyed most is getting to look at other people as they were looking at me, seeing their reactions, which were excitement and awe—even a glimmer of fear," he added.

Starring in two *Star Wars* films understandably changed Christensen's life. Still, he said, "Fame is not something I obsess over because there's no real equilibrium in this business. The amount of success you achieve is not directly related to the amount of work you put in" (Christensen *Evening Standard*). Despite the hard work involved in acting against blue and green screens, and the physical rigors of lightsaber fighting, he said, "I feel privileged to have been a part of these films" (ibid.). He recalled an experience back home in Toronto where kids came to his door at Halloween sometimes dressed as either Anakin or Darth Vader. "They were very excited when I would occasionally go to the door and give them candy," he said ("Visions ..."). As a young actor, "I think I've learned the most, from all the actors I've worked with, from Ian [McDiarmid]," Christensen said, citing his experience on set during the filming of the opera scene as "an eye-opening experience" ("Seeing ...").

Ian McDiarmid faced a unique situation when he agreed to return to reprise his role in *The Phantom Menace*: he had aged more than a decade since the release of *Return of the Jedi*, yet his character was several decades younger. When speaking about his role in the final prequel, he joked, "It's been a long time, hasn't it? I was 120 when I started, and I've gotten much younger" (Schaefer "Back ..."). McDiarmid enjoyed having the opportunity to act in the final film of the saga, which provided him with the excuse to play the role of the ultimate villain of the story. "My character is the blackest of the black. He's totally irredeemable," said McDiarmid, who summed up Palpatine's sole motivation as attaining power at any cost (ibid.). The character has one redeeming value according to McDiarmid: "You see in the movie he goes to the opera ... he's a patron of the arts" (McDiarmid). By contrast, Anakin's other mentor, Obi-Wan, has many redeeming qualities.

Ewan McGregor, despite his excellent work on the *Star Wars* prequels as Obi-Wan, had voiced numerous complaints about the work on the films and the fans. "The fighting in *Episode II* was unsatisfactory, I think," he said (C. Robertson "Ewan ..."). "I don't think the fight was nearly as good as it should have been and I certainly didn't have as big a crack of the whip as in the first one," he added. McGregor seemed to enjoy the choreographed fighting on set for the final prequel, however. Christensen said of his co-star, "He's really fast and he's got all the twirls down. He's quite extraordinary with his moves and spins. And he puts 110 percent into it" (Christensen *GQ*). Despite his problems with the prequel filming process, nobody with whom McGregor worked complained about his attitude or work ethic on set.

McGregor had previously trashed the first prequel by calling it "disappointing" and "flat" (C. Robertson "Ewan ..."). He also called the films "very tedious to make—there's no two ways about that," but the comment is more reasonable given that acting with characters to be added later could prove tedious to anyone (Wiltshire and Goodridge). Even Christensen said acting against screens all day is tough work. Regardless of his feelings about the first prequel, given his continuing working relationship with people who labored to bring the movie to fans, McGregor should have kept his opinions private. A professional would not bash successful film projects to the media when doing so harms a working relationship.

The quirky, outspoken actor also admitted to struggling with a drinking problem, saying the directors with whom he worked "must have known" he had shown up to work drunk in the past (Meller). He quit consuming alcohol after realizing that it was not only hurting his work but also making him depressed. While his relationship with alcohol was rocky in his younger years, his relationship with *Star Wars* fans is not too strong, either. "There's this huge following, which is weird. They have big meets and conventions, and I find it all a bit frightening," he said of the fans (Wiltshire and Goodridge). He must think thousands of people gathering to watch a sporting event is equally ridiculous.

McGregor is also notoriously against people seeking his autograph, feeling that everyone who wants an autograph plans to sell it on eBay or elsewhere at an inflated price. In fact, he described autograph-seekers as "fucking leeches" (Culley). He skipped the Cannes premiere of *Revenge of the Sith*, which other stars attended, because "the musical [*Guys and Dolls*, which he was working on at the time] doesn't stop for *Star Wars* so I just can't schlep off. I'll fit in what I can" (Culley). By contrast to McGregor's attitude, Christopher Lee, veteran actor and star of more than one hundred films, showed up to the United Kingdom premiere of the film and signed autographs for hours, saying, "These fans are very dedicated" (Culley). McGregor showed up briefly, then left. Anthony Daniels loved working with McGregor on the final prequel, though. "He's a national treasure, Scotland should be very proud" (Fulton "I've got ...").

Reprising his role, and appearing in all six *Star Wars* films, Anthony Daniels played C-3PO and enjoyed the distinction of having the final line in the last *Star Wars* movie ever. "I have the last line of the movie and I had the first line of the first movie, so there's a kind of neatness," he said (ibid.). Lucasfilm architects and crew had to rebuild the set of the *Tantive IV* that appears at the end of *Revenge of the Sith*, which Daniels described as "a real *Doctor Who* time travel experience," having been on the original set and the rebuilt one nearly thirty years later (ibid.).

At times, Daniels thought being known only as C-3PO overshadowed other work in his career, but he eventually embraced the popularity of the character and the saga, becoming somewhat of an unofficial spokesman for the saga. "I like the character and I want to safeguard him. I get paid for it, too, so it's no bad thing," he said (ibid.). In 2005, he kept busy with *Star Wars*–related work and appearances almost constantly. "It's dreadful if you want to do other things, but I'm proud to be a spokesperson and have a great time going around the world," he said (ibid.). By contrast, Natalie Portman has tried to distance herself from *Star Wars* fandom, much like her co-star, McGregor.

Portman keeps her personal life private, not even using her real last name, and has avoided the pitfalls of being a young star, like constant partying and substance abuse. Portman has always prided herself on academic success and intelligence, attending Harvard for a psychology degree. "She may be one of the most famous women on the planet but few people truly know her," one friend of hers told *The Mirror* in London (Portman). Christensen enjoyed Portman, though. "She's a real sweetie and articulate, astute, and very easy to play off. She's also a fantastic kisser and it's not hard to look at her with loving eyes" (Christensen *Evening Standard*).

Though presenting her with the opportunity to become famous worldwide, Portman seemed somewhat casual about the *Star Wars* phenomenon. "I don't really see *Star Wars* as a bigger deal than *Leon* [the 1994 Luc Besson film that helped catapult her to fame]. I just see it as another film, another experience and event in my life," she said (Portman). Perhaps to her, each *Star Wars* film is just another project, but to the public, Portman is much more recognizable as Padmé Amidala than any other character she has played. An older, wiser co-star in the prequels, however, has a much better appreciation of the importance of *Star Wars*.

With such a vast resume of successful films to his name, both commercially and artistically, Samuel L. Jackson had a different view from some of the actors and actresses who have appeared in the *Star Wars* saga. "I'd have been happy to play a stormtrooper. I'd have put on that white helmet and just run across the screen. As long as I knew I was in it, I'd have been happy," he said (Wiltshire and Goodridge). Far from being worried about his appearance in *Star Wars* and any possible detrimental effects, such as forever being remembered as a Jedi Master (hardly a tragic fate), Jackson said, "It's amazing to know that, no matter whatever else I do, no one will forget that I was in *Star Wars*" (ibid.). Still, Jackson shared some of McGregor's concerns about people taking the mythology a bit too seriously. "There's a faction of people in the world that actually believe I am a Jedi, which is very bizarre," he said (ibid.).

One of the minor characters in *Revenge of the Sith*, Bana Breemu, created a controversy near the release of the film because Lucas cut the character's only scene in the movie. Actress Bai Ling, who played Breemu in the prequel and had appeared in American films such as *Sky Captain and the World of Tomorrow* (2004), *Wild Wild West* (1999), *Red Corner* (1997), *Nixon* (1995), and *The Crow* (1994), among others, posed for the June issue of *Playboy*, which was an excuse for the magazine to tie-in with *Star Wars* and sell extra issues. Bai Ling posed as a Jedi on the cover, despite being a senator in the film. The issue hit newsstands well before the release of the final prequel.

Bai Ling was understandably disappointed with not appearing in the final cut of the movie, but she incorrectly assumed it was because of her *Playboy* shoot. The actress said, "I did not know that *Playboy* was going to come out the same time as *Star Wars*. I saw them as separate projects, I see the human body as beautiful and not pornographic, but maybe the *Star Wars* producers did not see what I did. I am in shock" (Chung). Lucas denied her assumption, saying, "My daughter is in that same scene. My daughter was cut as well" (Gensler). He further added, "My other daughter was in another scene and that was cut." The cuts were not vindictive or personal, but related to the length of the film and Lucas's decision to refocus it around Anakin, cutting the various scenes relating to the formation of what would become the Rebel Alliance.

Suffice to say, all of the actors and actresses had different experiences on the set of *Revenge of the Sith*, but in general everyone agreed that filming was fun and filled with funny stories and good memories. At the same time, filmmaking is hard work, especially with the physical prowess required of several of the actors and the blue and green screen acting expected of everyone in a *Star Wars* movie. While opinions about the significance of *Star Wars* to their careers varied between the cast members, the older, more experienced actors seemed to understand the phenomenon with a greater degree of perspective. Though many of the stars did not seem to understand the intense fan devotion to the saga, *Star Wars* fans had numerous Web sites online to learn more about the cast and the production process, including Lucasfilm's Official *Star Wars* Web Site.

Navigating Hyperspace and Beyond

As with *The Phantom Menace*, the Internet played a significant role in promoting *Star Wars*, both to casual and die-hard fans. Existing fan sites like GalacticHunter.com, JediNet.com, Lightsabre.co.uk, RebelScum.com, StarWarz.com, and TheForce.net, among others, continued to provide information for fans and collectors about news regarding the final prequel and about its various product tie-ins. Fans again had to decide how much they wanted to know about the upcoming movie before its release, especially with many spies reporting intricate details about the movie and its production to the fan sites. The Official *Star Wars* Web Site joined the fan sites in providing inside information and access to fans with an exclusive look into the movie's production, with photos from the set, journal entries with daily filming updates, and a webcam of the movie's production.

Much to the chagrin of freeloaders everywhere, access to all of the features of the Official *Star Wars* Web Site was not free, but it was fairly inexpensive. Beginning on June 10, 2003, Lucasfilm offered a paid version of the Official Site, called Hyperspace, giving fans much more material for a low subscription price of $19.95 annually. "It's less than a subscription to a magazine. And it's a way to have a little bit of *Star Wars* with you all year," said John Singh, a Lucasfilm spokesman ("Lucasfilm to Launch …"). Fans signing up for Hyperspace could have their own e-mail accounts with the Web site, too. At the time, starwars.com attracted about 4 million fans per month.

Among movie sites, even looking at just the free content, starwars.com is a behemoth, arguably the most extensive, most impressive official film site on the Internet. In the years since *The Phantom Menace* came to theaters, Web sites for movies have become much more impressive and significantly more important to studio marketing plans. In 1999, film sites were either an afterthought or not part of marking plans at all, which made starwars.com unique. By 2005, movie sites had become extremely innovative, with flash animations, games, quizzes, pictures, news items, and promotions available to Internet users. Because teenagers and young adults spend large portions of their time online, as a group, and they also see movies more frequently in theaters than older generations, studios know they need unique Web sites to establish buzz and set their films apart from the competition in the marketplace.

Hyperspace also joined the blog revolution, allowing its members to create their own blogs at blogs.starwars.com ("Blog ..."). For readers still unfamiliar with the concept, "blog" is short for "weblog." Blogs are like online journals, but often focus on particular topics, like politics, hobbies, or news. They are, in a sense, the ordinary person's tool to comment upon the world for everyone to read, though most blogs have small readerships of friends and family. Blogs have allowed people to take part in commenting upon issues themselves and have opened up the world of online publishing and writing to anyone who has a computer and can type. On blogs.starwars.com, the blogs are divided into categories such as gaming, collecting, Original Trilogy, prequel trilogy, and others, all allowing fans to take an active role in discussing the saga and its many subjects.

The live webcam, courtesy of Hyperspace, offered fans a behind-the-scenes look from Sydney, Australia, but fans also could see later pick-up shoots at Elstree Studios in London, where *A New Hope* filmed decades earlier. Hyperspace members could watch a live webcam to see John Williams and the London Symphony Orchestra record the soundtrack. One lucky fan jokingly asked Producer Rick McCallum in an online chat exclusively for Hyperspace members if he could visit the *Episode III* scoring session at Abbey Road Studios ("*Star Wars:* The Best ..." 6). To the fan's surprise, McCallum responded, "It's too late for today. But if you're here at 10:30 tomorrow, I'll let you have a little peek" (ibid.). The fan, going by the screenname GazelleUK and named Peter, showed up as requested. "I thought he was just joking," Peter said (ibid.). He reaped the benefits of Hyperspace membership with an extra, unadvertised perk.

Perhaps one of the best features of Hyperspace was the "Set Diary" section, where Pablo Hidalgo wrote daily updates to fans from the set of *Revenge of the Sith*. While being the official set diary writer would seem to be a great job, Hidalgo still spent long days on the set, waking up at 5:00 a.m. each day and finishing his diary entry for the day by around 9:00 p.m. (Hidalgo "Jump ..."). Hyperspace gave one lucky fan the opportunity to visit the set and write a set diary for starwars.com.

Although the experience of writing a widely-read set diary provided a nice opportunity for one fan, every fan on Hyperspace could participate in a small way in the decision-making process on *Revenge of the Sith*. Lucas and the *Episode III* Droid Unit agreed to allow fans to vote and decide between four different designs for Obi-Wan's astromech droid, with the winning design to appear in the final prequel ("Episode III: You Pick …"). At the end of 2005, Hyperspace gave away ten sets of three *Cinefex* magazines about the making of the prequels to selected members of the site, chosen randomly, as a way to thank fans for their support ("*Cinefex* …").

Though offering extensive coverage of the final prequel and a wealth of information about the saga, Hyperspace still drew criticisms from a segment of fans. The detractors complained that Lucasfilm should have offered the service for free and should not try to profit from loyal fans of the franchise by forcing them to pay for Hyperspace. The argument, with all due respect to its adherents, is ridiculously childish as none of the content already on starwars.com required fans to pay. Hyperspace only added additional content, not available before, that fans could access for a nominal fee. The extra video content, addition of more deleted scenes from *Attack of the Clones*, and greater coverage of the final prequel's filming resulted in more work for the staff of Lucas Online, which controls starwars.com.

Given the price of bandwidth and hiring employees to run Lucas Online, asking fans to pay less than $2 per month is not a hardship that warrants a backlash. Expecting a major company to operate a part of its business at a loss is unreasonable and demonstrates a lack of any real-world economic sense from fans suggesting such an idea. Besides, nobody forced fans to pay for the service. If they did not want access to the additional features at less than the price of a cup of coffee per month, they could choose not to sign up for Hyperspace. Despite some backlash, many people loved the additional content and welcomed the opportunity to have greater access to the production.

In April 2004, Hyperspace merged with the Official *Star Wars* Fan Club, putting all of the services for fans under one subscription and back at Lucasfilm for the first time since 1987. The one-year subscription package of $39.95 included access to Hyperspace, six issues of the *Star Wars Insider*, and a membership kit complete with various items, including a letter from George Lucas ("IDG …"). "Now that Hyperspace is the online component of a larger Fan Club experience, we're looking forward to new opportunities to make that fan experience even better this year," said Paul Ens, director of Lucas Online ("The Hyperspace …"). Lucas Online promised to offer more exclusive webcam access and photos for fans, besides its regular news updates and exclusive set diaries. "The Internet has redefined what the concept of a community can be, and it only makes sense for the Official Fan Club to embrace and facilitate this important aspect of being a fan," Ens said (ibid.).

In the weeks leading up to the release of *Revenge of the Sith* in theaters, traffic increased to the LucasArts *Episode III* game page by 120 percent, Yahoo's site for the prequel by 107 percent, and the Official *Star Wars* Web Site by 106 percent, according to an independent study conducted by Feedback Research, a division of the Claria Corporation (Claria.com). Even traffic to the Internet Movie Database (IMDb.com) increased 196 percent in the weeks leading up to the film, showing its broad appeal and cultural impact. The Official *Star Wars* Web Site collected 52 percent of total visitor traffic to *Star Wars*–related sites, among the random sampling Claria collected ("Sith Happens …").

Besides the Official *Star Wars* Web Site, the fan sites provided much of the news coverage and product coverage for fans on a daily basis. While TheForce.net and Rebelscum.com, both under the ownership of Philip Wise, remain the most popular destinations for fans and collectors, many other great sites provided, and continue to provide, high-quality destinations for *Star Wars* aficionados. JediNet.com, once one of the largest fan sites and still one of the oldest, remains a popular destination for many fans, as does StarWarz.com, where Lou "T'Bone" Tambone provides a wealth of information for fans. The site managed to report many spoilers related to the final prequel, too.

Over the years of the prequel trilogy's release, Tambone broke many stories about the films and spoilers relating to key plot points. "With *Episode I*, the site was popular but I was still sort of under the radar as far as breaking prequel news went," Tambone said.[1] He mentioned that other sites occasionally incurred the wrath of Lucasfilm, but usually in a friendly way with letters asking webmasters to remove content. With *Attack of the Clones*, Tambone and his site had gained popularity, leading to an alliance with Cinescape.com for a while, but Lucasfilm still treated the fan sites cordially. "I'd get an e-mail from someone at starwars.com or Steve Sansweet and they'd ask me to remove something. I'd always do so when it came like that," Tambone said. Though he mentioned a few heated moments with Lucasfilm over content, ultimately there was "nothing that wasn't resolved nicely."

With *Revenge of the Sith*, as Tambone describes the interactions, Lucasfilm took a harsher stance toward fan sites, or at least StarWarz.com. "It seemed like whoever was in charge over there decided they were just going to stop screwing around and send out legal letters instead. Forget all this politeness with the fan sites," he said. Instead of sending friendly letters, Lucasfilm instead sent legal cease-and-desist letters. "The threats of lawsuits flew and it was just a generally

---

1.   All comments from Tambone come from an interview with the author.

uncomfortable time," Tambone said. He also thought the situation was a bit strange because "a few clicks away, other sites were posting stuff way worse than I was and no one was saying a thing." Tambone called the Lucasfilm policy "selective enforcement." Despite the threats, the site survived, with Tambone doing his best to keep the peace.

Tambone sees his site as a place where fans like himself visit, so "not the thirteen-year-old fanboy," but more "the Original Trilogy generation, really." He thinks of StarWarz.com as a place for "the older, wiser fan," though acknowledges that "the occasional kid ... drops in looking for cool stuff to read or look at." Fan sites, in his estimation, grew from the early days of fandom where local fans gathered together to talk about the movies. With the advent of the Internet, fan sites became "hubs for people to come to and perhaps learn something or chat with other fans."

Going forward, Tambone said he does not plan to change much but will report on the television shows "as they develop," provided people send him information as they did with the prequels. Tambone is guarded in his optimism for Lucasfilm's television efforts, but hopes the live-action show will be more like *24* and not just "*Buffy* in space." Speaking of the change in traffic to the site between 2005 and 2006, Tambone said it "took a hit, no doubt," but that his normal traffic "is actually nice" because he can keep up with e-mails easier. Tambone enjoys running StarWarz.com mainly for "the interaction. I've made a ton of friends on the net because of this site and I've done things I probably would have never been able to do if I hadn't started it," such as having one of his parody films play at Cannes in 2005, where *Revenge of the Sith* premiered.

Over in the United Kingdom, Mark Newbold's Lightsabre.co.uk is a fantastic Web site with some of the best interviews with key *Star Wars* cast and crew members available anywhere. The site has, in some form, operated since 1996 (though only under its current title and at its current address since 1999) and offers fans a wealth of fan fiction set in the *Star Wars* universe besides more typical fan site product reviews and news items. When asked about what type of fans visit his site, Newbold joked, "A very smart, sexy, and well-read visitor I hope!"[2] Because Lightsabre is mainly a fan fiction site, it has perhaps a slightly different readership from other fan sites, but "nowadays we are best known for our star and webmaster interviews, which go live every two weeks," always drawing many additional visitors.

---

2.   All comments from Newbold come from an interview with the author.

Newbold described his experience running Lightsabre leading up to and during the release of *Revenge of the Sith* as an exciting time because "it was the final [film]," so fans had many hopes and expectations pinned on the movie. He applauds Lucas for his marketing of the final prequel online, saying, "Lucas was able to tease us with images, webcams, set visits, sneak production peeks, and glimpses of what was to come like never before," using Hyperspace. After the final prequel's release, Newbold noticed that many fan sites slowed greatly, not reporting much news nor adding much to the conversation about the saga. Newbold, who applauded the quality of the final prequel, also noted the absurdity of none of the prequels receiving an Oscar for Best Special Effects.

Newbold sees sites like StarWarz.com, JediNet.com, and his own site as serving "a vital role" to fans, almost like the heart of the fan sites, whereas Aint-It-Cool-News.com and TheForce.net are the more mainstream, news-oriented sites with staff members more likely to keep in personal touch with Lucasfilm representatives. Still, Newbold only recently realized his site's growing importance and recognition from Lucasfilm. "Folks at Lucasfilm *are* watching us, and not only to check for spoilers and illegal pictures we might publish, but to actually read us as fans," he said. Lightsabre, while perhaps not as well known among fans in the United States, is a classy and popular destination for English-speaking fans in Europe. It continues to gain recognition worldwide for its high-quality interviews, a wealth of fan art and fan fiction, and plenty of news to keep fans current on any franchise happenings.

Since the release of *Revenge of the Sith*, Newbold said his traffic has increased, but mainly because the site underwent major renovations in March 2005, so traffic bottomed out for a bit before it rebounded strongly. He works hard to promote his site to other fans, including through a Hyperspace blog, which has nearly tripled his readership. Newbold spends 12–15 hours a week running his site, not including writing fan fiction for it. Like Tambone, he most enjoys "the interaction with fellow webmasters and fellow fans on the blogs." He also loves interviewing the stars. "There's nothing better than receiving an e-mail from a childhood hero," Newbold said. "If you'd told me when I was seven that Chewbacca would be writing to me, I wouldn't have believed you, and not only because my first goldfish was named Chewbacca," he added.

Looking into the future, Newbold does not see his site changing much, but he thinks Lucasfilm faces a few challenges ahead with the franchise. The live-action television series will be a big deal, he thinks, especially the first episode, but with a new episode every week "there won't be the capability to delve in quite so deep" as with the films, where years passed between each entry. He cautioned, "Licensees will have to be more selective with what they release—greed in this instance could flood and kill the market [for licensed goods]." The quality of the live-action series is greatly important in its ability to hold fan interest in the franchise. "It will need to be something a bit special," Newbold said. With Lucasfilm planning one hundred episodes for the series, fans will stop watching quickly if the quality of the show is mediocre, Newbold thinks.

Both Newbold and Tambone thought Lucasfilm tried to maintain secrecy with the final prequel, but was either unsuccessful or managed to do so in a different fashion. "I think Lucasfilm tried to be much more secretive about the final [prequel]. The ironic thing about all that is, the more secretive they tried to be, the worse they were at keeping leaks plugged," Tambone said. When asked if Lucasfilm seemed less secretive with *Revenge of the Sith* compared to the two prior prequels, Newbold said, "I'm not so sure that [Lucas] was less secretive, it's more down to the technologies and avenues available to him compared with 1999," such as Hyperspace, where Lucas could release bits of information at a controlled pace.

In a message to Hyperspace members after a prize give-away, the Official Site wrote, "We at Lucas Online have viewed the site not as a traditional marketing tool, but rather as a celebration of *Star Wars* and true resource and community for its fans" ("*Cinefex* ... "). The unique access to *Revenge of the Sith*'s production, through Hidalgo's set diaries, the webcam footage, the news updates, and frequent behind-the-scenes photos gave *Star Wars* fans the opportunity to feel a part of the production of the final movie and watch as it came together. By the time *Revenge of the Sith* came to DVD, starwars.com had existed about nine years. With *Star Wars* fans a die-hard group and the franchise sure to remain popular into the future, the Official Site will continue to serve fans worldwide well into the future. Fans also will no doubt continue to enjoy the efforts of dedicated webmasters like Lou Tambone and Mark Newbold. Lucasfilm, though, had numerous other avenues to promote the final prequel besides the Internet.

Return of the Marketing Machine

Going Out With a Bang

Promotional tie-ins with well-known consumer brands and merchandising tie-ins with toy and collectible manufacturers for major films are not new, but they are almost inventions of the *Star Wars* franchise. Throughout the franchise's history, the movies have enjoyed numerous licensing tie-ins, from toys to food to bath towels to books and beyond. Find an item that exists in the world and a collector can show you the same item wrapped in *Star Wars* imagery, except perhaps condoms, cigarettes, and alcohol. "The very first *Star Wars* movie represented the birth of the modern movie merchandising business," said Martin Brochstein, executive editor of the trade publication *The Licensing Letter* (Tanaka). The first film revolutionized movie merchandising, but in the years since its release, Lucasfilm perfected the formula, eventually culminating in a massive push for the last prequel.

The Phantom Menace came to theaters with an incredible array of merchandising partners, including several fast-food chains, numerous toy companies, high-end collectible producers, and dozens of others offering T-shirts, soap, trash cans, beach towels, action figures, and lightsabers, among many other items. Despite the first prequel's merchandising blitz, Lucasfilm confirmed that *Revenge of the Sith* topped all other *Star Wars* films in number of merchandising partners. "This is the last big push for *Star Wars* marketing opportunities, and they are certainly going to go out with a bang," said Scott Krugman of the National Retail Federation (Yeldell). The more understated approach for *Attack of the Clones* was fine, for the middle film of the trilogy, but for the last *Star Wars* movie ever, Lucasfilm unleashed the full potential of the franchise.

In all, Lucasfilm had signed about four hundred licensees in more than thirty countries (Idelson "Timeless …"). Despite the massive number of licensees involved with *Star Wars*, Lucasfilm carefully controls the franchise and tries to make sure to pick companies that are going to have the best interest of the brand in mind, which means not making low quality goods. "We look for the best companies in any category," said Howard Roffman, president of Lucas Licensing (ibid.). The franchise could have more products associated with it, but Lucasfilm will not approve any license just for the money; the franchise is rich enough.

Over the years, though, Lucasfilm has received many unusual licensing requests. Roffman said, "As *Star Wars* fans have gotten older, we've been approached by more alcohol makers. But that's not really a match for us and so we won't consider tobacco and alcohol products" (ibid.). Lucasfilm is especially careful with the franchise and its product tie-ins to protect the long-term viability of the series as toys and other products still sell well in years without new films from the franchise coming to theaters. The company wants to manage *Star Wars* for decades into the future, not just the next few years.

Lucasfilm broke with tradition for the final prequel in a few instances, though. *Revenge of the Sith* marketing marked the first time the company had allowed the *Star Wars* characters to be used outside of the fictional film environment, or in other words interacting with humans in commercials promoting the film and its marketing partners (Ahrens). For instance, in a Cingular Wireless ad, viewers could see Chewbacca growl into a microphone in a recording studio to create the ring tones for the cellular service's phones while other characters like Darth Vader waited in the background. In a Diet Pepsi commercial, Yoda sits at a lunch counter and uses the Force to try to get a Diet Pepsi for his meal. The commercial, created by advertising agency BBDO New York, boasted effects from Industrial Light & Magic.

An article on the Official *Star Wars* Web Site at the end of 2005 read, "The enormous 1999 boom of *Star Wars* promotional activity was not echoed in 2002, leaving some fans a bit despondent that they couldn't go to a local restaurant and pick up a cup or a toy" ("*Star Wars:* The Best ..."). The article joked, "But that oversight was corrected in 2005 with partnerships with such well known brands as Burger King, Pepsi, Lays, Kellogg's, Cingular, Moviefone and M&Ms." In 1999, many retailers had massive quantities of left-over merchandise because of licensees overproducing items, while in 2002 the scant number of products by comparison surprised many fans. Howard Roffman said of the last prequel, "We will have a robust program, smaller than what we did behind *Episode I* and more than we did behind *Episode II*," though the number of promotional partners had reached a franchise high for *Revenge of the Sith* ("M & M's ...").

Many fans expressed surprise over the relatively small promotional and merchandising campaign associated with *Attack of the Clones*, especially after the massive hype of the first prequel. "*The Phantom Menace* was so over-saturated that Lucasfilm was frightened to do anything for *Attack of the Clones*, so there was almost no merchandising hype for that film," said Michael Kaminski of Toronto,

Canada (Kaminski). He continued, "With *Revenge of the Sith*, they reached a decent middle-ground—it was hyped up as you would expect a summer block-buster to be, but not unreasonably so." Lynde Roberts of Billings, Montana, agreed with Kaminski's assessment of the first two prequels, but not the final one. "There was such a big deal made over *The Phantom Menace* and then nothing from *Attack of the Clones*, it felt like they were overcompensating [with *Revenge of the Sith*]," she said (Roberts).

While many people undoubtedly thought Lucasfilm promoted its final *Star Wars* film too much, other fans thought the company's massive marketing campaign helped the movie attract more viewers who might otherwise not have been interested. Jason Rose from Derbyshire in the United Kingdom said, "The tie-ins seemed to help [the movie], since [they] drew a lot of people that weren't connected to *Star Wars* … and I doubt [they] put many people off" (Rose). Cody Powell from Texas agreed. "I actually thought that having many product tie-ins allowed for many people, especially younger viewers, to really get into the movies," he said (Powell). Diane Kovalcin of New Jersey thought Lucasfilm missed targeting a key demographic altogether, though. "*Star Wars* products are aimed mainly to boys and men, having very few things for girls and virtually nothing for women," she said (Kovalcin).

Tasting the Force

Darth Vader did his part trying to hawk various *Star Wars* licensee products. In an M&M commercial, viewers could see him holding a massive bag of M&M's while in an ad for Burger King he could be seen trying to con someone out of a hamburger. Spokeswoman Joan Buyce for Masterfoods USA, the company behind the M&M brand, said, "M&M characters are celebrities in and of themselves. This was an appropriate icon-meets-icon opportunity for us" (Tanaka). Various licensees focused on giving fans *Star Wars*–themed food, drinks, and candy for much of 2005.

Along with the April 2, 2005, debut of many new *Star Wars* toys tied to *Revenge of the Sith*, Masterfoods USA launched a special line of *Star Wars* M&M's. The company's marketing efforts, known as the "*Star Wars* M-Pire" promotion, encouraged customers to follow Anakin's fall to the Dark Side by trying limited dark chocolate M&M's. The "Darth Mix" of dark chocolate M&M's featured black, maroon, purple, dark blue, and silver candy coatings. Meanwhile, a "Jedi Mix" featured classic milk chocolate M&M's in colors such as beige, cream, pastel green, and "lightsaber blue." The Skittles and Kudos brands, also by Masterfoods, participated in the promotion as well.

On March 29, before the first huge merchandising push from companies hawking *Star Wars* products, M&M struck first in Times Square in New York, where a life-size X-Wing fighter, R2-D2 and C-3PO, a horde of Stormtroopers, and Darth Vader with his M&M counterpart M-Vader joined in a promotion of the new candy launch. M&M's had not come in dark chocolate versions before in the company's sixty-four-year history. "We continue to look for innovative approaches to launch products and know that dark chocolate is in great demand from our consumers," said Martyn Wilks, vice president and general manager of snackfoods at Masterfoods USA ("Darth ..."). Fans could collect seventy-two *Star Wars*–themed M&M packages with exclusive "Galactic Gossip" under the wrappers featuring trivia relating to the two brands.

Aside from the promotions from Masterfoods, Pez Candy introduced limited edition Giant Pez Dispensers, twelve inches tall, featuring characters like Darth Vader, Yoda, and C-3PO. The Giant Pez Dispensers also spoke lines or played music from the movie when activated to dispense the candy. Pez had produced many *Star Wars* dispensers before the final prequel, however, and is one of the rare candy companies with a sizable group of hardcore collectors. Many old Pez dispensers sell for hundreds of dollars on the secondary market. Besides Pez and Masterfoods, Hasbro's Cap Candy introduced *Star Wars* Spin Pops with characters like Darth Vader and Chewbacca on the handles.

Kellogg sold *Star Wars* Pop-Tarts, Frosted Flakes, Apple Jacks, Cheez-It crackers, and Fudge Shoppe cookies, among many other branded products. The company included "saberspoons," plastic spoons that light up, in cereal boxes to help boost product sales. "These promotions are very popular with consumers, and the excitement surrounding the film drives traffic to store shelves," said Jenny Enochson, Kellogg's senior director of marketing communications (Ahrens). Kellogg's promotional push reached fans in thirty countries worldwide as the company unleashed more than 200 million product packages from April through the early summer with *Revenge of the Sith* images and characters on them ("Kellogg ..."). The cereal based on the film consisted of toasted oat grains and *Star Wars*–themed marshmallows.

Burger King launched its first-ever global promotion to celebrate the release of *Revenge of the Sith* (Johannes "Star Wars ..."). Starting May 11, the fast-food company promoted the final film's release by celebrating the entire saga with thirty-one exclusive *Star Wars* toys spanning all six movies. The toys were Kids Meal premiums and represented five toy genres: pullback vehicles, wind-up figures, water squirters, plush toys, and image viewers of scenes from the episodes. The six-week promotion also included the *Star Wars* Choose Your Destiny scratch-and-win game. Customers could win a grand prize of $1 million or lesser prizes like toys, video games, and free food items with the sweepstakes lasting through June 13. In all, Burger King's promotion spanned restaurants in fifty countries.

The collaboration of Lucasfilm and Burger King was a reuniting of two companies that had earlier formed a partnership in the seventies and early eighties for promotions relating to the Original Trilogy. In 1978, Burger King had a premium poster promotion, the first of its *Star Wars* promotions, then the fast-food chain offered four collectible *Return of the Jedi* glasses to coincide with the final film of the first trilogy. The company is best known to *Star Wars* fans for its various collectible glasses, offered during limited promotions, which are now considered valuable collector's items. For *The Empire Strikes Back*, the chain had run three separate promotions spanning one year, a remarkably long time to promote a single film by modern standards. For fans nostalgic about the Original Trilogy Burger King promotions, the company's return to the saga after twenty-two years was a nice opportunity to relive old memories and create new ones with the chain's massive new promotion ("Doing *Star Wars* …").

Pepsi ran a large promotion centered around the final prequel, including a partnership with convenience store chain 7-Eleven, which offered Darth Dew Slurpees and four limited edition 3-D cups at participating stores. Pepsi launched the "Call Upon Yoda" instant-win sweepstakes on April 18, allowing fans to win one of ten $100,000 grand prizes by entering a code online, by phone, or by text messaging. For winners, Yoda responded by telling them the prize they won, but otherwise Darth Vader or the two droids, C-3PO and R2-D2, let fans know they should try again. The Darth Dew Slurpee was modeled after Mountain Dew Pitch Black, a popular drink originally introduced in 2004 as a limited edition soda with a grape flavor. "We know that black food does not generally sell well. Having said that, the inherent value of the *Star Wars* brand is good enough reason to try it," said Robert Passikoff, founder of brand research firm Brand Keys, when speaking about the Slurpee flavor (Meitner).

Frito-Lay also offered *Star Wars*–themed packaging for Lay's Classic and Lay's Wavy Potato Chips. Inside the bag, fans could receive one of twelve exclusive sticker designs. The company also offered a *Star Wars*–inspired Cheetos snack called Twisted Cheetos, which temporarily changed the color of consumers' tongues either to green or black. Frito-Lay had also been involved in campaigns with the previous two prequels. "As consumers line-up for *Episode III*, Lay's and Cheetos will be able to give them a 'taste' of the movie … before it opens," said Haston Lewis, vice president of shopper marketing for Frito-Lay ("Frito-

Lay …"). The company's final prequel promotion, known as the "May the Fun Be With You" program, gave fans a chance to win a trip for four to Orlando, Florida, a home entertainment system, or tickets to see the prequel through game pieces, doubling as stickers, included inside the *Star Wars*–themed bags.

From Taters to Sabers

In the toy realm, Hasbro had the license as "master toy licensee" and has been producing *Star Wars* toys for many years, since buying Kenner Toys in 1991. To promote the release of the final prequel, Hasbro launched one of the biggest toy lines in its history. "There is only one *Star Wars* and it has endured because of its passionate fan base," said Derryl DePriest, senior director of marketing for *Star Wars* at Hasbro (Coolidge). One of the most popular items the company made in association with the final prequel was the Darth Vader Voice Changer, a helmet and mask for children that alters voices to mimic the character's breathing patterns. "The final chapter of the *Star Wars* saga gives us the opportunity to roll out the most impressive line of *Star Wars* toys and games ever assembled," said Brian Goldner, president of Hasbro's U.S. toy segment ("Hasbro Brings …").[1]

Another of the most popular new products that Hasbro released in 2005, under its Playskool brand, was Darth Tater, the Darth Vader Mr. Potato Head version that came with a Vader helmet and lightsaber. The product came out several months before the April release of the *Revenge of the Sith* merchandise. Playskool Vice President of Marketing Todd Rywolt said, "A *Star Wars* Mr. Potato Head is always something we wanted to do … With *Episode III* focusing so much on Darth Vader, the time was right. Lucasfilm agreed and Darth Tater was born!" ("A Closer Look …"). The product spent about nine months in development, but marked a first for the icon of toys. "Mr. Potato Head has been Santa Claus and the Easter Bunny. But he has never played another movie character," besides himself in *Toy Story* (1995).

Darth Tater was a huge success with fans and kids, delighting retailers as well. "As soon as we get them in we sell them out," said Teresa Peck, product flow manager at a Toys "R" Us in Tennessee (Yeldell). Derek Donovan of the *Kansas City Star* called the toy "impossibly cute" and Peter Jenkinson of the *Daily Post* in Liverpool, England, said it appealed to "kids of all ages" and ranked it among the best new products for the franchise. The success of the toy prompted Playskool to give Darth Tater some company in the form of SpudTrooper, a Mr. Potato Head version of a stormtrooper. "Darth Vader had stormtroopers to protect him, so it's

---

1.   Hasbro promoted Goldner to chief operating officer in early 2006.

only natural that SpudTroopers would be created to serve Darth Tater," said Melissa Bernstein, Playskool brand manager ("SpudTrooper …"). At year's end, the Official *Star Wars* Web Site listed Darth Tater as #10 on its *"Star Wars*: The Best of 2005" list.

Hasbro made sure that fans would be able to enjoy more products for the final prequel than premiered with *Attack of the Clones*, where the company cut back because of the hype and oversupply that followed *The Phantom Menace*'s release. In early 2003, Hasbro signed a deal with Lucasfilm to extend its *Star Wars* license through 2018, an additional ten years from the original agreement (Fasig). Under the initial contract, Hasbro had to pay Lucasfilm a minimum of $590 million, of which it had already paid $470 million. Lucasfilm reduced the minimum payment by $85 million, to $505 million, a move that David Hargreaves, Hasbro's chief financial officer, said the company felt was necessary "to rebalance the economics of the deal" because "Hasbro under the original structure was struggling to make money with *Star Wars"* while "Lucas was making a significant amount" (Fasig). One can attribute most of the reason for the deal's imbalance to the incredible hype for the first prequel.

With many *Star Wars* video games and novels planned for release after *Revenge of the Sith*, not to mention the two television shows, the ten-year extension of the licensing agreement promised to give Hasbro a substantial economic boost, despite the end of the film franchise in 2005. "This extension provides us with a real economic benefit by allowing us to continue to build and expand on the success of this franchise property for many years to come," said Alan Hassenfeld, Hasbro's chairman and CEO at the time ("Hasbro Gets …"). Hasbro had an impressive line of toys and games prepared for the final prequel to capitalize on its long-term license. Lucas benefitted from the deal, too, by extending the time of the warrants granted to him to purchase 15.75 million shares of Hasbro stock by ten years.

Hasbro created a special toy tie-in with worldwide powerhouse retailer Wal-Mart to remind fans of the first days of *Star Wars* toy collecting. As part of the promotion, fans could buy an empty box, limited to only 50,000 total sets, and send a proof of purchase to receive four action figures. Eager fans had bought empty boxes in a similar promotional arrangement in 1977 when Kenner Toys, overcome with demand for action figures from the breakout success, had not produced any toys for the 1977 holiday season. "There's going to be a great emotional value to the package. This transcends movie hype; it's a pop culture phenomenon," said Eric Nyman, a marketing director for *Star Wars* at Hasbro (Choi "'Star Wars' …"). Analysts thought the move was perfect to build hype among adult collectors because of the limited availability of the item and the unlikelihood of younger kids wanting to buy empty boxes.

Other retailers also had special promotions, like at Toys "R" Us, where customers purchasing more than $35 in merchandise were given free holographic Yoda action figures. Target received an exclusive toy, "Lava Reflection Darth Vader," that Hasbro limited to 50,000 figures. Also at Target, fans could purchase an exclusive gift card complete with a sound-chip featuring Vader's breathing and lightsaber hum. The two toy promotions with Target and Wal-Mart marked the first times that Hasbro had disclosed production numbers for *Star Wars* toys, adding interest among collectors. The three exclusives were linked together with a hidden symbol on the package of each one. "Once you find all three symbols, go to the Hasbro Web site and try to crack the code for a secret prize," Nyman said (Bhatnagar).

Star Wars fans over the years have had numerous companies from which to choose when buying collectibles. Undoubtedly, the highest quality collectibles related to *Star Wars* over the past several years have come from Master Replicas, the Walnut Creek, California–based licensee that makes high-end, adult collectibles such as replica lightsabers, blasters, helmets, and studio scale models from the saga. Although its finest collectibles are far above the price range for many collectors, Master Replicas offers extensively researched replicas of some of the most popular weapons and props from the *Star Wars* saga.

The *Revenge of the Sith* line from Master Replicas was no less impressive than the company's past efforts, though limited edition runs were higher to meet increased demand. "Sales have definitely accelerated around the film," said Steve Dymszo, a founding member of Master Replicas and the company's vice president of product design at the time (Laidman). Howard Roffman said, "They had a good mixture of technical skills and marketing talents and understanding of the collector customer base. They did present product prototypes to us that are of really great quality," and thus Master Replicas was born (ibid.).

Although Master Replicas had annual revenues less than $30 million in its young history, it had already started to branch out into other licenses (ibid.). Besides *Star Wars*, the company produced products for franchises such as Marvel, *Pirates of the Caribbean*, *The Lord of the Rings*, *The Chronicles of Narnia*, and *Star Trek*. Although hoping to expand its reach, *Star Wars* launched Master Replicas and remained its primary focus. In fact, in 2005, *Star Wars* products accounted for more than 93% of total company revenue, according to a securities and exchange commission filing when Corgi International merged with Master Replicas in late 2006 ("Proxy …").

Dymszo, a former engineer who spent much of the nineties running a small entertainment collectibles business, partnered with Michael Cookson, a San Francisco entrepreneur, to start the company. "If you look at the *Star Wars* fan base, it has 2 million core fans that have been with the franchise now for twenty-eight years. Many of those people are in their 30s and 40s, so I felt there was an opportunity to develop a range of products to appeal to passionate fans" (Laidman). Master Replicas strictly limits production of full-scale prop replicas, with edition sizes ranging from five hundred to around four thousand. Fans with lower budgets, though, can still buy .45 scale lightsabers and .33 scale blasters for affordable prices often under $50.

Prior to the 1990s, high-end *Star Wars* collectibles were not a significant segment of the collecting galaxy, but as the first group of young fans grew into adults and accumulated disposable income, the demand for high-quality adult collectibles rose, creating a profitable market for several companies. Before Master Replicas, a company called Icons Authentic Replicas had the *Star Wars* prop license in the mid-1990s, producing several lightsabers and a few beautiful studio scale pieces. Nonetheless, the quality of workmanship on its lightsabers was vastly inferior to the high standards that Master Replicas has set for its high-end products. Aside from Master Replicas, other prominent high-end collectibles companies making *Star Wars* items at the time of release for the final prequel included Sideshow Collectibles, Gentle Giant Studios, and Rawcliffe.

For Japanese *Star Wars* fans, toy company Medicom offered a high-quality Darth Vader toy with a removable mask as part of its Real Action Heroes line. Happinet Corporation offered fans in Japan a new umbrella with a lightsaber handle grip, using the Master Replicas .45 scale Darth Vader lightsaber hilt as a reference. Tomy gave Japanese fans an opportunity to buy mini-dioramas, mini-helmets, and mini-lightsabers. Numerous other companies joined in releasing products in the country, with GE Consumer Finance offering *Star Wars* credit cards, like MBNA had done in America ("*Star Wars* Collectibles ...").

The Ubiquitous Force

Video rental chain Blockbuster helped feed the hype machine, encouraging fans to come into its stores for movies, games, and exclusive merchandise. "The legacy of *Star Wars* is enormous, whether you experienced the excitement of the first movie in the theater or just recently learned the difference between an Ewok and a Wookie," said Curt Andrews, senior vice president and general merchandise manager of Blockbuster ("Blockbuster ..."). He said, "Blockbuster is the complete source for *Star Wars* entertainment for the legions of faithful fans that are waiting for the movie premiere" (ibid.). Blockbuster ran a survey to find fans' favorite non-human character from the saga; Yoda won, with 27 percent of the vote compared to 24 percent for Chewbacca. Jar Jar Binks barely beat out Jabba the Hutt, 3 percent to 2 percent (ibid.). Blockbuster also announced a gaming event on May 4 at its Game Rush Blockbuster locations, with events starting at 11:00 p.m., in advance of the midnight release of the *Revenge of the Sith* game.

To help sell its soundtrack to *Revenge of the Sith*, aside from the great music John Williams provided for it, Sony Classical included a bonus DVD with the product that offered a surprise for fans of the saga. On the bonus disc, titled, "*Star Wars*: A Musical Journey," appears sixteen music videos with seventy minutes of footage and music from all six *Star Wars* films. The music videos tell the *Star Wars* story in a clever way with a mixture of music and dialogue played alongside carefully edited footage. The music videos, with titles like "A Hero Rises," "A Hero Falls," and "An Empire is Forged," help demonstrate themes of the saga or convey messages about the characters and story in just a few minutes each with the added emotional pull of Williams's powerful music.

Another aspect of promoting the theatrical release of the new *Star Wars* film, or at least satiating fan enthusiasm to some extent, was to pick an author capable of translating Lucas's filming script and additional character ideas to a novel, a task assigned to Matthew Stover. The author, a part-time bartender as well as acclaimed writer, had previously written *Star Wars: The New Jedi Order: Traitor* (Del Rey 2002) and *Star Wars: Shatterpoint* (Del Rey 2004). "We chose Matt because we liked the way he handled characters and character development, and we knew that would be a key element of doing the novel for *Episode III* ... what motivates a character to make a horrendous choice in his life," said Howard Roffman (Caterinicchia). The novelizations for the first two prequels focused more on fleshing out events in the films, whereas with the third novelization Stover focused on the inner thoughts and feelings of the characters (Italie).

Lucasfilm chose Stover, in the author's estimation, because of his ability to handle writing about dark situations and moral complexities, part of which is also what publisher Del Rey told him after selecting him for the project. Stover is best known for, in his words, capturing "the psychological breakdown of characters under extreme moral pressure," which applies to Anakin perfectly (Stover). Because of the time schedule he had to work on the project, "almost triple the amount of time given to the usual novelization," the *Revenge of the Sith* book should not be seen as a fast-and-loose translation of the film from one medium to another (ibid.). Rather, Stover wrote it "as I think it might have been if [Lucas] had been making the film based on" his book, instead of the reverse (ibid.).

Aside from his other professional pursuits, Stover has a martial arts background spanning several decades, which helped him detail a few of the fight sequences in his books. He reportedly earned an advance of about $100,000 for the prequel novelization with a small royalty scale (Italie). Though not a huge payday for such a large project destined for high sales, Stover was excited about the opportunity to boost his popularity. "It raises my profile in a way no other single project could. This takes me from being a respected, but little-known fantasy writer to being one of the best-known fantasy writers in America," he said (ibid.). Stover concluded, "That's something you can't figure in dollars and cents." Lucasfilm, however, could begin counting its dollars and cents once the book hit shelves April 2 with the rest of the first wave of merchandise.

Besides the novel, fans could purchase a souvenir guide to the movie, from IDG Entertainment, that featured a wealth of information about the final prequel, from both pictures and text. The souvenir book had exclusive behind-the-scenes information, cast and crew interviews, and enough details about the plot and characters to help viewers learn more about the film. Thin programs with black and white imagery followed the first *Star Wars* film to theaters in 1977, but Paradise Press created much larger guides to *The Empire Strikes Back* and *Return of the Jedi*, the latter of which was the first of the guides to be sold primarily through retail outlets, rather than in theaters. Topps picked up the souvenir guide duties with *The Phantom Menace*, but in another example of the relative dearth of merchandise and promotions for *Attack of the Clones*, the movie had no domestic souvenir guide ("Souvenir …").

Many theaters and theater chains offered special events and in-theater promotions to amuse fans and take advantage of captive audiences waiting in long lines to attain quality seats. For instance, Decipher, which has long produced the *Star Wars* Collectible Card Game (SWCCG), launched the premiere issue of *FLIcK Magazine*, which boasted nothing but *Star Wars* coverage and was available exclusively to *Revenge of the Sith* ticket buyers, with all 2.5 million copies given away free. "We are excited to launch the first issue of *FLIcK* in conjunction with one of the most anticipated and beloved films of all time and we can't wait for the most passionate *Star Wars* fans to get copies of the magazine," said Decipher CEO Warren Holland ("Free …"). For fans unable to get a copy, available at Loews, Cinemark, and Carmike theaters, the entire issue was online at FLIcKMagazine.com.

Promoting *Revenge of the Sith* to a worldwide audience required different marketing tactics than Fox and Lucasfilm had used in 1999 for *The Phantom Menace*, in part because of changing technology and emerging opportunities. Ivan Pollard at the Ingram Partnership, a media strategy firm in London, helped advise the studios on how best to make international audiences aware of the saga and its final film. Pollard suggested more sophisticated tie-ins, like cell phone promotions in European markets, events, like *Star Wars* Weekends at Disneyland Paris and other locations, and more marketing partnerships (Pfanner). "I think we did challenge a lot of what Fox was thinking. They certainly get it now," Pollard said (ibid.). *Star Wars* ice sculptures appeared at the Sapporo Snow Festival in Japan, again demonstrating the more creative marketing approach that Pollard advocated.

Lucasfilm also agreed to team with British tabloid newspapers, trading exclusive content for editorial space. "It's a win-win. They contribute to our noise, and we contribute to their sales," Pollard said (Pfanner). The media has always appreciated help from *Star Wars* in selling magazines and newspapers or attracting television viewers, so Lucasfilm probably had little trouble arranging such an agreement. Nonetheless, the media can be a feisty partner, sometimes promoting a movie on the cover to sell magazines and tearing it apart inside the issue.

In another example of quirky and innovative marketing, Lucasfilm teamed with the California Lottery to bring *Star Wars* Scratchers to fans. The California Lottery offered a set of collectible coins, featuring six characters (Vader, Luke, Leia, Yoda, C-3PO, and R2-D2), as a bonus to consumers, who could purchase the coins for $1 each with a Scratchers purchase costing $2 per ticket. Even the Scratchers themselves, of which there were twelve, could be considered collectible items. "The scenes [on the tickets] make these tickets an instant collector's item," said Chon Guttierrez, interim lottery director ("Join ...").

The Scratchers were available in April and gave fans a chance to win up to $10,000. "We were looking for a concept that would uniquely connect the fun of Scratchers with the tremendous fan base linked to *Star Wars*. We found the perfect solution in a film-based collectible that also serves as a scratching device for the lottery game," said Denise Kimes, group account director at Alcone Marketing Group, which was in charge of the promotion ("California Lottery ..."). The group had just four months to arrange the promotion, create the coins, and sell the program to retailers, the last of which a dedicated sales team managed in ten days (ibid.).

For *Star Wars* fans looking to combine their love for gambling with their love for the saga, International Game Technology (IGT) had developed a *Star Wars* gaming machine more than a year before the release of the final film. The first gaming machine was based on *A New Hope*, developed as a MegaJackpots progressive system game on the company's Advanced Video Platform (AVP). "AVP is the next generation of slot machines, with enough computing power to produce vibrant 3D-like video and theater-style audio, which should be a perfect match for this material," said John Sears, vice president of MegaJackpots for IGT ("IGT ...").

IGT first previewed the *Star Wars* gaming machine in September 2003 at the Las Vegas Convention Center, though it was not in casinos until later. The Nevada Gaming Commission had to rule on whether the gaming machines were appropriate given that *Star Wars* appeals heavily to young people who are not yet of gambling age. Nonetheless, the Commission voted unanimously in August 2004 to allow the machines in casinos. Commissioner Sue Wagner said of the machine, "It is a real grabber. Certainly it is directed at middle-aged guys" (Vogel). Most machines make it through regulations, despite state codes warning against approving machines that might appeal to minors, because regulators are anxious to help the gaming companies retain their edge in a competitive industry.[2]

In another bit of innovative promotion, racing fans could watch *Star Wars* Racing team members Elliot Sadler, Dale Jarrett, Jeff Gordon, and Kyle Busch race in *Star Wars*–themed cars in four events from late April through late May. The events included the Subway 500 in Martinsville, Virginia, the Aaron's 499 in Talladega, Alabama, the Chevy American Revolution 400 in Richmond, Virginia, and the Monaco Grand Prix Formula One race in Monte Carlo. Promotional sponsors of the cars included M&M's, UPS, Pepsi, Kellogg, and Red Bull ("*Star Wars* Racing ..."). When Gordon won the Aaron's 499, a race in which one crash disabled twenty-five cars but left Gordon's untouched, he said, "I told you guys the Force was with me" (Triplett).

While millions of racing fans love watching cars move at incredible speeds, flying makes many people sick just thinking about it. For sick travelers, Virgin Airlines in a collaboration with Activision and LucasArts released 100,000 limited edition airsickness bags to promote the release of the *Revenge of the Sith* video game. "Of course, we hope that our flights are as smooth as normal so that passengers don't need to use the sickbags. We want them to see the funny side ... not the inside," said the airline's owner, Richard Branson (Yancey). Four different bags, all with the same front design, offered different tips on the back, including: Knowing Your Lightsaber, Lightsaber Etiquette, The Art of Jedi Combat,

---

2.   Other popular themes approved in the past include gaming machines based on the *Betty Boop* and *Pink Panther* cartoons and popular television programs like *The Munsters* and *The Addams Family*.

and Seating Jedi and Sith. "The reaction has been really positive. Some crew will make passengers aware of them, others allow them to discover them themselves," said Lysette Gauna, head of media for Virgin Atlantic ("All Too …").

Revenge of the Sith had numerous mobile phone marketing partnerships and cell phone promotions worldwide for *Star Wars* fans. "The new group of movie-goers [compared to past generations] digest media in a different way that isn't that passive, and the cell phone is a much more active way to engage people," said Jim Ward, senior vice president of marketing and distribution at Lucasfilm (Idelson "Hollywood …"). Orange, a mobile phone company owned by France Telecom, joined the hype by offering a variety of promotions relating to the film for fans across Europe, including a service that enabled customers to have a *Star Wars* character read out their text messages. In Thailand, cellular operator Advanced Info Service (AIS), the largest mobile phone company in the nation, gave customers the opportunity to purchase refill cards featuring forty designs linked to the saga ("AIS …"). AIS produced nearly 40 million cards over a three-month period (ibid.). The company also offered special ringtones with movie themes.

Cingular Wireless users could access a variety of exclusive content, including more than one hundred ringtones, more than two hundred wallpapers, and nine games based on the events in the final prequel from developer THQ Wireless. "The *Star Wars* brand is recognized and loved by people of all ages. Fans of the *Star Wars* saga will appreciate the virtually anytime, anywhere access they'll have to their favorite *Star Wars* moments and characters directly from their Cingular handset," said John Burbank, vice president of marketing at Cingular Wireless ("CTIA …"). Likewise, Jim Ward said, "We're excited that Cingular is giving our fans the ability to download so many of their favorite *Star Wars* sounds, music, and graphics directly to their Cingular handset" (ibid.). Cingular had a base of about 50 million customers at the time of the announcement.

The primary cellphone game, with the same title as the film, did not provide as many spoilers to game players, but it offered many hints about the plot and a handful of surprises from the film. Another game the cell phone company offered was "Ask Yoda," which allowed cell phone users to seek advice from the Jedi Master through a Magic Eight Ball type of program with Yoda phrases and animations. THQ also had games like *Star Wars: Republic Commando Order 66* and *Grievous Getaway* planned for later in the year, after the film's release. The games cost about $5.99 each while the wallpapers, ringtones, and other sounds and graphics cost $1.99 each.

Another company took advantage of cell phone customization popularity, too. Cellfan.com, a division of Global Wireless Entertainment (GWE), offered the largest collection of *Star Wars*–themed vinyl skins for more than five hundred consumer electronics devices, like mobile phones, iPods, PDAs, and gaming devices. "This is another fun way for *Star Wars* fans to show everyone how excited and enthusiastic they are about the saga," said Casey Collins of Lucas Licensing ("Global ..."). The skins came available in eighteen designs, including ones featuring characters like Yoda and Darth Vader. Prices ranged from $12.95 to $29.95, available directly from the Internet site and shipped worldwide. "With Cellfan.com's reputation as the online brand source for mobile device personalization, the *Star Wars* skins are a great addition to our collection. Now *Star Wars* fans can choose a skin reflecting their favorite character from the most popular film series of all time," said CEO Paul Buss (ibid.).

In association with Lucasfilm, Disney launched *Star Wars* Weekends in 1997, well in advance of *Revenge of the Sith*. The event had become a popular attraction at Disney World (Disney-MGM Studios) in Florida, where it reappeared in 2000, 2001, 2003, 2004, and 2005; oddly, it was not running with the release of *Attack of the Clones*. Each weekend for at least a few weeks per year, *Star Wars* fans could see their favorite characters and droids at the theme park and experience the Star Tours ride as part of their visits, too. Various actors and crew from the films, like Peter Mayhew, Jerome Blake, Anthony Daniels, Warwick Davis, Daniel Logan, Amy Allen, Rob Coleman, and Don Bies, among others, appeared at Disney World to greet fans and talk about their work on the films or their contributions to the saga.

In 2005, Lucasfilm extended *Star Wars* Weekends by two weeks, making for six weeks total, the longest run in the history of the promotion. "Our guests told us they want more *Star Wars* Weekends this year and we're looking forward to extending the fun through the end of June," said Executive Vice President of Walt Disney World Marketing and Brand Management Linda Warren ("More 'Star Wars' ..."). As part of *Star Wars* Weekends, even Mickey Mouse could be seen walking around the theme park with a Jedi outfit, having his picture taken and signing autographs. In all, more than forty characters from the saga walked the theme park, signing autographs, posing for pictures, and creating a *Star Wars* atmosphere. For 2005, the theme park added the "Hasbro Zone" and an exclusive film presentation that chronicled the making of *Episode III*, which had officially received its title, *Revenge of the Sith*, in the summer of 2004.

Building Anticipation

The official naming of a *Star Wars* movie is always one of the first marketing decisions in which fans take great interest. The titles for the first two *Star Wars* prequels initially drew some criticism from fans, especially *The Phantom Menace*, which managed to befuddle a number of critics who still could not identify the character of the film's title after seeing the movie. With *Attack of the Clones*, which confirmed Lucas's desire to make the titles sound like old movie serials, fans had suspected a more simple title like "The Clone Wars," perhaps, but because the Clone Wars do not officially begin until the film's ending, the title Lucas chose is more appropriate. As with the film itself, the title for *Episode III* drew the least criticism of the three prequels.

Comic-Con International in San Diego is the biggest convention of its type every year, drawing more than one hundred thousand comic book and film fans from around the world every July.[3] Studios make many major film announcements at Comic-Con every year, where high profile actors, actresses, and filmmakers sometimes appear to promote their movies. At the convention in 2004, Lucas announced the title of his final *Star Wars* prequel, comparably early when one considers *The Phantom Menace* title did not reach the public until late September the year before its release.

On Saturday, July 24, fans could see Steve Sansweet, head of fan relations for Lucasfilm, wearing a black T-shirt with the words "Revenge of the Sith" printed on it. Instead of a fancy announcement or press release, Sansweet pulled off a baseball jersey to reveal the shirt to fans, many of whom immediately expressed their approval. Sansweet told about 6,500 convention attendees, "For some time now, the naming of a new *Star Wars* movie has taken on some special meaning among core fans who love to take part in guessing games before a title is announced, and then engage in debate once it is. Let the debates begin" (Breznican "Lucasfilm ..."). Other titles thrown around by fans included "Rise of the Empire" and "Birth of an Empire."

The Official *Star Wars* Web Site also announced the title through a "Special Announcement" to fans on July 24. The press release summarized what Sansweet had already told the fans in attendance at Comic-Con International in San Diego, though it also mentioned that the shirt Sansweet wore would be available to fans through StarWarsShop.com or in San Diego at the *Star Wars* pavilion. The red text on black fabric was supposed to mimic the 1982 Fan Club *Revenge of the Jedi* logo before Lucas changed the title.

The title of the final prequel also provides a great parallel between the two *Star Wars* trilogies. While the first trilogy ends in tragedy, thus the title *Revenge of the*

---

3.   According to the Comic-Con Web site, Comic-Con.org, 114,000 people attended in 2006.

Sith, the second trilogy ends in triumph with *Return of the Jedi*. As fans know, the original title of *Return of the Jedi* was "Revenge of the Jedi," until Lucas realized that Jedi do not seek revenge; Jedi seek retribution and justice. Sansweet joked in San Diego, "This time, George tells us he's going to keep 'Revenge' in the title" (Breznican "Lucasfilm ...").

The Sith have their revenge in the final prequel, but by the end of the saga, the title *Return of the Jedi* refers not to Luke specifically, but to both Anakin Sky-walker and the Jedi in a more general sense. In other words, one could take the title to mean that because the Sith are defeated, Palpatine overthrown, and the Empire no more, the Jedi (the "good guys") have returned, led by Luke, who the Expanded Universe books[4] suggest restarts the Jedi Order. More appropriately, however, Anakin is the Jedi, and while he fell from grace and joined the Dark Side in *Revenge of the Sith*, he has returned to his pre-Sith form, as the film sug-gests by showing Anakin in spirit form, as a Jedi. After announcing the film's title, Lucasfilm did not wait too long to show fans the first glimpse of the movie.

Trailers, as always with films big and small, still played a significant role for the promotion of *Revenge of the Sith*, though did not have the same revolutionary impact as the ones created for *The Phantom Menace* at the end of the nineties. The first teaser for the final prequel debuted on starwars.com's Hyperspace mem-bers area, for paid subscribers only, on November 4, 2004. For fans wanting the full experience of the teaser, the two-minute preview debuted on Friday, Novem-ber 5, in front of Pixar's *The Incredibles* for North American fans. Beginning on Monday, November 8, the Official *Star Wars* Web Site posted the trailer for all to see.

Besides Hyperspace members, the teaser trailer also premiered for AOL users through Moviefone.com on November 4. "Millions of fans look forward to every new *Star Wars* installment with great anticipation. As one of the largest online movie destinations, we are excited about giving our growing audience a first look at the *Revenge of the Sith* [trailer]," said Steven Yee, vice president and general manager of AOL Movies and Moviefone ("AOL ..."). Fans could access a special *Star Wars* section at AOL Keyword "Star Wars" with additional content from the saga helping to create enthusiasm for the final film. By the time of the film's release, Moviefone.com had streamed the teaser trailer a whopping 20 million times ("MovieTickets.com Sells ...").

The teaser trailer starts with footage from *A New Hope*, where Obi-Wan tells Luke that Jedi Knights had guarded the Republic for a thousand generations

---

4. The *Jedi Academy Trilogy* by Kevin J. Anderson, specifically.

before "the dark times." Footage from *The Phantom Menace* and *Attack of the Clones* then plays with Obi-Wan's quote as voiceover as he continues to tell Luke about his apprentice, Darth Vader, and how he hunted down and destroyed the Jedi. Footage from *Revenge of the Sith* follows in the final minute of the teaser trailer, which runs about 1:45 total. Fans could only glimpse a few scenes, but enough to stir the excitement. Dave Gohman of Schaumburg, Illinois, said, "To me the most effective example of [drawing in long-time fans disappointed with the first two prequels] was the nostalgia trailer ... It really made the point that this [film] was the realization of that hut scene recollection from *A New Hope*" with Obi-Wan and Luke (Gohman).

For the full-length trailer promoting *Revenge of the Sith*, Lucasfilm announced fans had several more ways to see the new footage. First, though, the trailer made its premiere on Thursday, March 10, during an episode of a Fox television show, *The O.C.*, which aired at 8:00 p.m. After the broadcast, Hyperspace and AOL members could view the trailer online at around 9:00 p.m. on the West Coast. Fans in North America could also wait a day to see the trailer in theaters in front of *Robots*, Fox's computer animated film. For fans in no hurry, the trailer made its public debut on starwars.com on March 14. The trailer generated intense interest among fans. Moviefone.com later reported, shortly after the film's release, that it streamed the trailer more than 15 million times ("MovieTickets.com Sells ...").

The full-length trailer showcases much more footage from *Revenge of the Sith* than its shorter predecessor, starting with Palpatine explaining the Dark Side of the Force to Anakin. It focuses on Anakin's moral struggle and relationship with Palpatine, then mid-way through plunges into action sequences showcasing the film's breathtaking special effects sequences. The trailer gave fans a glimpse of the entire plot, showing the final battles between Yoda and Palpatine and Obi-Wan and Anakin. It ends with a shot of Darth Vader and the message: "The Saga Is Complete May 19th." The trailer lasts almost 2:30.

The placement of the final *Revenge of the Sith* trailer during *The O.C.* was supposed to have the added effect of attracting new viewers to the Fox show, not just showing viewers of the program a preview of the upcoming film. Steven Mallas discussed the cross-promotion in an article for *The Motley Fool*. Pondering the effectiveness of the Fox-Lucasfilm crossover, he wrote:

> Let me use myself as an example. I knew nothing about *The O.C.*—nothing. I had heard about it, but, quite frankly, I thought it was on another network. Then, just last night, I read about the trailer promotion while surfing around starwars.com.... Now, I'm looking forward to seeing both the *Star Wars* trailer *and The O.C.*

Mallas concluded that "the synergy worked." Fox hoped that other fans and casual viewers would feel the same way, not only by watching *The O.C.* but also by going to theaters to see *Robots*.

The final trailer for *Revenge of the Sith* started to convert a few skeptics, at least. Brian Lowry of the trade paper *Variety* wrote, "Damn that George Lucas. Just when I thought I was out, he pulls me back in." Lowry expressed a bit of disappointment with *Return of the Jedi* after his love of the first two films in the Original Trilogy and "shared in the frustration" of the fans who did not wholly care for *The Phantom Menace*. He also bashed *Attack of the Clones*. "Yet after the trailer for *Episode III: Revenge of the Sith* … damned if I'm not getting excited again, figuring this installment's darkness quotient must render it vastly superior to its predecessors," he wrote. Many older fans felt the same way, yearning for a darker film more akin to *The Empire Strikes Back*.

Brian McIver of the *Daily Record* in Glasgow, Scotland, called the first two prequels "two of the most disappointing movies ever made," which is a fairly ridiculous sentiment given how many fans enjoy both movies. He further ruined his credibility by suggesting that "the effects in the first movies are light years ahead of the computer-generated" effects of the prequels. Despite numerous paragraphs of negativity, though, he admitted that "it's time to start queuing" because "the effects look more impressive in this new trailer than anything we have seen before" and "the fights … look great." The final trailer showed many disgruntled fans that their film, the one with "Darth Vader running around killing people" as Lucas said to the Associated Press when describing what many fans wanted, was about to become a reality (Germain "'Star Wars' mastermind …").

Along with the first teaser trailer for the film, Lucasfilm released a teaser poster, as had been customary for the *Star Wars* prequels. In 1998, the teaser poster featured a young Anakin Skywalker standing against a building on Tatooine with his shadow casting a Vader-like image on the building. The teaser for *Attack of the Clones* had text reading, "A Jedi shall not know anger. Nor hatred. Nor love." It showed Anakin and Padmé with their backs to one another, suggesting the forbidden love that blossomed in the film. In the teaser poster for *Revenge of the Sith*, Anakin is almost falling off the right side of the picture while his cape flows in the background and reveals the visage of Darth Vader. It is a nice bit of marketing suggesting not just the transformation of Anakin to Darth Vader, but the disappearance of "the good man" who had great promise as a Jedi to the "twisted and evil," "more machine now than man" Darth Vader, Dark Lord of the Sith.

George Lucas helped the marketing effort for his final film by appearing on an episode of Fox's *The O.C.* a week before the movie's theatrical premiere. In the episode, Lucas played himself and his character expresses interest in a graphic novel by Seth Cohen (Adam Brody). "We were looking to take the 'Seth graphic novel' storyline to its apex in this episode and it felt like the Holy Grail, the top of Everest to have Seth come face to face with Lucas," said Josh Schwartz, the show's creator (Coyle "As 'Star Wars' ..."). In the episode, Seth has to face the (incredibly obvious) decision of whether to meet Lucas or go to the prom. *The O.C.* had earlier promoted the final prequel with the trailer premiere, though Lucas's appearance drew yet more *Star Wars* fans to watch the show.

At the time Lucasfilm and Fox had discussed debuting the *Revenge of the Sith* trailer on *The O.C.*, Lucas had no idea he would also be making a cameo on the television series later in the season. Schwartz, also a writer on the show, had often used *Star Wars* references on the series in its first few seasons, especially with Seth, a comic book and sci-fi geek. Schwartz explained to the Official *Star Wars* Web Site, "*Star Wars* and the mythology of the *Star Wars* characters are woven into the fabric of life and for a show that makes a lot of pop culture references, that's obviously the biggest one. It's pretty much unavoidable" ("'The O.C.' ..."). Schwartz encouraged Lucas to make a cameo on the show and Lucas's daughter, Katie, further prodded him to do so.

In another television tie-in, sports network ESPN started airing a new round of SportsCenter commercials in late 2004, one of which featured characters from *Star Wars*. SportsCenter commercials have always been rather humorous and unconventional, but the *Star Wars* tie-in gave fans of sports and *Star Wars* a few laughs. "In the typical spirit of 'This is SportsCenter' fun, we're delighted that these heroic characters from *Star Wars* came to the rescue to help us run our new ESPN HD studio," said Ann Daly, executive vice president of marketing for ESPN ("New Round ..."). In the ad, the ESPN staff is having trouble with their new HD studio, so they have to hire Chewbacca, C-3PO, R2-D2, and other *Star Wars* characters to help with the new technology.

Even the NBA joined in promoting the last *Star Wars* film, with Lucasfilm and the NBA joining forces in an unusual alliance. As part of the promotion, NBA sponsor TNT aired the "Ultimate Battles" series in early May, which showcased memorable battles between both basketball legends and *Star Wars* characters. Six short segments offered parallels between various duels in the *Star Wars* saga and classic playoff confrontations between legendary players, like Julius Erving, Magic Johnson, Larry Bird, and Shaquille O'Neal, to name a few. Each montage showcased clips from one of the *Star Wars* films with footage from the playoffs during the same year the film was released. Lucasfilm evidently wanted to please sports fans who love *Star Wars*, and *Star Wars* fans who love sports ("NBA ...").

Size Does Matter

Not everyone was happy with the huge promotional hype and the vast array of merchandise, though. With such a massive number of *Star Wars* products available, Earth 911, an environmental protection organization supported by corporate partners and the U.S. Environmental Protection Agency, became concerned with how much garbage and waste the new film's merchandise could generate. "We love *Star Wars* as much as anybody, but it doesn't mean we should emulate the destructive power of the Death Star by harming the environment," said Anne Reichman, director of Earth911.org ("Yoda ..."). She noted how toys for the films cannot be recycled and "will sit in landfills long after we're gone." Apparently, Yoda could live to be 900 in our galaxy as well, even if he spends the last 895 years of his life in a more miserable environment than Dagobah.

Earth 911 released suggestions for reducing waste and recycling, such as recycling lightsaber batteries, recycling packaging from various items, donating *Star Wars* clothing to charity, and giving unwanted action figures away to schools and daycare centers ("The dark ..."). Die-hard collectors may cringe at the idea of kids discarding their toys, given how valuable the originals from the late seventies and early eighties became. The prequel era toys, however, are mass produced and, especially once opened, not likely to be worth a fortune in the future.

Christian Toto of *The Washington Times* surveyed the merchandise available for the new film as well as its various promotional tie-ins, making special note of Yoda selling Diet Pepsi and Chewbacca pitching cell phones, and concluded it was all too much. "Mr. Lucas is pulling out all the stops. And his beloved franchise is taking a hit in the process," Toto wrote. He thought marketing tie-ins had become a necessary part of the movie business and effective in many cases, but he thought the ubiquitous presence of the hype, including media hype, promotional tie-ins, and product releases, went too far. "Despite past successes, Mr. Lucas and his cohorts are behaving as though no one knows his little independent film is coming out next week," Toto wrote. He also felt the marketing could damage moviegoers' perceptions of the characters, like the M&M Darth Vader taking away from the power of the real Darth Vader character.

While many cultural commentators and analysts noted the incredible hype for *Revenge of the Sith* and expressed at least mild annoyance with it, fan opinions differ. Many fans love seeing *Star Wars* everywhere and feel that such a penetrating cultural presence was one of the great joys of a new *Star Wars* movie, while others agree to some extent with Christian Toto that the massive hype was excessive and took away from the film somewhat. Brian Kunkle of Sayre, Pennsylvania, said, "I'm sure that the whole thing must have been quite overwhelming for non-fans, but as for me, being inundated by *Star Wars* at every turn for a few months only enhanced the experience of anticipating and then watching *Revenge of the Sith* for the first time" (Kunkle).

Most fans shared Kunkle's view of the marketing and merchandising, admitting that Lucasfilm heavily promoted the film but not too much for their tastes. "I think they did good, but I don't think I would have ever had 'too much,'" said Dave Gohman. Richard Story of Acworth, Georgia, disagreed, saying there was "too much. I prefer quality over quantity" (Story). Many fans thought Lucasfilm placed too much emphasis on Darth Vader imagery, especially considering Anakin Skywalker only becomes Darth Vader near the end of the film and only wears the classic suit toward the last few minutes of it. "It was too much of Vader and not enough of Obi-Wan and Anakin," said Diane Kovalcin. "They used Vader's iconic image as much as possible, which I thought was very misleading seeing as he has about two minutes of screentime," Michael Kaminski said in agreement.

Mark Newbold of fan site Lightsabre.co.uk applauded Lucasfilm for its marketing efforts on the last prequel. The marketing was "very impressive, with excellent designs for the packaging and a wide and varied scope of items," he said (Newbold). Newbold noted how marketing tie-ins fell from the first to the second prequel, but with the final one, "The Force returned ... and *Sith* was awash with products." He cited Hasbro, Gentle Giant, and Master Replicas as having product lines that "never fail to impress." As with many fans and analysts, Newbold agreed that Lucasfilm finally "found the balance they were looking for," which further raised the profile of the final film, "if that's at all possible," he said.

Despite the presence of hundreds of new products, Lucasfilm made sure to work with licensees to ensure a more reasonable production of goods than happened with *The Phantom Menace* in 1999, where oversupplied retailers had to discount many products. "I think we all learned from that. We and retailers both scaled back. We decided to chase consumer demand rather than go out with so much product at the outset," said Howard Roffman (M. Rose). As a result of better information gained from the first two prequels about what sells best and which products fans prefer, the formula worked almost perfectly for *Revenge of the Sith*. The film received a massive worldwide promotional and merchandising push, but not disproportionate to the anticipation and excitement fans and the public had for the last prequel and for the saga. Aside from Lucasfilm's own marketing hype machine, the numerous worldwide media outlets also started their coverage months in advance, trying to capitalize on fan enthusiasm for the saga.

Galaxy of Hype

The Rise of Darth Vader

In 1999, *The Phantom Menace* had set new highs for media hype for a feature film, grabbing the cover of every major entertainment magazine, numerous news magazines, fashion magazines, and even specialty magazines. The media quickly learned that *Star Wars* sells magazines and newspapers, sometimes in record numbers. With *Attack of the Clones*, the media seemed more guarded because of the excessive hype and subsequent backlash with the first prequel. Although *Attack of the Clones* still graced its share of magazine covers, it seemed more like a normal blockbuster to the media rather than a special event. For *Revenge of the Sith*, however, the media geared up for a massive campaign, at times rivaling the hype for *The Phantom Menace*. After all, the last *Star Wars* film ever deserved the attention befitting a retiring champion.

Rolling Stone, which had featured the much-maligned Jar Jar Binks on its cover in 1999, chose a more popular character for its June 2, 2005, issue in the form of Darth Vader. The appearance marked the fifth time *Star Wars* had made *Rolling Stone*'s cover, beginning almost thirty years earlier. *Attack of the Clones*, as befitting its lower profile, did not earn a cover appearance. The 2005 magazine featured an interview with Lucas where Gavin Edwards asked him numerous questions about the world's favorite Sith Lord. Perhaps the best inclusion in the magazine was an article titled, "The Many Faces of Vader," where the people involved in bringing Anakin Skywalker and Darth Vader to the screen over the years gave their thoughts on the character and the experiences they had. The magazine also had a humorous piece, "Behind the Mask" by Rob Sheffield, that was supposed to be from Darth Vader's viewpoint, speaking of his career and personal difficulties since the Original Trilogy ended.

Aside from the interviews and the Vader story, director and *Star Wars* fan Kevin Smith wrote an over-the-top piece about his relationship with *Star Wars* and Darth Vader over the years. Besides some raunchy sexual humor and enough swear words to compare to a decent episode of *South Park*, Smith had a few nice rants about the fans who harassed Lucas over the first two prequels. He wrote that the group of fans who obsesses over their disappointment with the prequels is "populated by the joyless, cynical, übertrolls who, sadly, take up the most space on the Internet" (Kevin Smith).

Smith felt that many of the disappointed fans expected the impossible of Lucas. He continued, "These are the hollow men and women who marched into the prequels demanding that Lucas recapture their lost *Star Wars* youth for them—that simple time in their lives when they had the excuse of prepubescence to explain why they were still virgins." Smith also mentioned his glowing review of *Sith,* which contrasted sharply with the two-star, negativity-laced review Peter Travers wrote in the back of the magazine.

Cinefantastique, a film magazine published nine times annually in Los Angeles, also featured Vader on the cover, though with the left side of his mask being transparent enough to see Hayden Christensen as Anakin. The magazine had a brief article on points of interest in *Revenge of the Sith*, both for casual and die-hard fans, as well as a fascinating timeline of Lucas's comments about when the prequel trilogy would start filming and how many total *Star Wars* films he expected to make. Late seventies speculation had him making twelve movies total, then in the early eighties the number became nine, where it remained until the prequel trilogy came closer to existence in the late nineties and he insisted the story he wrote only covered six films. The issue also included a rather nice defense of Lucas's changes to the Original Trilogy over the years. Besides the in-depth articles, the magazine had reviews of both the video game and musical score for *Revenge of the Sith*.

Cinefantastique had the good sense of humor to make fun of itself, running a sidebar with critical acclaim from 1977 of the original *Star Wars* film, along with a damning review blurb from its film critic at the time. The magazine included a conversation with Gary Kurtz, John Dykstra, Richard Edlund, Ben Burtt, Dennis Muren, and Carrie Fisher, all of whom worked on the first *Star Wars* film in 1977. The issue also had a brief article in which Lucas explained the deeper side of *Star Wars* and how he intended the films to influence people. Looking back at the beginning of the saga, the magazine examined its own coverage of the production of what was originally *The Star Wars* and the various problems it faced before completion as well as its historic journey to theaters. All told, *Cinefantastique*'s coverage of *Star Wars* and *Revenge of the Sith* far exceeded that of other magazines and newspapers, most of which never went beyond the most superficial, widely publicized information.

Nickelodeon magazine, the official publication of the kids cable network, featured a *Revenge of the Sith* related cover for its May 2005 issue, putting Wookies

Chewbacca and Tarfful on the front. Inside, the magazine interviewed Hayden Christensen, Peter Mayhew (Chewbacca), and Trisha Biggar, costume designer on the prequels. *GQ* also went the interview route, featuring Christensen on its May cover. The actor talked about his role in the film, his acting career, and what made him decide to become an actor. Looking ahead, Christensen said he was not worried about the future after *Star Wars*. "I'm not really concerned about it, either, though maybe I should be, given how many times I'm asked about it," he said (200). Also in the magazine, Mark Hamill talked a bit about his career path and how he has tried to deal with post–*Star Wars* life.

Premiere magazine put Anakin Skywalker on its May cover, lightsaber ignited, for a "*Star Wars* Blowout." The primary article had commentary from Christensen, Lucas, and Rick McCallum, speaking of the prequels primarily and specifically how *Revenge of the Sith* ties the entire story together. The complexity of the special effects work also received mention. *Premiere*, in line with its promise of previewing summer films, gave a brief plot description of the film in its coverage. In the summer movie preview section, the magazine predicted a gross of $400 million and listed the film, justifiably, as first on its list of anticipated films. Editor-in-Chief Peter Herbst wrote, "It's clear that not only sentiment about this being the last *Star Wars* movie is at work [in exciting fans]—how Anakin becomes Darth is primal stuff, and *Episode III* looks like the real deal." Other entertainment magazines found their own ways to capitalize on the enthusiasm of eager fans.

Entertainment Weekly gave *Star Wars* a few cover stories in 2005, including one on its April 1 issue, which featured six different character covers, one for each episode of the saga. The characters included: Darth Maul, Yoda, Anakin Skywalker, Han Solo, Darth Vader, and Princess Leia. The issue had a nice quiz that began with extremely easy questions for *Star Wars* fans but offered a few tough questions at the end, like what real life person inspired the name Anakin Skywalker and which *Cheers* regular also played a Rebel Alliance officer in *The Empire Strikes Back?*[1]

The April 1 *Entertainment Weekly* issue also had a brief article on Lucas's plans to re-release the *Star Wars* movies in 3-D, which is covered more in the epilogue of this book. Finally, the issue had a small sidebar about a few key events in *Revenge of the Sith*. The covers appeared more as gimmicks to sell magazines than attempts to promote any significant *Star Wars* coverage inside the magazine. *Entertainment Weekly* had already learned by 2005 that *Star Wars* helps sell mag-

---

1.   Director Ken Annakin and Cliff (John Ratzenberger).

azines. Its March 26, 1999, issue with Obi-Wan on the cover had become the best-selling issue ever at the time.

Closer to the film's release date, *Entertainment Weekly* put Anakin on the cover of its May 20 issue with the headline, "Will *Revenge of the Sith* Save the Lucas Legacy?" As one of the most vehement Jar Jar Binks attackers and general prequel bashers, the staff at *Entertainment Weekly*, as a whole, felt that Lucas had to redeem himself. Regardless, any excuse to put *Star Wars* on the cover, whether to bash it or praise it, was good enough for the weekly publication. In fact, in the May 20 issue, the magazine wrote, "*The prequels have stunk like bantha poodoo*" (24). *Entertainment Weekly* has not been on the list of publications that *Star Wars* fans consider friendly to the franchise for a long time, especially because the magazine consistently uses franchise images to sell magazines yet bashes the films inside its covers.[2]

The article in the May 20 issue focused significantly on how much fans hated the first two prequels (and why the final one would be better), which is one version of events but not the one supported by any facts whatsoever, either in the magazine or elsewhere. Selectively piecing together Lucas quotes between mostly incorrect editorializing, *Entertainment Weekly* managed to twist what he said until it sounded like he agreed that the first two prequels had little plot (26, 28). In fact, Lucas only said that most of the backstory he had written earlier for the prequels related to Anakin's ultimate fall from grace in *Revenge of the Sith*, not the events of the first two prequels, for which he only had thin outlines that he later fleshed out during writing. Criticizing films because they do not fit with one's preconceived notions is easier than trying to understand them properly, but any such idea is lost on the staff of *Entertainment Weekly* as well as many critics and a loud but small group of frustrated fans.

Natalie Portman tried to deflect another *Entertainment Weekly* assumption, namely that Lucas was never altogether interested in the prequels but made them out of obligation, which would explain the fans' disappointment, according to the magazine. Portman countered, "He loved these films. He loved this story. I don't think he could have devoted such a significant portion of his life to them if he didn't" (30). As another example of the magazine's attempt to twist what Lucas said to them, the writer asked if he cared whether fans view the Original Trilogy first, then the prequels afterwards, and Lucas said, "No. [People] can

---

2.   Whether the fact that *Entertainment Weekly* is a Time Warner company, which also owns the Warner Bros. film studio that competes with *Star Wars* distributor 20th Century Fox, has anything to do with its negativity is debatable, but not entirely unlikely.

view it any way they want. I don't really care" (30). The magazine then wrote, "But just when you think he deems the prequel project irrelevant, he starts making a case for watching the saga episodes one through six" (30). Lucas's comment never suggested the prequels were irrelevant, only that he could care less how fans want to view his movies in their own homes.

Not surprisingly, *Sci Fi* magazine, the official magazine for the Sci-Fi Channel, also covered the final prequel, with a Darth Vader cover for its May issue. In another nice ploy to sell magazines, hardly original but always entertaining, *Go! Magazine*[3] ran an issue with prequel coverage featuring four covers, each with different characters (Palpatine, Yoda, Anakin, and Obi-Wan), that collectors could place side by side to reveal Darth Vader in the background. *TV Guide* also liked the multiple cover idea, which was popular internationally as well, and decided to offer five lenticular covers featuring characters and scenes from *Revenge of the Sith* for its April 28 issue. Ironically, *TV Guide* subscribers only received a non-animated cover, so fans had to go to newsstands to pick up the collectible editions ("Always …").

A Newsworthy Force

A number of news magazines and non-entertainment magazines also featured *Star Wars* stories or actors and actresses from the final film on their covers. *Time*, which had previously featured both of the earlier prequels on its cover, also put Darth Vader on the cover for its May 9, 2005, issue. The issue covered many of the normal subjects toward which the media seemed to gravitate, like whether *Revenge of the Sith* would "redeem" the franchise and the past two prequels, why Lucas told the story the way he did, and some of the plot details of the final prequel. It also included a "*Star Wars* Family Tree" for readers, which gave an overview of the saga's most important characters. John Cloud's article, "How *Star Wars* Saved My Life," detailed the influence the films had on his childhood and how they provided a sense of escape from life as a young man struggling to make sense of his sexuality.

Besides the article about the final prequel, designed more for the casual enthusiast than the die-hard fan, Lucas also granted *Time* an interview, which had a few funny comments from Lucas and good insight into what he planned next. Regarding his image as a pariah living an isolated, privileged life, Lucas responded, "Part of that comes from not being in a media center. I'm not in L.A.,

---

3.   *Go! Magazine* is the entertainment magazine for the *Times Herald Record* in Middletown, New York.

I'm not in New York, and therefore I must be out in the wilderness, sort of sitting in the Himalayas somewhere" (62). Lucas noted that he has hundreds of employees who work closely with him, no matter that they are not in Hollywood. At the end of the year, *Time* placed Darth Vader on its "People Who Mattered 2005" list, making him the only fictional character on the list.

In a rare front-page article for a movie, *USA Today* put Dark Side Anakin Skywalker on the top half of its weekend paper for April 22–24, 2005, to coincide with *Star Wars* Celebration III. The article focused on how Darth Vader, or rather Anakin Skywalker, is the central character of the saga. Lucas gave a number of quotes about what he hoped to convey through the final prequel and in the *Star Wars* saga as a whole. Though *USA Today*'s coverage of *Revenge of the Sith* did not match its hype for *The Phantom Menace*, it came close. For the April 29–May 1 weekend edition, *USA Today* had a picture of a battling Obi-Wan Kenobi and Anakin Skywalker on the front cover just below the paper's name with the headline, "War of the blockbusters." Though the article was more of a general preview of summer films, what better movie to highlight the summer than the last *Star Wars* film ever? Besides, *USA Today* had to follow the simplest media rule: *Star Wars* sells.

The final prequel made the front page again for the May 13–15 weekend edition of *USA Today* with a story, "'Star Wars' vs. 'Star Wars',", that pitted the Original Trilogy against the prequel trilogy. The next paper again had *Star Wars* on the front, but in the upper right corner with a picture of Yoda and a glowing blurb about the prequel reading, "Final film may be best." Two days later, the publication put Lucas on the right corner of the front page of its May 18 paper with the headline, "Politics hidden in the Force?" *USA Today* put *Star Wars* on the front again for *Revenge of the Sith*'s May 19 premiere. Though the story was in the Life section, a picture on the front page showed a fan in a Darth Vader costume accompanied by the headline: "'Star Wars' re-enters orbit." In a two-month period, one would think *Star Wars* set a record for most *USA Today* cover appearances by an entertainment franchise; it seemed to be on the cover almost every week.

William Booth of *The Washington Post* wrote an article in early May that accomplished two tasks: it gave readers information about the final prequel and looked into how Lucasfilm treated the press and organized a press junket for the film. Booth wrote about touring Skywalker Ranch, noting the secrecy of the company but also the impressiveness of its layout and architecture. For the early May press junket at the ranch, about sixty members of the press assembled at the Embassy Suites Hotel in the area. After a brief tour of Skywalker Ranch, the press had the opportunity to see the movie, where Booth described the response as pleasant and in several cases very impressed; he also seemed satisfied. The following morning, the press returned for roundtable interviews with Ian McDiarmid, Hayden Christensen, and George Lucas. Afterwards, some members of the group sought autographs from Lucas, or bought items from the Skywalker General Store. In all, Booth described the experience as calculated and well planned, thus the tight schedule.

Teen People put Hayden Christensen and Natalie Portman together on the cover of its June/July 2005 issue and featured them in an article titled, "The 25 Hottest Stars Under 25." The article mentioned why each of them are considered big stars, though Christensen's inclusion might be considered a bit flattering considering the other celebrities are probably better known among the public. *Cosmo Girl!* did not have a *Star Wars* cover, but it did run an article with a George Lucas interview, by Katie Lucas, his seventeen-year-old daughter. The article focused on George Lucas's artistic ambitions and how young girls aspiring to be creative can succeed at their dreams. Christensen also had an interview in the June issue of *Seventeen* that focused on the darker roles he's had in his film career, his private life and friends, and his goals for the future, which include screenwriting.

Esquire's June issue featured Ewan McGregor on the cover wearing a *Star Wars* T-shirt and a headline reading, "3 *Star Wars* Movies & All I Got Was This Lousy T-Shirt." The article and interview with McGregor was, to say the least, unorthodox. Numerous paragraphs focused on the appearance of McGregor's own "lightsaber" in various films throughout the years. The magazine tried to make McGregor wear a shirt with the cover's headline on it, with the addition of a swear word, but he refused, saying, "But it's not *true*" (94). The interview was humorous, despite being filled with insults about McGregor and loaded with profanity. The interview, which took place at a zoo, hardly had any mention of *Star Wars*, besides the interviewer's negative opinion of the films that he snuck in toward the end of the story.

Vanity Fair featured one of the most impressive, original covers for its February 2005 issue, thanks to the work of renowned photographer Annie Leibovitz. The cover photo, spread over four pages, showed most of the major cast members and characters from the saga, including: Ewan McGregor, Hayden Christensen, George Lucas, Natalie Portman, Yoda, Darth Vader, R2-D2, Anthony Daniels as C-3PO, Samuel L. Jackson, Jar Jar Binks, Jimmy Smits, Christopher Lee, Liam Neeson, Pernilla August, Jake Lloyd, Ian McDiarmid, General Grievous, Billy Dee Williams, Carrie Fisher, Harrison Ford, Peter Mayhew as Chewbacca, and Mark Hamill.

Leibovitz's cover picture is marvelous to behold simply because few cast photos like it are available anywhere else. It gives fans a nice glimpse of many of the people who made the *Star Wars* saga the most successful in cinema history. Leibovitz's photograph also made international magazines, such as the Italian edition of *Vanity Fair* and the Korean edition of *GQ*, which featured her photos on the cover and inside. *Star Wars* had also made the cover of *Vanity Fair* for both of the previous prequels, albeit not in as grand of fashion.

Inside *Vanity Fair*, Jim Windolf's article looked into the work that hundreds of people put into *Revenge of the Sith* to make it a bridging episode between two segments of the *Star Wars* story. The article was refreshing because Windolf took the saga seriously, calling *Attack of the Clones* "melancholy and ambitious" instead of the usual words the media used, like "disappointing" (110). Windolf showed a level of originality and insight that other media writers could not muster. Along with excellent photos of the sets, costumes, and behind-the-scenes work from Leibovitz, Windolf described the huge scale and epic feeling of the production process.

LIFE magazine, one of the oldest and most well known magazine publications in the United States, featured a look at the costumes in *Revenge of the Sith* for its weekend edition supplement on April 8. The magazine also had an interview with Trisha Biggar about creating the costumes for the prequel. *LIFE*, originally published as a weekly in 1936, ceased publication for several years in the seventies but returned by 1978 as a monthly magazine. It then turned into a newspaper supplement published weekly in 2000, where it enjoyed distribution to more than seventy newspapers across the nation with a circulation exceeding 12 million ("*LIFE* …"). The costume design in the prequels, because of its immense scale, interested a number of publications, though was overshadowed by special effects coverage.

Industry Admiration

As with both of the previous prequels, *Cinefex*, a quarterly industry magazine that features in-depth coverage of the best in special effects from Hollywood movies, looked at *Revenge of the Sith* extensively in its July issue, which featured General Grievous on the cover. The issue offered excellent insight into the technical details of creating the visual effects, both computer generated and otherwise, for a film with not only an unprecedented number of special effects but also a level of complexity never attempted previously.

The in-depth *Cinefex* article spanned twenty-eight pages of text and pictures, delving into many of the most challenging elements of the film's creation. Lucas took out a one-page ad in the magazine addressed to ILM and a few of the key employees reading, "Thank you for your hard work, passion, and dedication you poured into Episode III. You are an amazingly talented group of artists. I am so proud of your extraordinary work" (65). Jody Duncan, who worked on two of the three "making of" books for the prequels, also interviewed Lucas for an hour in what became an insightful eight-page section of the July issue.

In the same industry, *3D World*, a United Kingdom–based magazine, put a fierce-looking Yoda on the cover of its July 2005 issue. Under the title, the magazine also included a nice Yoda reference, reading, "The Magazine for 3D Artists, It Is." The magazine had more coverage of the special effects work in the final prequel, but it also included a small editorial from a disgruntled employee who felt the need to bash the first two prequels in an illogical rant. For instance, the author called the prequels merely "backstory," which is completely wrong as the trilogy represents half the *Star Wars* story (28). The saga story is not just about Luke Skywalker, Han Solo, and Princess Leia, but primarily about Anakin Skywalker. The other characters are important insofar as they relate to Anakin's journey and the complete story arc. Unfortunately, the media taking swipes at the past two films or the prequels in general was a recurring theme.

Make-Up Artist Magazine featured two covers, one of Padmé Amidala and one of Sith Lord Darth Sidious. The industry magazine, printed in the United States, focuses on make-up work in film, television, theater, and print. The magazine featured a fascinating article on the make-up work in *Revenge of the Sith* with some truly shocking photos of Anakin after his tumble into the lava. Although he looks disgusting in the film, somehow the magazine's photos were even more disturbing. Besides the work on Anakin, the article looked into the make-up work for Palpatine, various senators including Padmé, the Jedi, and Lucas, who had a cameo. All of the high-quality photographs the magazine included with the article made it a great resource for fans.

Post magazine, which focuses on post-production and Hollywood special effects, put Darth Vader on the cover of its May magazine and devoted a story to ILM and *Revenge of the Sith* with interviews of several key visual effects artists involved with the film. *Millimeter*, a monthly magazine directed at film, video, and multimedia production professionals, featured Darth Vader on the cover of its April issue with a story about the pre-visualization process for the film through its production and special effects workload. In the May issue of *Film & Video* magazine, ILM Visual Effects Supervisor John Knoll and High-Definition Supervisor Fred Meyers talked about using state-of-the-art, high-definition video equipment to make *Revenge of the Sith* as visually sophisticated and sharp as possible.

Wired magazine featured a cover with half of Lucas's face on the left side and half of Darth Vader's face on the right with the headline, "George Lucas, Unmasked." The magazine offered another interview with Lucas, where he talked about his post–*Star Wars* future as well as the state of movie technology and the industry in general. The interview appeared within an article, so his comments were sprinkled throughout, but *Wired* writer Steve Silberman successfully weaved Lucas's influences and past together with his current ambitions and opinions about film. The magazine also included a guide to how *Star Wars* changed moviemaking and influenced the lives of numerous people in the film industry.

A Galaxy of Coverage

Empire, the #1 movie magazine in the United Kingdom, pushed the traditional boundaries of publishing with its *Revenge of the Sith* coverage. The June magazine, a special collector's edition, featured Darth Vader on the cover with a sound-emitting (removable) card inside to simulate his breathing when readers opened the magazine ("Take …"). Inside, the publication boasted fifty pages of *Star Wars* coverage, looking at the entire saga but with a focus on the final prequel. The magazine had quotes and commentary from numerous people involved in the production and post-production of *Revenge of the Sith*, including stars like Christopher Lee, Ian McDiarmid, Natalie Portman, and Samuel L. Jackson, among others.

Empire's special edition magazine also had interviews with a number of actors from the Original Trilogy, along with a look into the initial casting sessions for *A New Hope*. The issue featured a roundtable discussion of the *Star Wars* films with Kevin Smith, Simon Pegg, and Edgar Wright, providing more commentary for fans to digest. An inside report from Hasbro about the making of its *Revenge of the Sith* action figure line further assured that *Empire* left no subject untouched in one of the best jobs of covering the final prequel and celebrating the saga.

Numerous U.K. magazines put *Star Wars* on their covers in summer issues. The June 2005 issue of *Martial Arts* magazine, a U.K publication, featured Obi-Wan on the cover, lightsaber drawn, with the headline, "*Star Wars*: The Greatest Martial Arts Movie in the Galaxy?" *Star Wars* appearing on the covers of film magazines is never surprising, but the franchise's appearance on magazines unrelated to film always seems the most impressive. The U.K. magazine *Arena* featured two versions of its June issue, a Light Side one with Ewan McGregor and a

Dark Side one with Hayden Christensen. The magazine featured an interview with both actors in an article titled, "Till Death Do Us Part."

Hot Dog magazine, another U.K. publication that had earlier featured Darth Sidious on its March cover, gave readers twenty pages of *Star Wars* coverage and a glaring Anakin Skywalker on the cover, while *SFX* gave fans three separate covers in May, featuring Mace Windu, Anakin, and Obi-Wan. *Total Film* magazine offered some of the best coverage in the United Kingdom, giving fans a thirty-five-page supplement with its June magazine that looked into the entire saga. The cover featured a simple image of a red and a blue lightsaber locked in combat on the front.

In Italy, weekly fashion magazine *iO Donna* put Natalie Portman on the cover with an interview of the actress inside along with a brief summary of George Lucas's filmmaking career. *Best Movie*, an Italian magazine as well, devoted eleven pages to coverage of *Revenge of the Sith* that included photos, an interview with Lucas, and a summary of the saga from start to finish. Italian *TV Film* magazine had a short preview of the final prequel, too. Another popular magazine in the country, *Ciak*, put Batman and Anakin on the cover in a "Batman vs. Star Wars" battle of the summer's biggest blockbusters. Even non-film magazines in the country, like the weekly magazine *Panorama*, gave readers a look at the upcoming prequel.

In France, *Kids' Mania* featured Anakin and Darth Vader on its cover while *Le Cinema SFX* (also sold elsewhere in countries like Canada, Belgium, Luxembourg, and Switzerland) put Anakin and Obi-Wan on the cover of its April–May edition. Also in France, *Score* magazine devoted more than twenty pages of coverage to the prequel, a saga chronology, and various character comparisons. *Premiere* magazine in France had Darth Vader on its cover months before the film's premiere, offering a retrospective on Anakin's life from innocent young boy to translucent ghost.

In Germany, *Widescreen* magazine featured a four-page preview of *Revenge of the Sith*, putting Darth Vader on its cover, while the March edition of *Cinema* magazine had two covers, one with Obi-Wan and one with Darth Vader, a fairly common theme. *K-Club*, a youth magazine, gave German fans *Star Wars* coverage about the characters, story, and toys of *Revenge of the Sith*. The magazine came in an oversized printed polybag featuring Anakin Skywalker.

Numerous other countries also greeted *Revenge of the Sith*'s release with fanfare. *Film Valley*, a monthly movie magazine from Holland, had two covers to celebrate the film's opening, one with Chewbacca and the other with the two droids, R2-D2 and C-3PO. Inside, the magazine ran a nine-page story about the film. In Mexico, *Cine Premiere* magazine featured Darth Vader on the cover and boasted an exclusive interview with George Lucas. The magazine also printed four special covers to celebrate the third prequel, featuring four characters: Anakin Skywalker, Darth Vader, General Grievous, and Chewbacca. The Australian *Empire* magazine covered the final prequel with an article by Ian Freer that focused on the making of the film with quotes from Rick McCallum and John Knoll. Its cover, like the U.K. version, featured Darth Vader.

Puerto Rico's city magazine, *San Juan Magazine,* featured Jimmy Smits on the cover, who discussed his role as Bail Organa in the final prequel. In Russia, *TV Park*, the best-selling weekly entertainment magazine in the country, offered an interview with Anthony Daniels along with information about the saga as a whole and the various worlds of *Star Wars*. In Hungary, *Vox Mozimagazin* published two covers, one with Anakin and one with Darth Vader, offering readers twenty-five pages of *Star Wars* coverage inside.

At Home With *Sith*

Aside from newspapers and magazines, television stations also had the opportunity to profit from *Star Wars* fever and in the process hype the new movie. Fox had already taken advantage in March, with the premiere of the final *Revenge of the Sith* trailer during *The O.C.* In an odd pairing, Animal Planet ran a one-hour special that Anthony Daniels narrated, which premiered on May 18 at 9:00 p.m. Eastern with the title, *Animal Icons: Star Wars Creatures.* Maureen Smith, general manager and executive vice president of Animal Planet, said, "We are thrilled to present viewers with the fascinating stories behind the creatures of [the] *Star Wars* films" ("Animal Planet …"). Although the otherworldly animals seen in the films seem unrelated to the programming on Animal Planet, the show examined the terrestrial origins of many of the extraterrestrial animals. As a bonus, the show offered footage from *Revenge of the Sith* for eager fans.

A *Star Wars* program on Animal Planet may have seemed strange to some viewers, but the network had several compelling reasons behind its production decision. Kevin Burns, who had earlier created the documentary *Empire of Dreams* for the Original Trilogy DVD boxed set, was also executive producer on the Animal Planet *Star Wars* show. "It was Kevin's idea to do a special on *Star Wars* creatures," Writer and Supervising Producer Steven Smith said ("Go …"). *Star Wars Creatures* was not the only time Animal Planet had ventured outside of normal programming. "We've done programs on comic book creatures inspired or influenced by animals, animal symbols used in politics like the donkey and the elephant, and so on," Smith said (ibid.). The program gave viewers, as well as the producers, insight into the thought process and research behind the various creatures in the *Star Wars* galaxy.

Aside from the Animal Planet show, the Discovery Channel featured three programs relating to technology and *Star Wars* that ran from May 16 through May 18 at 8:00 p.m. The "Science of *Star Wars*" specials included: *Man and Machine*, about droids, bots, and artificial intelligence; *Space Cowboys*, looking at hovercrafts and futuristic rides; and *War Weaponry and The Force*, looking at the future of warfare. Anthony Daniels and Kenny Baker hosted the shows. All three shows also aired on Discovery HD from 8:00 through 11:00 p.m. on May 18.

In a promotion with MTV, the band Good Charlotte performed at Skywalker Ranch in a celebrity-filled party[4] where guests had the opportunity to see *Revenge of the Sith* and give their verdicts. The *Star Wars* special, made for *Total Request Live* (*TRL*) on MTV and hosted by Damien Fahey and La La Vasquez, aired on May 13 at 5:00 p.m. Good Charlotte lead singer Joel Madden said, "When we heard about this MTV *Star Wars* party at Skywalker Ranch, we had to be there. We are huge *Star Wars* fans and never thought we'd even get the chance to visit the Ranch, much less perform there in front of George Lucas" ("Good …"). Like fans around the world, the band was anxious to see the last film in the franchise. "We can't wait to finally see the movie—this will be a big day for us and our fans," Madden said (ibid.).

CBS's *60 Minutes* featured an in-depth look at both *Revenge of the Sith* and Lucas's personal life in two separate segments of its news program in March. The first segment had reporter Lesley Stahl watching segments of the final prequel with Lucas, who explained a bit about the movie's darker themes while in the editing room looking over footage. Stahl asked Lucas about the criticisms his first two prequels endured, which led to some insights into how Lucas sees negative opinions about his work. Unfortunately, Stahl had not done her homework with comments like, "But most film critics hated *Episodes I* and *II*." In fact, only a few critics hated either film; most generally liked them.

Lucas told Stahl when asked about the criticisms of his films, "It hurts a great deal. But part of making movies is you get attacked, and sometimes in very personal ways." He compared the way he has made the prequels to painting a house white instead of green: there is no right color for a house to be painted, but ultimately whoever owns the house makes a creative decision that others will be able to judge. In the second segment, Stahl pestered Lucas about still being single, to which he responded that he has no drive to get married just for the sake of it.

---

4.   Covered more extensively in the chapter titled, "A New *Empire*."

Rather, he wants to find the right person before thinking of marriage. The segment concluded with a look into Lucas's business operations and the move to his new headquarters at the Presidio in San Francisco, as well as his future in filmmaking.

An Empire of Connections

Internet sites also joined in the hyping of the final *Star Wars* film. ESPN published an article in the Page 2 section of its Web site, ESPN.com, where writer Nick Bakay compared *Star Wars* to the New York Yankees, or more specifically the Evil Empire of the *Star Wars* films to the most successful baseball franchise, which detractors and jealous fans of teams the Yankees perennially steamroll like to call the Evil Empire as well. The hilarious article compared the two franchises in categories like uniforms, tactics of victory, hired guns, and theme songs. Bakay concluded, "In the battle of the $200 million opening weekend versus the $200 million payroll, the advantage goes to … *Star Wars*. You know they'll be in first place next week, but hang in there George." Although Bakay wrote the article to lambast the Yankees terrible start to the 2005 season and bury the team, the Bronx Bombers went on to have a great summer and steal an eighth consecutive AL East title from the Red Sox on the season's final weekend.

HowStuffWorks, which runs an Internet site at Stuffo.com, celebrated the release of the final prequel with a week of special features devoted to George Lucas and *Revenge of the Sith*. The site boasted articles on subjects like the inner workings of lightsabers and the mysteries of the Sith. HowStuffWorks describes itself as covering "anything and everything that reverberates in popular culture." *Revenge of the Sith* drew attention online from numerous sites, not just the normal fan sites that post *Star Wars* news every day of the year. When Ask Jeeves, a popular search engine at Ask.com, released its 2005 list of the most popular search queries on December 22, *Star Wars* topped the list for film related searches, ahead of *Harry Potter and the Goblet of Fire*, *The Pacifier* (seemingly misplaced given its more modest box office gross), *Batman Begins*, and *Madagascar* in second through fifth places, respectively ("What Do …").

Many of the media articles with *Star Wars* connections showed how far the franchise penetrated into every aspect of the culture, leading to a few funny or amusing connections. Rodd Zolkos of *Business Insurance* magazine wrote an article about *Star Wars* where he claimed he would not be surprised if "employers are seeing an unusual rash of claims on their health plans" because of the excitement surrounding the final film and the "inadvertent eye pokes sustained in the midst of heated plastic light saber battles or backs wrenched trying to squeeze into 25-

year-old Wookie costumes." Zolkos detailed his own *Star Wars* experience, indicating he had fallen from the faithful though was interested in the final film partially because of nostalgia, but also because of another, more esoteric reason. "I've been thinking about how it may well be possible to view the new film … as a metaphor for some of the events making headlines in the insurance industry in recent months," he wrote. Other writers also tried to tie together current events with *Star Wars*.

Rick Hiatt of *The Cincinnati Post* used nothing but *Star Wars* analogies to explain the status of the University of Cincinnati's athletic programs, "in honor of *Star Wars* Episode III coming out this week," he wrote. As an example of the writing style, he wrote, "Entrance requirements will be raised for future Jedi requesting training. Deviants and ne'er-do-wells will be banished from in and around the perimeter of Campusant [a parody of the planet Coruscant] by a collaborative effort of expensive structures and investment of significant Republic credits." He went on to explain the situation in non–*Star Wars* language for the infidels, though ended with another *Star Wars* reference alluding to University of Cincinnati President Nancy Zimpher: "But who is willing to take down a Sith?"

Another ongoing connection between world news and popular culture involved the "Star Wars" missile defense system, a project Ronald Reagan started decades earlier, before the end of the Cold War, officially known as the Strategic Defense Initiative but derisively called Star Wars by the media. *The Independent*, a London newspaper, ran a story about the $58 billion–plan the Bush administration was considering to create a missile defense shield for the United States. The article, which was negative of the preemptive strike and space superiority policies Bush and others in the United States advocated, was full of *Star Wars* references. One commentator compared U.S. missiles in space to the Death Star, while the writer suggested a ban of all weapons in space to avoid "the fictional *Star Wars*" coming true (Cornwell).

The June 2005 issue of *MAD* magazine, which parodies popular culture and entertainment, had its own special tribute to *Revenge of the Sith* with Obi-Wan and Anakin dueling in front of a cross-eyed emperor Palpatine on the cover. The issue boasted two comics, "A Day in the Life of George Lucas" and "Monroe and *Star Wars*," along with a few other funny features. *MAD XL* magazine also featured a *Star Wars* cover, with Yoda on the front holding a flaccid lightsaber. *MAD*, started in 1952, is one of the most famous humor and satire magazines. It is, according to the magazine Web site, "virtually impossible to think of any important trend or moment in our country's past 50 years that did not originate in our pages" ("About ..."). Clearly, *Star Wars* found itself in a privileged publication.

Lingering Bias

Although poor media coverage for *Revenge of the Sith* did not begin to compare with the negativity that *The Phantom Menace* suffered, it still plagued a few publications and tainted what should have been a celebration of a popular saga coming to completion. One common media trick, which is not hard to see present whether in sports, politics, or film, is to quote celebrities selectively, taking what they say out of context and then framing it within another context. A great example is the May 20 issue of *Entertainment Weekly*, where almost all of the quotes are framed within the context of fan disappointment.

In the *Entertainment Weekly* issue, when Lucas says that the first two prequels "got killed" by critics, instead of perhaps mentioning that both films received over a 60 percent approval rating, the magazine writes, "[Lucas] blames everyone but himself" (26). Given another spin, one could have mentioned that *The Empire Strikes Back* and *Return of the Jedi* both received much worse reviews than either prequel, yet they became classics, so perhaps Lucas's vision is simply ahead of film critics of the time. Whether one agrees with such an assertion or not, the point remains that quotes taken out of context and put within a negative, cynical framework have a different effect upon readers than the same quotes put in a positive light.

A few examples of poor journalism are worth analyzing, not primarily to criticize specific publications or writers as much as to underscore that the media affects individuals' opinions about an event even when the facts do not support such opinions. In other words, not everyone reads enough articles on the same event to form an unbiased view of what happened. As a result, the media's constant repetition of the great disappointment that the first two prequels caused fans is often frustrating because it threatens to undermine the opinions of the majority of *Star Wars* fans, who enjoyed and appreciated the prequels, to varying degrees.

As an example, consider a May 23, 2005, article from *The Daily Mail* in London, which showcased hilariously inept writing. One wonders if the journalist covers film at all. The article read, "The success of [*Revenge of the Sith*] is a welcome boost for creator George Lucas after the disappointment of the last two installments of the saga, *The Phantom Menace* and *Attack of the Clones*. Both had modest opening weekends after being savaged by the critics." In fact, *The Phantom Menace* became the fastest movie ever to gross $100 million, doing so in five days. It broke the non-holiday weekend record and it broke the opening-day and single-day gross records. *Attack of the Clones*, as previously discussed, opened strongly with one of the best four-day debuts in history. As well, neither film was savaged by critics; they both received many more positive than negative reviews. Not one part of the article had any basis in fact.

In another curious example, *The Sunday Telegraph* ran an article on May 22, 2005, that had a couple of questionable statements, as though the author, Matthew d'Ancona, was not sure what to write of the franchise. First, d'Ancona wrote that the final prequel "has been ridiculed by critics" and that they "gleefully trashed both its acting and dialogue," even though it was one of the best reviewed films of the year with more than four out of five critics giving it a positive rating. Later in the article, he called Lucas "the most successful film director of all time," which also seems questionable. While perhaps Lucas is the most financially successful director of all time, he is not primarily a film director but a film visionary and technology pioneer. Having directed only six films (*THX 1138*, *American Graffiti*, and four *Star Wars* films), Lucas would not seemingly be in the running for such an exalted title yet.

Business Week's Ronald Grover wrote one of the most embarrassingly poor pieces of journalism about the film in a May 4, 2005, article, which focused on the money that Lucas stood to earn from the final prequel. Grover wrote that the movie "could also end up being a big disappointment" because it is "part of a faded franchise." Furthermore, he made a big deal of the smaller box office gross for *Attack of the Clones* compared to *The Phantom Menace*, even though the same pattern happened with *A New Hope* and *The Empire Strikes Back*. Had Grover done his research, he would have known *Return of the Jedi*, the trilogy's final entry, increased its box office gross over its immediate predecessor to near the levels of the first film.

Grover obviously did not care much about facts as he incorrectly wrote that *The Phantom Menace* opened in 1997 instead of 1999. Furthermore, he wrote that "not a lot of overage Wookie lovers were walking out of *The Phantom Menace* humming a John Williams tune," which apparently is supposed to mean that fans were disappointed with the film, despite all the facts to the contrary covered in *Anticipation*. Grover wrote that the last prequel's PG-13 rating would hurt business, yet *Titanic*, the highest grossing movie of all time, is rated PG-13.

Grover also wrote that people were hoping *Revenge of the Sith* would leave behind the "dopey characters" and "pointless plot" of *Attack of the Clones*, which is curious because the characters in the second prequel are largely the same as the final installment.[5] Additionally, whether one likes the film or hates it, the plot of

Attack of the Clones is anything but pointless as anyone who paid attention realizes. Without the film, the Clone Wars are not set in motion, Anakin's turn to the Dark Side is not well established, Palpatine's rise to power is left largely unexplained, and how Padmé ends up pregnant or with Anakin would be a mystery. How well or poorly Lucas handled each of the events is for moviegoers to debate and decide for themselves. Whether the plot is pointless or meaningful to the saga is not up for debate as it clearly advances the six-film story arc.

Grover further defended his opinions about the business prospects for *Revenge of the Sith* by undermining its potential success. He wrote, "Doing very big business in a lackluster year isn't that great an accomplishment." When moviegoers are not going to theaters, bringing them back can be even harder than drawing audiences in a strong year with already high ticket sales. Doing great business in a lackluster year proved that *Star Wars* still mattered to millions of people, despite the failure of other Hollywood films. In general, Grover's poorly researched, biased article came across as little more than jealousy for Lucas, a man who runs several successful businesses rather than one who merely writes about them.

Another business article, from The Tribal Mind column of the *Sydney Morning Herald* on July 12, 2005, was just as poor as the one from *Business Week*. The final *Star Wars* film bombed in Australia, according to David Dale in an article titled, "What sank the Sith?" Because the movie did not pass the *Lord of the Rings* films, two *Harry Potter* movies, and "most embarrassing of all [made] less than its own truly terrible predecessor, *The Phantom Menace*," Dale felt it failed. For *Episode III* not to top the first prequel would not have been an embarrassment because *The Phantom Menace* was the third highest grossing movie of all time after its release. The article called *Revenge of the Sith* "a dwarf" because it only was able to reach #11 on the all-time list of blockbusters in Australia at the time of the article's writing.

The Dale article became even more ridiculous as time passed, however, to the point where one wonders how any news organization could allow such shoddy research from a journalist. *Revenge of the Sith* finished as the highest grossing film of the year in Australia, so if it was a bomb, apparently so was every other 2005 release in the country. More importantly, Dale spoke too soon of the prequel's ranking because it eventually finished its box office run well ahead of *The Phantom Menace*. It became the sixth highest grossing movie in Australian box office

---

5.   Not to mention that Yoda and Obi-Wan are present in the Original Trilogy and are hardly "dopey," unless one just does not like *Star Wars* at all.

history, beating two of the three *Lord of the Rings* films, every *Harry Potter* movie, and every previous *Star Wars* entry.

Dale also suggested that the final prequel only did "marginally better" in the United States, where it was the year's highest grossing movie by nearly $90 million. No other film broke $300 million and at the time no film was even within $150 million of the prequel's gross. In the opinion of the writer, "All the forces were aligned for *Sith* to sail past *Titanic* as the biggest moneymaker in our history." Additionally, Dale provided reasons he thought the movie failed, one of which was "audiences losing interest in science fiction," which is supported apparently by the fact that the last *Star Wars* movie did not beat *Titanic*. As he already mentioned, though, five fantasy films, a genre of which *Star Wars* is more a part than science fiction, ranked in the top ten of all time in Australia. Unrealistic expectations combined with no knowledge of box office grosses lead to disappointed media writers, apparently.

The article was fallacious enough to draw attention and ire from Lucasfilm, which first called the organization to ask why it would term such a successful movie a flop. When Dale asked, "Surely you must have been disappointed that it made so much less then [*sic*] you expected," Lucasfilm responded appropriately in a written statement via e-mail (Dale "The Lucas ..."). The statement read:

> *Revenge of the Sith* has been a remarkable success in Australia with $35 million [Australian] at the box office since its release on May 19. We are thrilled at the reception it has had, and appreciate the passion that *Star Wars* fans throughout Australia have shown for the movie. *Episode III* is nearing $800 million (U.S.) at the worldwide box office, and only recently opened in Japan, where the response has been extraordinary. Lucasfilm and Fox could not be happier about the response *Episode III* has received in Australia and around the world and the immense enthusiasm of tens of millions of *Star Wars* fans (ibid.).

Despite Lucasfilm's response stating the facts, the newspaper received 430 comments from various moviegoers who tried to give reasons for the film's "failure" at the Australian box office. When a newspaper tells moviegoers a film failed and asks for reasons why it could not meet expectations, of course it will receive responses from readers who do not know any better, especially from people who did not like the film. Even so, 430 people whining about a movie that millions of Australians enjoyed hardly seems like a reasonable sample size. One wonders about the journalistic integrity of a newspaper that supports such lousy reporting.

Aside from the poor journalism of a few writers and critics, the media largely threw *Star Wars* and its fans a party to remember in 2005. Instead of seeming nerdy or cultish, *Star Wars* was embraced for being the most popular, most influential franchise in film history, adored not only by fans worldwide but by directors, actors, actresses, musicians, and other creative people who at times have looked to *Star Wars* not only for entertainment but also for inspiration. A starwars.com article read at year's end:

> In the past, *Star Wars* fans have had to occasionally endure mean-spirited swipes from pop culture mavens who take umbrage with the saga's latest inspiration. In 2005, though, the overwhelming majority of this spotlight coverage was positive—the entire world was eager to see how the *Star Wars* saga was going to end ("*Star Wars:* The Best …").

For fans of the saga, 2005 was sweet revenge, as "it seemed almost everyone was a *Star Wars* fan," the article concluded. In a rare twist, even the critics joined in praising *Star Wars*.

The Fan Alliance

Creative Homages

Star Wars fanatics have existed almost as long as the franchise itself. The first fans were the entranced moviegoers who saw *A New Hope* (titled *Star Wars* at the time) in theaters in 1977, only to line up to see it again almost immediately afterwards. Millions of people became fans in dark movie theaters around the world while watching the *Tantive IV* try to escape the grasp of a monstrous Imperial Star Destroyer. Their passion for the film led to two sequels in the early 1980s, each building more interest in the saga.

With numerous generations of fans part of the Force faithful, fans have found many ways to express their love of the *Star Wars* saga, which continues to interest the media as writers and commentators search for answers as to why the films have captivated generations of moviegoers. In a *USA Today*/CNN poll conducted May 20–22, almost two-thirds of Americans surveyed said they were not specifically fans of *Star Wars*, but 30 percent said they considered themselves fans, 6 percent said they were somewhat interested in the movies, and 1 percent had no opinion ("'Star Wars' fans miss …").

For many years, fans have shown their love of the *Star Wars* saga by creating their own films set in the *Star Wars* universe showing new adventures of familiar characters or imagined ones, parodying the films, or documenting fan events. Fan films, as they are called, have gained Lucasfilm approval with the annual Fan Film Awards at AtomFilms.com, which hosts many of the fan films with Lucasfilm permission. The modern fan film craze arguably started with Kevin Rubio's 1997 short film *Troops*, a parody of *Cops* and *Star Wars* that has since attained cult status in the fan community. The first major parody, however, was twenty years earlier, with *Hardware Wars* (1977) boasting flying toasters and steam irons that made it highly successful for its time. The film "sort of set the mark for how funny and how clever people could be making a parody out of *Star Wars*," said Steve Sansweet, head of fan relations for Lucasfilm (Wells "No …").

Instead of combating the fan film phenomenon, which often breaks various copyright laws, Lucasfilm has embraced the creativity of fans, realizing that as long as fans are not collecting profits, they are not only expressing their enthusiasm in creative ways but providing good publicity for the saga. In 2000, Lucasfilm and AtomFilms launched a fan film network at AtomFilms.com, which led to the annual *Star Wars* Fan Film Awards beginning in 2002. Any satires or noncommercial spoofs running less than fifteen minutes were eligible in the competition, which excluded films adding content to the *Star Wars* universe in favor of parodies on existing material.

One of the most notable fan films was *Star Wars: Revelations*, released online April 18, 2005. The film is about forty minutes long and focuses on the Jedi purge, where Vader is hunting escaping Jedi while a former Jedi, Zhanna, who joined the Imperial cause, is in pursuit of an artifact to help eradicate her former comrades. Meanwhile, Jedi Taryn Anwar, working with a smuggler named Declan, vies for control of the artifact from ex-Jedi Cade through a series of battles. Director Shane Felux also played Cade. He maxed out a credit card trying to make the film, admitting that it "got bigger than even I thought it would. We just never really tried to limit ourselves" (Wells "'Star Wars' ..."). The $20,000 *Revelations* also earned a significant *USA Today* article, which mentioned the popularity of the fan film on TheForce.net and the work required to complete the ambitious project (Breznican "'Star Wars' fan ...").

More than two hundred people assisted in the production of *Revelations*, mostly for free. Many people contributed, especially to the special effects, with the hope that their talents would later be appreciated for potential employers. Mostly, though, fan films are a labor of love, created to celebrate the *Star Wars* saga and tell a story within the galaxy or capture part of the enthusiasm that fans have for the films. *U.S. News & World Report* also mentioned the fan film, with writer Marc Silver calling it "the most technically sharp amateur flick ever, with special effects as visually compelling as in the real movies." With increasingly advanced off-the-shelf software, dedicated fans with time to spend can create much more realistic effects than had ever been possible before the age of powerful personal computers.

Another fan film, a parody called *Forcery*, took the form of a fifty-four-minute film about George Lucas having recently finished the final script for *Episode III* in a remote area of the Rocky Mountains when he is in a serious car accident. An obsessed fan, Frannie, discovers Lucas, reads his script, and goes crazy. Chris Knight, former humor editor at TheForce.net, spent four years making his movie, which the site would not host because, "It's the worst parody we've ever seen," Knight recalled being told ("'Star Wars' Spoof ...").

After putting *Forcery* up on his site and receiving more than ten thousand downloads just weeks after the release of *Revenge of the Sith*, Knight felt vindicated when "Weird Al" Yankovic wrote to him expressing approval. "Weird Al thought my first movie was funny. Dude, that was so cool," Knight said (ibid.). The fan film parodied both *Star Wars* and *Misery*, the 1990 Rob Reiner film about a famous novelist rescued from a car crash by an obsessive fan.

Even the Organic Trade Organization took advantage of the fan film craze, making its own parody of the original *Star Wars* trilogy to promote its message against chemicals used for vegetables (Welych). The animated parody, *Grocery Store Wars*, which appeared at storewars.org, featured characters like Cuke Skywalker, Princess Lettuce, and Darth Tate, all drawing on the ways of the Farm to fight against chemically-infected Dark Side foods. The concept of using popular culture icons to promote a message is innovative as well as humorous in *Grocery Store Wars*.

In the United States and elsewhere, parodies enjoy protection under the law regardless of whether they may seem to infringe upon copyright laws. Because filmmakers making strict parodies need not worry about lawsuits, a few high-profile parodies of the saga made an impact over the years, not just the aforementioned *Hardware Wars*. In 1987, Mel Brooks released his comedy *Spaceballs* with characters like "Dark Helmet" (Rick Moranis) and "Lone Star" (Bill Pullman), not to mention "the Schwartz," instead of the Force. *Spaceballs* has gained a large cult following over the years and is one of many great comedies from Brooks's career. Steve Oedekerk of *Ace Ventura: Pet Detective* (1993) fame also made a thirty-minute parody, *Thumb Wars* (1999), with thumbs as all of the main characters. Although high-profile parodies like *Thumb Wars* and *Spaceballs* enjoyed more attention in the last century, fan films have taken over the spotlight in the twenty-first century.

Stories of fan filmmakers later earning jobs in Hollywood are not uncommon as such amateur films are increasingly seen as opportunities to showcase one's skills and creativity. For instance, John Hudgens of TheForce.net said, "Ryan Wieber got hired at Lucasfilm directly because of his fan film *Ryan vs. Dorkman* and his lightsaber creation tutorials" (Munk). Trey Stokes, who made the fan film *Pink Five* (with a clueless valley girl as the pilot trying to destroy the Death Star), later worked on *The Polar Express*, the high-profile animated blockbuster (Munk). Kevin Rubio used his *Troops* fame to work on a variety of small television projects as a writer-director and later landed a job with Dark Horse Comics writing *Tag and Bink*[1] and various offshoots (Rubio).

One group of fans, about three thousand of them, formed the R2 Builders Club in 2002 with the goal of promoting *Star Wars* robotics and constructing droids from the *Star Wars* films (Szadkowski "'Star Wars'–inspired …"). The group showed some of its creations at *Star Wars* Celebration III. The fans' projects cost between $500 and $8,000 and ranged from fairly simple to significantly complicated. The group runs a Web site at astromech.net, where fans and builders exchange information on how to construct droids. Other fans celebrated the saga by altering their cars to resemble *Star Wars* vehicles. A few dozen fans started a group known as Road Squadron, at roadsquadron.com, in which the members paint and modify usually inexpensive cars to look like famous craft from the saga (Collier).

Many fans found ways to be part of the *Star Wars* universe in some small way through their enthusiasm for the franchise. Ken Tarleton, also known as the Elvis Trooper for wearing a Stormtrooper costume with Elvis-like head accessories, had the opportunity to be part of Hasbro's *Star Wars* Trivial Pursuit DVD, after the company gave twenty-one fans the chance to ask and answer questions for the game. "I started growing my sideburns out just for a different look. I was playing cards with friends one night, and one of the guys asked me if I was trying to look like Elvis. So when I was in Las Vegas, I bought a pair of Elvis glasses," said Tarleton, who is also a member of the 501st Legion costuming group (Bentley "'Star Wars' …"). Soon enough, he was a minor celebrity at the conventions as everyone wanted pictures with him.

Clarke Reynolds in the United Kingdom took his devotion to an extreme by attempting to devote every inch of his skin to *Star Wars* tattoos in honor of Lucas's epic. He put lightsabers and droids like R2-D2 and C-3PO down his arms and a huge *Millennium Falcon* on his back complete with images of Han Solo and Chewbacca. Another fan with numerous tattoos, Eric Negron, is a tattoo artist specializing in *Star Wars* body art. With tens of thousands of dollars in merchandise in his collection, Negron also had numerous latex masks that he crafted himself. He even dumped his girlfriend of ten years over *Star Wars*. "She said it was me or *Star Wars*. My reaction was: *Star Wars!*" (K. Smith). If forced to choose between *Star Wars* and a girlfriend, most male fans pick the one they have loved longer. After all, the world has plenty of girls, but only one *Star Wars*.

One of the most famous displays of fan enthusiasm came from Charles Ross, whose show, *The One-Man Star Wars Trilogy*, has become popular with thou-

---

1. *Tag and Bink* is a humorous comic series focusing on the misadventures of a pair of Rebel Alliance operatives.

sands of fans who have attended a performance. Ross manages to recreate the events of the Original Trilogy in a fifty-eight-minute performance without any other actors or props. His show became such a hit that he toured across the United States for three months in the summer of 2005, was invited to perform on *The Late, Late Show* on CBS, and was interviewed for *Esquire* and *Spin* magazines. "It's an absolute thrill to take my love of something like this and commune with other fans," he said (Humphries). Ross spent three years perfecting his act and building popularity at fringe festivals and small performances. His big break came in 2004, when Lucas asked him to appear at Comic-Con International in San Diego, where three thousand fans watched and applauded him.

Another fan, renowned card stacker Bryan Berg, made an impact at *Star Wars* Celebration III with a nine-foot tall, twelve-foot wide recreation of Cloud City using seventy-five thousand *Star Wars* Wizards of the Coast trading cards from the *Revenge of the Sith* set. Berg had previously created huge card structures such as the New York City skyline on ABC's *Good Morning America*, but never otherworldly structures. "While I've built replicas of dozens of Earth-based buildings and skylines in my career, this will be the first time I've built something from a galaxy far, far away" ("Renowned ..."). Berg uses nothing but the cards to hold his structures together, not relying on tape, glue, or any adhesives. At the end of the Celebration, Berg used a lightsaber to destroy his creation.

The Light and Dark Sides of Fandom

Unfortunately, a few fans took their enthusiasm for the saga too far, resulting in unnecessary bodily harm. A few days after the opening of the final film, a report from London indicated that two young fans critically injured one another by trying to replicate lightsabers by filling glass fluorescent light tubes with fuel. One of the two lightsabers exploded, injuring the fans in the woods of Hemel Hempstead, north of London. Both were in critical condition at a burn unit in Essex after the incident ("Report ..."). For future reference, fans would be in better physical and financial shape spending $100 or so on a Master Replicas Force FX Lightsaber than potentially thousands of dollars in medical bills as a result of moronically trying to create their own lightsabers with accelerants.

Another fan also suffered an unfortunate fate, leading to perhaps more long-lasting emotional damage than the physical damage of exploding lightsabers caused the fans in England. Ghyslian Raza from Quebec, fifteen at the time, recorded himself twirling a golf ball retriever like Darth Maul wielded his double-bladed lightsaber in *The Phantom Menace*, at first nothing more than a silly home video. Raza had recorded the footage while doing a school project, but never intended the world to see it. A few classmates posted his two-minute video online, though, and before long millions of people downloaded the clip, soon giving Raza the nickname "*Star Wars* Kid." He became an immediate Internet celebrity in 2003, but the unwanted attention was embarrassing to the teen, who told the *National Post* newspaper, "I want my life back" (Irvine).

While many people watched the *Star Wars* Kid video to laugh at the poor teen in an embarrassing moment, others enjoyed his enthusiasm and had no malicious intent, often remembering their own make-believe lightsaber practice as kids. Web surfers created fan sites devoted to Raza, started fund-raising campaigns for him, and more than 180,000 people petitioned Lucasfilm to cast him in *Revenge of the Sith*; Lucasfilm declined (Moore). In August 2003, Lucasfilm spokeswoman Jeanne Cole said, "We are deeply saddened by this current situation and any difficulties this uninvited publicity might be causing (Ghyslian) and his family" (Irvine). In the years since its appearance, the *Star Wars* Kid video has only grown in popularity.

More than one hundred edited versions of Raza's video clip also appeared online, adding sounds and lightsaber effects or sometimes completely new footage. Many of the variations are not even *Star Wars* related; *Terminator* and *Matrix* versions also exist. Ghyslian's parents sued the parents of the four teenagers who posted the video online, arguing that it caused their son great emotional damage, forced him to drop out of school, and led him to seek psychiatric help (Thomas). In November 2006, a British net-tracking firm named the *Star Wars* Kid video the most seen viral clip on the net, with more than 900 million downloads of various versions of the footage (Moore). Raza's performance bested the Numa Numa lip-synch video by 200 million views and Paris Hilton's sex video by 500 million. While the *Star Wars* Kid quickly became one of the best-known fans, another fan spent years making a name for himself.

The ultimate *Star Wars* fan, author of multiple books on the subject over the years, is Steve Sansweet, who has amassed the largest privately held collection of *Star Wars* memorabilia in the world. His devotion to the saga earned him a job with Lucasfilm, where he works as both the director of content management and head of fan relations. His books on the franchise include collectible guides like *Star Wars: The Action Figure Archive* (Chronicle Books 1999) and *The Star Wars Poster Book* (Chronicle Books 2005), and archival books like *Star Wars: From Concept to Screen to Collectible* (Chronicle Books 1992) and *Star Wars Chronicles: The Prequels* (Chronicle Books 2005).

Sansweet's relentless pursuit of every *Star Wars* collectible worldwide has earned him immense respect in the collecting community, where fans envy his astonishing assortment of old and new items. Speaking about his collection, he joked, "I spend so much [money] I might as well sign the back of my paycheck and give it straight back to Lucasfilm" (Waugh "Space ..."). He is also the perfect person to represent Lucasfilm to the fan base. Sansweet says, "I speak for the fans because I am a fan."

Star Wars also has its share of musician fans, including a rapper named MC Chris and a band named Snow Patrol. MC Chris voiced Hesh on the Cartoon Network's *Sealab 2021* and wrote a rap song devoted to the *Star Wars* saga named "Fett's Vette." MC Chris put on a show at the WOW Hall in Eugene, Oregon, then the *Star Wars* party moved to Cinema World at Valley River Center, where WOW Hall reserved an entire auditorium for the opening of *Revenge of the Sith*. MC Chris said, "I'm as much of a nerd as my fans" (Lamberson). Snow Patrol guitarist Nathan Connolly, like MC Chris, first became interested in *Star Wars* with the release of *Return of the Jedi* in 1983. Connolly, an avid collector as well, said, "I kind of pride myself on my *Star Wars* knowledge" ("Snow ..."). He saw *Revenge of the Sith* opening day at 8:00 a.m., despite a busy show schedule.

Fan enthusiasm for *Star Wars* did not just manifest itself in box office grosses, costumed fans at premieres, and fan films, but also online. One Web site arose for the sole purpose of thanking creator George Lucas for the saga. The site, ThankYouGeorge.com, gave fans the opportunity to sign a thank-you letter to Lucas as well as adding personal comments about how the movies impacted their lives. The idea, which former Official *Star Wars* Fan Club President Dan Madsen started, culminated in thousands of fan signatures being presented in bound form to Lucas at the end of the year.

The fan appreciation Web site also sold logo T-shirts with "Thank you, George!" printed on them. Madsen said, "Many fans were there at the beginning twenty-eight years ago and have followed the *Star Wars* journey through the years with friends and family, to its culmination. This is a unique opportunity for them to mark the event by signing the tribute and wearing a visible symbol of gratitude and appreciation" ("Thank you ..."). Mark Hamill was the first to thank Lucas on the site.

A few days before the release of *Revenge of the Sith*, BlogPulse.com reported that the film had sustained a higher level of "buzz," or word-of-mouth and chatter between moviegoers, than any other action or fantasy movie scheduled for 2005 and both of the year's top grossing films at the time, *Robots* and *Hitch* ("'Star Wars Revenge of the Sith' Sustains ..."). BlogPulse measures trends, personalities, popular phrases, and top blogs daily, using nearly 11 million blogs at the time for its analysis. From November 2004 through March 2005, the final prequel maintained a steady level of discussion in 0.2 percent of all blogs daily, but the number rose to 8 percent in the first weeks of May.

Revenge of the Sith had also received more discussion on blogs than other big blockbusters on the horizon at the time, such as *War of the Worlds*, *Harry Potter and the Goblet of Fire*, and *Charlie and the Chocolate Factory*. Peter Blackshaw, chief marketing officer for Intelliseek, a marketing intelligence firm that monitors consumer feedback and discussion of brands, said, "They [Internet users] are building terrific momentum on blogs and message boards, and the intensity of what we call consumer-generated media (CGM) before a film's launch can have a huge impact on box office sales, merchandising potential, and even post-movie DVD sales" (ibid.).

For the week ending May 21, 2005, Lycos announced that "Star Wars 3" was the most searched term on its search engine at Lycos.com, surpassing other popular celebrities and terms like Pamela Anderson (#2), Paris Hilton (#3), American Idol (#6), and War in Iraq (#10). Activity for the search term doubled since the previous week, overtaking its rivals easily. The term first entered The Lycos 50 in August 2004, rising steadily ever since the title announcement for the final prequel. Six times as many people typed "Star Wars Episode 3" into their searches as "Revenge of the Sith." Among *Star Wars* searches, "Star Wars" ranked first while "Star Wars Episode 3" and "Star Wars Episode 2" ranked second and third, respectively. Other notables were "Light Saber" (#5) and "Padmé's Wardrobe" (#6), the latter indicating some additional female interest in the saga ("Lycos ...").

Setting Priorities

For the May 19 premiere of *Revenge of the Sith*, the entire sixteen-person staff of a Web development firm in Boston, Miller Systems, took much of the day off to see the film. The company paid for popcorn and soda, too. Seth Miller, president and CEO of Miller Systems, said the tradition started with *The Phantom Menace* and had continued with the second prequel. "It speaks to our culture. It's the benefit of not working at a giant monolithic—dare I say 'Imperial'—type company" (Fuentez). The answering machine at Miller Systems said, "Greetings. Our offices will be closed after 12:30 p.m. on Thursday, May 19th, in observance of George Lucas's latest epic, *Star Wars: Episode III—Revenge of the Sith*" ("Profile: People ..."). Other companies had similar plans.

At Serious Magic, a video software and special effects producer, the owners paid for tickets for all forty of their employees to see the film on its opening day.

"We think of the expedition benefitting the company in terms of inspiration and imagination. That's the lifeblood of our business," said President Mark Randall, who also called May 19 St. Lucas Day (Osterman). Only smaller companies could offer their employees such nice treats, however. Intel had no such plans, for instance. Dan Francisco, a spokesman for Intel, said that its employees "work in a global, competitive technology industry that does not rest" (ibid.). While employees of Miller Systems and Serious Magic had no trouble seeing the movie opening day, all expenses paid, other employees, like those at Intel, had a bit more difficulty.

NPR ran a special segment, hosted by Melissa Block of *All Things Considered*, in which Art Silverman went to talk with fans waiting in line for the final prequel at a theater in Washington, D.C. One fan, Adam, said he called in sick. "I gave no cough. I just said I wasn't going to be in," he told Silverman ("Profile: People ..."). Another fan replied, "I called in sick. I didn't even call my boss. I just called my co-worker and told him to tell my boss. I told him—I was like, 'Yeah, I'm dressed up as Darth Maul, and I'm in D.C. trying to see *Star Wars*.'" Randy Cook, a senior engineer for an Internet host in Virginia, joked, "I think in the IT industry it's not as much considered skipping work as it is a requirement" (Kelley). He skipped work for every *Star Wars* opening since 1977.

Fans missing work for *Star Wars*, though amusing on the surface, cost employers millions of dollars in lost wages and provided at least a minor problem for many businesses, especially those in technical fields with higher percentages of employees likely to be fans. According to a report from outplacement firm Challenger, Gray & Christmas, lost productivity from fan absences could have cost employers as much as $627 million (Kelley). The firm calculated the statistic based on the number of full-time employees, courtesy of the U.S. Bureau of Labor Statistics (51 percent), the two-day total attendance for *Attack of the Clones* on its Thursday opening and Friday second day (9.4 million), and the $130.60 average full-time daily pay for employees.

Other big events like the Super Bowl ($1.1 billion in days leading up to the event) and NCAA March Madness ($890 million) also cost businesses hundreds of millions of dollars in lost productivity each year, according to the firm's estimates. Nonetheless, Challenger spokesman James K. Pedderson cautioned not to take the large numbers too seriously. "They're definitely meant to be taken kind of lightheartedly," he said (Kelley). Many employers may have felt otherwise if their employees did not schedule vacation time but instead faked illnesses.

Best Buy's Geek Squad, which provides technology support to customers, offered help for fans eager to see the final prequel on opening day. The company created a form letter allowing fans to plug in their names, an excuse, and an assurance that the planned absence had nothing to do with "a long awaited prequel/the final installment of the greatest story ever/the #$%%!! BEST THING EVER." Fans could use a pulldown menu to select "move along" or "this wasn't the excuse note you were looking for" instead of "sincerely" ("Eyes …").

To help compensate for employee shortages, Geek Squad held rather unorthodox auctions for emergency IT employees in major markets like New York, Los Angeles, San Francisco, Seattle, and Boston to help small companies experiencing too many *Star Wars*–related absences (White "'Star Wars Flu' …"). Renee Link, a Sacramento *Star Wars* fan, planned far ahead: she requested time off for future *Star Wars* premieres when she interviewed for her job at a printing company five years earlier (Osterman). Not all fans prepared as well as Link, but many notified employers early that they intended to skip work.

Star Wars fans like Diane Kovalcin of New Jersey planned honest ways to miss work. Kovalcin said, "I went to the midnight showing and took a vacation day the next day to sleep and see it again. I told my boss that it was the last *Star Wars* and I wanted to be part of the opening night. They already knew I was a *Star Wars* fan" (Kovalcin). Dave Gohman of Schaumburg, Illinois, found himself in a similar situation. "I took that day and the rest of that week off. Everyone at work knows how much I love *Star Wars*, so it was no surprise to them," he said (Gohman). Absenteeism did not just occur on opening day, however. "I did call in sick one day at my job … It wasn't on opening day, but I had just got paid and had the money to go and see it. I decided to play sick … and I'm glad that I did," said Cody Powell of Texas (Powell).

American troops overseas in Iraq looked forward to the final prequel, but they had even more trouble seeing it than employees who had already used up their vacation time and sick days. At Camp Liberty in Western Baghdad, troops were excited to learn of big-screen showings of *Revenge of the Sith*, but the excitement dissipated when insurgents fired a rocket into the base, damaging shops and fast-food restaurants near where the movie was showing, killing one soldier, and forcing cancellations of future screenings (Castaneda).

The end of the *Star Wars* saga in film form generated numerous media articles about what fans were going to do with the story concluded and Lucas moving on to other projects. *The Hollywood Reporter* ran an article asking, "Does the final 'Star Wars' mean the death of the superfan?" With Paramount officially putting the once-proud *Star Trek* franchise on hiatus after the demise of the television show *Enterprise*, and Lucas ending his *Star Wars* saga with *Revenge of the Sith*, *The*

Hollywood Reporter and many other cultural pundits wondered what sci-fi fans would do with the two biggest franchises seemingly ending.

Star Trek has already had rough times before, but has always come back with new entries and will probably exist forever in one form or another. Likewise, *Star Wars* fans are not prepared to abandon their posts. The first generation of fans remembers its own "Dark Times," the period in the mid-to-late 1980s when the franchise seemingly had ended. Having survived such a period of inactivity and seen the franchise spring to life bigger than before with the *Star Wars: Special Editions* and the prequels, the true fans have already endured the longest *Star Wars* dry spell. Now, for the die-hard fans, the Force will be with them … always. The same devotion to the franchise that led fans to dress up, skip work, obsess about the movies online, and create fan films based on the movies also led thousands of die-hard fans to wait many hours in line for the final prequel.

The Final Countdown

Sleepless in Seattle

As with all important *Star Wars* events, fans lined up many hours and sometimes many days to be first to see *Revenge of the Sith*, or at least obtain the best possible seats. No other entertainment franchise has ever inspired such long lines as the *Star Wars* movies, especially the prequels, with a small group of fans having waited more than a month outside of Mann's Chinese Theatre to see *The Phantom Menace* in 1999. The craziness of lining up weeks early reached epic proportions with *Attack of the Clones*, when fans John Guth and Jeff Tweiten started lining up for the film in Seattle on January 1, 2002.

For *Revenge of the Sith*, Tweiten again returned to line up in front of the Cinerama in Seattle an amazing twenty-two weeks before the film's release to theaters. When the media asked him what would happen if the movie did not show at the Cinerama, he said, "If it isn't, I'll be more than happy to move to a different theater. It's really about the wait. *Star Wars* is about independence and freedom, and that's really what this wait is about" ("'Star Wars' fan …"). Of all the places to wait in line during the winter, Seattle is not at the top of the list for best locations. Not only is rain a constant feature of Seattle, but temperatures on winter nights often dip below freezing. Tweiten came prepared with several sleeping bags. "I've got another sleeping bag coming, so that's sleeping bag number three," he said in early January soon after starting the lineup (Haeck).

With such a long wait outside of theaters for the final film, which to most casual moviegoers is "just a movie," people often questioned how Tweiten could devote such a significant portion of his life to waiting in line. "A lot of people say, 'Get a life,' stuff like that. But I'm having the time of my life out here," he said (Haeck). Tweiten had saved enough money to manage the lineup financially. When speaking of people who had accused him of being a slacker, he said, "I make enough money to be able to do this. But I also challenge the idea that you're wasting your time if you're not stuck in a cubicle all day" (Paynter "The Force …").

Although many media members saw Tweiten's lineup as a great opportunity for comic relief and poking fun of *Star Wars* fans in general, Susan Paynter of the *Seattle Post-Intelligencer* thought he provided necessary character to the city. "Frankly, with a shortfall of characters, pranksters, goof-ups and gadflies, Seattle sorely needs Jeff Tweiten" (Paynter "'Star Wars' Fan ..."). A few people wondered about the legality of Tweiten's lineup for *Revenge of the Sith* early in his journey, though.

A number of people complained privately that Tweiten was breaking city ordinances, though the police had received no formal complaints in the first month of his wait. The ordinance reads, "No person shall sit or lie down upon a public sidewalk, or upon a blanket, chair, stool, or any other object placed upon a public sidewalk, during the hours between 7 a.m. and 9 p.m." At least one unnamed person with way too much time on his or her hands complained to the Seattle City Council and the City Attorney's Office that Tweiten was receiving preferential treatment compared to transients who would be booted if they loitered outside of a downtown business. Nonetheless, like many laws, the enforcement of the ordinance is driven more by complaints than the wording of the law, so as long as Tweiten was not damaging business or disrupting pedestrian travel, Paynter assumed he would not be banned from his wait (Paynter "'Star Wars' Fan ...").

For the start of the 139 day lineup, Tweiten lived on a periwinkle blue futon on the sidewalk with his sleeping bags and a sign behind him reading, "Waiting for *Star Wars*." He joked, "It feels more like home than any apartment I've ever lived in" (Dizon). Although many people assumed without further thought that Tweiten must be a fanatical lunatic with no life, the graphic artist, twenty-seven at the time he started lining up, attended the Art Institute of Seattle and described himself as having many other interests, like classical music, fine dining, working out, and reading about contemporary art. Tweiten played football and ran track in high school, so he did not fit the traditional stereotype of a nerd. "I don't really care how people label me. If they are so narrow-minded and can only see that one aspect of me, I kind of pity them," he said (ibid.).

Tweiten took a philosophical approach to his lineup. "Coming out here and sitting and waiting—embodying the anticipation—I think people need to see that. Maybe they'll slow down. So many people are in such a hurry that they miss the savoring of time," he said (Dizon). With many hours in line to fill, Tweiten maintained an online blog at waitingforstarwars.blogspot.com, writing to keep friends and fans informed of his wait, and spent much of his time on media interviews and answering e-mails. "I think I'm working the hardest I've ever worked," he said (ibid.). Tweiten had experienced media scrutiny before, though. As the release of *Attack of the Clones* neared in 2002, Tweiten had to answer hundreds of e-mails per day, conduct up to ten radio interviews, and speak with people greeting him in line. He even appeared on *Jimmy Kimmel Live* on ABC.

In the first few weeks of the lineup for the final prequel, Tweiten lost ten pounds, consumed two pots of coffee a day, slept only about five hours per night, and smoked a fair number of cigarettes. He admitted to Kristin Dizon of the *Seattle Post-Intelligencer* that the first few weeks seemed longer than he expected, partially because of the cold, "But I don't want to regret not doing this. If I end up not making it, and my will is broken, and I go home, at least I'll have tried." Tweiten's will, though, was not the problem; the pesky city ordinance started to haunt him, after all.

Despite receiving no complaints for weeks, an anonymous caller finally complained to the Seattle Police Department, which in late January told Tweiten that he was violating a city ordinance and needed to remove his couch and give up his camp by the next day. The police were reluctant, according to Tweiten, but still had to enforce the law. "They told me they didn't really want to do it. In fact, one said they felt like asses," he said (Paynter "The Force ..."). Quickly hoping to execute Plan B, Tweiten asked a representative of nearby Diamond Parking if he could relocate to the company's lot, but had no luck. He also tried applying for a street use permit, but the Department of Transportation declined his request.

Seemingly out of options, Tweiten was far from defeated. Instead of ending his lineup quest and quitting, as he could have done easily given the cold weather, police annoyances, and existing difficulties of waiting such a prolonged period outside, Tweiten was more determined still to see his goal to completion. He vowed to return the next day, without his couch, and planned to stand until May 19 if necessary. Tweiten was not pleased and vowed a new determination. "I figure I can stand sixteen hours a day if I take little breaks," he said (Paynter "The Force ..."). Furthermore, "This time I'll either leave in shackles or an aid car. And, as soon as I get out of the hospital, I'll be back," he said. Nobody could accuse Tweiten of being lazy. He showed more ambition and perseverance than many people manage in their daily lives.

Many people expressed indignation at Seattle's ridiculous reaction to Tweiten's lineup, blasting a city full of rules and restrictions that harm individuality and reduce the freedom of expression people are supposed to enjoy. Paynter covered the issue in a February 2 column, writing, "Did this guy (Tweiten) pester pedestrians for money, they ask? Sell drugs? Even spit on the sidewalk? No!"

Whoever complained probably has about as much intelligence and individuality as pond scum on Dagobah, many people reasoned.

Instead of lining up outside of the Cinerama again, Tweiten returned to his mission, but in front of the Pacific Science Center, where an IMAX screen had debuted *Polar Express* and *The Matrix Revolutions*. He hoped the Center also received the final prequel. As the release date neared, though, he became less and less certain. Nonetheless, the Pacific Science Center provided a good place to continue the epic wait. On April 15, Tweiten wrote on his blog:

> Tickets went on sale yesterday at the Cinerama. I got the call from Ken around 3:50 [p.m.]. I took [off] running down to the Cinerama. I was about half way there when two men moving a sofa into an apartment [were] taking up the entire sidewalk. I didn't have time to go around, and these are *Star Wars* ticket[s] and seconds [matter]. Over the sofa I [went] like the old days of high school track no stutter step, three perfect strides. Seconds later I was at the Ticket Booth, out of [breath] the only words I could say was can I still get tickets for 12:01.. Moments later I had pure gold in my hands[:] tickets for *Star Wars*.[1]

By early May, Tweiten had moved back to the Cinerama for the final days of the wait.

A Tradition Derailed

Another group of die-hard fans, as became a tradition with the first two prequels, prepared a long lineup outside of the historic Grauman's Chinese Theatre (called Mann's Chinese Theatre at various times in the past) in Hollywood, arguably the most famous moviegoing venue in the world. Core members of the Countingdown.com group, who had waited for *The Phantom Menace* under the organization of Lincoln Gasking, continued the tradition with *Attack of the Clones* independently of Countingdown.com, which had no plans arranged for fans to wait for the second prequel. The core fans from previous lineups launched LiningUp.net, the new home of Hollywood prequel lineups, which gave interested fans information about the event and how they could be part of the final countdown.

On Saturday, April 2, forty-seven days before the film's release to theaters, a group of fans from LiningUp.net started their lineup. The Chinese Theatre has special meaning for many *Star Wars* fans as it was one of the few theaters that

---

1.   Spelling mistakes corrected for readability are placed in brackets.

played the first *Star Wars* movie on opening day in 1977. It also was the locale for the lineup for *The Phantom Menace*, at the time a record for the longest wait outside of a movie theater. "This is still the epicenter for *Star Wars* fans. For the big iconic pictures of the 1970s, people lining up were here. They weren't at the Cinerama Dome," Sarah Sprague said, referring to the nearby ArcLight theater, which Fox had scheduled to play the prequel (Snyder "Inside …").

One major problem confronted the group immediately, however: Fox did not intend to show *Revenge of the Sith* at the Chinese Theatre, only at the ArcLight. "We've heard all this before," said Sprague, speaking of rumors that the first two prequels also would not play at the Chinese (ibid.). Luis Lecca, a thirty-two-year-old karate instructor who had joined the lineup, said, "We really hope they do just one midnight screening at Grauman's for us" (Shuster "'Star Wars' Fans …"). Paramount had already arranged to have *The Longest Yard* playing at the Chinese Theatre a week after the opening of the final prequel, so the outlook for fans in line looked bleak.

The fans in line, though they knew the final prequel may not play at the theater at which they planned to wait for many weeks, had a good sense of humor about the situation. "We have this thing where we act panicked, like we didn't know, when somebody tells us" that the movie will not play at the Chinese Theatre, said Mike Lund, who celebrated his twentieth anniversary while in line (Rock). The group had built an impressive setup in the area, too, complete with a twenty-foot-long shelter built of tarps and PVC piping. The fans also had access to wireless Internet, a webcam, power from Hollywood Souvenirs, and the use of bathrooms in the Hollywood & Highland complex.

As with the lineups for *The Phantom Menace* and *Attack of the Clones*, the organizers of the final prequel lineup had established rules for line members. Each person officially registered had to contribute a minimum of $50 to charity, helping to aid the group's goal of $30,000. Nobody could leave the line for more than thirty minutes without signing out first. Everyone had to be present for the final twenty-four hours of the wait. By the time of the film's premiere, each person's place in line was determined by the total number of hours waited.

Because of the organization of the Chinese lineup, with tens of thousands of dollars raised through the wait going to charity, it was the most famous lineup effort for *The Phantom Menace*, though Tweiten stole some publicity for the subsequent prequels with his longer wait time. Fans flew from around the country and across the globe to be part of the Chinese lineup, though, still making it the largest and most impressive line, if not the longest by wait time. Caroline Ritter, a twenty-three-year-old fan who estimated she had spent $60,000 on *Star Wars* by 2005, flew from Australia to take part in the queue. "What can I say? I love the *Star Wars* movies. They are my life. They mean everything to me; everything that is important," she said ("'Star Wars' fans …"). Other fans in line came from Britain, Canada, Japan, Germany, and other states like Ohio, though most still lived throughout the Los Angeles area.

As with past lineups the group organized, fans could choose to wait in line in shifts, logging hours to gain better spots in line. Initially, dozens of fans took part in the lineup, a far different operation than Tweiten's setup as the solitary camper in Seattle for months. Part of what made the lineup experience great for dozens of people in Los Angeles was the sense of community the group had built over several premieres. "*Star Wars* is not just a movie—it's about the high quality of people you meet through it. It's an absolute blast to be able to spend a month and a half with a bunch of awesome people who are fans," Lund said (Rock).

The lineup received rampant media attention, including Jimmy Kimmel coming to poke fun of the group by hosting a dating show using three people from the lineup. In late April, Matthew Wood, the voice of General Grievous in the final film, came to visit the lineup. Bai Ling had also made an appearance earlier in the week. Even tour buses stopped near the lineup to give tourists a glimpse of the die-hard fans. The lineup coordinators asked that fans in line who were interviewed ask for business cards from media members to keep track of everyone covering the lineup.

For the lineup at the Chinese Theatre, fans had devised a color-coded system of identifying fans' preferences regarding spoilers. "Reds" avoided spoiler information of any sort, while "greens" searched out every spoiler with enthusiasm. Sympathizing with both groups, the "blues" took a moderate stance between the two extremes. As is probably inevitable with people who stake such a large portion of time on such a relatively short event (a two hour movie), many of the fans who lined up at the Chinese for the previous two movies had expressed disappointment. Sprague said, "We're a little beaten down. But this one could be it!" (Snyder "Inside …").

On Wednesday afternoon before the film's opening, Lucas had his company arrange for a group of about fifty actors in stormtrooper costumes to escort the fans in line at Grauman's Chinese Theatre in Hollywood to the ArcLight on Sunset Boulevard. The escort was a nice gesture of goodwill from Lucas toward the fans, many of whom have given much of their time to his saga and kept the franchise strong through almost thirty years. In all, nearly two hundred die-hard fans took part in the lineup and were present before opening day when the stormtroopers came for them. A small group of fans, however, declined the invitation. Jerry Anderson, a fan in line with the group since its inception, said, "A lot of us are set to go with the stormtroopers, but some decided to politely say no thank you. It's heartbreaking. The series opened here—why not end it here?" (Shuster "Some ...").

When the Chinese Theatre lineup crowd finally saw the movie after weeks of waiting, most felt it was an incredible experience and a vindication of their long waits. "There was a lot more emotion in this movie and that is something I've been looking for in these prequels. It's the emotions of Anakin turning evil—it was just powerful," said Peter Genovese, who helped organize the lineup for *Revenge of the Sith* outside of the Chinese Theatre (Hernandez "'Sith' Set ..."). Lund wrote on his blog for the BBC after the wait, "The movie itself was absolutely amazing ... The reviews that said this would redeem Episodes I and II from the criticism they've had were so very right." Lund was unsure whether he would reach the minimum seventy-two hours in line when his journey began, but he had no trouble becoming one of the most die-hard line dwellers, finishing fourteenth in the group. In all, he logged 513 total hours.

By the end of the wait for *Revenge of the Sith*, the Chinese Theatre lineup group had raised more than $30,000 for the Starlight Starbright Children's Foundation. The group raised the money by individuals in line convincing friends and family to pledge money for each hour they waited in line, the same as the group had done for the previous two films. "This is the end of *Star Wars* [as a film series] and our line experience. We're going to miss it. I don't think we'll ever do anything as grand as this [again]," said Genovese (Hernandez "'Sith' Set ..."). In all, line members logged twenty-five thousand hours waited in line. It was the most successful of all three prequel lineups the group had organized, with more people than both of the previous efforts.

A Nation in Line

Seattle and Los Angeles were not the only locations nationwide for major lineups; other cities had their own die-hard fan bases ready to wait long hours for the final prequel. One of the other significant lineups occurred at the Ziegfeld Theater in New York City, one of the nation's most famous theaters. Fans started lining up as early as April 30, not as die-hard as their West Coast counterparts, but still impressive. Tents lined the street on West 54th Street as fans prepared to wait weeks for the final movie's premiere. Like the fans in Hollywood, the Ziegfeld lineup, known as NYLine Stand-A-Thon, raised money for Starlight ("Clearview ...").

Fans from other locations also took part in the Ziegfeld line, like Emma Sparks and Tom Minter from the United Kingdom, who planned two weeks of their total three-week vacation to wait in line for *Star Wars*. The couple had tickets for two showings per day after opening day for enough tickets to allow them to see the movie ten times in theaters. Matthew Wood also visited the Ziegfeld line, in a nice gesture of equality for fans on both coasts of the country. Steve Lorenzo, who waited in line outside of the Ziegfeld, said of the end of the film franchise, "There will always be something. Even though it's the end of the movies, it's not the end of *Star Wars*" (Hafetz). In all, 250 people signed up for the Ziegfeld lineup from twenty states, Brazil, Great Britain, the Netherlands, Peru, Mexico, France, Sweden, Spain, and Germany. At the Ziegfeld line, only thirty people at any given time could be in line outside in the days leading up to the premiere.

Another significant lineup took place in Washington, D.C., outside the Uptown Theatre and started several weeks before the film's opening. A small group of about a half-dozen fans, including Halit Sari of Maryland who spoke with *The Washington Times*, took turns guarding the spot at the front of the line, where they had placed a chair and mattress with a *Star Wars* sleeping bag. In case of rain, the group had a tarp ready to place over the area. Halit's wife, Adrienne Maul-Sari, organized the lineup at the Uptown. "We've all become friends, and we only see each other [at the premieres]. We have a good time at night ... and this is the last chance we'll have to do it," said Vance Rego, an executive manager at a Target store who took time off work for the lineup (Lively).

Although not everyone could line up for *Revenge of the Sith* for weeks at a time, almost every fan arrived hours early for midnight showings, enough time to build more anticipation and enjoy the festive atmosphere that always accompanied the release of a new *Star Wars* film. "We started lining up at the theater around eight or nine in the morning, and didn't see the movie until midnight," said Dave Gohman of Schaumburg, Illinois (Gohman). Speaking of his lineup experience, he said, "There was this awesome guy with a Jar Jar mask who was running around with a sign that said 'Stop the Hate.' Also I was amazed with all the really hot chicks who were lining up just as early as the guys."

For most people, nothing is more aggravating and boring than waiting in long lines, but many *Star Wars* fans understand that the experience can be positive. Having waited twenty-four hours in line for *Revenge of the Sith* myself with my good friend and fellow *Star Wars* fan Erik Sogn, I have fond memories of the experience, which far from being unpleasant and grueling was instead a highlight of the year. I had already seen the film at a charity premiere in Seattle, but I still chose to wait one full day to be first in line at Evergreen Parkway 13 in Hillsboro, Oregon, for the final *Star Wars* movie's national premiere. As the line grew in the early morning hours and throughout the day, then as day turned into night, I had the opportunity to speak with many fellow fans, making the moviegoing experience much more social than it is for most films.

Most people fail to understand that *Star Wars* is not just a movie. People do not wait days, weeks, and months in line for just another movie. Rather, *Star Wars* is a social experience for many fans, a hobby to share with other people, and lining up with many other fans creates a party atmosphere the same as at a sports event during the playoffs or a rock concert. Many media members and writers dismissed fans lining up early to see the prequels as a waste of time, claiming fans could see the movie without having lined up for numerous hours. They missed the point, though. Lining up is part of the event itself and part of the experience. For fans able to overcome the impatience of modern day living long enough to converse with other fans and enjoy the festive atmosphere of the last hours before a new *Star Wars* film, lining up one last time was rewarding and exciting.

No matter how different people may be, when gathered for the same cause, a sense of camaraderie exists that is often lacking in society as people go about their daily lives, mostly avoiding anything more than superficial contact with one another. At a meaningful baseball game, fifty thousand people could represent all of the world's major religions, socioeconomic backgrounds, and political ideologies, but for a few hours, none of their differences matter. All that matters is fifty thousand fans are all present to support their team. *Star Wars* creates a similar feeling among fans, at the *Star Wars* Celebrations, lining up to buy toys and to see the movie, and talking on message forums on the Internet. *Star Wars* Celebration III, which took place before most fans started to line up, gave fans another opportunity to meet one another and enjoy the saga together.

Pilgrimage to Indianapolis

Colder than Hoth

To celebrate the upcoming release of *The Phantom Menace*, Lucasfilm held a massive *Star Wars* party known as the *Star Wars* Celebration in Denver, Colorado, at the Wings Over the Rockies Air and Space Museum starting on the last day of April in 1999. The three-day event attracted tens of thousands of fans, despite awful downpours and near-record cold temperatures for late April and early May. For *Star Wars* Celebration II in April 2002, Lucasfilm moved the three-day event to Indianapolis, Indiana, at the Indiana Convention Center. At Celebration II, twenty-six thousand fans from across the nation and around the world descended upon one location to celebrate the franchise as a whole and count down the days until the newest entry arrived. For the final prequel, Lucasfilm announced in January 2004 that the event would take place once again in Indianapolis at the same location.

For Celebration III, Lucasfilm informed fans that the event would occupy the entire Convention Center, except the RCA Dome, and would last not three days, but four, from April 21 through April 24. "We had such a great experience with Celebration II that it just made sense to return to Indianapolis. Only this time, we're going to do it bigger and even better," said Steve Sansweet, head of fan relations for Lucasfilm ("Celebration III Set ..."). He also explained that the company made its announcement early to "give our fans all over the world" plenty of time to prepare vacations and set aside time to attend the event (ibid.). Gen Con LLC agreed to manage the convention on behalf of Lucasfilm and the Official *Star Wars* Fan Club. "Together I know that we will produce an event that will not only meet, but exceed fans' expectations. With Lucasfilm behind this show 100 percent, it's going to be the biggest party in the history of the franchise," said Peter Adkison, owner of Gen Con (ibid.).

Lucasfilm's official logo for the event, released in April 2004, showed Darth Vader's helmet with flames beneath it and the text "*Star Wars* Celebration III" at the bottom of the emblem. The logo closely resembles a cast and crew patch originally designed for *The Empire Strikes Back* ("*Star Wars* Celebration III ..."). For fans to have total access to the event, they had to be members of the Official *Star Wars* Fan Club and order four-day badges. The four-day passes along with a special Fan Club lanyard also allowed fans to enter the event an hour early and hang out at the Fan Club Lounge, along with a few other relatively minor benefits.

The weather from the first *Star Wars* Celebration returned for the third. While fans attending the previous Celebration in Indianapolis enjoyed great weather for almost the entire time, with rain following the day after Celebration II ended, fans in 2005 were not as fortunate. Just days before the Celebration started, Indianapolis had enjoyed seventy-plus degree weather with a nice breeze and sunshine. By Saturday, however, Indianapolis was one of the coldest cities in the continental United States as temperatures dipped below freezing and scattered snow showers appeared throughout the city.

Even with the winter weather, fans were not going to turn back because of cold, rain, or snow. At least a fair number of them had already lived through the first Celebration, which was largely outdoors and consistently cold and rainy. In all, 22,500 advance passes sold for the event, with more tickets available at the door (Britton). Visitors to Indianapolis were expected to bring in $16 million in direct spending for the city (ibid.). Local bars also benefitted from the increased downtown presence. The Ram brewery, for instance, became the headquarters for the 501st Legion costuming group, featuring menu items like "Boba Fettuccini," in honor of the bounty hunter Boba Fett (Soriano).

The line of thousands of fans that stood outside of the Indianapolis Convention Center was awe-inspiring and virtually indescribable. The line of people bent around the building, up a staircase, coiled through numerous aisles at the top of the stairs, twisted back down another set of stairs, snaked through a tunnel, and somewhere at the end of the line, seemingly in another world entirely from the door, were hundreds more fans huddled into dozens more aisles. Walking the length of the line took ten to fifteen minutes and one could swear every *Star Wars* fan in the world must have been in attendance. The massive scale of the line also distracted traffic at times apparently, as with a scary incident on Thursday where one car careened off another near the front of the line at an intersection, fortunately landing near the opposite sidewalk, away from the line.

In all, more than thirty-four thousand people attended *Star Wars* Celebration III, leading to booked hotels across downtown Indianapolis ("Star Wars Celebration IV ..."). Every major media outlet and many smaller ones sent representatives to cover the event. Sansweet said some fans from Japan, Mexico, and countries in Europe chartered jets to the event (Montgomery). Fans could keep busy from early in the morning until almost midnight every day, with events ongoing throughout the day all over the Convention Center. At night, fans could watch the saga with fellow enthusiasts as *A New Hope* showed Thursday, *The Empire Strikes Back* and *Return of the Jedi* played back-to-back Friday, and the first two prequels screened Saturday.

The official Opening Ceremony took place on Thursday night in Hall B, where Steve Sansweet welcomed the audience. Sansweet joked, "Would you believe there have been *Star Wars* fans lined up for two weeks to see Saturday's George Lucas presentation?" ("starwars.com at Celebration III; Let …"). Knowing *Star Wars* fans, he may have been serious, but continued, "There's only one small problem: they're lined up in front of the Denver Wings Over the Rockies Air and Space Museum where Celebration I was held!" The joke eerily foretold a later event where the fans who had lined up outside of Grauman's Chinese Theatre, weeks before the Celebration started, eventually learned that the film would not play at Grauman's after all.

Even Howard Roffman, president of Lucas Licensing, came on stage to crack a few jokes about the merchandising side of the Force. After all, nobody is naive enough to think that merchandising is not a huge part of *Star Wars* fandom. "As the chief merchandiser for Lucasfilm, I can tell you that I never, ever dreamed that over almost-a-lifetime career, my crowning achievement, my finest glory of my professional life … would be the creation and launch of Darth Tater," he said to much laughter (ibid.). Many others involved in the Celebration came onto the stage not only to welcome the fans, but to talk about what to expect from the event and what panels and shows fans should attend.

The highlight of each *Star Wars* Celebration for many fans, and a must-see for fans who did not mind spoilers, was the *Rick McCallum Spectacular*, where the producer showed fans new footage from the upcoming prequel. With Celebration II, fans seeing Yoda fight had burst into applause. The same type of enthusiasm greeted footage for *Revenge of the Sith*, which McCallum showed using a Christie Digital Cinema projector. With only weeks left before the final movie premiered, the *Spectacular* gave fans a final glimpse of preview footage, just enough to satiate them until the movie's release. McCallum also answered questions from fans, many relating to *Star Wars* in 3-D and future *Indiana Jones* plans.

The most hyped appearance of all at Celebration III was George Lucas, who had finally agreed to speak with fans in person for the first time since 1987 at the first official *Star Wars* convention and express his appreciation for their support. Fans were equally anxious to show their gratitude to the *Star Wars* creator, lining up hours in advance for the opportunity. "We were delighted that he was able to carve some time out from a heavily-booked schedule to share some of his thoughts with fans in person as he completes this amazing thirty-year screen saga," said Sansweet ("George Lucas to Attend ..."). Lucas took three question-and-answer sessions, along with speaking to fans about his personal journey with *Star Wars*. Each session could hold three thousand fans, so fewer than one in three fans at the event could potentially see Lucas speak.

Supposedly, the first and second Lucas question-and-answer sessions were to consist of 70 percent Fan Club members and 30 percent public, with the third session consisting of 70 percent public and 30 percent Fan Club members, though many fans claim the scenario played out differently (Britton). Although seeing Lucas made the question-and-answer sessions worthwhile for many fans, he made a major announcement about the future of *Star Wars* on television, confirming two planned projects to keep the franchise vital. Many of the questions Lucas answered were not especially new to *Star Wars* fans, though he was able to confirm Lucasfilm's greater interest in television in the future, also hinting at other projects that would hinge upon the success of the first few *Star Wars* series.

Apart from answering questions about the upcoming film and the future of *Star Wars* beyond the movies, Lucas gave a bit of insight into his understanding of healthy fan appreciation versus obsessiveness. "*Star Wars* is something to enjoy and take away what you can from it that maybe helps you in your lives. Don't let it take over your lives. That's what they all say about Trekkies, and I know *Star Wars* fans don't do that," he said ("starwars.com at Celebration III; Thank ..."). Lucas continued, "The point of the movies is to get on with your lives, to take that challenge, to leave your uncle's moisture farm, to go out in the world and change it to save the universe."

Before fans could save the universe, they had to save themselves from the bitter cold just to hear Lucas talk. "I was prepared for the cold but not the rain. I had layers so it wasn't too bad. Some of the fans were dressed much too lightly but people seemed to share what they had," said Diane Kovalcin of New Jersey (Kovalcin). Dave Gohman of Schaumburg, Illinois, added, "It was cold and rainy, but most of us grabbed garbage bags to make ponchos, which worked well" (Gohman). Linda Pellerito from Michigan, who started lining up at 3:30 a.m., was not pleased with the rain and snow, either. "The weather really made the waiting miserable," she said (Pellerito). "No one was really prepared; we went from perfect weather to a January thaw," Pellerito continued.

Fans tried to help one another out with the miserable weather, especially because most people were simply not prepared for arctic weather in April. "A lovely person next to me had brought blankets and plastic sheeting so about eight or nine of us huddled under that," Kovalcin said. Gohman also had similar experiences. "Everyone was really cool to each other. Saving their place in line when they had to go find a bathroom; some people made coffee runs to help warm us all up," he said.

Many fans braved the cold and the rain, despite the possibility of long lines. By 3:30 a.m., Pellerito said "over fifty" fans were already in line with more arriving "by the minute." A few hours later, the line had grown into triple digits. "I would say at least a hundred," Gohman said of the fan count when he arrived before dawn, "but with the way the line wrapped around the building it got hard to tell after a while." Kovalcin, who showed up at 5:00 a.m., agreed that "a lot" of fans showed up, but "I think a lot more were scared off by the idea that they could wait in line and not get in," which was common sentiment at the Celebration before Saturday's Lucas sessions. Many fans figured the wait was not worthwhile without any guarantee of gaining entry to see the *Star Wars* creator.

Pellerito thought Gen Con's organization of the lineup was unfair, not to mention poorly planned. "A huge amount of people just showed up [not long before the first Lucas session] and were allowed in front of us with great seats while we were relegated to the second to last back row," she said. Lineup confusion led many people to cut in front of the line, Pellerito said, without having waited cold, miserable hours outside like the more die-hard fans. "Our following the rules resulted in the worst seats in the house. We who paid a later price in the form of colds and other health problems," she said. Other fans "got out of bed, had breakfast, were well rested, and just walked in ahead of all of us who had been there hours before dawn," Pellerito continued. Many other fans at the Celebration who had waited in line for Lucas also complained of line confusion and people cutting in front of the fans who had spent more time in line.

Both Gohman and Kovalcin had few complaints about the line organization, though, besides the cold. "I thought the lineup worked somewhat. They gave us wrist-bands as soon as we got into the building," Kovalcin said. Gohman said, "It seemed really well done.... Also it was great the way the volunteer 501st members helped usher the line along. They got us across streets and held the doors open for us when they finally let us inside out of the cold." He also reported positive experiences with other fans in line throughout the wait. "The people in line were all in good spirits despite the weather, and everyone was respectful of everyone else. [I] didn't notice any cutting or anything like that," Gohman said.

Gohman and Pellerito differed with Kovalcin on whether the wait was worthwhile. Kovalcin said the lineup was "probably not" worthwhile. "It was really too cold. I think they could have arranged the line better so that we wouldn't be standing out in the cold for that long. Perhaps giving out timed tickets might have been a better idea," she said. Gohman enjoyed the experience, though. "It was a bit cold outside, but still fun," he said. He described various trooper volunteers helping round up the fans, with a few giving commands using voice changers such as, "Please move all the way down or you will be shot." Once Lucas appeared, "The energy in the room was absolutely electric," he said. Pellerito, while unhappy about the line organization, agreed with Gohman that seeing Lucas was worth the wait.

Immersed in the Force

Although he could not attend, Hayden Christensen spoke with fans live from Rome, Italy, where he was filming on location for *The Decameron*. As with other main events, Jay Laga'aia hosted the session in the Sagamore Ballroom. Christensen spoke about becoming Vader, training with Ewan McGregor, and the future of his career in film. Though Christensen could not attend, the voice of another villain, Matthew Wood (General Grievous), showed audiences how his voice became that of the primary action villain of the final prequel. Wood, who was also the supervising sound editor on *Revenge of the Sith*, brought other examples of his work from the film, too.

Fans had many opportunities to learn more about the making of *Revenge of the Sith* from professionals who worked on the project. For instance, Visual Effects Supervisors John Knoll and Roger Guyett gave presentations on effects secrets on the *Star Wars* movies, Original Trilogy included, and answered fan questions about the difficulties of the post-production process. In *Knoll Vision: Inside Revenge*, Knoll shared a humorous bloopers reel that showed what happens when computer graphics technology fails to do what the programmers and artists want.

The cape movement and modeling software, as Knoll described to fans in attendance, was supposed to make the clothing and capes move naturally with characters like General Grievous and the Jedi, saving animators valuable time. Sometimes, though, the software made capes and robes land directly over characters' heads. The computer simulation continued to run while the characters had clothing covering their faces, leading to frustrated effects artists but funny bloopers for fans to see.

Dan Gregoire, previsualization supervisor for *Revenge of the Sith*, gave a presentation, *The Vision Before the Film*, showcasing television spots for the film, with animatics footage instead of final effects shots to demonstrate the work that his team completed on the prequel. "Our shots are aesthetically not the same as ILM but conceptually almost the same. The framing and animation are very similar," he explained, but at a later point, "ILM then takes it to another level—by cleaning up the shots and doing the fine implementation of what you see" ("starwars.com at Celebration III; Previsionary ..."). Gregoire noted that his department saved the production $7–10 million in costs. The *Episode III* art department coordinated closely with the animatics department because "they'll have their ideas and we have ours and we mix them together," Gregoire said (ibid.).

In *The Art of Revenge*, seven members of the *Episode III* art department discussed the conceptual and design challenges they faced. Speaking of Lucas's mindset with the final prequel, Design Supervisor Ryan Church said, "He told us he wanted to show the galaxy at its height before its corruption. When you think about the opening shot of *Episode IV*, it's a pretty dreary universe. We were directed to highlight that contrast" ("starwars.com at Celebration III; Behind ..."). The artists also talked about design work on General Grievous, who had already become a fan favorite.

Aside from the post-production work that occupied much of the total time required to complete *Revenge of the Sith*, Stunt Coordinator Nick Gillard came to Celebration III to talk about his work on the climactic lightsaber duels and the type of choreography required to make them work. "When you see the duel in the script, it's huge! It's ten to fifteen minutes and they have to travel a distance of about half a mile," he explained to the audience ("starwars.com at Celebration III; Master ..."). Fans in attendance cheered with approval when he mentioned that a third to a half of the movie is fighting.

Gillard made no secret about being displeased that much of the lightsaber duel at the end of *Attack of the Clones* did not make the final cut of the movie, but he assured fans that for *Revenge of the Sith*, Lucas did not restrain his choreography. "I always try to make the films much more violent, but for *Episode(s) I* and *II* George would stop me. This time, he didn't stop me. In *Episode III*, *all* the Jedi are literally fighting for their lives" (ibid.). Gillard also talked about the creation of different moves for different characters, the point of which is not only keeping the fighting fresh, but also allowing characters' personalities to show in their fighting styles.

Lou and Dave Elsey, who worked as members of the creature shop for the prequel, also had their own panel: *Makeup Masters*. The two artists crafted many impressive makeup creations for the prequel, but the most memorable and significant work was devising Anakin's burns. "Surely, this could be the most famous burns in history, because I had known Anakin was going to take the tumble since I was about ten years old," Dave Elsey said ("starwars.com at Celebration III; Makeup ..."). He had done extensive research into real-life burns to see what he would need to create for the role, but worried about how far Lucas would allow him to push the grotesque appearance of the wounds. As part of the panel, the husband-wife duo applied makeup to a fan picked randomly from the audience to make her into an alien from the *Episode III* shoot.

Because the *Star Wars* Celebrations have focused as much on fans as on official merchandise and events, many opportunities arose for fans to show their enthusiasm for the saga or to see how other fans express theirs. For instance, the Fan Fair Exhibit Hall (Hall C) offered fans the opportunity to be involved in building a diorama of the Death Star, with instructions and supervision from Frank D'Iorio, a fan and film industry professional who is an expert on creating *Star Wars* dioramas.[1] *Star Wars* car enthusiasts from around the nation drove painted and modified cars to the event, which were on display for other fans to see. A *Star Wars* tattoo art show also allowed fans to show their body art or see how other fans express their love of the saga through tattoos. Various fan groups from around the country organized tables and other contributions to the Fan Fair Hall.

Chris Alexander and a team of about ten assistants, some from the audience, folded a giant origami figure or craft each day, using paper measuring twenty feet by twenty feet. On the first day, the team created a Naboo N-1 spacecraft, then a Jedi Starfighter on the second day, Jabba the Hutt on the third, and Anakin's starfighter on the final day. Fans could buy the origami creations, signed by at least eighteen celebrities in attendance at the event, via auctions that raised $3,716 for the Koret Family House charity ("Life Size …").

The Droidyard 500 let fans race their droids against one another, with many fans watching the spectacle. Regional 501st Legion Garrisons offered a Stormtrooper Olympics with various events for costume-clad fans who were members of the organization. Aside from numerous members of the 501st that came to Indianapolis to help Lucasfilm with crowd control and to enjoy the festivities, fans also had an opportunity to compete in a costume contest that proved popular for costumers and fans who enjoyed seeing the variety of costumes on display.

Anne Brown, costume contest coordinator, explained how the judges broke the contest into numerous categories like Hero, Villain, Outer Rim, Child, Padmé, and Best in Show, to award more prizes and make the judging easier. "Having a Best in Show winner is only natural. What's fun is that we let the audience vote for Best in Show from among the first-place winners," Brown said ("starwars.com at Celebration III; *Star Wars* …"). Earl Burkist won Best Villain

---

1.   GalacticHunter.com hosts his site at NiubNiubsUniverse.com.

and Best in Show for his General Grievous costume. All winners received an octagonal trophy engraved with the Celebration III logo.

Another popular contest was the Fourth Annual Fan Film Awards, with more than one hundred entries. Sixteen finalists made the last round of competition, where they competed in their own categories but also for the ultimate award, the "George Lucas Selects Award," given by the revered creator himself. Eight of the finalists won for at least one category. Lucas said, "We had a lot of great films this year ... There are a lot of good stories being told" ("starwars.com at Celebration III; Meet ..."). The categories included: Spirit of Fandom, Audience Choice, Best Comedy, Best Animation, Best Crossover Spoof, Best Original Concept, Best Song, and Pioneer. Barry Curtis and Troy Metcalf won the George Lucas Selects Award for their film, *For the Love of the Film*.

Merchandise Bonanza

Fortunately for organizers of the event, *Star Wars* fans are mostly peaceful, amiable people who enjoy talking to one another about the saga, rather than trying to riot because of ridiculously long lines and occasionally poor planning. Embracing the Light Side of the Force, fans exercised patience in waiting four to six hours, sometimes longer, to gain access to the Celebration III Store, which was the biggest disaster of the event. The tiny store could only accommodate a handful of fans at a time, relative to the vast army of Jedi anxious to have a crack at the exclusive Celebration III items, especially the talking Darth Vader action figure. Some fans bought the figure at the Celebration III Store, then sold it in the dealer area for a profit almost immediately, turning their time in line into cash.

Event organizers tried, unsuccessfully, to avoid the huge store lines that plagued both of the first Celebrations, especially the 1999 gathering in Denver, where fans waited in pouring rain and cold for many hours to see the new merchandise. An article on starwars.com read:

> Every day of the convention the Celebration Store will be open long hours, ready to handle large crowds efficiently with a Fast Path system. The Fast Path pass will allow shoppers to enter the store at the appointed time, within controlled half-hour segments, avoiding long lines and having more fun! ("Celebration III Shopping Spree!").

Unfortunately, the Fast Path system apparently did not work too well because it never cut down on long lines whatsoever. Dave Gohman joked, "I spent five hours in this line. If this was the 'fast track' I would have hated to see the long track."

Fans were not impressed by the line for the Celebration III Store, but many forgave the staff because of the huge number of fans in attendance. "I think the problem was there are just so many attendees [to *Star Wars* Celebrations]. I don't think there was a good way to make that a lot easier than it was," said Gohman. Diane Kovalcin did not bother with the store at all. "I didn't go to the Celebration III Store because I'd had such a bad experience with [the one from] Celebration II," she said.

The incredibly long lines throughout the event might have bothered other people more than *Star Wars* fans, though, who are accustomed to long lines. Joseph Szadkowski of *The Washington Times* noted in an article, "Although organized lines were further organized into more lines, the only thing quelling a riot was the pleasant attitude of attendees, who spent time chatting about everything 'Star Wars'" ("Fans …"). Most fans tried to enjoy the lines and make the best of the waiting. "I loved the lines. Where else could you be around thirty thousand other fans and talk *Star Wars* non-stop? Even waiting for shows to start, you could get into a philosophical discussion or talk about costuming or fan films or fan fiction. It was great," said Kovalcin.

As with past conventions, Celebration III provided a great opportunity for the various licensees to reach fans and announce upcoming products and services. Many companies used the event as an opportunity to sell exclusive items, like a new .45 Black Chrome Obi-Wan Kenobi Lightsaber variation from Master Replicas, an *Empire Strikes Back* collectible movie poster sculpture from Code 3 Collectibles, and a Sand Trooper Corporal exclusive from Gentle Giant. Topps, Acme Archives, Anthony Grandio Company, and Comic Images also had their own exclusives.

Burger King, Cingular, Masterfoods USA (M&M's, etc.), Intec (developer of video game accessories), and Target (the hotel sponsor) were all official sponsors of Celebration III. In a press release, David Garver, executive director of segment marketing and sponsorships for Cingular, said, "Celebration III is the perfect backdrop for Cingular to showcase our extensive collection of *Star Wars*–themed content and products. After all, who better to appreciate and enjoy [them] than official *Star Wars* fans?" ("Cingular …"). Other sponsors also took advantage of a captive audience of their core clients. Burger King offered young fans the opportunity to learn lightsaber moves at its Jedi Academy in the Fan Fair Hall. Hotels in the area offered key cards with *Revenge of the Sith* imagery and the Target logo on them.

Fans interested in *Star Wars* art and lithographs could buy limited edition prints from numerous leading artists in the business, like Steve Anderson, Matt

Busch, Joe Corroney, Tom Hodges, Cat Staggs, and Sarah Wilkinson, among numerous other talented artists. Each artist could create one limited edition lithograph for the Celebration with no more than 250 copies printed, or several images but totaling no more than 250 copies. The lithographs, varying in popularity by artist and content, ranged from cartoon style to more realistic, usually focusing on themes and characters in *Revenge of the Sith*.

Artists in attendance had to stay at their tables most of the time to meet with fans and sell their work, but the experience proved rewarding for most of the artists. "As an official artist working on the promotion and merchandise for *Revenge of the Sith*, the Celebration III show was quite an earth-shattering event," Matt Busch wrote by e-mail. "I had been working long hours on these products in anticipation for the movie for over a year. So to finish and be able to interact with the fans who love your work is really just the most rewarding feeling you can have," he continued. Other artists at the event expressed similar enthusiasm to fans who approached them at their tables.

Aside from being passionate about his work, Busch, and many other artists in attendance, also shared the fans' passion for the franchise. Busch explained, "Many folks don't realize that I, too, am a fan. The whole reason I got into this line of work is because of what I saw in 1977 that followed the words, 'A long time ago in a galaxy far, far away....'" For Busch, *Star Wars* provided a spark of creativity that lasted a lifetime. "As the saga grew, so did my personal and professional journey," he wrote. "Celebration III was also my own celebration," Busch wrote. The event gave him the opportunity to celebrate his fandom and his professional accomplishments through his artistic contributions to the *Star Wars* franchise.

For autograph hunters, Celebration III boasted dozens of actors from the saga who came to sign photos, toys, programs, or whatever else people brought them. Though no major stars like Natalie Portman, Harrison Ford, Ewan McGregor, or Mark Hamill appeared at Celebration III, fan favorites like Kenny Baker, Ray Park, Peter Mayhew, Billy Dee Williams, and David Prowse attended the event. A few stars received unexpected fan attention, notably Amy Allen, who was a production assistant at ILM until playing Aayla Secura in the final two prequels.

Allen's popularity did not come from her role as a blue alien Twi'lek, however, but because she is absolutely gorgeous, which at a convention full of mostly male *Star Wars* fans makes an impression. Allen had to switch booths because her line was causing chaos in the section where the less popular actors were signing. Allen's line was never much less than an hour-long wait, part of which came as a result of everyone wanting pictures with her.

Another popular autograph was Matthew Wood, who voiced General Grievous in *Revenge of the Sith*. Wood also spoke to fans in other rooms of the Convention Center, so he had more limited signing time. Celebration III host Jay Laga'aia signed autographs briefly as well. The autograph prices for the stars ranged from $10 to $30, making a complete set of autographs fairly expensive, but many fans had no trouble paying the price to meet their favorite stars and have them sign various items.

For fans who did not care about meeting the actors and actresses but still wanted their signatures, Official Pix, the company running the autograph hall, sold pre-signed, limited edition photographs to fans. The organization of the lines to meet the stars was effective and well planned, in contrast with the Celebration III Store. Once a line reached a significant length, fans received numbers that broke the line into smaller groups. Only people with a specific group number could be in a crowded line at any time, limiting the chaos and making for a much smoother process than one might expect given the mass of people in attendance.

Celebration III also offered a variety of collecting panels, which Gus Lopez of ToysRGus.com put together; Lopez is a renowned *Star Wars* collector. The panels ran Friday through Sunday at the Celebration, covering *Star Wars* posters, food collectibles, strange and comical collectibles, store displays, and the future of *Star Wars* collecting. Another panel looked into a few of the best private collections from fans, through pictures and descriptions. Fans could also bring their prized collectibles for a Celebration III Collectibles Road Show panel, which continued a popular idea from the previous Celebration in Indianapolis. Additionally, a Collectors' Social Hour gave fellow collectors a chance to meet one another and discuss their collecting habits and strategies.

For fans interested in seeing *Star Wars* items but not buying them, the Lucasfilm Archive Exhibit provided the perfect opportunity. The exhibit was always fairly popular as an alternative to scheduled shows and featured many items from *Revenge of the Sith* that fans had never been able to see previously, like a Mustafar Volcano model, Darth Vader's *Episode III* costume, an AT-TE production model, a Wookie shield and blaster, and several Wookie costumes. Items from the previous movies also were on display, like a Wampa puppet, *Millennium Falcon* production models, an Imperial Star Destroyer model, and Darth Maul's lightsaber, among many other pieces.

Star Wars Celebration III provided a great opportunity for fans to convene so they could discuss and celebrate the saga, learn more about *Revenge of the Sith*, buy merchandise and collectibles from the movies, and see upcoming products from various licensees. Despite a few problems with the store lines and crowd control in general, organizers still did a great job on providing many entertaining, informative events and discussions. For Celebration IV, Lucasfilm promised a twenty-four-hour store and a five-day event instead of four, setting up the event to be even larger than its predecessors. Fans who had money left over after Celebration III and after buying more merchandise from the franchise could spend yet more of their hard-earned cash on charity premiere tickets to see the movie days before their fellow fans.

Waging *Wars* for Charity

As with the first two prequels, *Revenge of the Sith* premiered first for charity before its global theatrical release. In North America, charity premieres in ten cities occurred a full week before release, allowing deep-pocketed fans to see the movie early and support worthy causes. Lucasfilm selected charities relating to children and families in an effort to raise money and awareness for their causes. "These charitable organizations are the leaders in direct services and advocacy for children and families," Lucas said ("Ten Charities ..."). The list of charities included: Alliance for Education (Seattle), Artists for a New South Africa (Los Angeles), Children's Defense Fund (Washington, D.C.), Children's Memorial Hospital (Chicago), City Year (Boston), Colorado Children's Campaign (Denver), Hughes Spalding Children's Hospital (Atlanta), Koret Family House (San Francisco), Miami Children's Hospital Foundation (Miami), and The Children's Health Fund (New York City).

Tickets for events nationwide ranged from a few hundred dollars to thousands of dollars for sponsorship packages, with most tickets costing in the $300–500 range. At the Los Angeles premiere in Westwood at the Mann Village Theater, Mark Hamill made an appearance, delighting fans in attendance. Stars Jimmy Smits, Bai Ling, and Billy Dee Williams also attended the screening, which Texas Instruments helped present digitally. Before the Los Angeles screening, Lucasfilm Licensing President Howard Roffman told moviegoers in attendance not to record the screening, saying, "We have monitors inside the theater. And when I say monitors—this is the company that invented the Evil Empire" (Higgins).

In New York at the famous Ziegfeld Theatre, where fans had lined up early to see the national premiere the following week, Liam Neeson, Samuel L. Jackson, Frank Oz, and Ray Park attended the charity screening, which like its Los Angeles counterpart was shown digitally. As with everything in New York City, charity premiere tickets were at the high end of pricing, with a $600 minimum for general admission and $1,100 for access to the party after the screening.

The Children's Health Fund had the opportunity to show a video of the work it has done to help the community before the charity screening in New York, which was common for the charity premieres and allowed the organizations to inform attendees about their operations. Much effort went into planning the event in New York, with four to five staff members on the project working part time or full time for roughly nine months. "It does take an organizational infrastructure to take full advantage of this type of opportunity," said Karen Redlener, executive director of the charity (Wellner).

In San Francisco, the premiere took place at the Loews Metreon Theater, where Lucas made an appearance to greet fans and be part of the first digital screening of the movie in the city. In Washington, D.C., Carrie Fisher attended the premiere. Neither Hayden Christensen nor Natalie Portman could attend any of the charity premieres; both were filming other projects. McGregor also did not support the charity effort with an appearance.

In Chicago, fans had access to food before the charity premiere at the Adler Planetarium and could also play video games to pass time before the film started. The theater the charity selected to show the film could only seat 402 lucky patrons. The screening did not entirely sell out, but came close. "This is certainly raising a significant amount of money and attracting a lot of attention for the [Children's Memorial Hospital]," said Arla Silverstein, a spokeswoman for the hospital (Davis). Famous chef Wolfgang Puck prepared food for the event, providing at least a bit of star power, though none of the stars from the films attended the event in Chicago.

In Denver, a silent auction gave fans the opportunity to bid on many great items, mostly related to *Star Wars*, spread across several tents. Fans also enjoyed various giveaways and a free dessert after the premiere. Many fans appeared in costume, including the Denver contingent of the 501st Legion costuming group. Neil Guggenmos of Longmont, Colorado, who attended the event, said, "It was a great party. I got to see the movie a few days early, and a wonderful charity benefitted. Everyone was a winner!" (Guggenmos). Guggenmos said he budgets a set amount for charity each year, so the opportunity to donate to charity while also satisfying his desire to see the final prequel as soon as possible proved too good to resist.

Each premiere had its own unique elements, such as special after-screening parties or pre-event entertainment. In Seattle, where the movie premiered at the famous Cinerama Theatre, general admission gave fans access to a variety of food items and drinks before the event along with various giveaways from local sponsors. Patrons paying additional money gained access to a more formal pre-premiere dining experience across the street. In Miami, organizers re-created the Mos Eisley Cantina for post-party entertainment, complete with characters from the *Star Wars* saga and an alien band to provide music. Fans in Miami could also play the newest Xbox games on giant movie screens.

At the charity premieres nationwide, members of the 501st Legion, the largest *Star Wars* costuming group, offered their support for crowd control and other assistance. Since its inception in 1997, the group has grown to more than three thousand members worldwide and has provided a growing force for good in local communities with visits to children's hospitals, help with charity premieres, and assistance at various Lucasfilm events. "We consider the members of the 501st part of the extended Lucasfilm family," said Steve Sansweet, head of fan relations for Lucasfilm (*"Star Wars:* The Best ..." 9). "It's inspiring how the members of the 501st will step up when called upon no matter how grand or humble the need. From huge events like Celebration III and the DVD release to local visits at children's hospitals—this group can be counted upon to do their best," added Mary Franklin, events manager for Lucasfilm (ibid.).

In all, *Revenge of the Sith* raised $2.5 million for charity, making it one of the top charitable films of all time (Higgins). "George's mandate has been consistent for the last five *Star Wars* films. Use the goodwill and desire to see the film as a way to raise money for charities that help families and children," said Howard Roffman (ibid.). Among reported takes, the Seattle premiere raised more than $290,000,[1] New York City contributed $330,000 after expenses,[2] Chicago netted about $150,000,[3] and Los Angeles was the big winner with $900,000 raised.[4] The event not only allowed die-hard fans to see the movie a week before its worldwide release, but it also helped ten charities nationwide with their fundraising goals and helped inform the public about various ongoing charity efforts in their communities. Several of the charity premieres also gave fans a chance to see the movie digitally.

1.   According to a letter mailed to attendees.
2.   Wellner.
3.   Davis.
4.   Higgins.

A Digital Force

In 1999, *The Phantom Menace* became the first major movie ever projected digitally, though it only played in two theaters in New York City and two in Los Angeles. *Attack of the Clones*, the first major movie filmed entirely using digital equipment, was also projected digitally and at many more venues than its predecessor, but still only around ninety in North America and thirty-five across the rest of the world, both tiny numbers compared to the thousands of theaters that showed the film. For *Revenge of the Sith*, only about 80 theaters projected the film digitally in North America, but the international number swelled to 350, a tenfold increase from 2002, according to Producer Rick McCallum (McCallum).

Many problems have stood in the way of the rapid adoption of digital projection, the primary of which is cost and who bears financial responsibility for the new equipment. Theaters do not feel they should have to pay all of the costs to buy new projectors, which can be $100,000 each, because studios benefit from not having to create prints of every movie to ship to theaters, a cost that skyrockets into the tens of millions of dollars for major releases. Studios, however, believe that theaters benefit enough to make the purchases worthwhile. With digital projection, theaters can mold supply to meet demand. If one movie is playing on a single screen but selling out every showing, and another expected blockbuster is taking up three screens but barely half full for each showing, the theater can easily switch one auditorium from the blockbuster film to the surprise hit.

Digital projection provides a number of advantages for studios and theaters, but also for moviegoers. Over the course of several years in a theater, digital projection saves money for studios and increases security for intellectual property through Digital Rights Management (DRM), which is technology allowing for only specific uses of digital media to prevent its illegal copying or distribution. Digital projection also grants theaters more flexibility with film presentation and a higher quality product (crisp movies) to provide to moviegoers. Though early digital projectors drew occasional criticism from traditionalists, current technology is much crisper and far superior visually to film stock, especially after numerous viewings.

Digitally projected movies are visually clean and sharp, free of any markings or lost film frames, and look as good on their thousandth showings as on their first screenings. No quality loss occurs with repeated viewings of a digitally projected film. The differences between the two formats, film and digital, and their qualities are similar to VHS technology versus DVD quality, only film as a format is far more antiquated than VHS as it has been around for more than one hundred years. Nobody denies that digital projection is the future of the industry, but every year since 1999 industry analysts keep wondering when the change will finally occur.

Unfortunately, because of the number of studios and major theater chains all trying to protect their financial interests, coming to an agreement across the industry is a complicated and time-consuming process, wrought with legal difficulties as well as logistical issues. Another major issue had been the lack of a uniform standard for digitally projecting movies, which the Digital Cinema Initiative (DCI) addressed before the arrival of the final prequel. The limited liability corporation, established in March 2002, included members like Disney, Fox, MGM, Paramount, Sony, Universal, and Warner Bros.

The studios involved in creating the DCI wanted to establish exact specifications for digital cinema components to ensure high technical performance for all approved systems as well as ensure reliability and security. In March 2005, the organization completed its 176-page document outlining the standards and criteria for digital projection. "There were so many different formats for the content, and every packaging stream had to be different," said Brian Claypool of Christie Digital Systems (White "Star Wars Remains ..."). With no standards, theaters were even more reluctant to adopt digital projection, fearing their projectors might not be compatible with all possible formats. Claypool explained, "The big studios finally said this was ridiculous—there needed to be the same kind of standards that there are for 35mm film" (ibid.). He continued, "You can send reels of film anywhere in the world and they can be viewed in any theater. They decided you need that kind of plug-and-play for the digital film."

By the end of July, the consortium of studios had officially completed its work on the Digital Cinema Initiative, meaning the responsibility for realizing the goal of widespread digital cinema projection fell upon investors and Wall Street to raise the necessary capital to put digital projectors in many of the nation's thirty-six thousand auditoriums. The primary plan the industry had envisioned to solve the financial problem of digital cinema adoption involved raising about $3 billion from Wall Street investment banks, which would be paid back with the savings in distribution costs from the studios, a number J. M. Dutton & Associates LLP estimated to be about $750 million annually ("*Star Wars* Tests ..."). The plan was to start a massive nationwide rollout, with studios hoping for late 2007 or sometime in 2008, outfitting almost all of the nation's screens with digital projection capabilities in several months, rather than the sluggish pace evidenced previously.

Although digital projectors and server equipment are still expensive, the price of a digital projector had dropped to between $80,000 and $100,000. Ahmad Ouri, president of Technical Digital Cinema, the company responsible for the distribution of the digital master of the final prequel to theaters, said, "DCI is going to solve a lot of problems. But there were a number of factors—economic issues, distribution costs, [the] standardization issue, and quality issues" (White "Star Wars Remains ..."). Unfortunately, most moviegoers are not particularly educated about the technology and fail to understand the importance of the move, which translates to apathy for many theater chains. "I think the average consumer could care less about this and I think that also means exhibitors aren't necessarily in a hurry to adopt it," said David Hancock, a digital cinema analyst for Global Media Intelligence's *Screen Digest*, based in London (ibid.).

As the number of digitally released films has increased, exhibitors have started to take more interest in the technology, but the number of digitally distributed films remains small, so studios have not rushed to help exhibitors defer the costs. In 2002, when *Attack of the Clones* came to theaters, the studios released only sixteen movies digitally, a number that rose to twenty-three in 2003 and thirty by 2004. In the future, through the assistance of companies like Access Integrated Technologies (AccessIT),[1] studios hope to be able to beam digital copies of movies directly to theaters using satellites. With the small number of theaters equipped for digital projection, hard drives are generally used instead of satellites, but fiber optic networks can also accomplish the task.

Lucas, who has been the most vocal and powerful proponent of digital cinema, not only released the first-ever digitally projected commercial film, he also used digital technology to shoot the first-ever fully digital major movie. He has expressed annoyance and frustration with the slow adoption of the technology, however. He accused the film industry of "dawdling on purpose for various reasons, to see how they can control it [the showings of films in theaters by number of screenings and time of day], but they're not going to be able to, and it'll all

---

1.   AccessIT is a company interested in digitizing Hollywood's supply chain to theaters. The company assisted in the delivery of *Revenge of the Sith* for digital projection at a number of theaters, including the Pavilion Theatre in Brooklyn ("*Star Wars* Tests...").

work itself out," he said (White "Star Wars Remains ..."). "They deny that they're stalling, but six years is a long time to wait for this stuff to happen," Lucas continued. In 1999, one would have imagined that digital cinema would be a larger force in North America by 2005 than it had become.

Texas Instruments (TI) DLP Cinema technology was instrumental in the technological progress that the prequels pioneered. Aside from providing the digital projection technology used for *The Phantom Menace*, Lucas and McCallum had used a DLP Cinema Projector to view dailies during production, make various color corrections during post-production, and eventually project the film for the charity premieres in Los Angeles, New York, and San Francisco, along with theatrical releases worldwide. "Digital cinema projection is a vital part of the moviemaking process since it reduces production time and consistently delivers our desired vision to the screen," said McCallum ("DLP ...").

Robert Heron of ExtremeTech.com, who apparently did not like the last prequel, applauded the digital projection technology, having seen the film in San Francisco at a charity screening. He had seen the previous two films in 720p DLP cinema, but *Revenge of the Sith* showed in higher quality 1080p, with an increase in resolution by more than 1.2 million pixels. He wrote, "The results were breathtaking," noting that Texas Instruments DLP projectors could recreate 35 trillion colors. He urged readers, "If you are fortunate enough to live near a theater that offers digital projection, be sure to treat yourself to a show."

Many *Star Wars* fans who had the opportunity to see the prequels, or at least the final one, digitally projected became huge supporters of the format. Dave Gohman of Schaumburg, Illinois, said, "It looks much better than film presentations. To tell the truth I don't even see movies in the theater unless it's digital" (Gohman). Diane Kovalcin of New Jersey agreed. "Digital is far and away better than straight film. The picture never goes bad, it's much crisper, the colors more vivid and, in general, is just a better format," she said (Kovalcin). Michael Kaminski of Toronto, Canada, disagreed. He said, "I think HD, at least at present time, is an abomination to the organic beauty of celluloid film" (Kaminski). Most fans, though, wanted to see *Revenge of the Sith* digitally if possible because of its digital origins. "After having seen it digitally I couldn't believe how much worse it was on film," said Gohman. "The colors were washed out, the image had instability and even within the first week of release there were scratches and dirt that just aren't an issue with digital," he continued.

Lucas has observed on several occasions that theaters need to offer more of an experience to draw audiences they are losing to video games, high-definition television, and increasingly inexpensive home theater setups. Gohman agrees, saying,

"If the theater industry wants people to leave the comfort of their own digital home theaters, they are going to have to do something to make their experience somewhat compelling." In other words, the quality has to be better than what people can find for cheaper without getting in a car. "When you have to sit through a movie you can't pause when you need to hit the restroom, in a public area where you aren't allowed to smoke if you want, you can't have a presentation that is worse than what people can get at home," Gohman added.

With *Revenge of the Sith*, Dolby Laboratories announced the commercial launch of its Dolby Digital Cinema system in a number of theaters worldwide. The final prequel became the first movie to use the new technology, which debuted in markets like Berlin, London, Los Angeles, New York, Paris, and San Francisco. A company press release read: "Continuing its successful tradition of introducing technological innovations for cinemas in conjunction with *Star Wars* film releases, Dolby brings to market its digital cinema solution to provide the highest quality digital cinema experience for *Revenge of the Sith*" ("Dolby Launches ..."). In 1999, Dolby had premiered its Surround EX 6.1 channel surround sound with *The Phantom Menace*, offering moviegoers a back speaker and separate audio channel for fly-over effects, making for a more realistic moviegoing experience. Lucasfilm again used Surround EX to mix the soundtrack for *Revenge of the Sith*.

Dolby's experience working with Lucasfilm far predates 1999, however. In 1977, Dolby teamed with Lucasfilm and Fox to introduce multichannel Dolby Stereo sound for the first *Star Wars* film. "We're pleased to be working again with Lucasfilm Limited as our latest technical offering is commercially launched in theaters to advance the cinematic experience for movie fans worldwide," said Tim Partridge, general manager and senior vice president of the professional division for Dolby Laboratories ("Dolby Launches ..."). The company formally launched Dolby Digital Cinema in Japan with the release of the prequel July 2, but also used the technology for *Revenge of the Sith*'s first industry screening on June 18. The company made its technology available for premieres around the world, assisting Lucasfilm in showing fans and everyone in attendance the power of digital projection and the high quality in which Lucas intended viewers to see *Revenge of the Sith*.

Aside from digital projection, many fans wondered why *Revenge of the Sith* had no IMAX showings, especially with *Attack of the Clones* having enjoyed a special fall IMAX release in 2002. Rick McCallum did not sound too enthusiastic about IMAX or its conversion process when speaking with Joseph Kleiman from World Enteractive, a now-defunct Web site about cinema technology. McCallum said, "We didn't have a great experience working with IMAX on *Episode II*," telling Kleiman that "they promised us the world ... and never delivered on the number of screens they got for us."

McCallum also said IMAX is too expensive for a partnership or any working relationship and "you have to stop and ask, why is anyone paying millions of dollars for their overhead?" Lucasfilm considered having *Revenge of the Sith* projected on IMAX screens if In-Three, an innovative company able to take 2-D movies and make them 3-D, could convert part of the final prequel. Ultimately, the whole idea had "become too much of a drama," McCallum said (McCallum).

Since 1999, when digital projection first made its mark with *The Phantom Menace* (an historic occasion and another milestone for the *Star Wars* saga), technology companies and the studios involved have made much technical and logistical progress and laid important groundwork for a digital future. Unfortunately, the technology has not reached theaters as quickly as Lucas and other proponents had hoped, but the DCI was a huge step forward as all of the major studios worked together to support a uniform standard for digital projection technology, distribution, and security. With proper funding, the future is bright for digital projection technology. It will save money for studios, increase flexibility and profit margins for theaters, and most importantly give moviegoers a better experience in cinemas closer to how filmmakers like George Lucas intend viewers to see their movies.

Parents Strongly Cautioned

Star Wars has always been a family-friendly franchise that promotes values like courage, integrity, friendship, loyalty, bravery, and leadership, among others. Nearly every young boy growing up between 1977 and present day has watched the *Star Wars* films, usually many times. The movies have always been great family entertainment because kids, especially boys, can delight in the special effects, action sequences, cool gadgets, spacecraft, and weapons, while adults can appreciate the historical, religious, and mythological themes of the story that make it enjoyable on a repeat basis. *Revenge of the Sith*, however, broke from tradition by including such intense imagery and violence relative to the other *Star Wars* films that the Motion Picture Association of America (MPAA), the official ratings board in the United States, had no choice but to slap the movie with a PG-13 rating. The decision made the final prequel the first *Star Wars* movie not to earn the more kid-friendly PG rating.

Because of the events that had to occur in the story, many people had already wondered years before its release whether *Revenge of the Sith* would be too dark for younger kids. While 1980's *The Empire Strikes Back* was a relatively dark film compared to its predecessor, it did not have enough intense imagery to warrant a harsher PG-13 rating. Aside from Darth Vader lopping off Luke Skywalker's arm, the film is mostly full of what is often termed "comic violence," or not realistic enough violence (blood, guts, and gore) to warrant a stiff rating.

Lucas knew, even in 1999, that his final prequel would be "very, very, very dark," as he told *Empire* magazine after *The Phantom Menace*'s release ("*Star Wars: Episode 3 ...*"). He said of the film, "It's not a happy movie by any stretch of the imagination. It's a tragedy. People think of the *Star Wars* movies as happy movies. What they're going to do about a tragedy, I don't know" (ibid.). Before the MPAA slapped the film with a PG-13 rating, numerous media organizations began discussing the possibility.

The possibility of a PG-13 rating seemed much more realistic in March, when an interview with Lucas aired on *60 Minutes*. He said, "I don't think I would take a five- or six-year-old to this. It's way too strong." He predicted its final rating, too. "My feeling is that it will probably be a PG-13, so it will be the first *Star*

Wars that's a PG-13." In April, the inevitable came true. The MPAA's Classification and Ratings Administration (CARA) gave *Revenge of the Sith* a PG-13 rating for "sci-fi violence and some intense images." Whereas the PG rating merely warns parents with the phrase "Parental Guidance Suggested," PG-13 carries a bit harsher caution: "Parents Strongly Cautioned."

Other countries' review boards gave *Revenge of the Sith* similar ratings, though each country has different organizations and policies on film ratings. In the United Kingdom, four of the previous five *Star Wars* films received a "U" rating, which translates to "suitable for all," while *Attack of the Clones* was rated PG. The rating verdict was harshest in Australia, where the Office of Film and Literature Classification gave the final prequel an "M" rating, meaning the film was not recommended for anyone under fifteen, though underage moviegoers would not be barred from seeing it ("Fed …"). Rather, parents were simply cautioned not to bring children under fifteen. All five of the previous films had received more favorable PG ratings, like in the United States.

Parents had a difficult dilemma with *Revenge of the Sith*, especially if their kids had already seen the previous *Star Wars* prequels and were part of a borderline age group, like older than six and younger than ten, perhaps. The *St. Louis Post-Dispatch* ran an article, by Lorraine Kee and Joe Holleman, focusing on the marketing tie-ins that played on kids television networks for products like video games, soft drinks, and food items. With constant reminders of the coming of a new *Star Wars* film, kids, even young ones, had more opportunities to bother their parents about seeing the film.

Kellogg, a Lucasfilm licensee that promoted the film on many of its products, downplayed parental concerns. A spokesperson said, "We believe that the *Star Wars* toys and promotional items give consumers of all ages a chance to experience the excitement of *Star Wars* regardless of whether they see the movie. At the end of the day, *Star Wars* is the most popular film franchise in history" (Kee and Holleman). The popularity of the franchise, though, made parents' jobs harder if they thought their kids were not old enough to see the film.

Jane Horwitz of *The Washington Post* Writers Group, who writes a section called "The Family Filmgoer," did not think *Revenge of the Sith* was overly violent or intense for younger viewers. She told the *St. Louis Post-Dispatch*, "I don't think there's anything that would scare a ten-year-old boy. But you can't generalize" (Kee and Holleman). For parents who thought the content would be too extreme for their kids, they may have had to deal with wars at home with kids eager to see the newest and final *Star Wars* film. Though the movie is arguably not appropriate for younger kids, the tie-ins included action figures, Burger King Kids Meals, and toy sets from LEGO, all generally targeting children under thirteen years old. "It's very hypocritical. Is a fifteen-year-old going to buy a lightsaber? I'm sure parents find it terribly annoying," said Horwitz (ibid.). To be fair, many forty-five-year-olds buy lightsabers, as long as they are *Star Wars* nerds.

Some people were outraged by the tie-ins and marketing, claiming that Lucas and the companies involved had no right trying to draw in kids too young to view the content suitably. Nell Minow, a film critic who writes a column called "Media Mom" in the *Chicago Tribune*, blasted the film's creator, saying, "It's horrifying. What's the purpose of the rating system if not to make distinctions? I blame George Lucas and the studio for marketing to the age not recommended by the rating" (Quinn). Most promotional deals were signed and planned far before the MPAA decided upon its rating, though. Others agreed with Minow, however. "There is something inherently contradictory in giving [the film] a restrictive rating and then marketing toys and Happy Meals and things like that to little kids. And that puts parents in a very difficult spot," said child psychologist Douglas Gentile of the National Institute on Media and the Family (Gardner).

The indignation from various commentators and parents, while worth noting, was not serious for Lucasfilm or its licensees because the MPAA rating system lacks any legal implications. It is a voluntary system that the National Association of Theater Owners (NATO) adopted to give parents information about movies in theaters, so it serves as the industry's attempt to police itself. Neither filmmakers nor theaters in America are required to use any type of rating system, if they so desire, because film content is protected by First Amendment rights in the Constitution of the United States. Any organizations outside of the film industry, such as licensees, are not concerned about film ratings so long as they believe the demographics they are targeting will be interested in their products.

Burger King took the most criticism for its tie-ins, however, drawing ire from numerous groups. Bob Moon from the news bureau *Marketplace* came on NPR to talk about the issue with Madeleine Brand, the host ("Analysis: ..."). The Dove Foundation, a family advocacy group, took issue with the Kids Meal tie-in at Burger King. Kids Meals apparently target children ages four to nine, which is mostly the age group that should probably not see *Revenge of the Sith*, at least toward the bottom of the range. The group had earlier convinced McDonalds to apologize over a similar incident, a 1992 promotion of PG-13-rated *Batman Returns*. The Dove Foundation had only twice in its fifteen-year history asked a fast-food chain to end a film-based promotion, though (Johannes "Burger ...").

Burger King insisted that their promotional efforts celebrated the entire *Star Wars* saga and not just *Revenge of the Sith*. As evidence, only four of its thirty-one toys in the Kids Meals were exclusive to the final installment. Because the saga is much larger than one film, the promotions for *Revenge of the Sith* could be said, at least in a sense, to celebrate the entire movie series and the end of the story. The Official *Star Wars* Web Site in a March article cautiously called the promotion "adult-targeted," despite the toys coming with Kids Meals. Dove Foundation Chairman Dick Rolfe said, "We have no qualms about Fox or about Lucasfilm. We even think the MPAA got it right this time in awarding this PG-13 rating" (Johannes "Burger …"). Rolfe had mentioned that the film's violence made it inappropriate, in his opinion, for children under twelve. He continued, "But we don't want parents to think Burger King is endorsing this movie by including these toys in Kids Meals. That is exactly what is happening."

Burger King downplayed the allegations, re-iterating that the promotions not only followed established rules but also that the company was promoting *Star Wars*, not the final film exclusively. A Burger King spokesperson said, "The thirty-one toys in our collection clearly celebrate not just one film but the entire *Star Wars* saga, which is the most popular film franchise in history," echoing Kellogg's sentiments (ibid.). The spokesperson continued, "The reception at our restaurants and from our customers has been overwhelmingly positive. As with all our promotions, we review all consumer responses and suggestions." Additionally, the Children's Advertising Regulatory Unit (CARU) has established guidelines, "which, for PG-13-rated films, include no film clips in children's advertising, no direct call to action to see the film, and rating caution disclaimers in other targeted marketing materials," the spokesperson said (ibid.). Parents and advocacy groups seemed more concerned about the subliminal advertising than direct marketing, however.

Advertising Age, a specialty industry magazine on advertising and marketing, ran an article about the differences between the tie-in campaigns for *Revenge of the Sith* and *Batman Begins*, both of which earned PG-13 ratings. While *Revenge of the Sith* had numerous promotional partners considered more family oriented, like Pepsi-Cola, Burger King, Kellogg, and Masterfoods, *Batman Begins* had tie-ins mainly with adult-aimed companies such as Verizon Communications, Symantec software, and Dell computers. Although family films used to fall under only the G and PG ratings categories, Brett Dicker, vice president of marketing for Buena Vista Pictures, observed how film franchises like *Spider-Man* and *The Lord of the Rings*, all PG-13 movies, became family films (Stanley "Tie-in …").

Ratings can also be a marketing concern for another reason unrelated to parental worries. Teenagers and young adults are unlikely to think of a PG-rated film as cool or edgy, so the PG-13 rating, a fair medium between the harsher R and more kid-friendly PG, can benefit box office performance. By the end of 2005, only one film in the top twenty highest grossing movies of all time in North America received an R rating, which was *The Passion of the Christ* (2004). Of the remaining nineteen, ten received PG-13 ratings and nine were PG rated, though four of the top five, all but *Titanic* (1997) in first, had PG ratings. The L.A. Office, a marketing consultancy for Hollywood, said 47 percent of marketers surveyed indicated their companies allowed cross-promotion with PG-13 films (ibid.). Film ratings, though not all-important, play a significant role in a company's consideration of whether to consider tie-ins with a film.

Many parents expressed anger over the PG-13 rating for the final prequel because they felt Lucas was disallowing their kids from seeing the film. Diane Lowery told *The Wichita Eagle* that she was "kind of irritated" that Lucas made the film PG-13, because "it just seems like he didn't really need to do that" (Tobias). Her comment seems a bit naive as the story clearly dictates that a PG-rated finale would be too tame to be successful artistically. Likewise, Laura Corbett of Myrtle Beach told *The Sun News*, "It's really terrible that they have done this because of all the young fans who loved the previous movies. Now, they have bumped up the rating. So children who have seen the five movies up to this point won't be able to see the culmination" (Wilson). As mentioned, though, only the parents could prevent kids from seeing the film because a PG-13 rating does not restrict moviegoers under thirteen; it only cautions parents.

Lucas reacted to some of the accusations of making the film too dark, especially from people who thought he had somehow betrayed his audience because they believed the films are supposed to be for kids. "We're getting a lot of flak from parents, a lot of people saying how can you do this? My children love these movies," Lucas told the Associated Press (Germain "Last ..."). He explained, "But I have to tell a story. I'm not making these, oddly enough, to be giant, successful blockbusters. I'm making them because I'm telling a story, and I have to tell the story I intended." Lucas told *Vanity Fair*, "I think children, young children especially, should be warned that this is not your average *Star Wars*. It's brutal in places and they should be aware of that" (Windolf 111).

To his credit, Lucas continually stressed the dark and violent content of his final prequel during numerous interviews with the media before and after the release of the film. He also emphasized that the MPAA rated the prequel PG-13 not just for its graphic imagery, but because of its greater emotional intensity, which the ratings board did not feel most younger children could handle. "The film censors said that it is too intense, which, of course, is what I was trying to do. The last movie [*Attack of the Clones*] was a PG-13 at first, but we went back and cut a few bits to get it a PG rating," Lucas revealed (Waugh "The Billion …"). He continued, "I wasn't willing for that to happen with this one. I'm ending *Star Wars* with tragedy because that's the way the story goes. It's not designed to be commercial."

Lucas also emphasized that parents ultimately have to be responsible for deciding whether their kids are mature enough to see the film. He said, "Who should be allowed to see (it) should be left up to the parents. But at least they're warned it's pretty intense" (Ryckman). Theresa Webb of the UCLA School of Public Health said of parents going with their children to see movies with questionable violence levels, "It appears to have a protective effect. See it with them, make sure to talk with them about it" (ibid.). Jane Horwitz agreed in her review, writing, "Particularly if parents decide to let their under-tens see it, they should sit with them in case they need reassurance."

Parents have differing views on the maturity of their children and the acceptableness of the content in *Revenge of the Sith* for kids. Diane Kovalcin of New Jersey said, "My kid had just turned eleven when she saw *Revenge of the Sith*. We've always been a *Star Wars* family so it was a given that she would see it" (Kovalcin). While Kovalcin mentioned that each child matures at a different rate, she said the movie is "definitely not to be seen if they are eight or younger."

Other parents disagreed with Kovalcin, though, like Lynde Roberts of Billings, Montana, who said, "My kids were six and three at the time. They saw the movie after I had seen it. I warned them to close their eyes during several parts" (Roberts). She admitted that kids should "probably [be] older than my kids" but she could not resist because "we are all really big *Star Wars* fans." Neil Guggenmos of Longmont, Colorado, took his three-year-old son to the film, but only because "I was able to discuss with him the good versus evil aspects of the film and show what wrong choices did to Anakin," he said (Guggenmos). Otherwise, "I would say ten years old" is the minimum age, Guggenmos said, if he had to make a fixed age for the film's viewing.

Although parents had to decide whether they could let their kids see the movie, most did not seem to agree with Laura Corbett's opinion that Lucas wronged the fans by making the movie PG-13 rather than PG. "No, I think it needed to be PG-13. Vader had to suffer for all the horrors that he inflicted on the Jedi and I think Lucas did a good job of showing that without going overboard," Kovalcin said. Roberts agreed, saying, "I was okay with the PG-13. It was a necessary part of the movie to see Anakin burned and to have the graphic fight scenes." Guggenmos added, "PG-13 was perfect for the intensity and darker themes of the movie," which he felt were necessary. After all, Lucas had cut *Attack of the Clones* to keep it PG, but could not cut *Revenge of the Sith* without sacrificing artistic integrity. Parents like Kovalcin, Roberts, and Guggenmos had to decide whether Lucas's final *Star Wars* film was acceptable to show to their kids.

Kevin Smith, famous director and *Star Wars* fan, also thought the movie was too dark for younger children. "It's a great movie, but I'm not sure any kid under eight should see that kind of violence. Even I was surprised by how insanely dark George [Lucas] made it," he told *USA Today* (Bowles "In 'Sith,' …"). Nonetheless, every parent had his or her own opinion of how old kids should be to see the film, from parents taking their five-year-olds and reporting no problems to others saying that children under twelve should not see the film. Most experts agreed, however, that parents had to decide for themselves whether their kids possessed the maturity to deal with the complicated themes and violence that the film contains.

The PG-13 rating left little doubt that Lucas would deliver on his promise of *Revenge of the Sith* at least being the darkest of the *Star Wars* films. In a poll that TheForce.net conducted in late February 2005 before the film's rating became official, 53 percent of fans said they would like the movie to be rated PG-13 while only 14 percent voted for PG; the remaining votes out of the 10,548 cast went to R (14 percent), NC-17 (12 percent, oddly enough), and G (only 4 percent). After the MPAA gave *Revenge of the Sith* its rating, critics gave the movie ratings of a different kind that also might have impacted moviegoers' decisions on whether to see the final prequel.

Critical Redemption

A History of Confusion

Making sense of the vast diversity of opinions about the *Star Wars* films is often difficult because time and perception have skewed facts and objectivity. For instance, judging from first reactions by the critical community, the only good film in the original *Star Wars* trilogy was the first, which received glowing reviews from many major publications including *Time* and *Variety*, but was dismissed by some critics as a shallow children's film. Both *The Empire Strikes Back* and *Return of the Jedi* received mostly mediocre to terrible reviews, especially *Return of the Jedi*. The passage of time, perhaps the best judge of true quality and appeal, was favorable to the first three *Star Wars* films. By the 1997 *Special Edition* re-releases, all three had gained the status of classics while *The Empire Strikes Back* had earned a place as one of the greatest sequels ever made, alongside films like *Terminator 2: Judgment Day* (1991) and *The Godfather: Part II* (1974).

The Phantom Menace, with the immense expectations of fans and an unprecedented amount of media hype, came to theaters greeted with mixed critical reaction. While critics praised its visual effects and action, most were not too happy with the story, acting, or dialogue, not surprisingly as critics also had ripped the previous *Star Wars* films for all of the above. Fans have not remained interested in the saga for visual effects alone, however, and the frequently quoted dialogue has played a major role in the popularity of the films. Because of the gap between perception and reality, created mainly by media bias, most ordinary filmgoers have the impression that critics not only disliked but hated *The Phantom Menace*. In fact, at the time of release, *The Phantom Menace* consistently hovered above 55 percent positive reviews on RottenTomatoes.com, a site that collects reviews from hundreds of sources online and in print and serves as a barometer for complete critical consensus.

Since 1999, the proportion of positive reviews compared to negative ones for *The Phantom Menace* has improved to the point where more than 60 percent of the reviews are positive, giving the film a "fresh" rating. Whether time has an extremely positive effect on the critical opinions about *The Phantom Menace* as well as *Attack of the Clones* decades after their respective theatrical releases remains to be seen, but with *Revenge of the Sith* being very well reviewed, a rise in respect for the first two films is far from unlikely.

In 2005, *The Phantom Menace* had a 62 percent positive rating, while one year later it had already climbed another point to 63 percent. *Attack of the Clones*, at 65 percent in 2005, had climbed to 66 percent one year later as well. While such small gains are statistically insignificant in many respects, over the years since each film came to theaters, the percentages have increased enough to speculate that critical opinions have perhaps shifted at least slightly, or rather that more critics favorable to the prequels have contributed reviews over the years.

Perhaps another reason why the first two prequels disappointed some fans and critics is the starting point Lucas chose for the trilogy. Instead of beginning with Anakin already as an adult and turning to the Dark Side, Lucas chose to start with Anakin as a child, then show him as a late teenager before his ultimate fall from grace. Lucas said in an interview with *Wired* magazine, "People expected *Episode III*, which is where Anakin turns into Darth Vader, to be *Episode I*. And then they expected *Episodes II* and *III* to be Darth Vader going around cutting people's heads off and terrorizing the universe."

The quality gap that many fans and critics perceive in the first two prequels compared to the third might largely be attributable to audience impatience. Lucas had one story to tell, a trilogy chronicling the rise and fall of Anakin Skywalker, but a segment of fans and many critics think the first two prequels are worthless exposition rather than useful chapters in the complete story. With such pre-conceived notions of how the story should evolve, no wonder many people found themselves disappointed in a trilogy with more political maneuvering and foreshadowing than death and destruction.

Although *Attack of the Clones* received widespread praise from fans and many critics, by the time *Revenge of the Sith* neared its release, most media outlets grouped both *The Phantom Menace* and *Attack of the Clones* into the category of major disappointments to fans and critics alike. In fact, most fans thoroughly enjoyed both films and most critics gave the movies favorable reviews. Very few critics ripped either movie. At worst, reviewers offered both praise and criticism, citing strengths and weaknesses of the movies.

The media would have the public believe that fans almost universally did not enjoy either of the first two prequels. The media, at least, felt that Lucas needed to redeem himself in the eyes of the fans and critics, to show one more time that he possessed the directing skill and filmmaking mastery to capture the magic of a galaxy far, far away. For the cynics, Lucas was prepared to deliver a masterpiece and have some semblance of revenge on his critics.

Before most of the critics published their reviews, however, *Revenge of the Sith* premiered at the Cannes Film Festival in France on Sunday, May 15. When *The Phantom Menace* was ready for its 1999 release, Cannes Chief Gilles Jacob had rejected the movie for the festival. To accompany the premiere of *Revenge of the Sith* at Cannes, fully clad Stormtrooper and Darth Vader look-alikes made their presences felt. Although the final *Star Wars* film was not in official competition at Cannes, it was nonetheless the most important event on Sunday, with hundreds of fans and media present to greet the stars and witness a cinematic milestone. One reporter said he felt "empty" after seeing the film, but not because of its quality. "No, because it is over," he said ("Final 'Star Wars' debuts ..."). Fans at Cannes applauded as Vader donned his suit for the first time and took his first breaths.

Stars Anthony Daniels, Samuel L. Jackson, Ian McDiarmid, and Natalie Portman, among others, were also at Cannes with Lucas, who received an achievement award earlier Sunday aboard the luxury liner *Queen Mary 2*. Portman stunned fans by showing up bald, because of her recent work on *V for Vendetta* (2006). Jackson said of the final prequel, "Now we know how [Anakin Skywalker] got to this particular place, so he seems more the tragic figure than an evil figure now" (ibid.). He also discussed his long-held desire to be in at least one *Star Wars* movie and his satisfaction with his role in the saga, not to mention his death scene. "I was pleased with my death. I asked [Lucas] not to kill me in my sleep," he said (Germain "'Star Wars' Tidbits ...").

Daniels talked about his influential role in the saga, as one of the few actors to be involved with all six films, and said of being behind the golden helmet, "There are moments when it's very nice to be recognized. A lot of moments when it's very nice not to be" (ibid.). Although McDiarmid appeared in the first two prequels, and much of the third, without much makeup, he said, "I hope it's the mask they remember and not my face" (ibid.). Not long after Cannes, the reviews from professional critics and fans alike began surfacing in greater numbers.

Lucas Strikes Back

Most fans, weary from years of tolerating naysayers and poor media bias, expected another mixed critical reaction to dampen the mood for opening day, but for once the seemingly impossible happened: a *Star Wars* film received glowing reviews. Not since the first *Star Wars* movie in 1977 had any of the franchise's films enjoyed widespread success with critics on first release. While *The Empire*

Strikes Back is now a critical darling, it barely broke the 50 percent mark on its first release and took a drubbing from many critics, before rising to prominence in the intervening years between its first release and its *Special Edition* re-release.

While Lucas always claims to have little concern for what critics think of his work,[1] focusing more on audience reaction, even he must have been surprised by the reaction *Revenge of the Sith* drew from critics. For Lucas and for fans of his work, *Revenge* truly was sweet. *Boston Globe* critic Ty Burr, often one of the harshest critics, wrote of the film, "It's good. I mean *really* good." Chris Hewitt of the *St. Paul Pioneer Press* called the film "triumphant," while David Foucher of *Edge Boston* called it "kick-ass." In an eloquent review praising Lucas for his steadfastness and vision, Michael Wilmington of the *Chicago Tribune* called the film "exhilarating" and the "most exciting" of the saga, awarding it four stars.

Many critics who felt Lucas lost his way on previous efforts returned to the bandwagon. Roger Ebert, who gave a "thumbs up" to *The Phantom Menace* but was not pleased with *Attack of the Clones*, wrote in a three-and-a-half-star review, "George Lucas has achieved what few artists do; he has created and populated a world of his own." Eleanor Ringel Gillespie of the *Atlanta Journal and Constitution* wrote in a glowing "A−" review, "Same logo. Same starry-night spacescape. Same music. Same crawl. Same everything. Only different. And so much better." The praise the film received did not stop at just being the best of the prequel trilogy; most critics felt it was one of the best in the series.

Many critics, likely the largest portion, called it the best *Star Wars* film since *The Empire Strikes Back*. James Berardinelli of *Reel Views* called *Revenge of the Sith* "a rousing and tragic sendoff to a beloved franchise, and the best installment in the *Star Wars* series since 1980's *The Empire Strikes Back*." *Variety*'s Todd McCarthy wrote, "Whatever one thought of the previous two installments, this dynamic picture irons out most of the problems, and emerges as the best in the overall series since *The Empire Strikes Back*." *Hollywood Reporter* critic Kirk Honeycutt wrote, "The final episode of George Lucas' cinematic epic *Star Wars* ends the six-movie series on such a high note that one feels like yelling out, 'Rewind!'" *Washington Post* critic Stephen Hunter wrote, "*Revenge of the Sith* is a brilliant consummation to a promise made a long time ago, far, far away, in a galaxy called

---

1. He told *60 Minutes* earlier in the year when asked about whether he was worried the critics would not like the final film, "Oh, I'm not worried at all. They haven't liked any of them, really, and they especially haven't liked the last two." He also said to the Associated Press, "You can't really worry about [reviews]. I make the movie I feel I want to make, telling the story I want to tell, and how it gets received is how it gets received" (Germain "Lucas…").

1977." Richard Roeper of *Ebert and Roeper* said of the film, "I think it's the best one since *The Empire Strikes Back.*"

Other critics ranked *Revenge of the Sith* as the best *Star Wars* film of all, or at least the most successful in some respects. *Oregonian* film critic Shawn Levy, a fan of *The Phantom Menace* on its release,[2] called the film "the darkest, most operatic, and technologically richest *Star Wars* movie to date." He continued in his "A–" review, "*Sith* is grim, stirring entertainment and a nearly complete vindication." Claudia Puig of *USA Today* gave the film three and a half stars, writing, "It's the darkest of the six-film opus, but it just may be the best of the lot." Jim Beckerman of *The Record* agreed: "The much-hyped last entry in the *Star Wars* saga is not only a return to form but—depending on your taste—arguably the best in the series." Given the high opinion most film critics and fans share for the Original Trilogy, such high praise seemed especially amazing at the time.

Critics who thought the final prequel ranked at least close to the best in the saga were hardly few in number. A. O. Scott of *The New York Times* heaved perhaps the most incredible praise on the film when he wrote, "This is by far the best film in the more recent trilogy, and also the best of the four episodes Mr. Lucas has directed. That's right: it's better than *Star Wars.*" Scott also wrote, "… the sheer beauty, energy and visual coherence of *Revenge of the Sith* is nothing short of breathtaking." He ranked it alongside *Empire* as "the richest and most challenging movie in the cycle." Philip Key of the *Daily Post* in Liverpool, England, said the *Star Wars* saga has sometimes been "a yawn," yet he gave *Revenge of the Sith* five stars out of five, called it "the best of the saga," and mentioned that Lucas is "so often unfairly criticized for his writing" despite the depth of the story.

Internationally, critics were generally favorable to *Revenge of the Sith*, though oddly reviewers from the United Kingdom were sometimes more negative than their counterparts in North America. *In Film Australia* critic Luke Buckmaster, who gave the film four stars out of five, said, "George Lucas's bombastic space soap opera thunders through its sixth installment in *Episode III—Revenge of the Sith*, a dazzling and gorgeously rendered send-off to one of cinema's most beloved science fiction franchises." Similarly, *SBS Movie Show* reviewer Megan Spencer in Australia said, "It remained very true to the original starting point of *Star Wars* all the way back in 1977." A few critics in the United Kingdom were not ready to join the party, however.

---

2.   He gave it an "A–."

Many U.K. newspapers absolutely panned *Revenge of the Sith*. Why there would be such a gap between U.S. critics and U.K. critics, when the two countries both have large, devoted fan bases, is hard to ascertain, except to attribute it to coincidence. Tim Robey of *The Daily Telegraph* wrote that the movie has "bad dialogue, poor acting, clumsy storytelling" and is ultimately "a big let-down." Among other U.K. critics, Cosmo Landesman of *The Sunday Times* called the movie "empty" at heart while Peter Bradshaw of *The Guardian* called it "dramatically weightless" and said everyone in the theater was "bored into submission." James Christopher of *The Times* (London) wrote, "I'm actually lost for words: amazed that I've held a candle so long for so little; and appalled by how irrelevant this marathon enterprise has become." Chris Tookey of *The Daily Mail* in London wrote, "If to the cinema you must go, a tiresome movie find you will."

Not every critic from the United Kingdom hated the film, however. *Empire* magazine gave *Revenge of the Sith* a positive review, even while bashing the first two prequels heavily. So also did *The People* of London, calling it the "second best of all the six." Richard Bacon wrote for *The People*, "I'm not gonna waste your time. This is good. Really good." Mike Davies of *The Birmingham Post* in England agreed, calling it "one of the best" *Star Wars* films. He wrote, "You knew it was coming, but who would have expected it to be so moving or so majestic[?]" Also in praise of the film, *The Evening Standard*'s Charlotte O'Sullivan wrote, "At once kitschy and compelling, overripe and disturbing, *Revenge of the Sith* makes you forgive Lucas's earlier indulgences and want to revisit the original three movies—if only to reassure yourself that it ends happily after all."

Many film historians and critics also appreciated the immense effort and vision required to tell a story over a twenty-eight-year period and six films. Andrew Gordon, an English professor at the University of Florida at the time of release for the final prequel, said, "What's rarer [than the mythology in the *Star Wars* films], though, is George Lucas's ambition. Hollywood movies tend to be isolated events" (Coyle "Star ..."). In other words, a phenomenon is difficult to duplicate with multiple event films. Gordon continued, "But to attempt to weave together a story this complex over such a long period of time, that's very rare. Going back through Hollywood, perhaps D. W. Griffith had that type of ambition." Farin Jacobsen of *The Fresno Bee*, who called the movie a "must-see," wrote, "One has to witness just how George Lucas masterfully fills in the missing puzzle pieces to complete the intricate jigsaw it took him almost 30 years to complete."

Numerous other articles around the time of release for *Revenge of the Sith* focused on the *Star Wars* phenomenon as a whole and its impact on popular culture. Gloria Goodale of *The Christian Science Monitor* wrote, "The sheer size and longevity of director George Lucas's vision alone rank *Star Wars* as unique in movie history." John Petrakis of *The Christian Century* wrote, "It's the movie equivalent of an ancient builder lowering the final massive block into a mammoth pyramid, knowing that unless this stone settles in perfectly against the others, the entire structure will collapse." Petrakis continued, "What's remarkable, given all this, is how successful *Revenge of the Sith* is and how closely it adheres to the ideals that accompanied the installments of the 1970s and 1980s."

Perhaps the best commentary came from Rick Curnutte Jr., editor of *The Film Journal*, an online film quarterly. He understood how *Revenge of the Sith* did not just complete the saga as far as entries, but it also made sense of the previous two prequels and added depth to the Original Trilogy in the process. It was a gift to the saga as a whole, improving all of the entries, not only offering a great new one. Curnutte, who called the movie "the best film of the year," wrote:

> *Revenge of the Sith* is a masterpiece. It shows Lucas as a filmmaker ferociously at the top of his game. *Sith* is, perhaps, the greatest bridging film in the medium's history. Never has a single film so decidedly wrapped up an entire mythology in one swoop. It is a heartbreaking, poetic, haunting, beautiful, powerful film. The political strategizing of the first two prequels which Lucas was so harassed for come together in such a gosh-wow explosion of sociological precision, the prescience of the director's vision is startling.

Curnutte's opinion of the final prequel echoed general fan sentiment, though not all critics wanted to jump on Lucas's bandwagon again.

Inevitable Backlash

As always, Hollywood is full of cynics who, perhaps out of jealousy, are eager to take shots at such a monumental filmmaker. In an *NPR Morning Edition* discussion on Lucas with Renee Montagne, Kim Masters, Lucas biographer Dale Pollock, and former Fox studio executive Bill Mechanic, the subject centered on Lucas's various perceived failures and shortcomings ("Profile: How …"). Mechanic complained that Lucas only wanted to use Fox for its distribution system for the prequels and had little interest in the studio besides being "a necessarily evil." Lucas, a shrewd businessman above all, completely financed the prequels, owned all the rights to the films and the merchandise, and gave Fox a cut of three of the largest blockbusters of all time for little more than taking care of distribution and marketing. Mechanic probably did not find too many industry executives' shoulders upon which to cry when he was at Fox.

Pollack compared Lucas to the fictional character Citizen Kane of Orson Welles's 1942 masterpiece. "The analogy is apt if you look at Skywalker Ranch as a kind of Xanadu and as someone who ... doesn't want a real world, he wants a created world that he can manipulate digitally," he said (ibid.). Because Lucas has earned the money, through technology and vision, to harness the power he wants independently, he must be a reclusive, anti-social, cold man who has lost touch with reality, apparently. Pollack sees Lucas as a victim of his own success. While Pollack makes cute analogies about old classics, Lucas is free to enjoy his billions of dollars and a feeling of accomplishment that accompanies creating the most successful movie franchise in history.

In a scathing editorial from *Esquire*, Mike D'Angelo likened *Revenge of the Sith*, without having seen it, to a "steaming glass of piss," blasting the past two movies and urging moviegoers not to see the third prequel. D'Angelo asked for a "provisional boycott" because he admits, "I haven't actually seen the film yet. I'm assuming it's going to reek." He adds the caveat that "if reviews suggest that the new film is light-years more entertaining," readers should "disregard everything" that he wrote. D'Angelo felt that most people would go see the third prequel because of a sense of cultural obligation, rather than from a sense of excitement, thus his call for a boycott of "at least ... the first week" of the film's opening.

Despite his negativity, and insistence that fans who liked the first two prequels must have had a lobotomy, D'Angelo at least made one meaningful observation. Unlike most media writers at the time of *The Phantom Menace*'s release, who bashed the movie while their parent companies made heaps of money on magazine sales, D'Angelo aptly noted the media's role in the hype. After mentioning that *Esquire* planned to feature a cover on one of the film's stars (Ewan McGregor), he wrote, "Why? Because *Episode III* is guaranteed to make a gazillion dollars and sell magazines. The media is part of the problem."

D'Angelo continued on his tirade, writing that the reason awful movies continue to come to theaters is because they continue to make money, which is a valid point and economically true, but his opinion of the *Star Wars* prequels is not in line with the majority. He seems to have thought he was speaking for the masses, though, as he wrote, "... most people were disappointed by the previous two films," which is patently untrue. Most people were not disappointed by either, as discussed earlier in the book.

Sam McManis of *The News Tribune* had his own cynical take on the positive reviews awarded to *Revenge of the Sith*. He wrote, "But part of me, the cynical and conspiracy-minded part, thinks the critics finally caved in to audience pressure." McManis observed how little critical opinion matters to shaping the success or failure of movies at the box office or with audiences. As he noted, many films like *Meet the Fockers* received mostly lousy reviews, yet made huge amounts of money, like $279.3 million for the popular *Meet the Parents* sequel. Despite tepid reviews, with only a few overwhelmingly positive ones, *The Phantom Menace* became the third highest grossing movie of all time on its first release. No matter what critics had to say about *Revenge of the Sith*, its success was assured.

As McManis mentioned in his article, because of the increasing use of the Internet by the core group of moviegoers, in other words mostly young people, critical opinions from major newspapers or magazines have lost their importance and relevance. They no longer are much more meaningful than small online review sources. RottenTomatoes.com includes reviews from numerous Internet sources alongside major publications, all weighted equally, while MetaCritic.com includes major critical reviews alongside user ratings. Critical consensus in major publications alone is not enough to sink a big blockbuster, at least with the proliferation of alternative review sources. While older audiences may care more about critical reviews, younger audiences are usually unconcerned or even openly defiant of critical reviews and film criticism in general. Hollywood is more interested in young moviegoers, too, as they make up a larger portion of the moviegoing public.[3]

McManis also observed how film criticism has become something of a form of entertainment, rather than a guide for moviegoers on which films to see. As an example, SomethingAwful.com has a hilarious database of film reviews, almost all focusing on awful movies that nobody would truly want to see, but the reviews are entertaining because of the lousy qualities of the films under review. As of December 2006, Google listed thirty-six review sites under the category "Humorous." Not surprisingly, many of the review sites that aim for a humorous edge focus on awful movies, like MoviesThatSuck.com and HorrorMoviesThatSuck.com. With more emphasis placed on entertainment than critical analysis, no wonder many serious critics are dismayed at their seeming irrelevance at times, though film fans still often appreciate their insights.

---

3.   For 2005, moviegoers 12–29 represented almost half of total admissions, according to the Motion Picture Association of America. In fact, moviegoers 12–24 increased 1.5 percent while the fifty and older demographic decreased by the same margin.

Drinking the Kool-Aid

Many critics applauded Ian McDiarmid's masterful performance as Supreme Chancellor Palpatine, who by the end of the film crowns himself Emperor Palpatine, otherwise known as Darth Sidious, Dark Lord of the Sith. McDiarmid was arguably the strongest actor in all of the prequels, and received well-deserved recognition for his role in the story arc, especially with *Revenge of the Sith*. Din Yalonen for the *Catholic New Times*[4] wrote that McDiarmid was "deserving of an Oscar for best-supporting actor" while Gary Arnold of *The Washington Times* was convinced that "Mr. Lucas has encouraged Mr. McDiarmid to steal his scenes."

James Verniere of *The Boston Herald* wrote, "British stage actor Ian McDiarmid, who first played the role in 1983's *Return of the Jedi*, channels Margaret Hamilton's Wicked Witch of the West brilliantly." Todd McCarthy from *Variety* called McDiarmid's performance a "dominant turn" and "worth writing home about." Looking through the reviews, one would have trouble finding a single negative word about McDiarmid's performance. Rather, most critics showered him with praise. If not for the reluctance of most awards groups to acknowledge *Star Wars* artistically, McDiarmid likely would have been at least nominated for an Oscar and many other accolades.

Once again, as with the second prequel, critics seemed unsure what to think of Hayden Christensen's acting as Anakin. While Yalonen compared Christensen to Robert DeNiro in *Raging Bull* (1980) and said that Christensen "handled complex and dramatic emotions with confidence, bravado, darkness, and humour," Peter Travers of *Rolling Stone*, who hated *Revenge of the Sith* as well as the other prequels, wrote that "to merely call him wooden is an affront to puppets everywhere" (87). Travers enjoys trying to be witty in his numbingly incoherent film reviews for *Rolling Stone*, though taking his opinions seriously is difficult when he does not seem to take his job of reviewing movies seriously enough to reduce the wit in favor of meaningful analysis.

As an amusing aside, fans adopted one of Travers's comments, which told viewers to "drink the Kool-Aid" (87) in reference to his belief that nobody could in fact enjoy the prequels, and used it humorously. On forums, fans began "Kool-Aid Brigades" or jokingly mentioned how good the Kool-Aid tastes. One could safely say that Travers takes himself more seriously than any *Star Wars* fans take him. For a critic to value his own opinion highly enough to judge that any fans who disagree with him must have "convinced themselves otherwise" (87), espe-

---

4.   According to its Web site, CatholicNewTimes.org, the paper ran into financial problems and has ceased publishing operations as of November 26, 2006.

cially when he is in the minority of the critical community too, is pompous and arrogant to the extreme. Why Travers has enjoyed such a long run with a large publication when he blasts almost every blockbuster that comes to theaters is puzzling. Suffice to say, he is not on the list of top critics for many *Star Wars* fans.

While Travers hated Christensen's performance, Jim Beckerman from *The Record* seemed to have no problems with it. "Christensen, to be sure, does convey the ominous pride that goes before the fall," he wrote in his overwhelmingly positive review. In another fairly negative review, Desson Thomson of *The Washington Post* was not impressed with Christensen, seemingly on superficial grounds, as he wrote, "How could Hayden Christensen, a pouty-lipped twenty-something you'd expect to see handing you a tall decaf latte over the counter, be Darth Vader?" Richard Bacon of *The People* disagreed, though, writing, "Christensen, who last round wasn't 100 percent convincing as Anakin, really nails the part—just as his evil nature grows, so seemingly does Hayden's ability to act." With such a wide range of dissenting opinions, one observation seems paramount: critics who liked the movie liked Christensen while those who did not like the movie did not like him. Perhaps the latter group did not consume enough Kool-Aid before reviewing the film.

Ewan McGregor drew praise for his role in the film from most critics, although fewer seemed to focus on his performance compared to Hayden Christensen, who was more of a polarizing presence. James Verniere from *The Boston Herald* wrote, "McGregor is best of all, alternating between urbane Hugh Grant–like quips ... and Alec Guinness–type gravitas." Chris Tookey disagreed, writing, "Ewan McGregor as Obi-Wan is abysmal," but he also hated the film in general. In a gushing review of the film, Rick Curnutte Jr. wrote, "McGregor is extraordinary in one of the most heartbreaking of all the *Star Wars* trajectories: the man who must destroy his best friend ... his brother."

Although not unanimously appreciated like McDiarmid's performance, McGregor drew a fair amount of praise. Todd McCarthy called McGregor "a steady presence" while Mark Rahner of *The Seattle Times* called his performance "terrific" and wrote, "McGregor settles into Obi-Wan's skin and brings such an irresistible Errol Flynn jauntiness that I'd watch a series of his adventures alone." In general, McGregor fared well, with few critics thinking he did less than a solid job and many applauding his great work.

Because of her diminished role, Natalie Portman did not receive much attention or praise from critics. Farin Jacobsen of *The Fresno Bee* wrote, in criticism of her role, not her acting, "The only featured female in Episode 3 is Padmé, who is only seen either crying or canoodling with Anakin." Other critics partially blamed the script for Portman's failure to shine as an actress. In a review for Zap2It.com, Daniel Fienberg wrote, "Portman ... still isn't enough of an actress to sell dialogue like 'Hold me like you did by the lake in Naboo' without checking out entirely." Jami Bernard of the *New York Daily News* wrote, "Portman's absentee senator paces her living room, displaying not the slightest interest in showing up for work." Claudia Puig of *USA Today* thought her performance was improved from *Attack of the Clones*, though, writing, "Christensen and Natalie Portman ... in particular seem more comfortable and less stilted." Aside from the acting, which adds much of the emotional weight to a movie, another integral part to the mood created is the musical score.

For the sixth time, John Williams composed the score to a *Star Wars* movie, ending an ambitious composing project that began when friend and fellow filmmaker Steven Spielberg introduced the composer to Lucas. Rather than strive for otherworldly sounds, Lucas wanted more of a traditional score to evoke familiar emotions in unfamiliar places. After all, while *Star Wars* takes place in a galaxy far, far away, its timeless appeal comes from the familiar themes of good versus evil, overconfidence versus humility, patience versus impulsiveness, and the numerous other lessons and dilemmas that everyone must confront, even in the Milky Way.

Because of the musical style in the *Star Wars* films, which feature a musical pattern called leitmotif where characters, objects, or concepts (like the Force) are often assigned recognizable themes, Williams had to compose music for roughly two-thirds of each *Star Wars* film. His efforts throughout the saga produced some of the most memorable themes in film history, specifically the Main Title music and The Imperial March. Both pieces of music routinely play at sporting events like football, baseball, and basketball games, and are often parodied or replicated in other films or mediums.

For *Revenge of the Sith*, Williams was able to bring full circle an impressive accomplishment with his prequel music, which was to "create a theme for the boy Anakin and, within it, try ... to suggest Darth Vader's Imperial March," as he told NPR in an interview ("Profile: Theme ..."). In other words, the music for Anakin progresses and darkens, much like the character himself, so the transformation of Anakin Skywalker is mirrored through the musical transformation Williams accomplishes through the prequel trilogy. By the end of *Attack of the Clones*, for instance, fans can hear the first hints of the Imperial March as peace in the Republic is threatened by the growing presence of the Dark Side and the slow but noticeable souring of Anakin's innocence and youthful goodness.

By the final prequel, Williams had perhaps the toughest job of all of the films on which he had worked. While Lucas had to focus on tying together the prequel trilogy with the Original Trilogy, Williams had to compose music that would bridge the gap between the two trilogies and offer a logical connection between the two parts of the *Star Wars* story. Williams recorded a total of about two hours and ten minutes of music for the final *Star Wars* film, an endeavor that took ten to twelve weeks total.

Another challenge of musical composition for film, Williams said in an interview, is trying to vie for attention with the visual elements of a movie. He said, "We may not notice the details of what we hear. And so, a lot of thought behind film composition, the creation of themes ... has to do with the management of the amount of attention we're going to get" (Williams). Williams also observed that a composer must work to make the music cooperate with "a lot of heavy sound effects and other materials that compete for the audience's attention" (ibid.). Nonetheless, during some of the most climactic scenes, the music plays a huge role in the audience's emotional connection to the material.

Williams received widespread praise for his musical work not just on the saga but on the final prequel specifically. Bill Gowen of the *Daily Herald* in Arlington Heights, Illinois, wrote of Williams's *Revenge of the Sith* score, "Williams has taken several of his earlier themes and interwoven them into a sophisticated musical fabric." Anthony Tommasini of the *International Herald Tribune* wrote, "Music plays almost throughout the entire movie, and much of the emotional resonance critics are finding is stoked by Williams's surprisingly subdued and murky score." In his review for *Variety*, Todd McCarthy wrote, "John Williams also seems to have put extra effort into his virtually continuous score, which increasingly invests familiar themes with darker and richer tones." In a three-and-a-half-star review for *Cinefantastique*, Jeff Bond wrote that the score "crowns an amazing 28-year musical achievement with grace and power."

Role Reversal

Though not applicable to reviewers of the films' musical scores, the usual role film critics have as experts in film knowledge compared to average moviegoers is somewhat reversed and made irrelevant with a franchise like *Star Wars*, a likely point of frustration for many critics over the years. For the average film release, blockbuster or art house film, one can assume that a film critic has a much wider base of cinema knowledge from which to draw than an average moviegoer, not only because most film critics are older than the core moviegoing audience, but also because film critics have made it their profession to study and analyze movies critically.

Critics look at movies from a different, usually more knowledgeable perspective than average moviegoers, comparing elements in films under review to past works and film movements or traditions. They try to make useful observations about similarities and differences to determine the merits of each movie. Critics' superior knowledge of film history compared to most moviegoers accounts for some of the gap in taste between the two groups. Film reviewers sometimes have seen the same type of movie repeatedly, while teen or young adult moviegoers may enjoy a new movie in the genre because it seems fresh to them, having seen fewer movies of the type.

With *Star Wars*, the usual critical advantage is dissolved for one significant reason: any fan knows more about *Star Wars* than any critic, unless the critic is also a fan. In other words, how could a critic who has seen the *Star Wars* movies only a handful of times possibly offer as educated of an opinion as a die-hard fan who has discussed the movies for hundreds of hours online, perhaps read extensive backstory, scholarly essays in journals and books, and has an immediately accessible databank of knowledge about the story as a whole? Critics were at a huge disadvantage for reviewing the last prequel. Even if they re-watched the previous films before reviewing *Revenge of the Sith*, critics almost always did not have the same knowledge and expertise in the subject area that a die-hard fan possessed.

Because of the gap in knowledge between the two groups, fans are justified for not caring much what critics have to say about *Star Wars;* the fans are the experts on the franchise, not the critics. Whatever comparisons film experts or critics make between *Star Wars* and other movies, or between *Star Wars* and classical literature and mythology, *Star Wars* fans usually already know, and probably much better and in more detail than most critics. After all, any *Star Wars* fan who has posted on Internet forums or read much about George Lucas or *Star Wars*, which would be most serious fans, is acutely aware of the mythological ties as well as the *Flash Gordon*, Saturday matinee serial connections.

Gargantuan hype or not, a new *Star Wars* movie to a critic was just another film to review, given probably about as much time and thought as any other, but to a *Star Wars* fan it was a monumental event, ready to be analyzed for years or decades after release. In a sense, the real experts on the franchise, the die-hard fans, hardly have a chance to express their opinions equally or to as many people as the critics, who are not the experts on the subject, a reversal of their usual role.

The ironic situation is exacerbated when the gap in opinion between the two groups is wide, as with *The Phantom Menace* and *Attack of the Clones*.

A large part of how much anyone will enjoy *Star Wars* beyond a superficial level is how much they put into it. On a purely visual level, few people are unable to appreciate the *Star Wars* films for their visual effects, costume design, set design, and action. Beneath the superficial surface, though, lies a philosophical and mythological core that one can only access through much study, reading, and discussion, each of which takes many hours of devoted effort. To illustrate the point, Mick LaSalle of the *San Francisco Chronicle* wrote of *Revenge of the Sith*, "The picture is laden with plot and difficult to follow, even for someone who has seen every *Star Wars* installment." Seeing every *Star Wars* movie once or twice is insufficient grounds to claim any authority in a review. Lucas makes his movies for himself and for his fans, who have no trouble understanding the plot because they have seen the movies dozens of times.

Jim Windolf for *Vanity Fair* gave one of the better written explanations of the criticisms launched at *Star Wars* and Lucas, though the February 2005 article also provided a nice opportunity for the filmmaker to strike back at critics with his own words. Critics have often contended over the past several decades that the *Star Wars* franchise ruined the art of cinema because it dumbed down audiences' tastes, creating a hunger for special effects and explosions over plot and character development. Ironically, *Star Wars* has more scholarly books published about it than virtually any other film or film franchise in history, focusing on subjects like its religious connections, political allegories, historical allusions, and mythological influences.

In general, Lucas is always unnecessarily humble about his franchise, reiterating that he made the films for adolescents, but in truth they are films deep enough to warrant decades of analysis and discussion from fans, philosophers, and film enthusiasts alike. Lucas addressed the issue in *Vanity Fair*, saying:

> The interesting thing about *Star Wars*—and I didn't ever really push this very far, because it's not really that important—but there's a lot going on there that most people haven't come to grips with yet. But when they do, they will find it's a much more intricately made clock than most people would imagine (Windolf 116).

As with many movies, Steven Spielberg's *Minority Report* (2002) being another great example,[5] audiences can choose to focus exclusively on the visuals and action sequences, but in so doing they miss out on a lot of the richness of the experience.

Film provides an ironic dilemma regarding the introduction of complicated themes to audiences. If a filmmaker has an important philosophical issue to address or complicated themes to present, the most direct way to accomplish such a task is to create a film that, because of its perceived seriousness, will only ever play in art house theaters or will fail commercially in larger cinemas, in all likelihood. If it plays in specialty theaters, the audience it draws will probably already sympathize with its message, thus the "preaching to the choir" dilemma.[6] If, however, directors choose to conceal their messages in commercial films with brilliant special effects, they risk not being taken seriously and having their insightful themes or messages ignored or left undiscovered by many or even most moviegoers, and perhaps critics, too.

By the time every critic online and off gave their opinions about the final *Star Wars* prequel, *Revenge of the Sith* had an approval rating above 80 percent, the highest of any *Star Wars* film on first release, including the 1977 original. Overwhelmingly, critics applauded Lucas's vision and ability to close such an ambitious film project on a high note, emotionally and visually. No comparable project exists in film history, which is to say a story spanning six movies and almost thirty years, all the vision of one man driven to tell a tale of mythological, moral, and cultural significance to many generations, past, present, and future.

With the mostly glowing reviews for *Revenge of the Sith*, RottenTomatoes.com published an objective look at the initial reviews for both *Star Wars* trilogies and all six films in the saga (Duong). The results would shock most people who have read how much everyone, critics and fans, hated the prequels, yet the research is valid and indisputable evidence that vindicates the recent trilogy from much of its unwarranted status as an inferior set of films. Upon their original releases, *A New Hope, The Empire Strikes Back*, and *Return of the Jedi* received 79 percent, 52 percent, and 31 percent positive reviews, respectively, for an average of 54 percent.

By comparison to the Original Trilogy, *The Phantom Menace, Attack of the Clones*, and *Revenge of the Sith* received 62 percent, 65 percent, and 83 percent positive reviews in the prequel release years, respectively, for an average score of

---

5.   *Minority Report* focuses on a deep philosophical issue, namely determinism and free will, but usually discussions about the subject are reserved for philosophy classes and intellectuals. By presenting the material in a blockbuster film with breathtaking visual effects, Spielberg thrust the debate into public consciousness in a way that a more clearly intellectual movie, such as a low budget art house film, could never have done.

6.   Realistically, for instance, probably not many hardcore conservatives see Michael Moore's films.

70 percent, or 16 percent higher than the Original Trilogy. The trend is also reversed: critical opinions of the Original Trilogy decreased with each movie, yet the percentage of positive reviews for the prequels increased with each successive film. While critics finally applauded a prequel for its artistic merits, fans also enjoyed the movie immensely, often ranking it higher on the list of *Star Wars* films than had the critics.

A New *Empire*

With the completion of the original *Star Wars* trilogy, fan and critical opinions of the films improved over time, until the entire trilogy gained its current classic status. *Return of the Jedi* suffered at least twice the percentage of negative reviews compared to any *Star Wars* prequel, yet is today regarded as a classic film, even by critics. History indicates that the prequels will grow in popularity well into the future. Movie fans will have an improved understanding and appreciation of the films as they receive more acclaim and as younger generations of fans become mature adults who grew up with all six *Star Wars* films. The rift between old and new will lessen as the younger fans without a voice in the media begin to enter the work force and assume prominent roles, with mostly fond memories of the prequels. Many young fans already prefer the prequels to the originals.

USA Today ran an article, "Generation flap," that compared the two trilogies and surveyed fans of each trilogy (Bowles). "I watched the originals to learn the whole story, but I couldn't watch them more than once. I like the worlds in the new *Star Wars*," Jean Burton, twenty-two, told the newspaper. Likewise, many fans online, though by no means a huge percentage, also feel more affinity for the prequels than the Original Trilogy. "Every fan I know who is under the age of fourteen seems to like the prequel trilogy more," said Sam Long, seventeen, from Castleton, New York (Long). Lynde Roberts of Billings, Montana, agreed, saying, "I don't know many younger fans who prefer the Original Trilogy, but there are plenty of older fans who enjoy the prequel trilogy" (Roberts).

Diane Kovalcin of New Jersey, though, did not see the connection that *USA Today* tried to make, and that Lucas has voiced, about younger fans versus older fans. "I haven't really seen any difference of opinion with age," she said (Kovalcin). Richard Story of Acworth, Georgia, agreed with Kovalcin, citing differences in the two trilogies as the source of fans' opinions. "I think it is the preference in filmmaking style more than age that creates fans of one set of movies over the other," he said (Story). Story explained that in his opinion, the Original Trilogy's "Saturday morning matinee" style is substantially different from the "grand epic style" of the prequels, leading to possible rifts between supporters of each trilogy, depending on one's stylistic preferences.

Neither Lou Tambone of fan site StarWarz.com nor Mark Newbold of fan site Lightsabre.co.uk thought much of the over/under twenty-five gap, either. "I honestly have a hard time gauging who likes what better ... I've seen all kinds of fans. I've seen young kids who are Original Trilogy fanatics and I've seen the opposite," Tambone said (Tambone). Newbold agreed, speaking more about the rift between prequel supporters and Original Trilogy enthusiasts than any gap between fans of specific age groups. "There is definitely an antagonism between prequel trilogy and Original Trilogy fans, especially those who have little time for the new films," Newbold said (Newbold). He thinks that in time, though, the prequel trilogy will receive more attention, especially *The Phantom Menace*, "a film that I believe matures like a fine wine and will, in time, be seen as the most mythological and biggest in scope of all six films."

The final *Star Wars* film impressed most critics, but it also delighted fans all over the world, including ones disappointed with the first two prequels. *Revenge of the Sith* had such an impact on the fan base that it arguably unseated *The Empire Strikes Back* as the fan favorite of the saga, an almost impossible feat given how entrenched the 1980 film had become with fans in over twenty-five years of viewings and adoration. In a poll on TheForce.net with 39,644 votes that started on May 31, 2005, and closed several months later, 31 percent of fans rated *Revenge of the Sith* the best *Star Wars* film, the largest percentage of any response, while 29 percent rated it second, 22 percent third, 12 percent fourth, and only 1 percent each for either fifth or sixth.[1] On another poll on TheForce.net from late May, fans were asked to rate the film from one to five stars. Eighty-five percent of fans awarded it four stars or higher while less than 5 percent of fans gave it fewer than three stars.

The Empire Strikes Back remains a favorite with many fans, especially the group still disenchanted with the prequels, but among fans surveyed for this book, *Revenge of the Sith* drew the most support, just ahead of its dark Original Trilogy counterpart. Diane Kovalcin cited *Revenge of the Sith* as her new favorite film instead of *The Empire Strikes Back* because "it changed the way I view the other movies." She added, "Frankly, I thought [Vader's] redemption at the end of *Return of the Jedi* was unacceptable—until *Revenge of the Sith*. Now I see Vader as a real person who made fatal mistakes and had a lifetime to pay for them." Lynde Roberts agreed, saying, "I really like all of them but *Revenge of the Sith* seemed to take all of the questions and anticipation from the other movies and really deliver on the expectations placed on it."

---

1.   Numbers do not amount to 100 percent because of rounding.

Sam Long chose *The Empire Strikes Back* as his favorite film, but said the final prequel followed "very closely." Many fans, especially older fans, rank the two darkest episodes of the saga, *Episodes III* and *V*, at the top of their lists. Kevin Gordon of Colorado also changed his favorite film from *The Empire Strikes Back* to *Revenge of the Sith*, like many fans. "Revenge was a darker movie. Bereft of comic relief ... and full of deep emotion. The action was fantastic and the effects were breathtaking," he said (Gordon). "So yes, though I might have done a few things differently, it is now my favorite *Star Wars* movie," Gordon concluded. Contributing to his fondness for the film, he said, "It was everything I had expected since I read the *Return of the Jedi* novelization. It evoked so many emotions that no other *Star Wars* movie ever had."

Lucas has his own take on the fan reactions to his three prequels, similar to the view promoted in *USA Today*. He said:

> We have two fan bases. One is over twenty-five and one is under twenty-five. The over-twenty-five fan base is loyal to the first three films. They actually are in their thirties and forties now, so they're in control of the media, they're in control of the Web, they're in control of everything, basically. So mostly, what you're hearing from are people over twenty-five years old (Germain "'Star Wars' Tidbits ...").

As usual, Lucas's analysis is insightful. In my own experience trying to promote my book on *The Phantom Menace*, I encountered several members of the media who would not talk to me about my book unless I was going to talk about all of the film's weaknesses and mistakes alongside its miserable commercial failures, even though my book not only argues otherwise but proves beyond any doubt that the film was a massive success financially. As a result of my unwillingness to renounce my positive position on the first prequel, I had no success promoting *Anticipation* with several media outlets.

Hope exists for the future, however, as the younger fans begin to make their voices heard. I had always hoped that *Anticipation* would serve as a tool for the younger generation of fans to combat the negativity that developed in the media and reverse the trend as fans warmed to the earlier prequels after the release of *Revenge of the Sith*. Echoing my own curiosity, Lucas said, "I'm curious to see what happens in about ten years when that other group starts to get their voice. How they'll remember it. I hope they remember it as one movie" (ibid.). Already, a significant minority of *Star Wars* fans prefers to consider all six movies as though they are one large film, one story, so that to ask which one is best or preferred is as ridiculous as asking which chapter in a great book is the best.

Because all of the films in the *Star Wars* saga are necessary to the complete story, each one contributes meaningfully like a chapter in a book, so many fans feel that to judge one movie qualitatively as better or worse than another is illogical or at least unnecessary. Sam Long said, "No one seems to really comprehend that each movie is a chapter of a story. They are too busy critiquing the movie by itself without looking at the broader view." Dave Gohman of Schaumburg, Illinois, agrees, saying, "Each movie is great not only because of what they each bring to the table, but because together they bring it all to the table" (Gohman). Long made a keen observation about a problem with many film critics reviewing films in the franchise. "Critics spend too much time attacking each movie separately. They fail to recognize the connections between the chapters.... The whole set of movies needs to be critiqued as one to truly understand the *Star Wars* experience," he said.

Many celebrity fans voiced their opinions about Lucas's new film, too. Director Kevin Smith, who is one of the most well known *Star Wars* fans in Hollywood, called the film "the prequel the haters have been [aching] for" (Rickey). Smith has included numerous *Star Wars* references in his films over the years, from *Clerks* (1994) to *Jay and Silent Bob Strike Back* (2001) through *Clerks II* (2006). Other celebrity reactions came after a screening for film and television celebrities at Skywalker Ranch, during a special edition of MTV's *Total Request Live* (*TRL*). The band Good Charlotte performed in front of the Main House at Skywalker Ranch before the screening. Billy Martin, guitarist and keyboard player for the group, said, "This movie is dark and it *should* be dark.... Hayden does such a good job holding back in the beginning of the film, that by the end of the movie your jaw is on the floor from how evil he becomes" ("Vader ...").

A few actors in attendance also voiced their support of the movie after it screened. Topher Grace from *That '70s Show* said, "I'm a big fan of the Original Trilogy, but I really found myself getting emotional as I was watching Anakin's fall in *Revenge of the Sith*" (ibid.). Michael Rosenbaum, who has done an excellent job showing the moral grayness and deterioration of Lex Luthor on television's *Smallville*, could identify with Anakin and his fall to the Dark Side. He said, "I was torn for Anakin Skywalker because the Jedi put him in this position in a way, so you feel more for the villain" (ibid.). Rosenbaum called the film, "... everything a *Star Wars* fan wants out of the final episode." Other stars like Elijah Wood, Seth Green, and Macaulay Culkin also attended the special screening.

Two lucky fans had the opportunity to watch the film with the celebrities for the *TRL* event. J. C. Reifenberg won a trivia contest months earlier that allowed him to take a friend, Neil James Cunningham, to see the movie at the private screening at Skywalker Ranch, with all expenses paid, including airfare, hotel, and prizes. "I think I was a fan since the first time I saw *Return of the Jedi*" at only two and a half years old, Reifenberg said ("MTV ..."). After the screening, Reifenberg spoke briefly with George Lucas, who gave him a hug after the conversation turned emotional. Cunningham, happy to be at the screening as well, said, "I went to film school because of [Lucas] and his movies, and it was very inspirational getting to meet him and talk to him just for a few minutes" (ibid.). Reifenberg gave his approval to the film, calling it "a perfect bridge from the two prequels to the Original Trilogy."

On the other end of the spectrum, M. Night Shyamalan had nothing but negativity for the prequels and much of *Star Wars* as he said, "The first *Star Wars* was religion, the second one was a great ride, but by the third, the series began its slide" (Rickey). He continued, "Has the Force lost its force? Who would not answer: yes?" First, perhaps the tens of millions of fans worldwide who were excited about *Revenge of the Sith* would answer emphatically no. Second, almost every *Star Wars* fan thinks of *The Empire Strikes Back* as at least equal to *A New Hope*, and usually *Empire* is the fan favorite of the Original Trilogy.

Third and finally, the same could be said of M. Night Shyamalan's directing career, which is to say it has lost whatever force it once had. *The Sixth Sense* (1999) was a great film. *Unbreakable* (2000) was a very good film, if not perfect or classic. By *Signs* (2002), everything started to deteriorate[2] until his 2006 film, *Lady in the Water*, which David Cornelius of eFilmCritic.com wanted to "punch in the face" and that forced Sean Burns of *Philadelphia Weekly* to question, "Has M. Night Shyamalan lost his damn mind?"[3] The film later won its creator Razzie awards for Worst Supporting Actor and Worst Director (Leopold). Maybe Shyamalan should consider trying to accomplish one-tenth as much as Lucas, or start with showing some filmmaking ability in the new century, before publicly criticizing the *Star Wars* master's work to the media.

For many fans, the prequel trilogy changed their views of the Original Trilogy and thus the saga as a whole. "Absolutely," said Diane Kovalcin, "the prequels really fleshed out the Original Trilogy, making everything they did sharper and more tragic." She added, "I think some of the characters became much more vivid—Palpatine and Vader, especially." Lynde Roberts agreed, saying, "All of

2.   Any time clichéd aliens come to a planet covered in water only to discover their weakness is exposure to water, one wonders who let the script pass through pre-production.

3.   Both quotes from "Lady..."

the characters from the Original Trilogy have more meaning ... you really feel more sympathy for Anakin/Vader that was never there before." Sam Long added, "Now we realize the much deeper connections between all the characters," and "we now truly appreciate Yoda's mastery of the Force, having witnessed him wield a lightsaber." Many fans appreciate knowing more about a few of the Original Trilogy characters, a task the prequels accomplished.

One article from *The Scotsman* provided an unusual look at the *Star Wars* saga from a franchise virgin, Emma Cowing, who claimed never to have seen any of the films before 2005. In an experiment for her column, she finally watched them all, in order of the chronology, *Episodes I–VI*. Her reactions were amusing to read as few fans can imagine what future generations might think of watching the movies not in the order they were produced, but in the order Lucas intended from a story-telling perspective.

Though Cowing did not seem too interested in the franchise or the story itself, she noted how many of the prequel foreshadowing scenes or in-jokes she simply could not understand. Having heard *The Empire Strikes Back* was the best of the series, she writes, "Nuh-uh." Instead, she "loved *Revenge of the Sith*" and wrote, "For my money it was by far the best film in the series. Brilliantly acted, amazingly shot, the true heart of the story in every sense." She also mentioned the saga's most annoying character, Chewbacca for her, who is "for my money 100 times more annoying than Jar Jar Binks," she wrote.

Cowing enjoyed the saga as a whole, calling it "two spectacular, if flawed, trilogies," but she did not come to the same conclusions as long-time fans, who lived through the *Star Wars* movies and grew up with them. She wrote, "If you watch *Episodes I–III* first, your heart belongs to these three movies and their main protagonists. Luke? Leia? Han Solo? Who cares? I didn't." She continued, "By the end of *Return of the Jedi*, the only character's fate I was interested in was Darth Vader's," which helps demonstrate the success Lucas achieved in crafting a six-part story about the rise and fall of Anakin Skywalker.

Fans who find Cowing's perspective shocking might want to consider the advice of a wise old Jedi who once said, "Many of the truths we cling to depend greatly on our own point of view." For future generations of fans, Chewbacca and his incessant growling may not always be "endearing" and Jar Jar's accent and dialect may not always be "annoying." Rather, fans are free to choose for themselves which characters they like best, after growing up with all six movies. Looking at the saga twenty years after the release of the last prequel will be a worthwhile undertaking, not only to study the effect of time on the series, but also to examine the changing opinions of fans toward individual parts of the story.

Original Trilogy purists, who blast the prequels and seem never to have been particularly interested by the other half of Lucas's epic story, often complain, as have critics, that the prequels' problem is no Luke Skywalker, no Han Solo, and no Leia Organa. The prequels are missing the old favorites many people grew to love having seen the films in the seventies and eighties, but a new generation of fans may respond similarly to the Original Trilogy: no Padmé Amidala, no Jedi Anakin Skywalker, no Yoda fighting, no Mace Windu, and no Jedi in their prime. In other words, attachment to characters is a matter of perspective and often nostalgia.

The Original Trilogy is not better than the prequel trilogy in any respect objectively, it is simply different, so while many fans love one and hate the other, many more fans are able to embrace both and appreciate their similarities and differences. If fans look at the two trilogies as interlocking stories that form one larger epic, they will probably have a more positive view of the franchise as a whole. The prequel trilogy is more politically detailed than the Original Trilogy, however, which drew widespread commentary from the media and stirred fan discussion as well.

The Politics of *Wars*

Critics often complained that the first two prequels had an overabundance of political dialogue and exposition, otherwise known as character and plot development, yet many of the same critics complained that *Star Wars* is too simplistic or childish and that Lucas emphasized special effects and action over deeper story elements. Din Yalonen wrote in his review of *Revenge of the Sith* for the *Catholic New Times*, "*Revenge* is edited masterfully; there is not a single line of slow-paced political dialogue, [like in] *Episode[s] I* and *II*. As a political 'junkie,' I personally missed that element." Because most of the first two prequels take place during peacetime, the point of the films, and thus why both have an abundance of political dialogue, is to show how the fall of democracy and the rise of injustice do not occur during war, but before it. Ultimately, *Revenge of the Sith* demonstrates how elected leaders can use war as the ultimate excuse to reduce personal liberties and solidify a dictatorship.

In his review, Yalonen called into question what critics in general wanted or expected out of the prequels. He suggested that the first two episodes had perhaps too much "slow-paced political dialogue," yet he also wrote that he enjoyed the political conversations. Yalonen seemed to be making the assumption that most moviegoers are uninterested in political dialogue, even when it is relevant to the plot, but he was interested in it as a political "junkie." One would assume that critics, being supposedly a more educated group of people than the general moviegoer, would applaud Lucas for engaging political issues in mainstream entertainment and trying to provide more than simple, mindless fun at the movies, yet sometimes the opposite was true.

Many critics, including the ones who gave Lucas's first two prequels positive reviews, still complained about the subject of the dialogue and how it weighed down the story, which is curious given that the prequel story is largely about the politics of the Republic and how it rotted from within. Lucas, in various interviews, emphasized that one of the biggest themes of *Star Wars*, besides the pseudo-religious redemption of Anakin Skywalker at the end of *Return of the Jedi*, is the cyclical nature of politics. Speaking about the greater message of *Star Wars*, Lucas said, "You start out in a democracy, [which] turns into a dictatorship, and rebels make it back into a democracy" (Goodale "Why …"). Complaints about the first two prequels' political dialogue and emphasis are simply without basis. The stories are political, so the dialogue is necessarily political as well.

In 1999, one of the big subjects for critics and detractors of *Star Wars* upon which to dwell was the supposed racism in *The Phantom Menace*, specifically the Jar Jar Binks character, who fans and critics derided on many additional levels. The racism allegations were ridiculous, but by 2005 mostly forgotten. In fact, in a July 1, 2005, editorial for *USA Today*, Lois Hatton explained all of the ways that the saga slays stereotypes and promotes understanding, not prejudice. She wrote, "Director George Lucas shows that we can't judge people (or otherworldly creatures) by their appearance. In his films, the most unlikely characters emerge as heroes." She explained how Yoda, while short and strange looking to Luke at first, is powerful and wise, while Obi-Wan, a "crazy old hermit" according to Luke's uncle, is in fact a great warrior and a brave man. Hatton also noted how Princess Leia defied the typical damsel-in-distress cliché by being a strong, independent woman. She concluded, "Age, race and gender are never adequate ways to measure a person's worth. At the very least, *Star Wars* taught us that."

In 2005, another controversial subject came along with the final *Star Wars* film, not as serious as allegations of racism, but still a popular topic of discussion. Many critics saw parallels between the politics of *Star Wars* and the Bush administration in the United States. Because the prequel trilogy is a cautionary story about how a dictatorship can arise from a democracy through staged wars and the removal of various freedoms, many people thought the trilogy was an allegory for the United States after the 9/11 attacks. The issue first arose publicly at the Cannes Film Festival, though many additional reviews brought up the subject as well.

A year earlier, *Fahrenheit 9/11*, the Michael Moore documentary, had raised much political debate at the Cannes Film Festival. Many people at Cannes in 2005 noted similarities between Emperor Palpatine's rise to power through war, from a senator to Supreme Chancellor to crowning himself Emperor of the Galaxy, to President Bush's war on terrorism and invasion of Iraq. The controversy at Cannes soon spread throughout many reviews of the film, launching commentaries and editorials around the world, also eliciting occasional mentions on political news programs.

One line specifically bears mention, as many critics later noted. Anakin says to Obi-Wan before the climactic battle that decides the fate of the Chosen One, "If you're not with me, then you're my enemy." The line is remarkably similar to Bush's comments after the September 11 attacks, where he told the international community, "Either you are with us, or you are with the terrorists." Both lines are absolute statements, and as Obi-Wan tells Anakin after his comment, "Only a Sith deals in absolutes." McDiarmid commented on the line, saying he did not think it was specific to Bush. "I know that's the line that George Bush said, but many other people who have run countries have said it before," McDiarmid said as he went on to cite Slobodan Milosevic, former president of Serbia and Yugoslavia who was guilty of numerous war crimes (Caro).

Although many people at Cannes noticed parallels and similarities, Lucas only half acknowledged them. He said, "As you go through history, I didn't think it was going to get quite this close. So it's just one of those recurring things" (Germain "Cannes ..."). He never mentioned the president by name, nor was the prequel trilogy written to reflect current events in any respect; the story started in the 1970s, after all. Bush was not even in office when the prequel trilogy began. Lucas joked, "When I wrote it, Iraq didn't exist" (ibid.). In fact, Lucas wrote the backstory to *A New Hope*, which later became the prequel trilogy, at a time when he was greatly influenced by the Vietnam War and the Nixon-Watergate scandal.

In an anonymous editorial published in *The Wichita Eagle*, the author saw the politicalization of *Star Wars* as a small tragedy at a time when the movie should have brought together people of many ideologies and political views. The author wrote, "The politicization of the film may play well on the fringes, and play into real-world battles ... but it also lends a lasting taint to something that had seemed like unadulterated entertainment" ("Even ..."). Despite praising the film's story as being told "extraordinarily well," the author felt that "in the process of gaining a last film in the series, we lost something, too."

Robert Denerstein of the *Rocky Mountain News* agreed with *The Wichita Eagle* editorial. He wrote in his review, "Some things made me wonder: *Episode III* speaks to the political moment in ways that are less than mythic—and possibly at odds with the *Star Wars* spirit." In an unsigned article, a writer from *The Wall Street Journal* disagreed, writing, "In truth, the themes of 'Star Wars' are so universal, and so familiar (like Darth Vader, Satan is a former good guy gone over to the dark side), that they can be read any way one likes." Other critics, though, took issue not only with Lucas including political allegories, but the specific references they read into the movie.

Six years earlier, John Podhoretz had written a positive review of *The Phantom Menace*, blasting critics who complained about the movie as "whiny." He wrote that his prejudice before seeing the film was "overcome by the movie's wondrous look and by its fascinating, multilayered plot." In the six years between the first and last prequels, Podhoretz seemed to undergo his own transformation to the

Dark Side, of film criticism. Podhoretz, a conservative political columnist with the *National Review*, blasted Lucas and *Revenge of the Sith* for the political connections in the film. He wrote in a May 17 blog entry on The Corner, part of the *National Review Online* (*NRO*) Web site, "Lucas has basically all but said Vader is George W. Bush." To be fair, the comment was somewhat of a side note to an attempt at humor in a post bashing the commercialism of *Star Wars*, specifically Vader marketing M&M's.

Understandably, a number of fans chose to e-mail Podhoretz about his review, as usually happens to critics or commentators when they bash *Star Wars*. In response, as part of another post on The Corner titled "Jedi Warmongers," Podhoretz called Lucas "an incompetent storyteller" and told fans to "move out of your parents's [*sic*] basements and join an Internet dating service before you lose all of your hair." The comments seem like pretty harsh criticism from a guy who praised Lucas's talent and storytelling six years earlier. Podhoretz's review of the final prequel, however, had few mentions of politics whatsoever; only on *NRO* did he blast the film politically.

The supposed political messages of the film, and the anti-Bush theme that some people found, offended one group enough to call for a boycott of the film. The "Patriotic Americans Boycotting Anti-American Hollywood," originally located at pabaah.com,[1] called for moviegoers to stay home rather than contribute money to a film that questions the value of politics and foreign policy based on moral absolutes. Clarence Page, a *Chicago Tribune* columnist, could not understand the uproar over the film's politics, writing that people will see what they wish to see. He concluded, "I think Lucas has a larger, age-old message: If democratic societies like ours are not eternally vigilant, the next evil empire might be us." Most critics had few problems with the politics in *Star Wars*, even if they noticed connections.

A. O. Scott of the *New York Times* also saw a connection between *Revenge of the Sith* and current political situations. He wrote:

> You may applaud this editorializing, or you may find it overwrought, but give Mr. Lucas his due. For decades he has been blamed (unjustly) for helping to lead American movies away from their early-70's engagement with political matters, and he deserves credit for trying to bring them back.

---

1.   The Web site moved to FireHollywood.com by the time of writing.

Scott noted that the film is about much more than current political situations, however, and has a more universal, timeless theme. He concluded his review with a mention of the *Star Wars* films' focus on a cyclical nature of history, writing, "Democracies swell into empires, empires are toppled by revolutions, fathers abandon their sons and sons find their fathers." In other words, political comparisons are possible largely because history repeats itself and at some point, current events are bound to mirror *Star Wars* as the saga portrays the full repeating cycle of history.

Aside from monopolizing entertainment media nationwide, *Star Wars* also made political news shows such as *The O'Reilly Factor* for its alleged political connections. O'Reilly said on air that Lucas, besides being a genius, is "also a Marin County liberal who sprinkles in some dopey political stuff. But in my opinion, it was so insignificant, I hardly even noticed." Although O'Reilly called many of the connections "political nonsense" and did not seem too interested in taking the allegories seriously, he applauded the film technically, saying, "And I've never quite seen anything as good, technically, as that movie. And you've got to go see it in the theater. You can't see it at home."

The discussion on *The O'Reilly Factor* included film critic Richard Roeper and Belinda Luscombe, arts editor for *Time* magazine. Roeper said of the anti-Bush allegations, "If [Palpatine's] the evil senator working from within, and really it's a large civil war that's in place here, what does that have to do with George Bush as the President of the United States and his policies?" Roeper did not see the connection, adding, "If George Lucas wanted to make a commentary on that ... I think he would have drawn a straighter line." Luscombe added, "I think clearly, it's not necessarily anti-Bush; it's anti-totalitarian, which a lot of people say is the same thing." In other words, people who are extremely anti-Bush are apt to see Palpatine, the personification of evil, as having much in common with Bush.

Lucas could not have foreseen that his prequels would in any way resemble current events when he first wrote the story, nor did Producer Rick McCallum expect such a connection at the time of filming. Padmé says after Palpatine crowns himself Emperor, "So this is how liberty dies: with thunderous applause," which is a line that drew a fair amount of attention from critics and political commentators. "I didn't expect that to be true," Lucas said of the line, then laughed (Caro). McCallum had his own commentary on the political connections:

> First of all we never thought of Bush ever becoming president, or then 9/11, the Patriot Act, war, [and] weapons of mass destruction. Then suddenly, you realize, 'Oh, my God, there's something happening that

looks like we're almost prescient.' And then we thought, 'Well, yeah, but he'll never make it to the second term, so we'll look like we just made some wacky political parody of a guy that everybody's forgotten' (ibid.).

McCallum added that he thought the French, and the rest of Europe, would love the movie because of its political commentary and that Europeans would be more likely to "respond to the film on the political level."

Political connections aside, Lucas has always been more interested in older history, which is partially why, for instance, the Imperial officers and troopers in the Original Trilogy bring to mind Nazi Germany. Lucas wanted to know, "Why did the senate, after killing Caesar, turn around and give the government to his nephew?" or "Why did France, after they got rid of the king and that whole system, turn around and give it to Napoleon? It's the same thing with Germany and Hitler" (Germain "Cannes ..."). Because of the nature of the *Star Wars* story, which has from the beginning focused on a galaxy in turmoil, Lucas grew interested in researching how democracies turn into dictatorships, sometimes with the full support of the electorate.

Lucas's research led him to craft a politically intriguing trilogy of films that slowly, deliberately demonstrates how a powerful, ingenious man, who is devious enough to forge such a goal, can impact the peaceful state of a republic behind the scenes. It also shows how such a man can then perpetrate a false war between Separatist forces threatening the Republic and a newly created army of clones to safeguard the Republic. The Separatists give Supreme Chancellor Palpatine the opportunity to wield a massive "Army of the Republic" to counter their threat, which then allows Palpatine to ask for ultimate control of the galaxy to safeguard it from war and restore the peace. In other words, a manufactured war allows for war-time actions, such as reducing civil liberties and increasing the powers of the Supreme Chancellor. In time, because of the war he created, he is able to convince many of the galaxy's inhabitants that dictatorship is preferable to the previous democracy, which failed in its attempts to preserve peace and safety in the galaxy.

Having done the historical research on how dictators come to power and how good governments are corrupted, Lucas used his knowledge to plot the prequels, and *Revenge of the Sith* specifically. He said:

> You sort of see these recurring themes where a democracy turns itself into a dictatorship, and it always seems to happen kind of in the same way, with the same kinds of issues, and threats from the outside, need-

ing more control. A democratic body, a senate, not being able to function properly because everybody's squabbling, there's corruption (Germain "Cannes …").

While many critics relentlessly blasted *The Phantom Menace* for its focus on "the taxation of trade routes to outlying star systems," the point of such political meandering and squabbling was to show, as Lucas did over the prequel trilogy, what happens when a political body is unable to act swiftly and appropriately even on minor issues. The senate, as one can see in retrospect, was primed for a takeover by a stronger man, like Senator Palpatine.

Despite the controversy over whether Lucas's film takes sides politically or criticizes the Bush administration, at least a few critics found the political allegories compelling. Raphael Shargel of *The New Leader* wrote, "This summer I am in the embarrassing position of finding my tastes corresponding with the box office numbers," apparently never a circumstance in which critics want to find themselves. He continued, "George Lucas' *Revenge of the Sith* strikes me as not only more entertaining, but also more politically astute and dramatically compelling than the serious drama *The Interpreter* or the critical favorites *Crash* and *Unleashed*." Shargel added later, "But whatever its shortcomings, *Revenge of the Sith* is a bona fide science fiction masterpiece." He also mentioned how the film was destined to be one of the few tragedies in the box office top ten for the year.

Despite Bush's low approval rating, many people were not happy with the idea of Lucas bashing a current political leader in a popular blockbuster, but Shargel observed that much of the film "borrows broadly from world history," such as "the rise of imperial Rome and Nazi Germany." Nonetheless, he conceded, "but [*Revenge of the Sith*] makes a few striking nods to the present day as well. Its plot concerns an unpopular leader who gains the adoration of a great republic by waging an unnecessary war." The parallel is less than perfect because Bush did not receive the adoration of many citizens for the Iraq War.

While most of the critics and commentators who saw political connections in *Revenge of the Sith* picked a side either for or against their inclusion, James Pinkerton, a columnist for *Newsday*, saw the connections and did not seem to care either way. Instead, he thought Lucas wanted some critical acclaim at last and possibly awards recognition, not to mention better overseas box office numbers. "Will American audiences flock to a Bush-bashing movie? Perhaps not. Maybe fewer tickets will be sold here, but more will be sold overseas, where Bush-bashing sells," Pinkerton opined. Nonetheless, he seemed more convinced that Lucas's political allegories came from a desire to achieve critical, not commercial, success. He wrote, "In the meantime, Lucas will have those awards, honors, and 'top 10' lists to look forward to. There are some things that can't be bought with money; they can only be bought with ideology."

Pinkerton, ultimately, should probably not quit his job as a writer and try to become a psychic. *Revenge of the Sith* won few critical awards and had more success in the United States than in most other countries worldwide. Additionally, international critics did not seem to applaud the political connections any more than their North American colleagues. For fans who saw similarities between the final prequel and the political situation in the United States, Lucas said, "You've got to remember that the rebels win in the end. Darth Vader is vanquished. Don't forget the ending. Don't get stuck on *Episode III*" (D. Cohen "The Darth …"). The *Star Wars* saga is a myth, after all, and through the six-episode story, Lucas conveys his optimism that good always triumphs over evil, eventually.

As far as adding political connections for awards attention, Lucas did not expect or give much thought to awards. He said, "I don't really care that much about that part of it. I like awards when they're given to me. I'm not going to go out and try to get an award. I don't really care. If they come to me, it's great" (Fulton "Leaving …"). Although the first *Star Wars* film received numerous award considerations, including Oscar nominations for Best Picture, Best Director, and Best Screenplay, Lucas and *Star Wars* have never had much success at major Hollywood awards shows thereafter. The films have continued to inspire generations of moviegoers and led scholars to examine their messages and stories, though.

Understanding *Revenge*

To some extent, Lucas understands the criticisms of his first two prequels, but he believes that most of the story criticisms come from improper expectations and misunderstandings, a view that many fans share. Lucas told fans in a newsletter from the Official *Star Wars* Web Site:

> The first trilogy—Book One—is about the father, while the second trilogy—Book Two—is about the children. When you combine them together they become one big piece. When I told people that Episode I was about a ten-year-old boy, people panicked, and they said it wasn't going to work because everyone wanted to see Darth Vader going around killing people. But I really wanted to be thorough about telling the story about where Darth Vader came from. When I did the second film, people were mortified that it was going to be a love story. But we got through both of those films, and people were excited for Episode III to see the rest of the story ("Braving …").

In other words, although fans might have thought the prequels should begin with *Revenge of the Sith*, much of what makes Anakin's journey worth watching and what makes the final prequel such a powerful movie is the setup that the first two prequels accomplished. Without being able to see Anakin as a young boy, full of generosity and promise, seeing his ultimate fall would not be as emotionally gripping or as potent.

Viewers' enjoyment of the prequels largely depends on whether they believe what Lucas says about the focus of the *Star Wars* story. While many casual enthusiasts and critics have complained that the prequels suffer from a lack of Harrison Ford, Mark Hamill, and Carrie Fisher, Lucas made the films to emphasize that the *Star Wars* story is primarily about Anakin Skywalker, not Luke and his friends; Luke's purpose is to redeem his father. "You can buy this or not, but I actually felt compelled to get the story I always wanted to tell on the record. It was Darth Vader who made the sacrifice by killing the evil Emperor who had seduced him," Lucas said (Lawson).

For fans who choose not to believe Lucas, the prequels could understandably seem like irrelevant backstory to the other main characters of the Original Trilogy. But when one considers Anakin as the main character, the prequels become invaluable in telling half of his story, focusing on how he rose to power and fell to the Dark Side. Without the prequel trilogy, Darth Vader in the Original Trilogy is a much more two-dimensional character, not to mention his redemption in the saga's final film is dramatically not as meaningful.

As with the other *Star Wars* prequels, *Revenge of the Sith* has jokes and references that only *Star Wars* fans are likely to understand. For instance, when Obi-Wan kills General Grievous with a blaster, he tosses it aside afterwards and says, "How primitive!" In *A New Hope*, Obi-Wan tells Luke that blasters are "clumsy and random," but that lightsabers are "an elegant weapon for a more civilized age." Thus, *Revenge of the Sith* underscores Obi-Wan's distaste for using blasters except out of necessity, which is a nice minor character detail. Ahmad Faiz of *New Straits Times* wrote, "Such a remark would have been more suited for the prissy [C-3PO] than the Jedi Master," demonstrating that many times critics who are not well versed in the saga simply miss important and witty references.

The close attention to detail and background stories help make *Star Wars* such a rich experience. The Official *Star Wars* Web Site published an article in late May about the visual details for which fans may want to watch in *Revenge of the Sith*, typically called "Easter Eggs." The article read, "You simply cannot take in all the detail of a *Star Wars* movie in one sitting. So intricate and meticulous is each shot that every image tells a rich story," which is part of the reason fans see the films again and again ("Episode III Easter ..."). The article continued, "In some cases, that story is kind of funny—a cleverly placed nod to audience members who know where to look." For instance, in a nice nod to fans and a small connection to the Original Trilogy, the *Millennium Falcon* is visible in an establishing shot of the Senate docking bays.

One valid criticism of *Revenge of the Sith*, which is not much of an issue in the complete *Star Wars* saga, is the limited presence of Senator Amidala. The original script of the film, which is a must-read for die-hard fans, contains numerous scenes with Senator Amidala and her colleagues talking about rebellion and the direction of the Republic. Unfortunately, because Lucas had such a large story to tell with *Revenge of the Sith*, he had to cut almost all of Natalie Portman's political scenes, choosing instead to focus the story almost exclusively on Anakin Skywalker and his fall to the Dark Side.

As a result of focusing on Anakin's story, much of the strength and depth of Portman's character is lost. Instead of being a strong, assertive woman as she is in both of the previous prequels, she becomes more of a plot device than a character. She exists to give birth to the twins, Luke and Leia, but her death is also a plot device. Because Anakin foresees her tragic demise, he betrays the Jedi Order to join Darth Sidious in an unsuccessful attempt to stop the inevitable. As a result of the limited number of scenes with Portman playing a significant role, many critics seemed not to comment on her performance at all, occasionally mentioning how little screen time she had or how the final prequel lacked a strong female presence.

Lucas admitted that the film had to focus on Anakin because of time constraints, a decision he perhaps regretted in some ways but that became necessary regardless. He said to *Premiere*, "It's Anakin's story, and so I said, 'Anything that does not involve Anakin I have to get rid of.' I had to kind of shove [material on Obi-Wan and Padmé and R2-D2] in sideways" (Roston 56). Many of the deleted scenes that Lucas filmed are included on the DVD release, though, which gives fans at least a knowledge of what happened off screen, if one wants to see them that way. Although she could have benefitted from more scenes in the final cut, Padmé's final pleas to Anakin, and her subsequent death knowing her husband has turned to evil, are some of the more powerful scenes in the film and in the saga.

Revenge of the Sith is a rare blockbuster because of its tragic ending, while the prequel trilogy is unique in film history because it ends on a downer. Although the box office champion, *Titanic* (1997), is also a tragedy, it is based on real events and it connected with audiences largely because most people are familiar with the tale of the Titanic itself. The Titanic story represents somewhat of a classic demonstration of a failed attempt on humanity's part to conquer the expanse of nature. By contrast, Lucas's story is fictional. The franchise itself encompasses numerous licensees that normally do not coordinate promotions with tragic movies. In general, tragedy does not sell commercially because people like to go to theaters to escape the many problems of the real world, so they expect to leave theaters feeling uplifted. No matter its quality as a film, *Revenge of the Sith* is not uplifting.

Fortunately, Lucas was uncompromising in his vision and never tried to lessen the tragedy of *Revenge of the Sith*. While many critics and less-observant fans thought the first two prequels were somehow upbeat, optimistic movies, Lucas had in fact set up the tragedy from the beginning of the trilogy. He showed the smallest tinges of darkness in *The Phantom Menace*, then established the framework in *Attack of the Clones* for the ultimate fall of the Republic, the rise of the Sith, and the betrayal of Anakin Skywalker.

By the end of the prequel trilogy, the hero has turned to evil, dictatorship has replaced democracy, the Jedi are mostly dead, and the primary female star dies at the darkest moment, having only her newly born twins to show for a life of service and dedication to the principles of democracy, justice, and equality. The audience knows Padmé's twins will together save her husband, form an alliance to restore the Republic, and bring peace to the galaxy, but she does not. She dies in desolation.

While perhaps the visual effects are almost not worth mentioning because everyone knows that the *Star Wars* films always broke new barriers in effects technology, the dramatic impact of the effects work should not be overlooked. Aside from the incredible planets and vistas created mostly with digital technology, present in all of the prequels, the best effects work in *Revenge of the Sith* is not a lightsaber battle or a planet or an amazing space battle; it is a character fans have known for more than twenty-five years: Yoda. The facial expressions that Yoda conveys, if the Academy of Motion Picture Arts and Sciences allowed digital characters to win Oscars, should have at least given Yoda a nomination. Critics and fans applauded the digital Gollum in *The Lord of the Rings*, but Yoda took digital character animation to new levels.

While Yoda has many great scenes in *Revenge of the Sith*, including a discussion with Anakin earlier in the movie about his spiritual crisis and dreams about a loved one's death, his best scenes come near the climactic finale. While on the Wookie homeworld of Kashyyyk, Palpatine gives Order 66, the infamous command to the clone troopers to destroy the Jedi. As the Jedi begin to die one by one, already a painful sight, moviegoers are shown a close-up of Yoda as his shoulders and body almost go limp, his expression conveying more pain than most accomplished human actors could manage. In one simple shot, with no dialogue, Lucas's effects crew added emotional weight to the events occurring in the galaxy and conveyed perfectly the sense of sorrow Yoda must feel at the time. For hundreds of years, he has trained Jedi, advised the Republic, and safeguarded freedom, but in one moment he can feel a ripple through the Force that threatens to undo all of his efforts and cast a dark shadow over the galaxy for years to come.

Revenge of the Sith, and *Star Wars* as a whole, has many messages beneath the incredible visual effects and amazing action sequences. Politically, *Star Wars* has much to say about history. The saga argues that people want democracy and freedom, but when they are not vigilant, and when they fail to heed the bigger issues in favor of minor squabbles like trade route taxation, tyranny and corruption soon develop, which if unchecked lead to dictatorship. It also indicates people are willing to surrender freedom and sometimes democracy itself for security. Even with many people fighting for good, like the Jedi and a strong group of senators, collective apathy and rampant corruption outweigh efforts to preserve democracy.

Revenge of the Sith shows the ultimate culmination of events that led to the fall of the Republic and dictatorship for the galaxy. The Republic failed not primarily because of the actions of one or two people, like Anakin and Palpatine, but because of the numerous people who failed to take action and instead fell into complacency, such as the Galactic Senate. British political philosopher Edmund Burke is often credited with saying, "The only thing necessary for the triumph of evil is for good men to do nothing."[1] With the Republic, as with Nazi Germany, to place all of the blame on the dictator at the top is to ignore all of the people below who tacitly approved through inaction or through compliance.

Aside from the historical sources from which Lucas drew some of his story, *Revenge of the Sith*, like the past *Star Wars* films, has numerous religious themes and connections.[2] Mustafar, the fateful lava planet where Obi-Wan and Anakin face each other for the first time in combat, brings to mind traditional Judeo-Christian visions of hell. If the *Star Wars* galaxy has a hell, surely it must be Mustafar. That Anakin would find himself in a physical hell at the same time as he is in emotional hell is not surprising given the presence of other Christian themes present in the prequel trilogy as a whole.

The prequel trilogy begins by showing Anakin as a Jesus figure, apparently the result of a virgin birth, according to his mother, Shmi Skywalker. Jedi Master Qui-Gon Jinn discovers Anakin on Tatooine, a planet similar to the desert environment where Jesus spent his youth as well. Like Jesus, Anakin performs miracles, like racing pods, which no other humans can do without Jedi reflexes. *Revenge of the Sith* shows Anakin as Jesus fallen from grace, a savior who has lost his way.

Anakin has great power and ability in the prequels, to use for good or evil, but tempted by Darth Sidious, as close to the devil as one will find outside of the Bible, he chooses a dark path. Obi-Wan screams to him during the duel, "You

---

1. Although Burke is given attribution for the quote, none of his works has the quote, of which there exist many variations, nor is it clear whether he said it at all, though his ideas and writings suggest a similar message (Porter).

2. Along with Dr. Rachel Wagner, I co-authored an essay titled, "'Hokey Religions and Ancient Weapons': The Force of Spirituality" in *Finding the Force of the Star Wars Franchise: Fans, Merchandise, & Critics* (Peter Lang 2006). For a more thorough discussion of religious themes running through the *Star Wars* prequels, especially Taoism, Buddhism, and Christianity, refer to our essay.

are the Chosen One! You were supposed to destroy the Sith, not join them! Bring balance to the Force, not leave it in darkness!" By the end of the prequel trilogy, Anakin has betrayed the faith that the Jedi had in him, demonstrating what would have happened had Jesus accepted the devil's offer of great power while in the desert (Matt. 4:8–9). Palpatine makes a similar offer to Anakin when telling him that the Dark Side offers the power to prevent death.

The parallels between Palpatine and the devil continue in other areas of the film, too, though less obviously to the casual viewer. Palpatine's Order 66, the ultimate act of cementing his place as ruler of a new empire, also has biblical ties. The number 66 is close in appearance to 666, which in the Book of Revelations 13:18 is the number of "the beast," which "stands for a person," although like much in the Book of Revelations, the passage is cryptic and unclear. The passage reads, "One who understands can calculate the number of the beast," but biblical scholars have made many attempts at such calculations and come up with wildly varying results.

A common suggestion about 666 seems to be that a society without cash, relying instead on computer chip implants, would fit with Revelations 13:17 (Blank). The passage reads in part, "no one could buy or sell except one who had the stamped image of the beast's name or the number that stood for its name." In some sense, then, worshipping the devil ("the beast") and the coming of the end of time is represented by 666. Without a means to buy or sell goods easily, chaos would ensue. Though Palpatine is not a perfect representation of the beast from Revelations, he sets in motion events that lead to chaos and war in the galaxy.

Lucas's inclusion of the number, or at least part of it, reinforces his desire to reference classical mythology and prominent religions. While 666 relates to the worship and acceptance of the devil, Order 66 has similarly sinister ramifications as it represents the victory of the Sith over the Jedi, evil over good, and the Dark Side over the Light Side. It also represents the coming of "the dark times," as Obi-Wan Kenobi calls Imperial rule in *A New Hope*. Despite the Christian parallels and references, the prequel trilogy is more strongly connected with Eastern religious traditions because of its moral ambiguity.

The Judeo-Christian tradition focuses much more on absolutes, like right and wrong, good and evil, and sinful or not sinful, whereas traditions like Taoism and Buddhism are not as dualistic. Consider, for instance, Obi-Wan's quote, "Only a Sith deals in absolutes," which is hardly favorable to dualistic religions like Christianity. One has to wonder, given Lucas's opposition to the Iraq War and the Bush administration, if he was trying to suggest that, in a time where nations rely on one another more than ever before, the types of absolute moral judgments that the Judeo-Christian West holds are incompatible with forming a peaceful world where differences are tolerated and other cultures appreciated. The same could be said of Islam, which bears more similarities to Christianity and Judaism than it does any Eastern religion.

The prequels introduce much more gray area into the morality of *Star Wars* compared to their predecessors. Instead of having just the Evil Empire, a clearly repressive, totalitarian regime full of similar-looking people with British accents, and a Rebel Alliance that employs the help of aliens of all sorts in an effort to restore democracy to the galaxy, the prequels show a murky Republic against Separatist forces whose motivations are somewhat unclear. In fact, the Separatists' motivations must be unclear because the organization is run by several competing interests. Many of the Separatist leaders are justified in their wish to secede from the Republic, which has turned sour and rotten with corruption. Darth Sidious, though, has encouraged and supported the Separatist movement while his alter-ego, Palpatine, has taken office as the Supreme Chancellor of the Republic with the intention of destroying the Separatists to hasten his political ascent.

The Republic, not only because of the corruption and bureaucratic ineptitude already witnessed in *The Phantom Menace* but also because of Palpatine's rise to power and the militarization of the government, is definitely not the clearly delineated force of good that the Rebel Alliance represents in the Original Trilogy. The Jedi Order is the only clear representation of good in the prequel trilogy, yet its ranks have also suffered from the presence of the Dark Side. Count Dooku left the Jedi Order to join the Sith and by the end of the trilogy, the most promising Jedi Knight, Anakin Skywalker, has betrayed and helped destroy the Order.

As the opening crawl reads for *Revenge of the Sith*, "Evil is everywhere." Coincidentally, the political situation in the prequels mirrored current events in much of the world at the time of the film's release. Instead of a clear enemy to attack and destroy, like the Empire in the Original Trilogy, often likened to the former Soviet Union, the presence of evil is felt but not clearly seen in the prequels, like terrorism in the twenty-first century.

Though the religious and political connections are fascinating to examine, ultimately what makes *Revenge of the Sith* such a powerful, masterful movie is the way the mythology is woven together, effectively joining the two trilogies and completing the story arc. While tragedy is not uplifting, the prequels try to show how unchecked ambition in an extraordinarily talented individual can lead to ruin not only for him but for the people and organizations his life touches. As an examination of what makes a villain along with how a republic turns into a dictatorship, *Revenge of the Sith*, and the prequel trilogy as a whole, is resoundingly successful.

At the end of *Revenge of the Sith*, a movie filled with death and destruction that seems to invite a feeling of hopelessness as ten thousand years of democracy ends, the guardians of peace and justice are massacred, and a savior falls, a sliver of hope remains. At twilight on a desolate planet in the Outer Rim, a survivor of the massacre uneventfully delivers a baby boy to two unassuming moisture farmers. Just like a seedling at the end of a forest fire, the boy is destined to help restore what was lost, for he is Luke Skywalker, son of the most promising Jedi ever; he is a new hope. At the box office, analysts saw *Revenge of the Sith* much the same way, hoping it could help bring new hope to a struggling year.

Light Speed to Prosperity

The Pedigree of a Savior

The *Star Wars* films have always been hugely successful at the box office, ever since the first entry in 1977 catapulted past *Jaws* (1975) to claim the title of highest grossing movie ever. It retook its crown in 1997 with the *Special Edition* re-release, defeating *E.T.* (1982) and climbing to $461.0 million, where it ranked second behind 1997's *Titanic* ($600.8 million) at the time of release for *Revenge of the Sith*. *The Empire Strikes Back* was also hugely successful in 1980, collecting $222.7 million before its 1997 re-release, though 1983's *Return of the Jedi* improved upon its predecessor's numbers with $263.8 million before its re-release.

By the time the final prequel arrived in theaters, *Return of the Jedi* ranked eighteenth on the list of the top grossing films with $309.3 million, compared to $290.5 million for *The Empire Strikes Back* in twenty-second place. Unfortunately, since their re-releases, the films have lost many positions to newer entries, with *Empire* having been ranked ninth after its re-release and *Jedi* seventh. With its massive gross, *A New Hope* had not been as assailable and had not lost a rank since 1998 when *Titanic* overtook it. Since it captured first place on its initial release, *A New Hope* has never ranked lower than second on the all-time list. With future re-releases, the movie may never drop out of the top five, especially as box office grosses continue to struggle with the rising popularity and success of the home theater market and other emerging technologies. Movie downloads on iTunes and the possibility of pay-per-view broadcasts coinciding with theatrical releases also threaten to cut into theatrical moviegoing in the future.

As for the prequels, the best indicators of success for *Revenge of the Sith*, they both proved formidable forces at the box office, though *Attack of the Clones* experienced more of a dip than many people expected. *The Phantom Menace* still reigned as one of the most successful summer blockbusters of all time when the final prequel came to theaters. It had only lost two ranks since 1999, one to the re-release of *E.T.* (pushing the classic film's box office gross to $435.1 million) and one to *Shrek 2* (2004), which barely passed the prequel with $441.2 million.

At $431.1 million, *The Phantom Menace* ranked as the fifth highest grossing movie of all time and had given the prequel trilogy a huge start at the box office.

Attack of the Clones made $310.7 million, good for eleventh place at the box office at the time of its release, but only nineteenth by the opening of *Revenge of the Sith*. The unusual number of big blockbusters in the three-year period pushed the second prequel far down the list. It also was the only *Star Wars* film not to be the highest grossing film of its release year, which is a dubious distinction for which *Revenge of the Sith* aimed to atone. The dip, however, was not wholly surprising as the middle installment of the first *Star Wars* trilogy also dropped significantly (almost 32 percent) from its predecessor's success, despite no drop in perceived quality. Likewise, many fans felt *Attack of the Clones* was superior to *The Phantom Menace*, but the box office results do not reflect fan opinion.

Because of a massive marketing campaign, incredible hype from fans and the media, largely fantastic reviews, and the reality that *Revenge of the Sith* would be the last *Star Wars* film ever, expectations for its box office performance were high among analysts and casual observers. Aside from mere speculation about its box office potential, analysts and studio executives again looked to *Star Wars* to save a down year from falling box office grosses. By mid-May, the box office for 2005 was already down 6 percent compared to the previous year, making the success of the final prequel more important for the collective psychology of film industry players. "Everyone is looking to this to turn things around," said Paul Dergarabedian of Exhibitor Relations, the primary box office tracking firm for major studios (Newman). When *The Phantom Menace* came to theaters in 1999, box office revenue was also down a few percent, but with a strong summer schedule the deficit evaporated and the year beat 1998 handily. Many people hoped the same would be true of summer 2005.

For almost three months preceding the release of *Revenge of the Sith*, every weekend's box office revenue was down compared to the comparative weekend a year earlier, an unprecedented losing streak in the multiplex era. Many analysts and cultural commentators wrote articles about the declining attendance, focusing not just on 2005 but the several years leading up to it as well, during which time attendance generally declined even when revenue rose.[1] Most analysts believe that competition from increasingly realistic video games, superior home entertainment systems with high-definition televisions and sophisticated DVD

---

1.   Ticket sales peaked in the modern era at 1.63 billion in 2002, but fell each year through 2005, down to 1.51 billion in 2004, the first full year before the final prequel's release ("Americans…").

players, and rising ticket prices have cut into the importance of the theatrical moviegoing experience. "People have their DVDs, their video games, their iPods—it just takes a whole lot more than before to get people to come out to the movie theater," said Paul Dergarabedian (Goodale "Will ..."). Consider, for instance, that DVD sales and rentals had reached $21.2 billion per year for 2004, compared to $9.5 billion for theatrical film revenue (ibid.).

According to an Associated Press-America Online poll of one thousand adults taken from June 13–15, 2005, most Americans would rather watch films at home than in theaters ("Summer ..."). In the poll, released June 16, a whopping 73 percent of adults said they prefer watching movies at home on DVD, videotape, or pay-per-view. Only 22 percent of respondents said they prefer seeing movies in the theater. Even more amazing, considering that moviegoing used to be a weekly event for many people in the Golden Age of cinema in the 1930s and 1940s, about a quarter of people surveyed said they had not seen any movies in theaters in the past year. Although many people, as with the introduction of television in the 1950s and VHS tapes in the 1980s, wrote about the possible demise of theaters, Lucas strongly disagreed. "Going to the movies is a social event, like going to a football game, like going to the ballet, like going to a play.... I don't think that's ever going to go away," he said ("Americans ...").

The poll called into question many analysts' opinions about competing technologies, however. Results indicated that people who use DVDs, watch films on pay-per-view, download movies from the Internet, and play computer games go to theaters more often than people with similar incomes who do not use the aforementioned technologies. Nonetheless, one still has to assume that competing technologies at least reduce the frequency of moviegoing as a whole. In other words, if nobody had video games or the Internet, they would likely go to more movies. Nobody should be surprised to learn that as a whole, people who watch more movies in general, whether on DVD or pay-per-view, probably watch more movies in theaters, too, but that does not mean the presence of numerous other forms of entertainment and technology have no influence on moviegoing habits.

With the box office returns diminishing and attendance slumping, *Entertainment Weekly* also focused an article on the future of the theatrical film business (Hayes). While David Tuckerman of New Line insisted that better movies would cure the slump, other people had more proactive ideas. For instance, filmmaker Steven Soderbergh had recently announced that he planned to release six films in theaters, on DVD, and on cable simultaneously, as part of a deal with 2929 Entertainment. The idea challenges the traditional business model for film distribution, where movies enter theaters, play for several months, then are available at home through pay-per-view or DVD. Other industry players, along with Lucas himself, pushed for upgrades in theater technology, like digital projection and IMAX, to give people an experience at the movies that they cannot duplicate at home.

Carmike Cinemas took advantage of the rough box office season by acquiring GKC Theaters in advance of *Revenge of the Sith*'s opening day. After adding 30 theaters with 263 screens in Illinois, Michigan, and Wisconsin from GKC Theaters, Carmike ran 311 theaters with 2,471 screens by June 30, 2005. "We were able to complete the acquisition of GKC Theaters on the targeted date of May 19th in order to take full advantage of the opening of *Star Wars: Revenge of the Sith*, the biggest film of the summer," said Michael W. Patrick, president and CEO of Carmike Cinemas ("Carmike ...").

With only three movies having crossed $100 million at the box office before *Revenge of the Sith*'s release, including *Hitch*, *Robots*, and *The Pacifier*, analysts expected the prequel to inject some life into the box office receipts. Early summer films with substantial hype, namely *The Hitchhiker's Guide to the Galaxy*, *xXx: State of the Union*, and *Kingdom of Heaven*, failed to generate much interest from moviegoers whatsoever; not one of them crossed $55 million total. "If anything can stop that kind of weak box office, it's *Star Wars*," said Fox Domestic Distribution President Bruce Snyder (Hernandez "The Force ...").

Most industry analysts wondered whether the box office weakness was more an issue of the quality of films in release, where *Star Wars* might save the day, or a fundamental shift in moviegoing habits. "We're seeing a real shift, and I think it's the beginning of a trend. There's the old adage that if you have good movies, people will come. But we're at the point when new technology has finally begun to eat into traditional moviegoing," said Peter Sealey, a marketing professor at University of California at Berkeley and former president of Columbia Pictures (Stanley "Can ..."). The increasingly large opening weekends, where new films not only break records for revenue but also for attendance, have shortened the waiting time for major films to come to DVD, too, which further encourages people to delay seeing films until their home video releases.

Traditional industry wisdom says that big blockbusters help the entire marketplace, not just the studio releasing them, because they expose moviegoers to more upcoming movies and, if they are popular with audiences, provide a good experience that people want to duplicate by returning to theaters. Paul Dergarabedian said, "Moviegoing begets moviegoing. It helps the other movies that are upcoming to have a big movie in the marketplace. If people aren't in theaters and [are] not exposed to trailers and marketing materials, it hurts future potential business" (Hernandez "The Force ...").

The industry hoped *Star Wars* would again bring moviegoers back to theaters and start a big summer at the box office. Bruce Snyder lamented the expectations heaped upon the prequel, saying, "Everybody is kind of laying the ills of the industry on this movie. I do think it's a big burden to put on the shoulders of one movie. But if there is such a movie that can handle it, this is it" (Halbfinger). The first prequel also faced such a burden, though it had plenty of help at the summer box office to make for a record-breaking summer.

Fans and moviegoers interested in betting for or against the success of *Revenge of the Sith* could place their bets online with PinnacleSports.com, which offered a bet on the opening weekend, three-day gross for the final prequel against *Spider-Man*'s $114.8 million record from 2002. In 1999, Intertops.com had offered a similar bet with *The Phantom Menace* against *The Lost World: Jurassic Park* (1997), but had lost money when the first prequel was unable to top the dinosaur film's opening weekend gross. Initially, PinnacleSports.com had *Revenge of the Sith* at a 6:1 longshot, but when 80 percent of bettors picked *Star Wars* to win, the odds changed to 11:5 ("Bettors ...").

Another bet on the prequel, which convinced 60 percent of bettors to stick with the Force, had the prequel beating the $134.8 million four-day opening record held by *The Matrix Reloaded* (2003). The opening odds were 2:3 while the odds immediately before release had moved to 5:9, so the betting site thought the prequel was a favorite to pass *The Matrix Reloaded*. Additionally, the over/under for the film's three-day opening was set at $96 million initially, though rose to $101 million. Finally, fans could bet on whether the prequel would make $300 million domestically by September 1, which strangely was set at 7:5 odds ("PinnacleSports.com ...").

PinnacleSports.com did not have a corner on the gambling market for the film's grosses, however; Sportsbook.com also joined the action. The gambling site offered a much lower over/under, at $85.5 million, and another over/under for the highest grossing day of opening weekend, at $35.25 million. Marketing Director Alex Czajkowski said, "*Star Wars* is the most famous movie series of all time. Offering people the chance to bet on the film just adds to the excitement" ("Sportsbook.com ..."). Like PinnacleSports.com, Sportsbook.com did not think *Revenge of the Sith* had a strong chance to beat *Spider-Man*'s three-day opening weekend gross.

As with other major blockbusters, such as *The Phantom Menace* in 1999 where the issue became particularly hotly contested, other studios wanted time slots

before *Revenge of the Sith* to play trailers for their films, anticipating huge exposure from the prequel. Many studio executives felt that if they shaved their trailers
down to sixty seconds, they would have a better chance to earn a coveted advertising spot (Horn and Lee). Ultimately, exhibitors have the final decision on which
trailers are to play before a movie. Several distributors, however, mentioned that
Lucas prohibited them from running more than five trailers before the film in an
effort to save fans the agony of absurdly long waits for the movie to start.

Trailers, so called because they used to follow the feature film not precede it,
are one of the most effective ways to let moviegoers know of upcoming releases.
Dick Westerling, a spokesman for Regal Cinemas, called trailers "one of our best
marketing tools, especially when you can program them in front of so many moviegoers" (Horn and Lee). Only 20th Century Fox enjoyed guaranteed placement
for its movies, though, because it distributed the prequel. As such, it attached previews for *Fantastic Four* and *Mr. and Mrs. Smith*. Other studios also sent trailers
for their high-profile films, which included: *Batman Begins, Cinderella Man,
Stealth, The Chronicles of Narnia: The Lion, The Witch, and The Wardrobe, The
Island, War of the Worlds*, and *Wedding Crashers*. Not all of the trailers sent
received placement before the film at each theater, however.

At Fandango.com, the nation's largest online and phone movie ticketing service,[2] advance tickets went on sale for *Revenge of the Sith* on April 15, more than
a month in advance of the film's release. For *The Lord of the Rings: The Return of
the King* (2003) and *Harry Potter and the Prisoner of Azkaban* (2004), Fandango
accounted for 8 percent of their respective opening weekend box office grosses
("May the Fandango ..."). For *Fahrenheit 9/11* (2004), the online ticket company accounted for an even more impressive 13 percent of its total first weekend
ticket sales (ibid.). Fandango President and CEO Art Levitt said, "We hope and
expect that online ticket sales for *Star Wars* will go through the roof" (ibid.). In a
poll on the Web site, 67 percent of moviegoers voted *Revenge of the Sith* the summer film they most wanted to see. Fandango film commentator Richard Horgan
wrote in a column that "*Sith* has a certain must-see factor because its the end of
the saga and a major event in film history" (ibid.).

By May 6, the prequel had accounted for 79 percent of Fandango's weekly
ticket sales, increasing its sales 75 percent from the previous week ("The Force is
Strong with Sith"). Additionally, a poll on Fandango's Web site indicated that 80

2.   Fandango at the time sold tickets to roughly 1,100 theaters representing 12,500
screens, or about 70 percent of all theaters in the United States with remote-ticketing
capabilities ("The Force is Strong with Sith").

percent of movie fans planned to see the film opening weekend. At two weeks before release, no movie had ever sold as many tickets on Fandango as *Revenge of the Sith*. Art Levitt said, "The final installment of the *Star Wars* saga is clearly attracting not only the long-time fans, but also mainstream ticket buyers throughout the country. Based on our advance sales, *Sith* will likely enjoy one of the largest opening weekends in box office history" (ibid.).

Fandango's results were duplicated by the Internet's other major ticket seller, MovieTickets.com, Moviefone's ticketing Web site. No film in the five-year history of MovieTickets.com had sold as many tickets before its release as *Revenge of the Sith*, which also set a record for the company by marking the earliest it had ever sold advance tickets for a movie ("Star Wars: Revenge of the Sith Selling …"). The company re-launched its Web site in time for the release of the final prequel to add power and ease of use for the millions of people logging in to buy movie tickets for the prequel and other upcoming releases ("MovieTickets.com Unveils …").

Not everyone in the film business was happy about the opening of *Revenge of the Sith*, which became clear when Quebec independent exhibitors boycotted the film (Tillson). In 1999 with *The Phantom Menace*, and again to a lesser extent with *Attack of the Clones*, many theater exhibitors complained about the harsh terms and strict conditions that Lucasfilm and 20th Century Fox set for the prequels to play in theaters. The studios demanded that *Revenge of the Sith* play in the largest auditorium for twelve weeks and that 70 percent of the ticket sales for the first two weeks be returned to the studio, with 65 percent returned for the three weeks following. Usually, studios ask for 70 percent from the first week, 60 percent for the second, then declining 10 percent each week until it hits the fifth weekend at which point the cut moves to 35 percent. Out of eight hundred screens in Quebec, the boycott affected only about fifty.

Most theaters did not want to miss the opportunity to have thousands of movie fans come through their doors. In one industry tracking report that *Variety* mentioned before the film's release, 45 percent of respondents knew *Revenge of the Sith* was opening during the weekend without being prompted first (Snyder "A force …"). More than half of males surveyed said it was their first choice at the movies for the weekend, while about a quarter of women responded similarly.

Theaters prepared for the unprecedented demand among the moviegoing public in various ways, including increased security and additional showings. AMC representative Pam Blase said, "We're already encouraging our theaters to add 6:30 [a.m. showings]" (ibid.). Likewise, Regal, the nation's largest theater chain, wanted to keep pace. Dick Westerling said, "In many of our locations, we are adding a second late-night show starting around 3:00 a.m. We also have some theaters that are going to run *Star Wars* around the clock on opening day" (ibid.). The opening for *Revenge of the Sith* dominated media reports, online ticketing, and the film industry to such a degree that rival studios had planned no other movie openings in wide release and the distribution heads for Paramount, Sony, and Universal were all on vacation the Tuesday before the film's opening (ibid.).

Despite the expectations for *Revenge of the Sith* at the box office from analysts and fans, George Lucas had revealed much more modest expectations. In an interview with *Empire* magazine in 1999, Lucas had said the final film would be "very, very, very dark" ("*Star Wars: Episode 3* ..."). Though *Titanic* is a tragedy and became the highest grossing movie ever made, Lucas was not as sure about the financial success of his final prequel. He said, "It will probably be the least successful of the *Star Wars* movies—but I know that" (ibid.). The filmmaker is notoriously humble about his expectations, however, and has often underrated the ability of his franchise to amaze and excite audiences.

Unlike Lucas, political commentator Bill O'Reilly had wild expectations for the box office success of the last *Star Wars* movie. In a discussion about the political messages a number of critics saw in the film, O'Reilly took the time to make a box office prediction that the movie would be the biggest ever. "You know why? The stoned slackers are going to see this ten times" for the visual effects, he insisted. When Belinda Luscombe of *Time* magazine asked Bill where they would find the $100 to see the movie ten times, he responded, "Trust me, ... stoned slackers, they may be ... but a lot of these guys are whizzes at what they do. They've got money. They wouldn't be stoned all the time if they didn't have money, Belinda. Come on. They need money to get stoned." Stoned or not, the Jedi faithful showed up in force for the movie's theatrical premiere nationwide.

Intergalactic Record

Revenge of the Sith opened on Thursday, May 19, in 3,663 theaters and roughly 9,400 screens. It became the second *Star Wars* film to open on May 19, along with *The Phantom Menace* six years earlier. The release date also mirrored the Original Trilogy pattern, where *A New Hope* and *Return of the Jedi*, the first and last of the trilogy, opened on the same date, May 25, while the middle install-ment, *The Empire Strikes Back*, opened earlier (May 21). *Attack of the Clones* had opened May 16, the earliest of any of the films.

No *Star Wars* movie had enjoyed such a wide opening as *Revenge of the Sith*, with *The Phantom Menace* premiering in 2,970 theaters and *Attack of the Clones* opening in 3,161. Of the total theaters playing the film, about 2,900 offered midnight screenings, which in the time since *The Phantom Menace* came to theaters had become commonplace among major blockbusters. Many film fans forget that prior to the first prequel, no blockbusters ever opened at midnight, no matter how anticipated. The final prequel began breaking records immediately, with $16,912,367 just from its midnight showings.

Many theaters offered at least three midnight screenings, with some theaters using every auditorium to screen the final prequel. "We'll be counting the grosses for a while. It's an absolutely remarkable number. It seems like the industry got kickstarted last night at midnight," said Bruce Snyder (Fuson). By comparison, the previous record holder for midnight showings was *The Lord of the Rings: The Return of the King* with $8.0 million, paltry by comparison. *The Phantom Menace* had earned around $7.5 million from midnight and early morning showings. *Attack of the Clones* made roughly $6.2 million from its first showings. "This is extremely impressive. It just says so much about how excited people are to see this film that they lined up at midnight and just got on board and went along for the ride," said Paul Dergarabedian of *Revenge of the Sith*'s midnight performance ("'Star Wars' grosses …").

The amazing midnight showing grosses were possible largely because theaters continued to add screenings of the film up to the last minute, molding supply to meet demand through a process known as interlocking, where one print can be used to show the film on multiple screens. One theater in metro Atlanta, the Regal Hollywood 24, showed the prequel on eleven separate screens at midnight, providing an astonishing number of seats for one theater (Longino). Even with many screens showing the film, numerous theaters sold out most or all of their midnight showings before opening day. The Loews Boston Common had already sold out nine of its ten midnight and 12:45 a.m. screenings by the day before release, for instance (S. McCarthy). The AMC Fenway 13 in Boston had sold out all five of its midnight screenings (ibid.). Digital screenings proved more popular where offered; the Boston Common sold out every digital showing through opening day by May 18.

In Tulsa, Oklahoma, the Starworld 20 sold out its first midnight showing weeks in advance of opening day, though the theater had five prints of the film ready to accommodate demand. Jonathan Potter, manager of the Starworld 20, said, "When there's a big show like this, it changes a lot of what we do" (Evatt). For instance, extra staff is required for such a huge event picture. "Midnight showings are a real hassle, because we have to have people here to 3:00 a.m.," Potter added. The theater also opened earlier to add more show times, which is a concession that many theaters nationwide made for at least opening day and often through opening weekend.

The South Barrington AMC 30 in Illinois sold out twenty-eight screens playing the movie at midnight. The fifty-two hundred moviegoers caused an hourlong traffic jam early in the morning, forcing the police to offer four officers in assistance. Sergeant Sam Parma of the South Barrington Police said, "When you've got two lanes to get people out there's only so fast you can move the cars" (Ordower). The Force apparently had a large presence in Chicago because the AMC Cantera 30 devoted all thirty of its screens to *Revenge of the Sith* and still sold every ticket available, filling all six thousand seats.

In Los Angeles, the ArcLight sold out nine "midnight" showings (12:01., two at 12:05, 12:10, 12:15, 12:20, 12:21, 12:30, and 12:40), a 3:30 a.m., and a 6:30 a.m. show, making for eleven sold-out shows before dawn (Snyder "'Sith' is already ..."). The ArcLight had showings at close intervals for twenty-four hours. Another nearby theater, The Grove, sold out six midnight showings. Aside from the ArcLight, AMC's Burbank 16 and 30 both boasted twenty-four hour screenings, along with the AMC Long Beach Stadium 26. In Cincinnati, the Newport on the Levee theater used all twenty of its screens to play *Revenge of the Sith*, selling out four thousand seats (Eigelbach). By the Sunday before its opening, midnight showings for the prequel had sold out in 75 percent of AMC theaters, 85 percent of Century theaters, 83 percent of Regal theaters, and 77 percent of Loews theaters, according to data Bruce Snyder shared with the media (Hernandez "The Force ...").

By the end of April, the AMC Lynnhaven 18 in Virginia had already sold out one auditorium for its midnight screening and nearly sold out a second, with plans already underway to add a third (Vincent). As the release date neared, many theaters added more show times at midnight or in the early morning hours, with the freedom to play the prequel in as many auditoriums as they had available. Bruce Snyder said, "Some theaters started with five or six screens and ended up showing it on fifteen or eighteen screens at midnight because they had that freedom with no other movies playing at that hour. They kept selling tickets and adding more screens" (Hernandez "'Sith' Set ..."). With Fox still counting the monstrous midnight grosses, *Revenge of the Sith* added to its massive total as the day progressed.

For its first full day, *Revenge of the Sith* set opening day, single day, and Thursday records with $50,013,859. The previous record holder for a single day was *Shrek 2*, with $44.8 million on its first Saturday in theaters, which was its fourth day of release. *Spider-Man 2* had held the opening day record with $40.4 million when it opened on a Wednesday in June 2004. "Fifty million is a good opening weekend, let alone a single day. This is the box office equivalent of a one-hundred-year flood," said Paul Dergarabedian (Gentile "'Star Wars' Breaks …"). As a result of its huge opening day, the prequel became the first movie to crack $50 million for a single day. Fox was happy with the result, too. "It's staggering. It's probably 20 percent more than I thought we could do," said Bruce Snyder (ibid.). The next highest grossing film for the day was *Monster-in-Law*, which grossed a relatively pathetic $1.5 million.

Before *Revenge of the Sith* opened, *Hitch* had the biggest opening weekend of the year with $43.1 million, a figure the prequel easily surpassed in its first day of release, which was even more impressive given that it started on a weekday in late spring. "When I consider it's a Thursday with kids in school, I'd figure it can't do that," said Bruce Snyder, who said he did not expect the prequel to beat the three-day gross of *Spider-Man* (Gray "'Sith' Destroys …"). Still, he predicted, "For the four-day, we'll be the biggest ever" (ibid.). Dergarabedian called the opening day "an unprecedented achievement" ("'Star Wars' day 1 …"). Lest anyone think that the higher theater count gave *Revenge of the Sith* the single-day victory over its two predecessors, consider that its $13,661 average per theater was 43.3 percent better than *Attack of the Clones* and 42.2 percent better than *The Phantom Menace* on their opening days.

On Friday, with most die-hard fans having already seen the film on opening day, ticket sales dropped 33.0 percent, but remained strong with a $33.5 million gross, which was the third best Friday of all time, behind *Spider-Man* with $39.4 million and *Harry Potter and the Prisoner of Azkaban* at $38.3 million. Saturday, ticket sales rose to $40.7 million, again good for the third best Saturday ever behind *Shrek 2*'s $44.8 million and *Spider-Man*'s $43.6 million. Sunday, the prequel nearly set a record with $34.2 million, just behind *Shrek 2*'s $34.9 million, but still ranked second on the all-time list. According to Fox exit polling, based on Friday's attendance only, 52 percent of moviegoers attending the film were older than twenty-five and 58 percent were male, not surprisingly (Byrne).

In total, *Revenge of the Sith* grossed $108,435,841 in its first weekend, the second biggest opening weekend of all time behind only *Spider-Man* at $114.8 million. The prequel averaged $29,619 per theater, compared to $25,317 for *Attack of the Clones* and $21,825 for *The Phantom Menace*, neither of which had as many auditoriums per theater in which to play. When comparing its first three days to the wall-crawler, however, *Revenge of the Sith* easily set a three-day record with $124.2 million. Additionally, its four-day gross of $158,449,700 handily defeated *The Matrix Reloaded*'s $134.3 million gross over the same time, giving the prequel one, two, three, and four day gross records. In the process, it had also set speed records for fastest movie ever to make $50 million, $100 million (a virtual tie with *Spider-Man* at three days), and $150 million. For the weekend, ticket sales for the final prequel represented about two-thirds of all tickets sold, showing utter dominance of the marketplace (Snyder "The 'Sith' …").

With its numerous records and stratospheric box office gross, the prequel had captivated the nation. "You can't really measure a film like this against anything else. It was unprecedented and phenomenal," Paul Dergarabedian said (Hinckley). Measured against any other openings, however, *Revenge of the Sith* dominated. If Lucasfilm and Fox had decided upon a Friday opening instead of Thursday, the weekend box office record would have belonged to *Revenge of the Sith*, though *Spider-Man*'s Friday through Sunday record was nearly the only one the prequel did not rewrite. Bruce Snyder said, "It's an international record [referring to the day-and-date release of the film around the world], a domestic record, and we also set the intergalactic record I believe. I can't find the old one, but I know we set it" (Byrne).

Despite a monstrous opening, *Revenge of the Sith* could not save the beleaguered box office. The top twenty movies grossed $160.2 million, but the number showed a decline of 3.6 percent from the previous year when *Shrek 2* dominated theaters alongside films like *Van Helsing* and *Mean Girls*. Behind the prequel, *Monster-in-Law* made $14.4 million, a solid hold from its prior weekend gross, *Kicking and Screaming* made $10.7 million, and *Crash* held steady with $5.5 million. *Unleashed* ($4.1 million) and *Kingdom of Heaven* ($3.5 million), in fifth and sixth places, took major hits, each falling more than 60 percent as their audiences dwindled in the wake of *Star Wars*. Ultimately, the prequel did not have enough help to stop the box office from falling for a thirteenth straight weekend. "It's shocking. We really thought this would end the slump," said Dergarabedian (Gentile "'Star Wars' Fails …"). The prequel did help the box office top twenty rise 62.0 percent from the previous weekend, however.

Online ticket sales proved hugely successful for Fandango and MovieTickets.com, with moviegoers purchasing a total of $30.5 million in tickets to see the final prequel during opening weekend from the two online sellers, representing almost 20 percent of the total box office gross ("Online …"). For the week before its release and during its opening weekend, the prequel represented 98 percent of all online ticket sales at Fandango.com (Lunsford). Regal Entertainment Group Marketing Manager Chad Browning said, "[*Revenge of the Sith*] has generated tremendous ticket sales out of all of our locations," partially thanks to Fandango kiosks in Regal Cinemas locations nationwide (ibid.).

On May 19, *Revenge of the Sith* was selling six tickets per second on Fandango.com, with the number increasing into the weekend. By opening day, the final prequel had already sold more tickets on Fandango.com than *Attack of the Clones* sold on the site for its entire first weekend. For Friday of opening weekend, Fandango.com sold an average of eight tickets per second, with as many as thirty-five per second sold during peak hours ("Revenge is Sweet: …"). The company also reached a new forty-eight-hour record in ticket sales for Thursday and Friday, on the strength of *Revenge of the Sith*'s success. "Even as of Sunday, we're selling tickets like gangbusters," Art Levitt said (ibid.).

MovieTickets.com also experienced torrid ticket sales for *Revenge of the Sith*, selling an average of ten tickets per second and as many as thirty during peak hours after its opening (Hernandez "Online …"). Opening day ticket sales for the final prequel set a single-day record for the company. Before the final prequel, *The Lord of the Rings: The Return of the King* reigned as the #1 seller on MovieTickets.com, with *Attack of the Clones* in fourth position (though at the time of its release in 2002, it was first). "We were pleasantly surprised by the pent-up demand," CEO Mitch Rubenstein said (ibid.). The site added more than two hundred thousand registered users on Friday and Saturday combined.

Still A Force

Revenge of the Sith's $14.4 million Monday, while only the eighth best Monday ever, ranked as the all-time best non-holiday Monday at the time. Every other film above it enjoyed extra business from Memorial Day or, as with *Spider-Man 2*, a day off following the July Fourth holiday. In 1999, *The Phantom Menace* had also set a record for a non-holiday Monday. With its Monday gross added to its previous total, *Revenge of the Sith* continued its dominating performance, setting the all-time mark for highest gross after five days with $172.8 million, well ahead of *Spider-Man 2*'s $152.4 million. The prequel had already secured the five-day record without needing to sell a ticket on Monday, though, as its four-day total was also better than the previous five-day mark.

Before its second weekend, and after only six days of release, *Revenge of the Sith* had become the highest grossing movie of the year with $182.7 million after its $9.9 million Tuesday gross. By comparison, *Hitch* had only reached $177.6 million.[3] Paul Dergarabedian said, "I think this very graphically demonstrates that people were waiting for something really big to hit the movie theaters. The fact that this has already eclipsed the top-grossing film of the year is a testament to that" (Hernandez "'Sith' Soars …"). Furthermore, once it became the highest

---

3.   It later finished its theatrical run with $179.5 million, ranking as the eleventh highest grossing 2005 film.

grossing movie of the year, it never ceded is throne despite a few potentially serious threats to its chances at becoming the fifth *Star Wars* movie to win its year at
the box office. *Revenge of the Sith* also set a record for best six-day gross, surpassing *Spider-Man 2*'s previous record of $180.1 million.

With $200.4 million by the end of its eighth day of release, *Revenge of the Sith*
tied *Spider-Man 2* for the fastest film ever to reach $200 million, before even ben-
efitting from a second weekend. "This is a phenomenal box office achievement.
The $50 million day was sort of a foregone conclusion it would be a sprinter to
$200 million. And it's already the top-grossing film released this year," Dergara-
bedian said ("'Sith' Hits …"). The prequel had to settle for second-highest gross
after eight days, however, as *Spider-Man 2*'s $202.1 million still ranked first, on
the strength of its eighth day being a Friday, a weekend box office day, versus a
Thursday for *Revenge of the Sith*.

Adding to the success of the final *Star Wars* film, fans were seeing it over and
over again not only to honor the last movie in the saga, but to catch all of the
details that one viewing cannot possibly reveal. In studio tracking during its first
full week, 10 percent of the moviegoers who watched *Revenge of the Sith* midweek
had already seen the movie at least twice. "That's the largest number I've ever
seen," Bruce Snyder said (Snyder "'Sith' smackdown"). Analysts saw the midweek
numbers for the prequel as very encouraging. *Shrek 2* had made $11.5 million on
its first Monday and in the $8 million neighborhood through the rest of the
week. "I'm startled by these midweek numbers, especially for a non-summer,
non-holiday week," Snyder said (ibid.).

Going into its second weekend at theaters, *Revenge of the Sith* still led advance
ticket sales on Fandango.com and MovieTickets.com. It represented 83 percent
of all sales at Fandango and 90 percent of sales at MovieTickets.com (Armitage).
Its closest rival was *Madagascar*, which despite being poised for success generated
little interest among online ticket purchasers. Art Levitt said, "The advance ticketing numbers for *Sith* are still very strong," so analysts expected a repeat at the
top for *Star Wars* (ibid.).

On its second Friday in theaters, *Revenge of the Sith* grossed $15.6 million,
declining 53.5 percent from the previous week. With $216.0 million, however,
the prequel set a new mark for best nine-day gross in box office history. Its Saturday gross of $20.9 million represented a fall of 48.6 percent from its previous
week, but again the film set a record for box office total after ten days with
$236.9 million. In all, the prequel set all-time marks for single day through ten
day box office totals, with the exceptions of the seven and eight day records, held
by *Spider-Man 2*. For its second Sunday, the prequel added $18.7 million, falling

45.3 percent from a week earlier. The total weekend gross of $55.2 million was down 49.1 percent from the massive opening. Adding its Memorial Day take of $14.8 million, slightly better than its opening week Monday, the prequel earned just more than $70.0 million for the four-day, holiday weekend, bringing its total gross to $270.5 million.

Because of its massive opening, *Revenge of the Sith* was bound to fall significantly in its second weekend, especially with stiff competition from *Madagascar* and *The Longest Yard*. For the four-day weekend, the animated kids film *Madagascar* made an impressive $61.0 million while *The Longest Yard*, a sports movie remake starring Adam Sandler, finished close behind with $58.6 million. Though *Revenge of the Sith* played in about five hundred more theaters than any previous *Star Wars* film, *Madagascar* had an even wider release, with 4,131 theaters playing the movie. The prequel generally occupied more auditoriums in theaters where both played, though, because of higher demand.

Despite three films making well more than $50 million over the long weekend, the box office still fell from 2004's level for a fourteenth consecutive weekend. The top twelve movies grossed $225.5 million, which was 5.5 percent behind the same weekend a year earlier when the top two films, *Shrek 2* and *The Day After Tomorrow*, had combined for $181.4 million. Dergarabedian said, "On the one hand, yeah, fourteen weeks, that's a terrible slump. But I'm optimistic, because this weekend proves you can still get a heck of a lot of people in theaters with the right movies" (Germain "'Star Wars' retains …").

Though *Revenge of the Sith* did not enjoy the same strong staying power *The Phantom Menace* had experienced in 1999, when it fell only 20.7 percent from its first to its second weekend, it also opened substantially bigger, so it could fall more and still make a massive second-weekend total. While *Spider-Man* only fell 37.8 percent from its record opening weekend, a remarkable accomplishment, most films opening with more than $80 million on their first weekends have fallen harder, often more than 50 percent the next weekend. *The Matrix Reloaded*, which like the final prequel also had Memorial Day Weekend to ease its fall after opening, still fell 59.8 percent. Even worse, *Harry Potter and the Prisoner of Azkaban* fell 62.7 percent on its second weekend in 2004. *Spider-Man 2* fell 48.7 percent from weekend one to two, comparable to *Revenge of the Sith*'s performance.

On Sunday, its eleventh day of release, *Revenge of the Sith* cracked the quarter-billion dollar mark in record time, besting *Spider-Man 2*'s twelve days and *Shrek 2*'s thirteen days. The prequel's second weekend also ranked as the fourth best second weekend ever, behind *Shrek 2*, *Spider-Man*, and *Harry Potter and the Sor-*

cerer's Stone (2001). With a solid hold given its huge opening, *Revenge of the Sith* was well ahead of *The Phantom Menace*'s $207.1 million total after two weekends and the $201.3 million mark for *Attack of the Clones*.

Duel of the Blockbusters

On its third weekend of release, June 3–5, *Revenge of the Sith* was unable to hold the top spot at the weekend box office as *Madagascar* and *The Longest Yard* both enjoyed smaller drops, probably because of the business that the prequel had already done earlier in its run. *Madagascar* was first with $28.1 million, ahead of *The Longest Yard* at $26.1 million and the final *Star Wars* film at $25.1 million. The prequel declined 54.6 percent, which was similar to the 56.1 percent decline *Attack of the Clones* had experienced in its third weekend. *The Phantom Menace*, falling 36.0 percent, also experienced the worst fall of its run (while in the top ten at the box office) between its second and third weekends. Because the third weekends for the *Star Wars* prequels always fell on the weekend after Memorial Day, they had comparatively harsher drops than most of their other weekends.

By the end of three weekends, *Revenge of the Sith* had climbed to $307.9 million. With its $10.5 million Saturday gross, adding up to $300.3 million total, the prequel became the fastest movie ever to reach $300 million, doing so in seventeen days, compared to eighteen for *Shrek 2* and nineteen for *Spider-Man 2*. "You have to be gratified when you have the fastest to $300 million. How far it will go, I don't know. The next few weeks will tell us that," said Bruce Snyder (Hernandez "'Sith' Marches ..."). Box office analyst and BoxOfficeGuru.com webmaster Gitesh Pandya had his own prediction. He said, "At the end of the day, I see [*Revenge of the Sith*] at a path toward $375 million to $400 million" (ibid.).

With its $2.4 million gross on Tuesday, June 7, *Revenge of the Sith* reached $312.7 million, passing the entire $310.7 million gross for *Attack of the Clones* in less than three weeks. As of Wednesday, it was the seventeenth highest grossing movie of all time, still moving up the charts with *The Lord of the Rings: The Fellowship of the Ring* (2001) close in sight at $314.8 million and *Harry Potter and the Sorcerer's Stone* just ahead at $317.6 million as its next target. *Revenge of the Sith* passed the first *Lord of the Rings* film on June 8, before its fourth weekend.

On Friday, with a gross of $4.0 million, *Revenge of the Sith* defeated *Harry Potter and the Sorcerer's Stone* to take fifteenth place on the list of the highest grossing movies in North America. With $14.9 million on its fourth weekend, June 10–12, *Revenge of the Sith* fell a much more modest 40.8 percent, stabilizing its box office performance a bit and retaining a third place ranking despite the opening of *Mr. and Mrs. Smith* with $50.3 million. *Madagascar* stayed ahead of the prequel with $17.2 million, but *The Longest Yard* fell back to $13.9 million. With its strong weekend performance, the prequel's $332.1 million total also beat *Forrest Gump* (1994) to move into fourteenth place on the all-time chart.

The Phantom Menace held strong every weekend during its release, routinely passing new releases and maintaining audience support, so Lucasfilm and Fox did not need to promote it much after its opening. *Attack of the Clones*, however, experienced steeper declines and never seemed to attract casual moviegoers in the same numbers as the other *Star Wars* films, perhaps because of a dearth of advertising. While running a series of television ads reminding audiences that *Revenge of the Sith* was in theaters, Lucasfilm also aimed to keep the fan base coming back for repeat viewings. On June 8, the Official *Star Wars* Web Site announced that from June 10 through July 4, fans could send their ticket stubs in and be entered to win a $2,500 *Star Wars* pinball machine as part of the "See *Star Wars* Episode III Again Sweepstakes" ("Win …").

Aside from the material prize the Official Site offered, the press release promised that the fan who sent in the greatest number of ticket stubs over the contest period would be featured on starwars.com and in *Bantha Tracks*. Additionally, the group that sent in the most ticket stubs from a single showing, demonstrating the largest "group party" at a theater, was also featured on the site. The article read:

> Your viewings of *Revenge* this weekend, and in the weeks to come, will also help you and your fellow fans enjoy this one last *Star Wars* summer, an opportunity to go back to the theater time and again to watch our favorite film in the best possible way—on a big screen with a banging sound system, and in the company of other fans (ibid.).

Although die-hard fan viewings only account for a small portion of the total box office gross of a franchise film, repeat viewings for a hit film can still squeeze out a few million dollars extra over the course of several weeks.

On the June 17–19 weekend, another cultural icon, Batman, returned to theaters with a new entry, *Batman Begins*, a movie that found favor both with critics and audiences. It stole first place easily, with $48.7 million during the weekend and $72.9 million for its opening five days. Still, many box office pundits were surprised by the relatively weak performance compared to other comic book films. Beginning to show some of the box office staying power that made *The Phantom Menace* a dominant performer six years earlier, *Revenge of the Sith* fell only 32.4 percent in its fifth weekend, marking the smallest decline in the top ten. Beating Sunday estimates by $300,000, the movie earned $10.0 million, ranking fourth for the weekend, still behind *Madagascar* but closing ground. The prequel raised its total to $348.1 million, eleventh on the all-time list of highest grossing films at the time, having passed *Finding Nemo* (2003) and *The Lord of the Rings: The Two Towers* (2002).

Again trying to boost already strong attendance, Lucasfilm announced via starwars.com that anyone attending *Revenge of the Sith* for Father's Day Weekend at participating theaters would get a free poster, while supplies lasted ("See *Revenge* ..."). The poster showed Darth Vader with an open hand in the foreground, the film's title at the bottom, and the text, "Who's Your Daddy?" centered in large capital letters below Vader's hand. The eleven-by-seventeen-inch poster provided a nice touch in an already strong marketing push to keep fans returning to theaters, an effort aided by the quality of the movie itself and its growing status as a fan favorite.

Though *Revenge of the Sith* achieved incredible success, other films in the marketplace simply did not attract enough audience attention to duplicate the type of performances from films in 2004, meaning that by the end of the June 17–19 weekend, the box office had suffered through a seventeen-week losing streak, so every weekend during the stretch was down from the previous year. Seven weeks into the summer season, as *Variety* noted, the revenue of $1.34 billion was the lowest since 2001 (Snyder "B.O...."). Compared to 2004, the summer box office lagged $120 million behind, or 8.2 percent.

Variety's Gabriel Snyder, in an attempt to explain the difference, blamed two movies specifically: *Kingdom of Heaven* and *Monster-in-Law*. Ridley Scott's *Kingdom of Heaven* was running $71 million behind *Van Helsing* from 2004, a useful comparison as both films started the summers of their respective years. Meanwhile, *Monster-in-Law* was $50 million behind *Troy*, which opened in the same frame a year earlier. The combined $121 million difference accounted for the summer-to-summer decline. Snyder noted, however, that "these two pictures are not the reason for the 'slump,' but they show that when you set out to break box office records, there is very little room for error" (ibid.).

On Thursday, June 23, for the first time in its box office run, *Revenge of the Sith* failed to make at least $1 million, ending a streak of thirty-five consecutive days. Nonetheless, it had to fall below the mark eventually, yet it followed with a strong weekend, falling a moderate 39.1 percent to $6.1 million in seventh place, losing rank because of the releases of *Bewitched* ($20.1 million), *Herbie: Fully Loaded* ($12.7 million), and *Land of the Dead* ($10.2 million). On Sunday, its thirty-ninth day of release, *Revenge of the Sith* finally entered the all-time box office top ten, standing at $358.5 million, barely above *Jurassic Park*'s $357.1 million total.

In a final holiday weekend push, Lucasfilm announced through starwars.com on June 29 another promotion for *Revenge of the Sith* over the July Fourth Weekend. Fans could buy three tickets to see the movie and get one free, good July 1–4. Bruce Snyder said, "Like a ride at their favorite amusement park, people are seeing the movie over and over again to make sure they don't miss anything before the movie leaves the big screen, so we're giving them a little Fourth of July treat to keep the fireworks going" ("May the Fourth ..."). Fox also printed a poster featuring Yoda holding his lightsaber with fireworks in the background and text at the top reading: "May the Fourth Be With You!" The image appeared in a full-page ad in *USA Today*'s Life section on July 1, page 5E.

With its first release in most theaters beginning to wind down, *Revenge of the Sith* earned $4.1 million over the three-day portion of the July Fourth Weekend and $5.0 million total including the holiday Monday. Its three-day gross fell 33.2 percent from the previous weekend, despite losing more theaters, down to only 1,759 from its high of 3,650 in early June. It ranked eighth for the weekend, passing *Land of the Dead* even as Steven Spielberg's *War of the Worlds* opened big and *Rebound* finished barely ahead of the prequel. The weekend gross boosted the total *Revenge of the Sith* box office gross to $366.5 million.

Revenge of the Sith enjoyed one more weekend in the top ten, falling 36.3 percent and grossing $2.6 million in tenth place for a total of $270.8 million through its eighth weekend, enough to pass *The Passion of the Christ* (2004) and move into ninth place all time. The nineteen-week box office slump also ended, thanks to a strong opening by *Fantastic Four* and a good second weekend from *War of the Worlds*, along with the contributions of other films in the marketplace. In its subsequent weekends, *Revenge of the Sith* continued to find small audiences, falling 34.5 percent to $1.7 million in its ninth weekend and passing *Spider-Man 2* to move into eighth all time.

A Champion Crowned

Revenge of the Sith played 155 days in theaters, through October 20, which was just two weeks short of the November 4 exit for *The Phantom Menace*. By the end of its box office run, the prequel had collected $380,270,577, passing *The Lord of the Rings: The Return of the King* and finishing as the seventh highest grossing movie ever. Despite the detractors and cynics who said *Star Wars* was no longer cool, and that it had been overtaken in popular culture by *Harry Potter* films and

The Lord of the Rings, the final *Star Wars* film passed every film from both franchises.

The financial success of the final prequel also assured the ultimate level of success for George Lucas's prequel trilogy. The combined grosses of the three films stood at $1,121,765,037, passing the original *Star Wars* trilogy ($1,060,779,251) as the highest grossing trilogy ever. The two trilogies formed a powerful one-two punch at the top of the all-time list, demonstrating the cultural impact the entire saga has had on generations of fans over nearly thirty years between the first and last films. In all, the nearly $2.2 billion combined for the two trilogies easily ranks the *Star Wars* franchise as the most financially successful series of movies in history, almost a billion dollars ahead of the *James Bond* series despite twenty *Bond* films at the time of the final *Star Wars* movie's release. No other franchise had ever crossed $2 billion in total box office revenue domestically.

After the summer ended, *Revenge of the Sith* was the highest grossing film in a lopsided competition, eventually beating the summer's next biggest blockbuster, *War of the Worlds*, by nearly $150 million.[4] Unlike in 1999, when Fox released almost nothing but bombs besides *The Phantom Menace*, the studio put together a strong slate of films for 2005, which allowed Fox to reach $1 billion in domestic grosses by the end of the summer, ranking as the second-fastest studio in history to reach the milestone (Hernandez "'Sith' is summer …"). The success of *Fantastic Four* ($154.7 million total) and *Mr. and Mrs. Smith* ($186.3 million) during the summer, combined with the massive *Star Wars* gross, put Fox in the market-share lead among studios.

Despite Fox enjoying a nice summer at the box office, the industry as a whole stumbled mightily, with box office receipts down 9.1 percent from $3.86 billion to $3.53 billion[5] according to *Variety* and attendance off almost 12.0 percent from 2004 to 562.5 million tickets sold, the worst number since 1997 (Fritz and Snyder). "I'm trying to figure out how many weekends out of this whole summer have been down. Basically, it's like the whole summer," Dergarabedian said (Vancheri). He called the summer "very disappointing" and noted it was "punctuated by certain films that did very well," like *Batman Begins*, *Charlie and the Chocolate Factory*, *Revenge of the Sith*, *War of the Worlds*, and *Wedding Crashers*,

---

4. *War of the Worlds* had grossed $231.8 million by the end of August, finishing with $234.3 million in North America. *Revenge of the Sith* had nearly finished its box office run and stood at $379.4 million.

5. The summer period lasts eighteen weeks and is measured from early May through Labor Day Weekend.

all of which earned more than $200 million (ibid.). Other significant hits included *Fantastic Four, Madagascar*, and *Mr. and Mrs. Smith*.

Variety writer Gabriel Snyder observed that the top films in the summer of 2005 performed as well as those of the previous summer, but the mid-level hits were lacking in 2005. Including *Revenge of the Sith*, five movies hit at least $200 million for 2005's summer, compared to only three the previous summer. Additionally, the top ten films of summer 2005 had grossed $1.92 billion by the time of the article's writing (August 21), compared to $2.06 billion in 2004.[6] Sony Vice Chairman Jeff Blake said, "Clearly, audiences chose to support the films they liked best, and there were some very big hits this summer" ("Summer …").

The next twenty highest grossing films from summer 2005, however, stumbled badly, grossing just $1.10 billion, compared to $1.34 billion for summer 2004's next twenty hits, representing an 18.0 percent drop and accounting for much of the summer depression (Snyder "Summer …"). The difference was too significant to ignore, leading many in Hollywood to conclude that perhaps moviegoers, frustrated by high ticket prices and encouraged by increasingly advanced home theater systems, were willing to wait for the second-tier hits to arrive on DVD. Especially with the DVD market having increased 15 percent in 2004, many industry experts thought a box office slowdown combined with strong DVD sales could signal a shift in moviegoing habits (Snyder "Who's on top?").

With numerous films failing to meet box office expectations, like *Cinderella Man, Kingdom of Heaven, Stealth*, and *The Island*, among others, studios had to hope for better DVD sales to offset production costs. "The middling-choice picture is tougher to create," Universal Vice Chairman Marc Shmuger said, because "people are choosing to own or rent it on DVD or see it in some other method of consumption" (Snyder "Summer …"). In support of Shmuger's theory, mid-level DVD releases continued to perform well in 2005, while big blockbusters were not selling as well on DVD as in the past relative to their box office grosses. Two primary groups of movie fans exist, one that sees movies in theaters often and another that waits for the DVD releases, so a film that few people saw in theaters may have a larger viewing audience once it reaches DVD. "Lots of titles in the middle box office tier [movies between $30 million and $80 million] are selling more than they would have a year ago," said Craig Kornblau, president of Universal Home Video (Snyder "Who's on top?").

---

6.   The top ten films from summer 2005 eventually finished with $2.04 billion, making the comparison even more appropriate.

To combat a slow year and bring in additional moviegoers, many theaters tried creative marketing, like the Brenden Theater Corporation's Modesto 18 in California. To boost concession and ticket sales, the company transformed its theater into a *Star Wars* space station, complete with props and stormtrooper displays. In-theater activities, a promotional giveaway of a Hyundai Accent with imagery from *Revenge of the Sith*, and an extensive media campaign helped boost the theater's ticket sales and concessions per capita by double digits. For its innovative marketing, the theater won an award, "Best Overall Promotion and Showmanship," from ShoWest in March 2006, the annual exhibitor's convention in Las Vegas ("Brenden ...").

The hype surrounding *Revenge of the Sith* and its subsequent success at the box office also helped sell many DVDs for the other five *Star Wars* films. For the week ending May 8, *Attack of the Clones* was the thirteenth best-selling title, up from eighteenth the week before. It was also the highest-ranked *Star Wars* film on the rental charts as casual filmgoers wanted to see the previous installment before the final entry in the franchise. *The Phantom Menace* was only one spot behind, though, and had been seventh the week earlier. By the week ending May 22, the *Star Wars Trilogy* DVD set had skyrocketed from unranked to seventh, while *Attack of the Clones* moved into tenth and *The Phantom Menace* took eleventh, meaning all of the five films were competing with and sometimes beating the new releases.

The *Star Wars* films continued to sell well during the summer, too, proving that interest in the prequels and the franchise in general was strong. For the week ending June 5, the *Star Wars Trilogy*, which had risen to sixth the previous week, was still ranked seventh. *The Phantom Menace* had a great showing with a rise to ninth, while *Clones* took tenth, putting all of the films in the top ten at once. On Buy.com, the two prequels were second and third ranked, respectively. The rental success and consumer interest for the other films in the franchise earned an article from *Video Business Online*, the Web site for *Video Business*, an industry publication owned by the same company that publishes *Variety*. Editor Carl DiOrio wrote, "The spillover effect [from *Revenge of the Sith*] for home video business has been impressive," noting that rental stores in the area had only five copies of each of the films and were completely checked out before the film opened in theaters ("Embrace ...").

By the end of the year, box office revenue reached $8.99 billion on 1.40 billion admissions, compared to $9.53 billion from 1.53 billion admissions in 2004. Revenue fell 5.7 percent from the previous year, despite higher ticket prices ($6.41 compared to $6.21), so admissions dipped 8.5 percent.[7] Unable to overcome its early deficit, 2005 was the third consecutive year that ticket sales dropped, after reaching a modern high of 1.63 billion tickets sold in 2002. Dergarabedian said, "2005 was not one of those years that was breaking all kinds of records. The one record we broke that we didn't want to was the nineteen-weekend slump" (Hernandez "Box ..."). Nonetheless, Fox enjoyed a strong year for its film slate, which succeeded despite the decline in admissions.

Star Wars nearly helped Fox win the market-share crown for 2005, with final receipts showing that Warner Bros. edged Fox $1.38 billion to $1.36 billion (Fritz "WB ..."). The winner for the year was still undecided up until the last weekend, with the two studios in a virtual tie for first. Fox was arguably the bigger winner, though, as it released twenty-one films compared to twenty-five for Warner Bros., representing a significantly higher average gross per picture. Fox had finished sixth in 2004 with $916.0 million, so the gross of *Revenge of the Sith* was nearly the entire difference between Fox's 2004 and 2005 totals. Aside from its success in 2005, Fox was undergoing a nice upswing under new management by Tom Rothman and Jim Gianopulos, co-chairmen who together led the studio to four consecutive profitable years, with profits almost tripling (Koehler).

Though a weak box office year could mean softer competition and thus more moviegoers available to see a big film, *Revenge of the Sith* still had to succeed in a year where moviegoers did not seem to have as much enthusiasm about the theatrical viewing experience. With more people waiting for films on DVD, the final prequel offered an experience that cannot be duplicated at home, not only because of its incredible visual effects, but also because of the communal experience of seeing a meaningful film with other fans who appreciate the saga. With a gross 22.4 percent greater than *Attack of the Clones*, which had failed to become 2002's highest grossing film, *Revenge of the Sith* beat *The Chronicles of Narnia: The Lion, The Witch, and The Wardrobe* by $88.5 million to claim first place for 2005. The final prequel enjoyed similar success internationally, breaking many records overseas as well.

---

7.   The National Association of Theatre Owners (NATO) Web site at NATOOnline.org provided the data cited. Exhibitor Relations data indicated a total revenue of $8.9 billion compared to $9.4 billion in 2004, a 5.3 percent drop.

Exporting the Force

Preparing an Invasion

Star Wars has always been an international phenomenon, encompassing a global fan base and attracting media attention in countries worldwide. George Lucas shot the first film in Tunisia and at soundstages in England, not to mention the movie had a strong contingent of British actors, especially in the Imperial ranks. The international film market, though, was not as strong when the first film premiered in 1977, but the global influence of the Force has spread considerably in the intervening decades and with each episode released. In 1999, *The Phantom Menace* grossed $491.4 million internationally, the fourth best international gross in history at the time. *Revenge of the Sith* was poised for similar success in the global marketplace, with the *Harry Potter* and *Lord of the Rings* films attracting hordes of fans around the world.

With all of its releases combined, *A New Hope* has grossed $775.4 million worldwide,[1] but 59.5 percent of its total has come from North America, which is high by modern standards. Newer films often make more than 60 percent of their total worldwide box office grosses internationally. The ratio for *The Empire Strikes Back* is not as lopsided, with 46.0 percent of its total $538.4 million coming from countries outside of North America. *Return of the Jedi* is the most skewed of the entire saga, with 65.1 percent of its $475.1 million gross coming domestically. In 1999, 53.3 percent of *The Phantom Menace*'s worldwide box office total came from outside of North America, reversing the trend of the Orig-

---

1.   Worldwide box office totals are from BoxOfficeMojo.com. Where available, revenue information from the popular box office tracking site is cited instead of *Variety*'s data for the sake of uniformity. Whenever possible, box office gross numbers will be given to one decimal place. Unfortunately, international box office grosses are a headache to pinpoint, especially for older films because of poor record keeping. As an example, if one territory tracked 115,000 tickets sold, and two sources have different data on the average price of tickets in 1977, two different results arise when trying to calculate revenue numbers. Readers should note that *Variety* puts *A New Hope*'s total at $798 million.

inal Trilogy. Likewise, *Attack of the Clones* earned 52.2 percent of its $649.4 million total from foreign markets.

Although the international grosses for the *Star Wars* films are impressive by most blockbuster standards, the films have not duplicated the type of international success that other major franchises have achieved. For instance, *The Lord of the Rings: The Fellowship of the Ring* (2001) made $314.8 million in North America, similar to the gross of *Attack of the Clones*, yet its international gross of $556.6 million far outstrips the second prequel's total in accounting for 63.9 percent of the total worldwide gross for the Peter Jackson film. *Harry Potter and the Sorcerer's Stone* (2001) is a more extreme example, having grossed $317.6 million domestically, also similar to the second prequel, but a whopping $658.9 million internationally, or 67.5 percent of its total.

For whatever reasons, which seem inexplicable given the epic nature of the *Star Wars* saga, Lucas's franchise has not achieved as much success internationally as other recent behemoths. *Shrek 2* (2004) is one of the only exceptions, having earned 47.9 percent of its $920.7 million from North America, though because of its numerous cultural references and jokes, one can easily understand why it would not appeal as much to many foreign audiences. Likewise, the patriotic themes of the *Spider-Man* films have led to similar ratios for domestic and international grosses; neither of the first two films made even 52.5 percent of their totals from overseas box offices.

Star Wars, like *Harry Potter* and *The Lord of the Rings*, is a more universal story that, because of its other-worldly locations and timeless mythology, would not seem to be a domestically skewed film series. The *Star Wars* films perform phenomenally well in several countries while only solidly in others. Nevertheless, fans around the world looked forward to the premiere of the final prequel with the same type of anticipation and excitement as fans in North America.

Unlike with *The Phantom Menace*, which premiered throughout the summer in countries worldwide, *Revenge of the Sith* came to international fans at roughly the same time as fans in North America, much like the release pattern of *Attack of the Clones*. Many territories did not start playing the final prequel until Friday of its opening weekend, but fans still had the movie on almost the same date as their North American counterparts. The only exceptions were South Korea (May 26) and Japan (July 9), the latter because July is the traditional month for *Star Wars* premieres, so Fox stayed with the typical release month.

The prequels proved much more successful internationally than the Original Trilogy, largely because of better marketing and distribution as well as more emerging markets in which to play. "We knew with *Phantom* that we could achieve a certain level of box office based on core male fans," said Jim Ward, senior vice president of marketing and distribution at Lucasfilm (D'Alessandro). "We wanted to grow the brand over time with a new generation of fans, so we talked to kids in an aggressive way as well as women," he continued. The marketing efforts aimed at women for the prequels included museum tours of costumes from the films and a Yves Saint Laurent makeup line inspired by Queen Amidala. With numerous merchandising partners creating products for children, Lucasfilm also had the youth market interested.

To introduce the *Star Wars* films to a global audience, Lucasfilm enlisted the help of artist Drew Struzan, who had previously done artwork for numerous *Star Wars* book covers and later drew the posters for the *Star Wars: Special Edition* releases as well as the prequels. Aside from Struzan's work, Lucasfilm partnered with New Wave Entertainment, a Los Angeles creative agency, to design six bold, aggressive posters featuring characters from *Revenge of the Sith* to promote the film outdoors on billboards, busses, and transit stations internationally. Though outdoor advertising is not particularly prominent in the United States, it is more significant in many foreign countries, where the need to familiarize audiences with the saga made outdoor advertising more worthwhile.

Four of the posters featured individual characters, namely Darth Vader, General Grievous, Mace Windu, and Yoda, another featured a Special Ops Clone Trooper, and the final one showed Anakin Skywalker and Obi-Wan Kenobi locked in combat. "We really wanted the [images] to be very active and feel like you're in the midst of Jedi action," explained Lucasfilm Director of Marketing Tom Warner ("Outdoor ..."). The Darth Vader image is particularly effective in displaying a sense of engagement with the viewer as Vader has a fist toward the virtual camera as though he is grabbing for the attention of people passing the poster. Lucasfilm worked on the image to maximize its appeal, changing the original design "with the idea of him reaching out and coming at you with that hand in a clutch that everyone knows," Warner said (ibid.).

Preparing *Revenge of the Sith* for international release was not an easy task for Fox, despite the iconic nature of the characters and historical significance of the saga's final entry. In a humorous bit of cultural confusion, Lucasfilm had to modify the film's title previous to release in several countries because it would not have the intended meaning otherwise. Danish fans would have thought Lucas had finally lost his magical touch when "Revenge of the Babysitter" hit theaters, for instance, and Turkish fans may have been almost as confused by "Revenge of the Government," which sounds more like an editorial on high taxes than a film about Anakin's fall to the Dark Side ("International Episode ...").

Aside from amusing title complications, a few of the original character names had even more ridiculous foreign translations. For instance, Chewbacca was "Chique-Tabac" in France, which literally means "chew tobacco." C-3PO and R2-D2 were D-3BO and C1-P8, respectively (Keaten "Around …"). Most of the characters eventually became known by their English names, but a few variations stayed, such as "Darth Fener" in Italy for Darth Vader and an altered spelling, "Vador," in France (ibid.).

While North American fans had Celebration III in Indianapolis, Indiana, at which to gather and show their enthusiasm for the franchise, European fans had an alternative in France in mid-May, before the film's May 18 premiere in the country. The three-day convention started Friday, May 13 and drew more than three thousand fans to a Paris movie theater, the Grand Rex, in a convention billed as the first of its kind in Europe. Fans in attendance had the opportunity to listen to theme music from the saga performed by the Paris Cinematographic Orchestra. Other activities included special effects demonstrations, fan film showings, and question and answer sessions with actors like Peter Mayhew and Jeremy Bulloch. A pass to attend the convention cost fans $101 (Keaten "Star …").

Although France is well known for promoting home-grown products and trying to minimize the influence of Hollywood on its popular culture, *Star Wars* transcends such ideas. "*Star Wars* is for everybody," said Patrice Giroud, who organized the three-day *Star Wars* convention and is also editor of *Lucasfilm Magazine* in France, a bimonthly publication with a circulation of about fifty thousand (Keaten "Around …"). All three major French dailies featured front-page photos of *Star Wars* characters on the Monday before the final film's release. One television station had shown the previous five films each week for several weeks before release.

One of the biggest international events was the first-ever screening of all six *Star Wars* films for the public, where one thousand fans in the United Kingdom had the opportunity to see an all-day marathon with a "Galactic Passport" ticket, costing about $100 but sometimes selling on the secondary market for more than $450 each (Butt). The tickets went on sale April 25 at the UCI Empire box office and sold out in less than thirty minutes. The marathon screening took place at London's Leicester Square on May 16, with Lucas, Hayden Christensen, Ewan McGregor, Christopher Lee, Ian McDiarmid, and Anthony Daniels, among others, attending the premiere at the Odeon Leicester Square. Leicester Square is a popular entertainment area in London with night clubs, bars, restaurants, and four separate theaters, so while the premiere took place at Odeon's theater, the screening was at the UCI Empire theater next door.

For the *Star Wars* marathon, Leicester Square transformed into a party zone for *Star Wars* fans, with stormtroopers from the 501st Legion's U.K. garrison patrolling the area and the Royal Philharmonic Orchestra playing music from the saga. Even a life-size X-Wing made an appearance. "*Revenge of the Sith* is a remarkable movie, and this extraordinary celebration reflects the fun and excitement that are the hallmarks of *Star Wars*," Producer Rick McCallum said (A. Singh). The marathon screenings started at 7:00 a.m. with *A New Hope*, then continued with the other two Original Trilogy films and the first two prequels, before *Revenge of the Sith* made its premiere in the country. Fans not lucky enough to get a ticket to the six-film marathon could watch the other films in separate screenings throughout the day at the Odeon West End Cinema and the Leicester Square's VUE cinema.

By the time of *Revenge of the Sith*'s London premiere, about 5,500 fans had shown up to greet Lucas and celebrate the final film's opening. Unfortunately, rain had slightly dampened the premiere, and not just literally, though it did not seem to deter many fans. "These fans have been waiting in the rain. That's dedication for you. These fans are hardcore," Christensen said ("Star Wars mania …"). Lucas agreed, saying, "The turnout here is excellent. In Cannes the people were standing in the sunshine; here they're in the rain" (ibid.). One vocal group of fans chanted, "Thank you, thank you!" to Lucas at the premiere, though the filmmaker thought they were saying "R2, R2" (Youngs).

Fox reported that advance ticket sales worldwide were often in line with the torrid pace that North American theaters had seen. In some territories, the final prequel sold more tickets before its release than either of the first two prequels had sold total during their entire box office runs. "We are seeing phenomenal advance ticket sales in many territories," said Paul Hanneman, executive vice president of sales and strategic planning for Fox International (Snyder "A force …"). In the United Kingdom, advance ticket sales for the final prequel were the second highest ever for Odeon Cinemas, behind only *The Phantom Menace*.

Not surprisingly given the monstrous hype and fan excitement in the United Kingdom, the final prequel ranked as the most searched film by U.K Internet users, according to Hitwise, a leading online tracking company ("Jedi …"). *Star Wars* collected almost 1 percent of all movie-related searches, with four of the top ten movie search terms relating to the prequel. The search term "Star Wars" ranked third, behind only "IMDb" [the Internet Movie Database] and "Odeon," the theater chain. Additionally, starwars.com was the second most popular movie site with U.K. Web surfers, behind only the IMDb; the Official *Star Wars* Web Site held a 3.5 percent market share.

Numerous other markets experienced the type of fan enthusiasm and excitement that led to thousands of sold-out midnight showings across North America. Every midnight showing in Belgium had already sold out before the film's release. Advance ticket sales hit $1.5 million in Australia, $160,000 in New Zealand, $375,000 in Singapore, and $40,000 in the Philippines; the grosses for Singapore and the Philippines set records. The Cineapolis chain in Mexico had already sold $500,000 in tickets during its first week of advance sales. Advance sales in Peru were the biggest for any film in history.

Worldwide Attack

Released in France on Wednesday, May 18, a day before its release in North America, *Revenge of the Sith* came to forty-eight more territories on Thursday, including countries like the United Kingdom, Germany, Spain, and China, among others. Midnight showings in numerous countries broke records, including $2.9 million from Germany, where 705,348 people saw the movie in the first twenty-four hours, also a record. Fox reported that midnight showings in Chile broke records, too.

Revenge of the Sith enjoyed the biggest opening day ever in Belgium, with $452,000 from nintety-nine screens while Switzerland contributed $393,000 from thirty-six screens. The prequel also set opening day records in Ecuador, Hungary, the Netherlands, and Puerto Rico. In all, the movie collected $38.4 million on Wednesday and Thursday from openings and previews, according to *Variety*, with just more than half the total markets opening the film on Friday (McNary "'Star Wars' hits …").

For its opening day in France, the final *Star Wars* film notched the best opening for an American film in history, with $5 million from 938 screens; *The Matrix Reloaded* had held the record previously. *Revenge of the Sith* sold 124,000 opening day tickets in Paris, the most ever at the time, surpassing the 113,000 tickets sold for local hit *Taxi 2*. Total admissions for the country reached 642,000, behind *Taxi* at 802,000 in first, but ahead of the 576,000 for *The Matrix Reloaded*. As in the United States, many fans dressed in costumes and waited hours in line to obtain desirable seats to the midnight showings. "It was extraordinary to see so many people queuing for a midnight show," said Jean-Francois Porcher, director of the EuroPalace in Nantes, a northern city of France ("New 'Star Wars' …").

Although Fox gave *Revenge of the Sith* a day-and-date opening internationally, meaning a simultaneous worldwide release instead of a gradual rollout as with *The Phantom Menace*, the film had a number of openings on Friday, May 20, a more traditional day of the week for films to open. By the weekend, the prequel was playing in 105 countries worldwide, the biggest aggregation of territories ever. Over the course of its opening weekend, it accumulated $145.5 million from 10,489 screens (a record) internationally, setting a new foreign opening weekend record and already ranking as the third highest grossing movie of the year internationally. The previous top film in the opening weekend category, *The Lord of the Rings: The Return of the King* (2003), had grossed $125.9 million in its five-day frame, while three years earlier *Attack of the Clones* had taken in a relatively tame $69.1 million in its simultaneous worldwide release. In all, the final prequel had made $303.9 million worldwide after only its first weekend of release.

Because of its Thursday opening, the prequel failed to set opening weekend records in most territories, mirroring its performance in North America. The prequel set weekend records in Chile and Peru, however, and its opening weekend totals worldwide were still impressive. In the United Kingdom, which contributed the most to the international gross for the weekend, *Revenge of the Sith* earned $27.5 million including previews from 485 screens, ranking in the top five of all time. It crushed the second prequel's opening by 66 percent and sped ahead of *The Phantom Menace*'s opening by 85 percent. For its opening weekend in France, the final prequel was even more dominant over its predecessors, grossing $22.6 million from 938 screens, a record in dollars, though not in euros. The take represented 73.7 percent of the entire box office gross for *Attack of the Clones* and 52.6 percent of *The Phantom Menace*'s lifetime total.

In Germany, another strong *Star Wars* country, the final film earned $17.8 million from 1,182 screens for the second biggest opening ever, just behind *The Return of the King*'s $17.9 million. The previous two prequels had opened with $12.4 million and $11.8 million, respectively. "It was a galactic opening. This is what we have been waiting for. You can't beat *Star Wars*—it's attracting a cross-generational audience that has crowded theaters across the country," one German exhibitor told *Variety* (McNary "Force ..."). While its opening weekend fell short, the four-day gross for the prequel nearly matched the five-day total for *The Return of the King*.

In Australia, where *The Phantom Menace* had achieved one of its best ranks internationally, *Revenge of the Sith* grossed $10.4 million from 535 screens, the best opening among the prequels and the second best debut of all time. Likewise, franchise popularity continued with New Zealand's $1.4 million from seventy-five screens, the second best opening ever, also behind *The Return of the King* as with many countries, but 69 percent ahead of the second prequel and 115 percent ahead of the first.

One of the biggest improvements over the previous prequels came in Spain, where *Star Wars* films had not enjoyed much success traditionally. *Attack of the Clones* only earned $15.5 million compared to $24.5 million for *Troy* (2004), for instance, a film that in North America was not even half as successful as the middle prequel. The $9.7 million gross from 495 screens for *Revenge of the Sith* was not only the second best opening ever in the territory, but also 126 percent ahead of *The Phantom Menace* and 143 percent ahead of *Attack of the Clones*. One exhibitor told *Variety* that the film set a record for costumed fans, besting the *Lord of the Rings* films, in his opinion (McNary "Force …").

Italy only offered $4.0 million to the final prequel during opening weekend, which was less than half as much as *The Return of the King*'s $10.3 million record, a disappointment that exhibitors blamed on sunny weather and economic recession. On a more encouraging note for Fox and Lucasfilm, the last *Star Wars* entry grossed $4.5 million in Russia, twice the combined debuts of both previous prequels and the fourth-best opening ever. Emerging markets like Russia helped boost the final prequel's total throughout its run, though the bulk of its gross came from more well established markets.

Revenge of the Sith had a robust opening in Mexico as well, where its $6.4 million from 914 screens destroyed the openings from the other prequels, besting *The Phantom Menace* by 88 percent and *Attack of the Clones* by 45 percent. It also ranked as the fourth best opening weekend ever in the country. Elsewhere in Latin America, the prequel collected $2.3 million from Brazil, $1.1 million from Puerto Rico, and a bit less than $700,000 from Colombia, all of which were considered fairly impressive starts. The Brazilian opening was a record for Fox.

An article from Christopher Bodeen of the Associated Press indicated that demand for the final prequel in China was minimal and that "theaters were all but empty for Thursday night's debut" of the film, but the numbers prove otherwise as do other reports. Although China only lets a few American films into the country annually, because of its efforts to promote local movies, *Revenge of the Sith* still took advantage of the burgeoning market. It was only the second movie ever to include China in a simultaneous worldwide release; *The Matrix Revolutions* was the first. China's State Administration of Radio, Film and Television had to approve the film for release and agree to an early review.

According to the *Xinhua News Agency*, the final prequel experienced incredible business in China. At a Warner cinema in Guangzhou,[2] the film set house records with $240,000. "We opened two halls with one thousand seats in total for the new episode's premiere," with almost all of the seats selling out, said Ye Xueying, deputy general manager of Warner Jinyi International Cinema ("Rocketing ..."). At Shiyigong Cinema, an older theater in the area, nearly fifteen hundred people paid $2.40 each to see the movie for its premiere. By Sunday of opening weekend, about $181,000 in tickets had sold at the theater. In all, *Revenge of the Sith* grossed $3.0 million from its three-day opening frame in China.

One of the problems with taking advantage of the huge potential moviegoing audience in China is the sizable disparity in currency values. Pirated DVDs sell for less than $1 on streets throughout China, so to pay sometimes up to $6 to see a movie in theaters is an incredible sum of money for the average, non-affluent Chinese citizen. With everyday items costing five to ten times less money in China than in the United States, charging similar prices for tickets or even a few dollars per ticket is too much money for many people to afford. Additionally, moviegoing has never been a traditional activity in China, having just recently started to gain popularity. Cultural disadvantages aside, analysts expected *Revenge of the Sith* to make 80 to 100 million yuan, or about $10 to $12 million (ibid.). By comparison, the first two episodes of the series had made $4.1 million and $5.4 million, respectively.

Most of the other Asian countries did not contribute impressive grosses to the final prequel, nor was the prequel's opening in most Asian territories relatively impressive either compared to the other prequels or other significant blockbusters. Thailand contributed $1.2 million, Taiwan $1.3 million, and the Philippines $0.8 million. Below is a chart showing other notable openings in smaller markets:

Country	Opening Weekend Gross (millions)	All-Time Rank at Opening
Sweden	$2.7	4th
Denmark	$2.2	4th
Norway	$1.6	6th
Poland	$1.6	5th
Czech Republic/Slovakia	$0.5	3rd

2.   The South China city is often known internationally as Canton.

Fox and Lucasfilm were pleased with the impressive international results. "We're all elated. It was a fantastic weekend. It's one for the record books. We're looking forward to continued excellent results for the coming weeks," said Joe Ortiz, executive director of sales administration for Fox ("'Sith' Rampage …"). The only country where *Revenge of the Sith* did not open in first place was Egypt, where *Kingdom of Heaven* held onto its throne, apparently because of two prominent Egyptian actors in the movie, which was a complete commercial failure in North America. Through the early part of the first week after opening weekend, *Revenge of the Sith* continued to boost its total, up to $171 million internationally as of May 24 with $13 million Monday and another $12 million Tuesday. The total already stood ahead of *Return of the Jedi*'s $165.8 million international total.

Ascending the Charts

During its second weekend, *Revenge of the Sith* grossed $61.5 million from 10,586 screens worldwide, boosting its foreign total to $246.2 million, but declining 54 percent from its opening weekend in the process, according to *Variety* (McNary "'Wars' …"). The trade publication mentioned warm temperatures in Western Europe cutting into moviegoing, though the prequel still boasted impressive figures. "We're very pleased with the results and expect to continue setting more records," said Joe Ortiz (ibid.). Only *The Return of the King* had performed better over a similar period, having grossed about $270 million after a dozen days compared to just more than $250 million for *Revenge of the Sith* by the end of Monday, the prequel's twelfth day.

After less than two weeks, *Revenge of the Sith* had already passed the foreign gross of *The Empire Strikes Back* ($247.9 million) and entered the top fifty foreign grossers of all time. The twelve-day gross for the final prequel had reached $520 million worldwide. In the United Kingdom, the film declined 50 percent to boost its total to $46 million, while France took a rougher fall, 59 percent to $8.9 million, for a total of $34.8 million. The prequel also opened in South Korea, one of its final markets, where it grossed $3.8 million from 306 screens, the sixth highest country gross for the weekend for the prequel and Fox's second biggest opening ever in the country, behind *The Day After Tomorrow* (2004).

In other notable markets, Italy disappointed again with a drop of 58 percent to $1.6 million. Germany added $6.6 million, a 54 percent weekend-to-weekend decline, Australia contributed $4.9 million, and Spain injected another $4.2 million. The prequel fell 46.7 percent in China to $1.6 million, an impressive hold because movies in China commonly fall 70 percent or more on their second weekends and disappear entirely by weekend four (Bresnan "… Still Huge"). In the international market, most studios avoided opening any significant competition against *Revenge of the Sith*, so the only other film performing well worldwide was *Kingdom of Heaven*, which significantly outperformed its domestic gross abroad. By the end of two weekends in release, the last *Star Wars* film ever had beaten the final grosses for *Attack of the Clones* in thirty-one markets and *The Phantom Menace* in five.

For its third weekend internationally, *Revenge of the Sith* showed better staying power, with $38.5 million and a decline of just 37.4 percent. As with its performance in North America, the massive worldwide openings led to sizable declines from the first to the second weekend. Fortunately, the positive word of mouth and popularity of the franchise contributed to a strong third weekend, where the film boosted its international total to $309 million, barely surpassing its domestic total. "We're still seeing very conservative dropoffs," said Joe Ortiz (McNary "'Sith' still ..."). While many countries are typically fast-burn markets for films, the prequel enjoyed solid staying power in most European nations.

In Germany, the prequel fell 19.7 percent to $5.3 million, an extremely impressive hold after a heat wave had cut into the previous weekend's box office take. France also reported a nice hold, down 31.5 percent to $6.1 million, raising the prequel's box office total to $42.3 million. The French cumulative gross stood barely below *The Phantom Menace*'s entire box office total in the country. In Belgium and Switzerland, the prequel fell just 2 percent and 15 percent, respectively. The 40 percent decline in the United Kingdom was one of the steepest, but with $5.9 million more, the prequel reached $60.8 million in the territory. The 49 percent drop in Spain was surprising, though. One exhibitor told *Variety* of the decline, "Pirate DVDs are taking people away from cinemas in general, and especially are discouraging people from watching the movie in the cinema twice" (McNary "'Sith' takes ...").

Asian territories, almost always fast-burn markets because of higher piracy rates, also experienced impressive declines for the prequel. *Revenge of the Sith* fell 35 percent in China and 30 percent in South Korea, where the film already was on course to pass both of the previous prequels the following weekend. Already, the film had topped *Attack of the Clones* in forty-nine markets and *The Phantom Menace* in seventeen, an impressive accomplishment for a movie competing with the sixteen years of anticipation and hype from which the first prequel had benefitted.

By its fourth weekend overseas, *Revenge of the Sith* could no longer dominate as it had for three consecutive weeks. The opening of *Mr. and Mrs. Smith* finally dethroned the prequel with $32 million, though *Star Wars* still earned $19.1 million after declining 48 percent. The total gross for the prequel reached $340.6 million internationally and $672.7 million worldwide, ranking twentieth on the all-time list. The box office grosses declined 41 percent in France, 43 percent in Germany, 43 percent in Australia, and only 36 percent in Spain, a reversal of the previous weekend's trend.

Falling to fourth place internationally behind *Batman Begins*, *Mr. and Mrs. Smith*, and *Madagascar*, *Revenge of the Sith* continued to climb the all-time charts with its $8.8 million gross from roughly 7,200 screens during its fifth weekend, falling 54 percent. Its worldwide box office gross crossed $700 million, placing it nineteenth on the list of history's biggest worldwide hits. By its sixth weekend internationally, the prequel lost more than 4,500 screens, consequently plummeting to $2.5 million in weekend grosses. It reached $362.2 million overseas for a worldwide total of $721 million, in desperate need of its final opening in Japan to catapult it further up the list and re-invigorate its box office.

Having soared well into blockbuster territory already, *Revenge of the Sith* had one major territory left in which to play: Japan. The Japanese have always had a special respect and admiration for Lucas's mythic saga, especially because of Lucas's incorporation of elements from famous Japanese director Akira Kurosawa's films, most notably *The Hidden Fortress* (1958). *The Phantom Menace* had achieved a massive box office gross in Japan of $109.9 million, the highest total for the film from any country outside of the United States, so Fox saw the country as a major territory for *Star Wars* films.

To promote its July 9 release, Fox made a specially cut, fifteen-second trailer that screened on tunnel walls of Tokyo's Ginza subway line from late June through July 14 (Frater). The unique marketing technology, based on the nineteenth century Zoetrope, came courtesy of Submedia, a New York company, though usually only static images are used. The *Revenge of the Sith* trailer marked the first time that Submedia had done moving images for a promotion of its kind.

Before the prequel opened in Japan, it enjoyed two sets of previews, one on June 28 and the last on July 2, collecting $7.5 million combined from both. The $4.6 million from the Tuesday, June 28 previews set a record, destroying the $3.5 million haul for *The Matrix Reloaded*. Many big blockbusters have preview showings leading up to their releases, which can account for significant percentages of the final box office grosses. Showing on 756 screens, the final *Star Wars* film earned $9.5 million for its July 9 weekend premiere.

The preview screening numbers are combined with the opening weekend numbers to calculate the total launch gross in Japan, which for *Revenge of the Sith* reached $17.0 million, the third best total ever. "In Japan, we've got a long way to go. Key markets will make it tough to reach [*The Phantom Menace*'s total]. But we've got a long way to go, and it's going to be close," said Joe Ortiz (Mohr "'Sith' …"). The figures lifted the prequel's total foreign gross to $391 million and its worldwide take to $782 million, placing it seventeenth all-time.

Before its second weekend in Japan, *Revenge of the Sith* crashed through $400 million in foreign grosses. Falling 26 percent from its opening weekend, the prequel made another $7 million in Japan to boost its total to $410 million internationally. It was tracking ahead of the earlier prequels after two weekends. During its third weekend, it declined a steeper 44 percent, to $3.9 million, but it held stronger the following weekend, falling 14 percent to $3.4 million despite losing 131 screens. The total in Japan had ascended to $52 million, lifting the foreign total to $431.6 million for a worldwide take of $807.4 million.

Even on its fifth weekend in Japan, the prequel ranked first at the box office, with $2.4 million, and maintained its dominance again with its sixth weekend gross of $2.8 million, an increase from the previous weekend because of the Obon holiday. The prequel beat both *Madagascar* and *War of the Worlds* to retain its first place ranking. *Revenge of the Sith* narrowly lost to *Madagascar* in its seventh weekend, but remained strong with $1.8 million. It collected another $1.3 million, falling only 27.8 percent, for its eighth weekend.

Summer of *Sith*

By the end of its massively successful worldwide box office campaign, *Revenge of the Sith* had grossed just a few dollars shy of $850 million, including $469.7 million from its foreign campaign. The worldwide total ranked as the eleventh best of all time, no small accomplishment given the massive worldwide success of the *Harry Potter* and *Lord of the Rings* films that clogged the charts between the release of the first and last prequels. In most countries around the world, the prequel ranked first for the summer box office season, although *Harry Potter and the Goblet of Fire* often topped the film in many countries once it came to theaters in late 2005.

Although the last prequel showed more strength in some markets than others, it proved very successful worldwide and reached impressive gross totals in many territories. The box office total for *Revenge of the Sith* reached $82.7 million in Japan, $72.8 million in the United Kingdom, $56.8 million in France, $47.3 million in Germany, $27.2 million in Australia,[3] and $23.8 million in Spain,

---

3.   The film's success in Australia is covered in more detail in the "Galaxy of Hype" chapter earlier in the book.

among major markets. The prequel ranked first for the year in Spain,[4] France, and Australia. Other notable final grosses include:

Country	Total Gross (millions)
Brazil	$7.3
China	$9.1
Denmark	$5.6
Holland	$4.9
Italy	$11.3
Mexico	$15.3
New Zealand	$4.2
Russia	$8.3
South Korea	$10.3
Sweden	$7.7
Switzerland	$4.8

In many major box office territories, *Revenge of the Sith* did not reach the heights that the first prequel achieved in 1999 with its amazing summer and fall campaign, but Lucas's last entry in the saga crushed *Attack of the Clones* in almost every key market. The final prequel also topped *The Phantom Menace* in countries like Australia, China, the Czech Republic, Denmark, France, Hungary, Mexico, New Zealand, Norway, Russia, South Korea, and Sweden, among many other small box office countries. In France, the prequel was by far the most successful summer film with 7.2 million admissions by the end of August, helping to offset deficits in other major countries between the first and third prequels. Even *Harry Potter and the Goblet of Fire* could not unseat the prequel as the year's top film in France.

The biggest discrepancies between the 1999 *Star Wars* phenomenon and the 2005 blockbuster came in territories like Brazil, Germany, Japan, and the United Kingdom. Although all of the aforementioned countries were solid performers for *Revenge of the Sith*, the grosses represented double-digit percentage declines from *The Phantom Menace*, thus contributing to the final prequel's inability to

4.   In Spain, *Harry Potter and the Goblet of Fire* overtook the prequel, as it did in many markets, but not until 2006, and then only by the tiniest margin.

reach the billion-dollar mark worldwide. While the Japanese gross for the final prequel was substantial, it was closer to the total for *Attack of the Clones* than for *The Phantom Menace*, which was a bit surprising given its superior reviews and greater anticipation when compared to the second prequel. Likewise, the impressive gross in the United Kingdom, which stood almost $10 million less than the 1999 prequel, was not seen as disappointing, but analysts thought it had a chance at passing the first prequel's gross, or at least approaching it.

The relatively disappointing Italian box office numbers do not mean Italy lacks *Star Wars* fans, only that the marketplace as a whole is not as interested in the franchise as most other countries. Before release, for instance, fans dressed in *Star Wars* costumes in Milan, Italy, had raised money for children's hospitals. Despite a contingent of die-hard fans, an unnamed exhibitor told *Variety*, "The public that would go see a *Star Wars* film in Italy is well-defined. It hasn't increased its fan base" (McNary "'Sith' wages ..."). None of the previous franchise films had increased the number of fans enough to make *Revenge of the Sith* a huge blockbuster in Italy, apparently. *Variety* ran an article about the film's difficulties in the country, citing an aversion to high-tech and science-fiction films in the country's Southern regions and a snobbish, elitist attitude against the saga that does not exist in other countries in Europe (Vivarelli).

European moviegoing in general, but Italian moviegoing especially, is highly dependent on the weather, another factor that damaged *Revenge of the Sith*'s gross potential. Before the first *Star Wars* film made the summer a big moviegoing time in North America, Americans mostly avoided movie theaters. Likewise, the Italians prefer beaches during the summer, not movie theaters, so 60 percent of the country's theaters do not operate during the summer. While Fox tried to remedy the situation in 1999 by opening *The Phantom Menace* in September, its box office gross ($12.9 million) did not prove particularly impressive. Warner Village Cinemas Italia Commercial Director Nicola Grispello said of the final prequel to *Variety*, "Italy is the only country in the world where *Star Wars* didn't work" (ibid.). The film's unimpressive gross by territorial standards contributed to the down year in Italy, frustrating local exhibitors.

In 2005, most European markets had as many problems with poor yearly box office totals relative to 2004 as North America. German box office receipts declined 17 percent, the Italian box office fell 7 percent, and both France and Spain lost 10 percent of the market from the previous year; only the United Kingdom posted a slight increase. The Australian box office also had fallen 10 percent. Markets like China, Russia, and South Korea continued to experience growth, however. Russian movie admissions had increased sevenfold in the previous five years, showing a market in a period of exponential growth. China experienced a 30 percent jump in admissions from 2004, a year that was also up 60 percent from the prior year.

Despite the strong emergence of several markets outside of Europe, most of the revenue from Hollywood films, between 60 and 65 percent, comes from Western Europe, which suffered a rough year. By year's end, the international box office had dipped about 4 percent from the previous year, totaling roughly $12 billion. Only four movies topped $300 million internationally, compared to seven the previous year, making *Revenge of the Sith*'s gross even more impressive. Only *Harry Potter and the Goblet of Fire* topped the prequel internationally for 2005, despite the film's inferior domestic gross. For the year, Fox ranked second among the studios in international grosses with $1.6 billion.

Among the highest grossing countries for *Revenge of the Sith*, China ranked tenth, marking the first time ever that China had been in the top ten biggest countries for an American movie since it started importing U.S. films in 1994. For 2005, about 55 percent of Chinese box office revenue came from locally produced films, not Hollywood products. Although Chinese film fans have become increasingly interested in science-fiction films, the number of periodicals devoted to the genre has shrunk from more than thirty to just one over the past twenty years.

The only remaining publication devoted to the genre at the time was "SF World," a monthly magazine with a circulation of more than five hundred thousand. Jin Tao, a senior science-fiction novelist, told *Variety*, "[Chinese science-fiction writers] cannot make a living by selling science-fiction books, and there are too many social shackles on them. Besides, the spirit of science fiction has not pervaded the public awareness" ("Chinese ..."). Compared to the United States, where science fiction is a huge commercial genre, China had less than one hundred professional writers in the genre at the time of the article's writing. Despite the struggles of the science-fiction genre in China, the *Star Wars* prequels enjoyed impressive runs in the country, relative to other American films in release in their respective years.

After a less impressive though still huge worldwide gross for *Attack of the Clones*, *Revenge of the Sith* was a behemoth in most markets, shattering opening day records and breaking Fox records for an opening weekend in almost every country. "Some people feel they didn't want to be left out of this last one," Joe Ortiz said (Mohr "'Sith' ..."). Fans worldwide who had waited patiently for the final installment in the saga made it a huge success, but so also did the casual moviegoers and new fans in territories not as familiar with the saga. *Revenge of the*

Sith lifted the prequel trilogy's worldwide box office total to more than $2.42 billion and the complete saga's haul to just more than $4.21 billion, a truly staggering figure for six movies. After all, the first three films originally came to theaters far before the international marketplace had blossomed into the cash machine it had become by the end of the 1990s. Unfortunately, rampant piracy worldwide made a difference in the final prequel's box office gross, especially because of the film's high profile.

Revenge of the Pirates

Although *Revenge of the Sith* enjoyed an immensely successful theatrical run worldwide, piracy haunted the movie's release, a common occurrence with major Hollywood blockbusters. In recent years, studios have started to release their largest blockbusters simultaneously worldwide in an effort to curb piracy in foreign countries. The idea is to give fans worldwide the opportunity to see the movie in theaters at roughly the same time, hopefully discouraging them from downloading pirated copies on the Internet or buying illegal VCDs on the streets.

Piracy is not only a foreign concern. Unfortunately, frequent piracy still occurs in North America, part of which stems from overpriced tickets, which studios do not directly control. Average ticket prices have not increased in line with inflation. Rather, they have far exceeded inflation and have continued to rise while the price of DVDs has remained unchanged. As a result, many people, especially high school and college students with limited funds and a frequent Internet presence, have turned to piracy. The music industry has faced similar threats, and responded accordingly by offering inexpensive music downloads through services such as Apple's iTunes.

Piracy was a huge problem with the first prequel in 1999, but it only became easier in the intervening years, at least online, because of the vast majority of Internet users switching from slow dial-up connections to high-speed access, making movie files much quicker to download. A file that could have taken nearly a day to download with a dial-up connection became downloadable in just a few hours. According to CNBC in 2004, *The Phantom Menace* was the most pirated movie of all time, increasing the likelihood that *Revenge of the Sith* would suffer from more piracy than most major blockbusters ("'Star Wars' Leads …").

Before the final *Star Wars* movie's release, *Variety* reported that clips featuring Hayden Christensen and Ewan McGregor performing stunts had leaked to the Internet in early 2004 ("Star Wars 3 …"). Lucasfilm sent cease-and-desist letters to various Web sites, all of which complied, but not before many fans downloaded the footage. By the time of the final prequel's release, the entire film had already become available online, easy to find on the BitTorrent file-sharing network. More than sixteen thousand people were downloading the film when Reuters published an article about the leaked film on opening day ("Final 'Star Wars' film ..."). The article noted that one copy seemed to come from inside the industry as it had time-stamping on it and did not seem to have been filmed in theaters.

George Lucas has worried about piracy for years, warning that it could destroy the Hollywood business model. He said, "I'm glad I'm getting out when I can because it's not going to be the same in a few years. Piracy is going to get much worse. I don't know how they'll [studios] survive" ("Star Wars leaked ..."). One major problem, as Lucas has mentioned, is people downloading movies illegally rather than buying them on DVD. According to the Motion Picture Association of America (MPAA), fewer than one in ten movies turn a profit from box office grosses alone ("Latest ..."). The other films that eventually become profitable achieve their success from DVD sales and other revenue streams, like cable television, pay-per-view, and network television, to name a few. To combat the growing piracy problem, numerous organizations joined forces in various efforts to stop Internet downloading.

In late May, the Department of Homeland Security, the FBI, and the MPAA joined together to shut down Elite Torrents, a Web site at EliteTorrents.org helping about 133,000 members find roughly 17,800 movies and software programs at the time, including *Revenge of the Sith* ("Revenge of the MPAA ..."). Users had downloaded the final prequel more than ten thousand times in the first twenty-four hours it was available on the network. Federal agents executed ten search warrants and seized the main server, afterwards posting a notice on the site that read, "This site has been permanently shut down by the Federal Bureau of Investigation and U.S. Immigration and Customs Enforcement" ("U.S....").

In Germany, a group called Media Control called the final prequel one of the ten most downloaded films in the country by the middle of the summer, citing roughly 9,500 illegal downloads between May 23 and May 29, 77 percent dubbed in German (McNary and Mohr). The prequel performed well in Germany, but one wonders how much of a dent piracy put in the box office figures. Aside from lost box office profits for the studios, other concerns plagued many businesses and networks.

Illegal downloading had become such a problem that Akonix Systems, a leading provider of enterprise-class business solutions that specializes in network security, warned businesses that employees downloading the movie illegally at work could cause two significant problems. First, downloading large media files could cause slowdowns across company networks, especially from multiple employees downloading large files, and second, the downloads could put companies at potential legal risk. "This latest *Star Wars* episode is causing great excitement among movie fans so it's inevitable there will be high demand for free copies of the movie," said Akonix Systems CEO Peter Shaw ("Star Wars Frenzy …"). He warned IT managers, "Organizations should immediately make sure that the use of BitTorrent and other file sharing applications are banned in company policies" (ibid.).

On Tuesday, September 27, 2005, eight Californians were charged with involvement in the illegal release of *Revenge of the Sith* before it reached theaters. According to court documents, the piracy began with a "screener" copy of the film at a post-production facility where one of the defendants, Albert Valente, worked. Valente then gave it to a friend, Jessie I. Lumada, who gave it to four other people who worked at a Los Angeles–based cable company. Stephani Reiko Gima, one of the cable company employees, then made a copy to give to her cousin, Joe De Sagun Dimaano. Soon after, Dimaano loaned the copy to Marc Hoaglin, who then released the stolen movie online a day before its worldwide theatrical release.

All eight people involved in the chain of custody for the pirated film faced charges of misdemeanor copyright infringement, carrying a penalty of up to a year in prison, while Hoaglin faced more serious charges of uploading the movie onto the Internet, a felony carrying up to three years of jail time. U.S. Attorney Brian Hoffstadt, the prosecutor for the case, noted the unusual nature of charging eight people in one case. He said, "Most of them, they didn't intend for it to be uploaded, but they knew they were passing it along. We take the crime of copyright infringement, particularly of movies, very seriously" ("Eight …").

In December, Hoaglin, the worst offender in the group, pleaded guilty to unlawfully posting *Revenge of the Sith* on the Internet. The upload was in violation of the Family Entertainment and Copyright Act of 2005, which made uploading a film before its release to DVD a federal offense. Hoaglin was just the second person convicted under the law. The other seven in the group pleaded guilty to charges of misdemeanor copyright infringement. "If they'd done it for financial gain or profit, then that could have become a felony, but … that wasn't the case for these folks," Hoffstadt said (Dobuzinskis).

None of the seven people convicted of misdemeanor copyright infringement seemed to have any intentions of damaging the film financially, though the movie industry is exceptionally sensitive to any type of copyright infringement. "Stealing copyrights is a serious problem, and the theft and illegal distribution of *Revenge of the Sith* was a glaring example of how the actions of dishonest people can cheat the movie-watching experience," wrote an MPAA official in a statement (ibid.). The unusually long chain of people involved in the copyright infringement case demonstrates how minor copyright violations can lead to a larger violation once one person decides to go beyond passing a movie to a few friends and instead uploading it to the Internet.

International piracy also remained a huge problem for *Revenge of the Sith*, especially in China, which never seems to have much respect for international copyright laws. In Beijing, Chinese pirates had the prequel available for 10–20 yuan, or about $1.20 to $2.40 (Coonan "Dark ..."). *The Evening Standard* in London claimed that many of the illegal DVDs had English subtitles that did not match the film, but were instead from the 2003 action movie *Detention* starring Dolph Lundgren ("It's revenge ..."). The visual quality, according to reports, was fairly good, though slightly blurry.

In North America, nobody could buy a small soda for the price at which pirates sold the prequel in China. While many people might picture shady individuals selling copies of Hollywood movies in dark alleys, their visions are inaccurate. The media often refers to the Chinese black market as a hidden exchange of money for illegal goods, but one need not go to any special, hidden location to find pirated films in China. In many cases, vendors approach people with bags full of illegal DVDs on the streets. Other times, though, the DVDs are sold at seemingly legitimate brick-and-mortar businesses that look like standard neighborhood video stores.

Having been to Beijing myself, I was shocked at how inexpensive and professional many of the DVDs looked from a packaging perspective alone. All types of movies were available for as little as 85 cents, many of which had not yet received official DVD releases in North America. In Beijing, stores selling illegal copies of movies for sometimes less than $1 are easy to find and they operate as normally as a local Blockbuster in the United States, despite the presence of police officers on almost every corner. The stores are not hidden or in areas with other illicit activities. Rather, they are common venues throughout the city and do not seem to elicit any attention from authorities.

China claims to be combatting piracy, citing nearly ten thousand prosecutions in 2004, but according to *Variety*, pirates have an 80 percent stranglehold on the DVD market, making legal sales difficult (Coonan "Dark ..."). Even at a paltry $3.60, which is the price Time Warner tried selling cut-price DVDs in 2004, legal discs seem like a rip-off compared to the inexpensive, pirated alternatives, many of which are burned directly from legitimate copies of the film and boast decent to great quality picture and sound (ibid.). In July, China signed a joint anti-piracy agreement with the United States. By late October, though, Washington officials were unimpressed. Trade Representative Rob Portman said the United States would invoke a World Trade Organization article requesting evidence of China's attempts to thwart piracy (Coonan "U.S....").

The MPAA believes Hollywood lost more than $280 million because of piracy in China in 2004 alone. "There will be no quick fixes to China's serious piracy problems," said MPAA Senior Vice President Mike Ellis (ibid.). While Zhang Xinjian, vice director of the Market Supervision Department of the Ministry of Culture, reaffirmed the importance of the countries' agreement and its mutual benefits to both film industries, MPAA officials were not impressed by early results. "The U.S. government's request for information on the administrative, civil, and criminal actions to enforce China's intellectual property rights obligations is critical to ensuring China's international commitments and to protecting the rights of the U.S. copyright industries," said MPAA President Dan Glickman (ibid.).

Piracy also reigned in Scotland, where black market traders reaped an economic windfall from the film's release. John McGowan of the Federation Against Copyright Theft (FACT) said that in Glasgow's Barras market, at least twelve traders were making twenty thousand pounds per week on the movie. "This latest *Star Wars* movie is making these traders a fortune," he said (Alexander). The traders bragged about their accomplishments, one having written, "It's been reported that *Revenge of the Sith* has broken the cash record for Scotland. This report was issued by the Barras Trust" (ibid.). The prequel became available several weeks before its official May 19 release. "This is the biggest film we've ever sold. I can't remember such demand for a film," one anonymous trader said (ibid.).

Far from only an international issue, illegal DVDs also were a problem in the United States, especially in major markets like New York City. Shortly after the movie's debut, the NYPD seized one thousand pirated copies of *Revenge of the Sith* from a Harlem storage facility, along with about forty thousand other illegal discs (Melago). In the raid, police arrested nine men. Bootleg DVDs were already for sale around the city at about $5, or half the price of a movie ticket. "The street vendors knew to come here to pick up the DVDs," said NYPD Deputy Inspector Kevin Walsh (ibid.).

Along the United States–Mexico border, in towns in both countries, piracy blossomed. "I'm all out [of copies]," said one vendor in Matamoros, Mexico (Chapa). In Brownsville, Texas, one vendor said he could burn copies of the film on his computer for waiting customers to meet demand. Pirates on both sides of the border agreed that the film was a blockbuster on the black market, too. Like

China, enforcing copyrights in Mexico and much of Latin America still proves difficult for the MPAA and other watchdog organizations. According to one report from the International Federation of Phonographic Industry, Mexico has the third highest level of piracy of movies and music in the world.

Piracy remains a growing problem for the studios, with the MPAA estimating that film theft costs the industry about $3.5 billion per year in lost revenues (Melago). If anyone thinks the MPAA overestimates the impact of piracy, a separate Smith Barney study concluded that the organization had drastically underestimated the impact. With illegal Internet downloads considered, Smith Barney put the figure at closer to $5.4 billion annually (ibid.). Police working with MPAA investigators seized more than 81 million illegal discs in 2005, up from 76 million in 2004.

With the proliferation of online piracy and continued illegal DVD sales, eternal vigilance is necessary to keep the movie industry from suffering the same fate as the music industry. Because of the growth of illegal file sharing networks, the music industry spun into rapid decline in the late nineties. Fortunately, Lucasfilm later offered a desirable DVD set for the final prequel, enticing millions of people to pay for home copies of the movie.

The Saga is Complete

After a successful global theatrical run, *Revenge of the Sith* made a speedy debut on DVD in time for the holiday shopping season, which is always one of the best times for DVD sales. By late July, Lucasfilm had announced the November 1 release date of both *Revenge of the Sith* on DVD and another highly anticipated sequel, *Star Wars: Battlefront II*, scheduled to arrive on the same day in a joint marketing push. As with its release to theaters, the DVD enjoyed a simultaneous worldwide release, meaning it came to DVD at roughly the same time in every major territory.

Global DVD releases, like global theatrical releases, are fairly rare. "The great news is, it's nearly thirty years in the making, [but] now fans old and new alike can enjoy the entire *Star Wars* saga whenever they want," said Steven Feldstein, senior vice president of marketing for 20th Century Fox Home Video ("'Star Wars' Movie …"). The DVD release marked a special event not only because any *Star Wars* movie's debut on a new format is event-worthy, but because fans for years had dreamed about being able to watch the entire saga, nearly thirteen hours long, from start to finish in their homes. Before the final *Star Wars* film came to DVD, Lucasfilm had sold tens of millions of copies of the other five films, including spikes in all of their sales with the release of the final prequel to theaters.

To promote the release of *Revenge of the Sith* on DVD and *Star Wars: Battlefront II*, Lucasfilm planned a $60 million global marketing campaign (James "'Star Wars' …"). "The combination of *Revenge of the Sith* on DVD and *Star Wars: Battlefront II* makes November 1 a watershed day for *Star Wars* fans. It's really going to be a terrific celebration of the entire saga," said Jim Ward, senior vice president of marketing and distribution for Lucasfilm ("The Ultimate …"). Prior to *Revenge of the Sith*'s release to DVD, Fox had sold an estimated 100 million copies worldwide of the *Star Wars* saga on VHS, laserdisc, and DVD (Hettrick "'Revenge' …"). Retailers and analysts knew sales of the final prequel would be huge, as did Warner Bros., which had scheduled *Batman Begins* for an October 25 release, but moved the date up to October 18 to give it more time before the prequel went on sale (Ault "Batman …").

Several promotional partners for the film's theatrical release also participated in its DVD release campaign, like fast-food chain Burger King, which released seventeen additional Super-D figures and vehicles to go along with its thirty-one from earlier in the year, for forty-eight total collectible toys for fans to enjoy. The new toys fell into four categories of four toys each: Cosmic Cruisers (rolling spring-loaded vehicles), Shadow Casters (figures where an image projects from the bottom of the toy), Galactic Spinners (tops), and Jedi Wisdom (figures with fortune-telling cubes beneath them).

Additionally, Burger King offered Darth Vader as the elusive chase figure and seventeenth toy, with a sound chip featuring his heavy breathing. Burger King also made available six collectible Destiny Watches commemorating each of the saga's films. Additionally, fans could buy Burger King *Star Wars* lenticular cards, coming in six different designs, which operated as gift cards but could be kept after their totals were depleted. Much like its earlier promotions, Burger King intended its new toys to celebrate the entire saga, not just the final movie.

Because of the problems DreamWorks Home Entertainment and Buena Vista Home Entertainment suffered with shipping too many *Shrek 2* (2004) and *The Incredibles* (2004) DVDs, both of which experienced high return rates, Fox strictly limited the allotment of *Revenge of the Sith* DVDs retailers could receive. Additionally, Fox made *Revenge of the Sith* its first major release not to come to VHS, which also made it one of the first big releases in home video history not to be available in the format (Netherby). Buena Vista Home Entertainment and Fox were the two studios leading the way in the death of the VHS format, although many retailers had already stopped stocking VHS copies of popular films.

According to an article in *Video Business*, an industry trade paper, many retailers received 20–30 percent fewer copies of the *Revenge of the Sith* DVD set than they felt they needed to satisfy first-week demand from customers (Ault "Fox skimps …"). Many retailers expressed surprise that Fox would want to limit sales of such a critical title in its fourth quarter release schedule. Steven Feldstein said, "Initially, the right amount of product is being placed. At Fox, our supply chain systems are extremely sophisticated, and we can replenish within twenty-four hours where needed" (ibid.). Other retailers and analysts understood Fox's desire to ship a more reasonable allotment of units to stores, after Wall Street lambasted DreamWorks and Pixar over high retailer returns.

The DVD package, which included two discs, one with the film and the other with numerous extra features, received great reviews. *Denver Rocky Mountain News* writer Mike Pearson gave the DVD release a "B+." Gary Frisch of *Video*

Business gave the two-disc set a glowing review, calling the picture quality "flawless" and wrote, "This is one of the best discs to come along all year and a fitting capstone to one of the most popular series of all time." Guido Henkel of DVDReview.com wrote, "The image is absolutely breathtaking ... The clarity of the image is unparalleled." The review concluded that "Lucasfilm [has created] a remarkable DVD" and a documentary for the second disc that is "as novel as it is exciting."

The extra features disc for the final prequel has five categories of special features: Documentary and Featurettes, Deleted Scenes, Trailers and TV Spots, Web Documentaries, and Video Games and Still Galleries. "From the beginning of production, George [Lucas] wanted to be sure we chronicled everything that went into the making of *Episode III* specifically to create an incredible DVD experience," said Jim Ward (Hettrick "'Revenge' ..."). As such, the bonus disc boasts an exclusive documentary, *Within A Minute*, that offers an in-depth look into the filmmaking process by examining a forty-nine-second clip from the film, which comes from the climax on Mustafar. The documentary shows how numerous teams of people from pre-production through post-production helped bring the planet and its scenes to life for moviegoers.

Within A Minute is an informative, seventy-eight-minute documentary that shows how many thousands of hours went into each minute of film and how many different talents were required to realize Lucas's vision. Producer Rick McCallum provided audio commentary for the feature, which director Tippy Bushkin and his team compiled using more than six hundred hours of footage from the film's production. "*Within A Minute* is almost a 'mini-film school' in which Rick and George examine the entire process of making *Episode III* in a fun and fascinating way," Bushkin said ("Feature-Packed ..."). Besides the primary documentary, the bonus disc includes two additional featurettes, *It's All For Real: The Stunts of Episode III* and *The Chosen One*.

The deleted scenes section of the bonus disc has six scenes total, five of which appear in completed form. Only the first deleted scene has elements that are still in animatics form, though it is nonetheless serviceable. "George worked with Industrial Light & Magic and *Episode III* Producer Rick McCallum to finish most of these scenes with complete visual effects and sound design, and they bring a new perspective to the movie," said Jim Ward (ibid.). Each deleted scene also has accompanying, optional introductions by George Lucas and Rick McCallum.

Within A Minute is a fantastic documentary, but the real gem of the DVD is the collection of deleted scenes, which greatly add to the experience of the film.

Although one could see them as "cutting room floor" material that, because of the artistic decisions of the director, do not exist in the *Star Wars* universe, Lucas cut them not because of quality reasons but to keep the story on track. He had to re-focus the movie on Anakin's journey to keep the film a manageable length. As a result, he made a few tough decisions to delete scenes that are not second tier as far as quality, but could be seen as expendable when focusing solely on Anakin's journey toward the Dark Side.

A few of the deleted scenes, however, are invaluable additions to the *Star Wars* story as a whole, especially as an early look into the foundation of the Rebel Alliance. While the first deleted scene, "Grievous Slaughters A Jedi; Escape From The General (Animatic)," is not high on plot, it features a few nice moments between Anakin and Obi-Wan and shows a nifty escape sequence through part of the General's capital ship, the *Invisible Hand*, which is filled with water. "We spent a couple of days in this big vat of water, and on paper, it seemed really cool. So that's something that I'll go see first on the DVD, because it wasn't in the movie," Hayden Christensen said (Ault "*Sith ... *").

The second deleted scene, "A Stirring in the Senate," focuses on a private meeting of senators, including Bail Organa and Padmé Amidala, and is dramatically powerful as well as relevant to the story. Organa knows the Republic is nearing its end, but says to the others, "We cannot let a thousand years of democracy disappear ... without a fight." He quickly amends his statement to suggest he wants a diplomatic solution to the problems at hand, however. Even so, viewers can see the first makings of a rebellion.

Revenge of the Sith offers enough scenes with Bail Organa to gather that he is a friend to the Jedi and a force for good in the galaxy, but the deleted scenes show that Organa is a man willing to stand by his ideals despite risking his safety to do so. Mon Mothma has a cameo with dialogue in the second deleted scene. The third deleted scene, "Seeds of Rebellion (Padmé's Apartment)," is also a nice insight into the politics and maneuvering behind the scenes in a last attempt to stop Palpatine's creation of an empire before he destroys the final elements of democracy. Viewers know that Mon Mothma and Bail Organa's talks of peace turn into preparations for violent rebellion between the two film trilogies.

The fourth deleted scene, "Confront the Chancellor (Palpatine's Office)," shows a Mon Calamarian behind Padmé as she is speaking to Palpatine on behalf of the "Delegation of 2000" (an alliance of senators trying to restore democracy to the Republic after Palpatine's executive orders; the group eventually becomes the Alliance to Restore the Republic, or the Rebel Alliance as the Empire calls them). Die-hard fans know that the planet Mon Calamari was instrumental in the war effort for the Rebel Alliance as it contributed the massive capital ships known as Mon Calamari Cruisers, seen in *Return of the Jedi*, where Admiral Ackbar commands the Rebel Alliance fleet in the Battle of Endor aboard *Home One*. The acting in the fourth deleted scene, from Ian McDiarmid, Hayden Christensen, and Natalie Portman, is commendable work, so its exclusion from the final cut is a shame.

One can see why, for time constraints, Lucas had to cut the fifth deleted scene, "A Plot to Destroy the Jedi?" Nonetheless, it gives great insight into the private thoughts of the Jedi, specifically Yoda, Mace Windu, and Obi-Wan, about the shift in the Force and the crumbling of democracy in the Republic. The final deleted scene, "Exiled to Dagobah," is a short scene showing Yoda's arrival on the swamp planet where he would spend the rest of his days, eventually training Luke Skywalker as the last of the Jedi Knights. Because it is such a short scene, it deserves inclusion in the film, more so than any of the other scenes as it would be a nice conclusion to the first trilogy. The look on Yoda's face after landing is also telling. The Jedi Master sighs and looks as though he cannot believe that after hundreds of years defending the Republic, his life will be spent in exile on a distant planet far from the galaxy's core.

Although extra features are always a huge part of the quality of a DVD release, especially as fans often expect two-disc versions of any major blockbuster, the most important part of a DVD release is still the quality of the film's presentation, both video and audio. "The fact that *Revenge of the Sith* was produced digitally means that the picture and sound on this DVD are truly extraordinary," Jim Ward said ("Feature-Packed …"). Additionally, fans can listen to an audio commentary track with Lucas and various key crew members.

For the audio commentary track on the feature film, most of the contributing members, besides Rick McCallum and Visual Effects Supervisor Roger Guyett, recorded their commentary individually with DVD Commentary Producer Gary Leva. For the project, Leva's job was to oversee the commentary, help the speakers deliver clear, compelling dialogue about the film and their work on it, and then edit together the various commentary tracks into one track with the best of their insights and observations. "I want the commentaries to be as informative as possible—to give fans a sense of the creative work that went into these films," Leva said (Burton). He also faced the challenge of prodding the visual effects gurus to speak in terms that people outside of the industry would be able to understand, as well as encouraging the commentators to relay their personal feelings about the film and their work rather than just technical details of the production.

Some fans may have noticed that when they put the *Revenge of the Sith* DVD into their computers, a desktop icon appears that reads, "CHARLOTTE." As with "Blue Harvest," a codename used for *Return of the Jedi*, "Charlotte" was the codename assigned to the *Revenge of the Sith* DVD project to protect it from publicity leaks. Prequel DVD Producer Van Ling said, "It is only seen on the very first batch of the Episode III DVDs, and is being 'retired' for future manufacturing runs, so it could be a collector's item that gives the fans a glimpse into the secret history of the *Star Wars* DVDs" ("'Charlotte's' ..."). The codename could not be a random word, however.

Ling explained to the Official *Star Wars* Web Site that the codename had to be a single word, but it also had to relate to a film that Fox owned or distributed, and furthermore it needed to be connected with a title that the studio planned for release around the same time as the final prequel, to make the codename believable. Ling chose "Charlotte" after the 1964 Fox film *Hush, Hush, Sweet Charlotte*. The article also mentioned the codenames for the first two prequels, "Laura" and "Mary," and for the Original Trilogy, "Eve."[1] Ling said, "Clearly, I was having *way* too much fun coming up with these things" (ibid.). The other films, though, did not carry their codenames with the desktop icons as the final prequel did. Besides quirky details like codenames, fans often have fun hunting for "Easter Eggs" on the *Star Wars* DVDs.

Easter Eggs are hidden elements on a DVD that fans can unlock by clicking on a specific spot or entering numbers or characters on a certain menu, for instance. One amusing Easter Egg hidden on the *Revenge of the Sith* DVD is "Hip Hop Yoda," a brief scene of Yoda surrounded by clone troopers as he demonstrates his dancing skills ("Behind ..."). Virginie Michel d'Annoville, a lead animator on the film, put together the joke sequence on weekends as "a side project" meant "as a surprise for the Animation Director, Rob Coleman" (ibid.). She was taking a hip hop class offered through ILM at the time, which helped inspire the sequence, put together by a team of animators. "It was the combination of all these amazing talents from ILM that allowed Hip Hop Yoda to reach this level of quality," she said (ibid.).

Keeping the Hip Hop Yoda project secret from Coleman proved difficult, though, because to render the sequence, the team had to use the *Star Wars* pro-

---

1.   "Laura" came from the 1944 film of the same name, "Mary" was inspired both by *There's Something About Mary* (1998), the hit Ben Stiller comedy, and *The Mary Tyler Moore Show*, and "Eve" came from *The Three Faces of Eve* (1957), where each personality of the title character—Eve White, Eve Black, and Jane—were the codenames for the individual films in the trilogy ("'Charlotte's'...").

duction processors. When he finally saw the completed sequence, Coleman was impressed, as was Lucas, who eventually saw it as well. Because the dancing was set to "Don't Say Nuthin'" by The Roots, Lucasfilm had to seek permission from the group to place the Hip Hop Yoda scene on the DVD, but "The Roots were *very* enthusiastic," according to Michel d'Annoville (ibid.). The group requested that Yoda perform a specific dance move characteristic of their style, however, so animators then integrated it into the final sequence seamlessly, which fans can enjoy on the DVD release.

When *Revenge of the Sith* finally came to DVD, it helped generate $210 million in retail sales alongside *Star Wars: Battlefront II*, though Lucasfilm did not specify how much each product contributed to the total. Jim Ward said, "The phenomenal sales underscore the enduring strength of the series. In many territories, DVD and game sales were nearly double what we initially expected" ("Combined Force …"). *Battlefront II* was also on course to break its predecessor's sales total, running 40 percent ahead of the first title after a week (ibid.).

Many larger retailers offered special promotions to help sell *Revenge of the Sith* on DVD. Target gave away a collector's coin with Darth Vader on one side and Anakin versus Obi-Wan on the other, Wal-Mart offered an enhanced *Star Wars* set that offered an extra DVD with sixty minutes of new content,[2] and Best Buy gave away a lithograph by artist Shepard Fairey. According to *Video Business*, the retailers with special promotions fared the best with DVD sales as many fans are interested in finding collectible exclusives, even when they are relatively minor additions to the product package (Ault "Starry …").

Retailers differed on whether Fox provided them with adequate inventory to meet demand for the much-anticipated DVD release. "There was a lot of demand, [but] we felt we had pretty good supply," said Best Buy spokesman Brian Lucas (ibid.). Virgin Entertainment buyer Chris Anstey disagreed, saying, "We would like to have been allocated many more units than what actually happened" (ibid.). Retailers had similar problems with other DVDs for the year, such as *Batman Begins*, which was unavailable in its two-disc special edition version at many retailers after unexpected demand for the film (Netherby and Ault).

Although Lucasfilm and Fox had kept supplies tight for past *Star Wars* films as well, the move still irritated retailers anxious to take advantage of customer demand. According to *Video Business*, distributor Baker & Taylor reported one

---

2.   The disc featured R2-D2 and C-3PO's "Chronicles of Luke and Anakin Skywalker" among its sixty minutes of bonus content and cost almost $10 more than the standard DVD version.

hundred accounts placing replenishment orders on the final prequel during the DVD set's first several days in stores (ibid.). The distributor was able to fulfill the requests, however.

In another promotional tie-in to help boost sales of the DVD release, Fox and Lucasfilm teamed with NBC and *The Apprentice* in an inventive cross-promotion. In an episode that aired November 10 from 9:00 to 10:00 p.m. on both coasts, the *Apprentice* candidates had to create compelling, effective marketing materials for the launch of the prequel on DVD and its video game counterpart. The two judges of the candidates were Jim Ward and Gary Arnold, senior vice president of entertainment for Best Buy. "*Star Wars: Episode III* is the biggest movie of the year and broke box office records," *Apprentice* Host Donald Trump said ("Donald ..."). "It's the DVD event of the year, and the candidates really have their work cut out for them making sure they please the creators of the most successful entertainment franchise of all time," he continued.

The promotion represented a unique opportunity for Lucasfilm to take advantage of the popularity of *The Apprentice* and the business sense of its candidates. Jim Ward said:

> We needed to create a massive retail event for the combined release of *Episode III* and *Star Wars: Battlefront II*, so we wanted to work with someone who really understands how to create excitement and generate interest—and who could be better than Donald Trump and some of the best young business minds in America? (ibid.).

The winning team's display for the dual release could be seen at Best Buy stores across America, as well as a full-size version appearing in New York City, Los Angeles, and Lucas's home turf of Marin County, California.

Although the *Apprentice* episode did not air until November 10, the campaign was created in May before the prequel came to theaters. The episode was also supposed to air a week earlier, but NBC pushed it back because of the show's season debut being delayed. Ward joked, "Fine to help out week two, it is. Enough going on in week one, we have" (Hettrick "Of Darth ..."). To promote the episode, NBC used teasers featuring Darth Vader, Chewbacca, and stormtroopers facing off against Donald Trump in the boardroom.

Aside from strong sales, *Revenge of the Sith* also led the rental market during its first week with $7.64 million, ahead of second place *Bewitched* at $5.96 million and *Batman Begins* in third with $5.58 million. Although rentals do not account for a huge portion of a film's revenue, they generate a nice additional revenue stream alongside already solid sales. According to *Variety*, *Revenge of the Sith* was one of only six titles in 2005 to generate more than $200 million in home video sales, helping distributor Fox to a strong year (Hettrick "Spending …"). The company also enjoyed success with releases like *Napoleon Dynamite*, *The Simpsons* television series boxed sets, *The Family Guy* original movie, theatrical hits like *Mr. and Mrs. Smith* and *Fantastic Four*, and continuing strong sales of the *Star Wars Trilogy* boxed set.

In Australia, *Revenge of the Sith* was the third best-selling DVD of the year, behind only *The Incredibles* in first and *Madagascar* in second (Boland "B.O.…"). Generally, successful animated films enjoy excellent DVD sales, as do kid-oriented titles in general, not only in Australia but worldwide. The number four and five sellers in Australia were *Shark Tale* and *Harry Potter and the Prisoner of Azkaban*, further demonstrating the dominance of such films. More revealing still, the tenth best-selling DVD in Australia was *Finding Nemo*, an animated film which had been in release for more than twelve months already (ibid.). Although the final prequel officially came to DVD in Australia November 2, fans could buy it a day earlier in Sydney at the BIG W in a special promotion for fans made possible by *Rove Live* and Fox Home Entertainment ("Sydney …").

Revenge of the Sith on DVD not only sold millions of copies to fans worldwide who were happy to complete their six-film collections, it also received a few awards. At the Ninth Annual DVD Awards with Leonard Maltin, hosted at the Los Angeles Hilton as part of the Entertainment Media Expo (EMX) on August 8, 2006, the DVD won awards for Major Video Presentation and Major Audio Presentation. The awards are a testament not only to the quality of work that Lucasfilm put into its DVD releases, but also the quality of the technology used to film the prequel, making its digital-to-digital transfer seamless and precise. As a result, *Star Wars* fans can continue to enjoy the full experience of the film for years into the future. The simultaneous release of *Battlefront II* with the final prequel on DVD helped push another major product category for Lucasfilm, with subsidiary LucasArts accounting for a large sum of the company's total profits over the years.

Controlling the Force

Small Band of Rebels

In 1982, a small group of programmers began researching video games for the Computer Division of Lucasfilm. After releasing two titles, the Games Group, as it had been known internally, officially became Lucasfilm Games. By 1990, the title changed to LucasArts Entertainment Company, LLC, which the company continued to use thereafter. In 1993, LucasArts released its first *Star Wars* game,[1] called *Star Wars: X-Wing*, a space combat simulator where the player pilots an X-Wing, A-Wing, or Y-Wing, and a new era in gaming had begun ("LucasArts History").

X-Wing spawned a series that continued with *TIE Fighter* in 1994, *X-Wing vs. TIE Fighter* in 1997, and *X-Wing Alliance* in 1999. "*Star Wars* didn't create video games but it totally influenced them," said Peer Schneider, senior publisher of video game Web site IGN.com (Rickey). He continued, "The Death Star trench run in the original *Star Wars* is the archetypical video game climax: fire a missile, hit a weak spot and everything gets destroyed." In the years after its first *Star Wars* game, LucasArts went on to produce numerous other games for the franchise, which naturally yielded itself to fast-paced, exciting games, though not all *Star Wars* titles are developed in-house by LucasArts.

Besides space combat simulators, LucasArts made several highly successful first-person shooters, starting with *Star Wars: Dark Forces* in 1995, which in turn started its own franchise, the *Jedi Knight* games. With its success in the genre two years earlier, LucasArts released *Jedi Knight: Dark Forces II* in 1997, with an expansion pack in 1998 called *Mysteries of the Sith*. The 1997 *Dark Forces II* won numerous Game of the Year awards from print and Web publications. By 2002, the company had a full sequel for fans called *Star Wars: Jedi Knight II: Jedi Out-*

---

1. Though the company had earlier made several *Star Wars* console games for the NES, SNES, and GameBoy systems in the early 1990s, the games came from partnerships with JVC.

cast. Star Wars: Jedi Knight: Jedi Academy, a less acclaimed sequel, came out the next year.

Though games based on *The Phantom Menace* received mixed reviews, LucasArts enjoyed great critical and commercial success with *Knights of the Old Republic*, a collaboration with BioWare. IGN Entertainment, with its site IGN.com being a huge portal on the Web for gamers, named *Star Wars: Knights of the Old Republic* Game of the Year for both the Xbox and PC, also awarding it the Overall Best Game of the Year award for 2003, beating out nearly one thousand other titles reviewed. Additionally, the International Game Developers Association (IGDA) crowned the LucasArts title Game of the Year in its fourth annual ceremony. The Game Developer's Choice Award is like the Pulitzer of gaming awards, decided by other artists in the gaming industry ("IGDA ..."). The character HK-47 from *Knights of the Old Republic* won Original Game Character of the Year while the game also took home an award for Excellence in Writing.

Knights of the Old Republic also succeeded with fans, receiving the Golden Joystick Award for Xbox Game of the Year, an award voted on by gaming fans. The Golden Joystick Awards started in 1982, drawing hundreds of thousands of fans annually to vote for their favorite games. In another victory, GameSpy named *Knights of the Old Republic* the 2003 Game of the Year, an award voted upon by the editorial staff of GameSpy.com. Other critics agreed, like Victor Godinez of *The Dallas Morning News*, who called it the best game of 2003 and lauded it for giving gamers choices between good and evil and for its intricate story ("Electronic ...").

Besides its critical success, *Knights of the Old Republic* did well commercially, too. GameFly, the world's leading online video game rental service, announced that *Star Wars: Knights of the Old Republic* was its #1 most-rented game for the Xbox and across all platforms ("GameFly ..."). The game also set a record as the fastest-selling Xbox title following its debut on July 16, as well as becoming the top-selling Xbox title for July and second highest for all formats in the month ("BioWare ..."). With a 94.6 percent average review score from GameRankings.com at the end of August 2003, the game became the eighteenth highest-rated of all time, second highest-rated title ever on the Xbox, and the highest-rated RPG game of all time, in any format (ibid.).

Another popular set of games that LucasArts released was the *Star Wars: Rebel Assault* series, which started in 1993 with a game that featured part interactive gameplay and part hands-off story, where fans could watch a new *Star Wars* story unfold with a few of the first full-motion video clips since *Return of the Jedi. Rebel*

Assault II—The Hidden Empire came out in 1995 and offered yet more full-motion video clips for fans, though it was especially notable for having the first live-action video footage since 1983 when the final film of the Original Trilogy came to theaters. LucasArts also introduced more console games shortly afterwards, with *Star Wars: Shadows of the Empire* (1996) and *Star Wars: Rogue Squadron* (1998) for Nintendo 64 and *Star Wars: Masters of Teräs Käsi* (1997) for PlayStation.

Besides shooters, combat simulators, and adventure games like the *Rebel Assault* series, LucasArts explored strategy games with 1998's *Star Wars: Rebellion*, a 3-D game where players choose to command Rebel or Imperial forces in both strategic plotting and tactical combat. Soon after, *Star Wars: Force Commander* (2000) gave players the opportunity to participate in the *Star Wars* galaxy in real-time strategy format, focusing on the Original Trilogy and recreating many events from the films. One year later, *Star Wars: Galactic Battlegrounds* gave fans another real-time strategy game, based on the *Age of Empires II* engine, but focusing on the entire *Star Wars* saga at the time, which included *The Phantom Menace* and some expanded universe references. The game expanded in May 2002 with *Star Wars: Galactic Battlegrounds: Clone Campaigns*, adding battle scenarios from *Attack of the Clones*.

Additional console games appeared in mass quantities with the first two prequels, including *Star Wars: Episode I Racer* (1999), *Star Wars: Episode I—The Phantom Menace* (1999), *Star Wars: Episode I Jedi Power Battles* (2000), *Star Wars: Episode I Battle for Naboo* (2000), and *Star Wars Demolition* (2000) around the time of the first prequel. The games appeared on systems such as Nintendo 64, Sony PlayStation, and Sega Dreamcast. On later systems such as Sony PlayStation 2, Microsoft Xbox, and Nintendo GameGube, LucasArts released *Star Wars: Starfighter* (2001), *Star Wars: Obi-Wan* (2001), *Star Wars: Rogue Squadron II: Rogue Leader* (2001), *Star Wars: Jedi Starfighter* (2002), *Star Wars: Racer Revenge* (2002), *Star Wars: The Clone Wars* (2002), and *Star Wars: Bounty Hunter* (2002). Little surprise, after such a huge list of games, that LucasArts was ready for tackling the final prequel and new fields of game development.

Force Resurgence

Though the company had drawn fire from many fans and critics for formulaic, unoriginal gameplay in many of the more recent *Star Wars* games of the time, LucasArts had a renaissance of its own as Lucas readied and delivered the most acclaimed *Star Wars* prequel. The upward trend, however, began after a series of mediocre *Star Wars* games that failed to achieve substantial success either critically or commercially. In September 2004, Jim Ward, named president of LucasArts only four months earlier, met with Lucas about the company's future and its current state.

LucasArts had already scrapped its bonuses for 2004, but Ward had a plan for Lucas, saying he could turn the video game division into one of the top five publishers (Holson "At LucasArts …"). In 2004, roughly one-quarter of the four hundred LucasArts employees lost their jobs. "I needed to free them up and get rid of the politics so I could institute a team. I told them they either get on board or they don't" (ibid.). LucasArts ranked thirteenth in sales for the year, though the company still accounted for about 25 percent of Lucasfilm's annual revenue (ibid.). With a promising slate of upcoming games as well as sales of existing titles, like *Star Wars: Galaxies*, LucasArts hoped for a triumphant rise.

Arriving in stores before Ward took over as president, *Star Wars Galaxies: An Empire Divided*, released on June 26, 2003, was a new type of game for the *Star Wars* franchise, representing the first foray into the massively multiplayer online role-playing game (MMORPG) genre for LucasArts. In an MMORPG, thousands of players can enter a virtual world, assume created identities within the game world, and build lives, experience adventures, and amass wealth and power within the context of the game's virtual environment. In *Star Wars Galaxies*, players had access to ten planets upon the game's launch. When entering the game for the first time, players create their virtual identities, having many elements to customize that allow for thousands of unique characters. Players also decide their professions, which can range from more adventurous, violent paths like bounty hunter to more laid-back vocations like entertainer and artisan. Players could even stake out real estate and build virtual houses.

Reviews for *Star Wars Galaxies* seemed mixed between cautious optimism about the future of the game and annoyance at its bugs and apparent premature release. *PC Magazine*'s Rich Brown called it "a half-baked experience in a rich universe" and mentioned that it continued "the irritating trend of premature game releases," though he expressed hope for the game's future if LucasArts "adds promised content." Ahmad Faiz of *New Straits Times* agreed, writing that it was "bug-filled, ill-patched," and that LucasArts "should have kept the game in beta testing stage" until fixing various problems.

Several critics gave *Star Wars Galaxies* fairly solid marks, though. *Newsweek*'s Peter Suciu called the game a "new hope" for fans disappointed with the first two prequels. The *Seattle Post-Intelligencer* gave the game a "B" and wrote that "the things that 'Galaxies' does right, it does very right." Nonetheless, the paper's review raised a few of the same gameplay issues that other critics had voiced, such as a lack of easy transportation around the game's various atmospheres and locales.

By late August, *Star Wars Galaxies* had reached 275,000 registered players, making it the second largest MMO game at the time ("Star Wars Galaxies ..."). It also set a record as the fastest growing MMORPG. "Almost immediately we were seeing thousands of players interacting simultaneously, building communities and creating in-game events like player weddings, store openings and many other inventive activities," said LucasArts President Simon Jeffery (ibid.). By its one year anniversary, *Star Wars Galaxies* had topped 500,000 registered users, with more than 115,000 logging in daily ("LucasArts Celebrates ..."). By December 2005, barely more than a year after release, *World of Warcraft*, an MMORPG from Blizzard Software, had attracted roughly 5 million registered gamers, dwarfing the more niche-oriented *Star Wars Galaxies*, despite the massive appeal of the *Star Wars* franchise ("World ...").

Although *Star Wars Galaxies* proved somewhat successful for Lucasfilm and its partner, Sony Online Entertainment, problems arose, which is to be expected for such a massive project. In an attempt to boost sales, Sony overhauled the game in late 2005 to increase the pace and offer more action-oriented gameplay (Musgrove). The changes also supposedly made the game easier to play, according to Sony ads meant to attract new players. Fans had reason to be angry. Sony eliminated numerous career paths in the game, often the less violent and less exciting ones, to streamline the content into a more action-packed game.

Instead of being satisfied with its niche audience and richer diversity of gameplay, Sony attempted to simplify the game to attract new players, causing numerous cancellations from veterans of the game. John Blakely, vice president of development at Sony Online Entertainment, was not surprised at the backlash. "It was a tough decision we had to make. We knew we were going to sacrifice some players ... [but] as a *Star Wars* license, we should do a lot better than we have been doing" (Musgrove). One fan wrote to *The Washington Post*, published in an article explaining the gaming situation, "The game for me probably will be a lost love. Sort of like seeing your spouse with Alzheimer's" (ibid.). He explained, "Outwardly, everything appears the same as it always has, but you know that beneath the surface, things will never be the same."

In *Star Wars: Battlefront*, launched the same day as the Original Trilogy on DVD, gamers can fight in many of the battles seen in the *Star Wars* films, as a Rebel Trooper or an Imperial Stormtrooper in the classic films or as a Republic Clone Trooper or a droid in the Separatist Army in the prequels, among other possibilities. In the game, players can also pilot various *Star Wars* craft, including

X-Wings, TIE fighters, and AT-STs. The game covers more than twenty-five ground and air vehicles in all and allows players to choose from one of twenty characters. It also has more than a dozen unique locations that are spread across ten planets, such as Hoth, Geonosis, and Endor. *Star Wars: Battlefront* proved wildly successful, becoming the best-selling *Star Wars* game of all time. It had already sold more than 3.5 million copies before its sequel hit shelves in late 2005 (Antonucci).

In July 2005, Aspyr Media released *Battlefront* for the Mac, giving Mac gamers the opportunity to play the popular title in single-player mode or online through GameRanger with other gamers. Peter Cohen of *Macworld* gave the game a thumbs up, writing that it "looks and sounds terrific" and "puts you in the middle of your favorite *Star Wars* moments—and does so with a great deal of style." By the end of the year, THQ gave gamers another option to play *Battlefront* with the announcement of *Star Wars: Battlefront Mobile.* The game, which arrived in November to coincide with the DVD release of *Revenge of the Sith* and the release of *Battlefront II* as well, allowed Cingular Wireless players to play head-to-head in a special version of the game created for wireless phones. "Fans of the *Battlefront* franchise can now experience the great battles, famous locations, and planets on their mobile phone, anytime and anywhere," said Casey Collins, director of domestic licensing for Lucas Licensing ("THQ ...").

John Gaudiosi of *Video Store* magazine called *Star Wars: Battlefront* "one of the best *Star Wars* games ever made." Every year, *Macworld* releases a "Game Hall of Fame Awards" list spotlighting "the most wonderful and imaginative" games of the year. For 2005, the year the game came to Macs, *Macworld* placed *Star Wars: Battlefront* on its list under "Best Use of The Force" (P. Cohen "Macworld's ..."). Joseph Szadkowski of *The Washington Times* gave *Battlefront* a positive review, calling the environments "an eye-popping experience" and the game a "fun adventure." Jeff Kapalka of *The Post-Standard* in Syracuse, New York, wrote, "The graphics, as one might expect, are excellent" and called it "a nifty little action shooter." Besides positive reviews and great sales, *Battlefront* has another uplifting story attached to it.

One young boy in Ohio who turned five in 2005, going by the name Jason for the media, used *Star Wars: Battlefront* to make it through a difficult time (Sabin). When his parents discovered a strange purple rash on his body and a series of bruises, they took him to the hospital, later to discover that their son had a rare case of anemia where the bone marrow stops working. Jason's body was fragile enough so that a strong touch could bruise him, a condition that forced him to stay in a padded room, awaiting a transplant procedure. When he transferred to a hospital in Cincinnati, the hospital had a copy of the Original Trilogy, which he watched daily. He passed most of his time, though, by playing *Battlefront*. His dad said, "If it wasn't for that game, I don't think he would have made it" (ibid.). Jason eventually received his transplant, from one of his sisters, and eagerly awaited the release of *Star Wars: Battlefront II*.

Released in late 2004 for the Xbox and early 2005 for the PC, *Knights of the Old Republic II* understandably carried with it high expectations because of the immense success of its predecessor, especially critically. The sequel takes place five years after the first game, which is still thousands of years before the *Star Wars* films. Paul Johnson of *The Record* applauded the game for its "rich plot that reacts to your choices" and wrote that it "unfolds like a compelling mystery novel." On GameRankings.com, the game had an average rating of 87 percent, including 8.7 out of 10 from IGN, 4.5 out of 5 from *GamePro*, and 87 out of 100 from *PC Gamer*. Although not as well received as its predecessor, it still earned a number of strong reviews and had fans clamoring for another sequel. The game later received a Saturn Award nomination for Best Science Fiction Video Game.

The 2005 Onslaught

In March 2005, LucasArts released *Star Wars: Republic Commando*, a first-person shooter for the Xbox and the PC where gamers can command a squad of clone troopers through various missions. The game gives clone commandos distinct personalities and attempts to make them more than faceless drones. The commandos of Delta Squad in the game are RC-1138 (nicknamed Boss), RC-1140 (Fixer), RC-1207 (Sev), and RC-1262 (Scorch), each with different specialties. The game tied in with the release of *Revenge of the Sith* by featuring General Grievous's bodyguards. Grievous became a staple of the Clone Wars era also featured in the cartoon series of the same name.

Republic Commando is notable also for its inclusion of the single "Clones," by Irish rockers Ash, as the title theme to the video game ("Star Wars 'honour' …"). "Clones" marked the first time Lucasfilm featured a band on *Star Wars*–related merchandise. "Being on the game is a dream come true and a great honor. It's the closest we'll get to being in our favorite films," group member Tim Wheeler said (ibid.).

Critical reviews of *Republic Commando* varied significantly, from 8.7 out of 10 on GameSpot.com to an unimpressive 62 out of 100 from *PC Gamer*. The game had an average rating of 79 percent from GameRankings.com. Levi Buchanan of the *Chicago Tribune* gave it three stars out of four, writing, "Where *Republic*

Commando surprises, though, is its grittiness. This is a side of the *Star Wars* universe we haven't seen before," specifically referring to soldiers stained in alien blood and combat that is not as elegant as Jedi with lightsabers or as sterile as pilots shooting other spacecraft. Several critics complained that the game was too easy or short, but Shaun Conlin of *The Palm Beach Post* wrote that its ease is "not a bad thing, just less 'hardcore' complex, more 'mass market' easy. Ergo, fun." He gave it four stars out of five, calling it a "rock-solid single-player game."

Geared toward young gamers, Eidos launched *LEGO Star Wars: The Video Game* in April 2005 for the Xbox, PlayStation 2, Game Boy Advance, and the PC. In the game, characters from the films are represented in LEGO form, serving as a strange promotion for both brands at once. *LEGO Star Wars* focused on the prequel trilogy era, with a number of amusing effects like ships and droids falling into LEGO block pieces when chopped with lightsabers, for instance. In the game, players can choose from more than thirty playable characters as they progress through fairly simple levels that are taken from scenes in the prequel films. The game, however, does not require players to beat the levels sequentially, so jumping around is possible within the prequel chronology. Jefferson Dong, Eidos global brand manager, said, "Anyone who has ever known the joy of building with LEGO blocks or been entranced by *Star Wars* will find themselves drawn in by this game" ("Eidos and Giant ...").

Levi Buchanan of the *Chicago Tribune* called it potentially "a marketing nightmare, a game based on toys based on a movie," but wrote that it "is by far one of the better child-oriented games in months." Victor Godinez of *The Dallas Morning News* gave the game a "B+," calling it "one of the most whimsical *Star Wars* titles ever" and "just so darn cute!" International video game critics applauded the game, too. Rob Waugh of *The Evening Standard* in London wrote, "It's a peculiar idea, but against all odds it's one of the most charming, funny—and naggingly addictive—games I've played this year." He added, "Visually, it's perfect." In a list of the ten best *Star Wars*–related products, events, or trends for 2005, the Official *Star Wars* Web Site listed *LEGO Star Wars* as #5 ("*Star Wars:* The Best ...").

By mid-May, Eidos had shipped almost seven hundred thousand copies of *LEGO Star Wars* in only one month of release ("Eidos Announces ..."). The company also had some of the most ambitious marketing plans of any licensee, attempting to make everyone aware of its product to boost future sales. "The LEGO and *Star Wars* brands have millions of fans spanning all ages. Eidos has put together an integrated TV, retail, print, and online campaign that offers both extensive reach and frequency," said Vice President of Marketing Communications Paul Baldwin (ibid.). Like many *Revenge of the Sith* products and much of its advertising, recalling memories of 1999 with *The Phantom Menace*, the company wanted its product to be ubiquitous. "This campaign is targeted at LEGO and *Star Wars* fans everywhere. You will not be able to turn on your TV or walk into a store without seeing the product advertised," Baldwin said (ibid.). At Target retail stores, gamers could get a free ticket to see the final prequel with a purchase of the game.

Eidos later released *LEGO Star Wars* for GameCube in advance of *Revenge of the Sith*'s DVD release. Aspyr Media also readied a Mac version of the game for a late summer release in 2005, giving yet more gamers and fans an opportunity to play through the events of the *Star Wars* prequels in LEGO fashion. When SCi Entertainment, a computer games publisher, purchased Eidos later in 2005, it also benefited from the success of the continuing strong sales for *LEGO Star Wars*, which had sold more than 3 million copies by early 2006. SCi Entertainment credited the game's surprising sales for boosting its internal budget by almost $30 million ("Lego Star ...").

The official *Revenge of the Sith* game for the Xbox and PlayStation 2 gave fans the opportunity to participate in the events that occur in the film interactively, rather than as viewers, and offered a nice preview of the film for fans not bothered by spoilers. The game included twelve minutes of film footage, accessed by completing each mission successfully. The LucasArts title received mixed reviews, with some complaints about character animation and gameplay sluggishness, but with high marks for its environments, fun play, and imaginative interactivity. The *Coventry Evening Telegraph* in England gave the game 8/10 and called it a "thrilling bit of classic console action."

A few critics blasted the *Revenge of the Sith* game for being too easy, while others forgave its formulaic design because of its close adherence to the film and the opportunity it gave to play the events that take place on screen. Paul Johnson wrote for *The Record*, "LucasArts has made many innovative games out of the *Star Wars* universe. This isn't one of them." He called the game "second-rate" and "unoriginal." Although not terribly reviewed, as it did receive some positive comments from players and critics, its review average on GameRankings.com hovered in the 65 percent range with major publications like GamePro only awarding it 2.5 stars out of 5 while IGN blasted it with a 4.5 out of 10 rating.

Because of its tie-in to the hugely anticipated film, the *Revenge of the Sith* video game drew a fair amount of press. EB Games (formerly called Electronics Boutique), with more than two thousand gaming destinations across ten countries, celebrated the release of the game with a special event at the Regal Cinema

Waterford Lakes in Orlando, Florida, on Saturday, May 21 from 4:00 to 10:00 p.m. ("EB …"). The event featured a live broadcast from a local radio station, O-Rock 105.9 WOCL, and an appearance by members of the 501st Legion, the *Star Wars* costuming group. Fans could demo the new game and win various prizes. In London, about one hundred fans, some in costume, lined up outside of Oxford Street's Virgin Megastore for the midnight release of the official *Revenge of the Sith* video game. One fan, forty-one-year-old Alan McNamee, said, "I couldn't wait until the morning, I had to get it as soon as it was available" ("Out …").

Intec, a leading manufacturer of video game accessories for numerous platforms, introduced *Star Wars*–branded video game controllers in February 2005, available for shipping by April. The controllers, specifically designed to enhance gameplay for *Revenge of the Sith*, offered programmable combination moves and numerous features like a turbo function, dual vibration motors, and auto-sensing technology allowing for up to sixteen players to play without interference. The company offered several different controllers, including the Jedi Hunter 2.4 GHz Wireless Controller and the regular Jedi Hunter Controller as well as a Sith versus Jedi two-pack. The controllers worked for both the Xbox and PlayStation 2 systems.

Another company took a more high-end approach to elicit interest from *Star Wars* fans, or perhaps die-hard *Star Wars* gamers. Alienware created the first officially licensed *Star Wars* PC, the Alienware Aurora: *Star Wars* Edition, based on AMD Athlon 64 FX-55 processors and featuring exclusive content from the saga, such as desktop skins, fan club membership, and movie soundtrack samples. Fans could choose their allegiance, with Dark Side and Light Side versions available, each of which featured artwork from the films on the cases. The desktop wallpapers on each model differed depending on the side of the Force chosen, too. "*Star Wars* indisputably ranks as one of the most popular movie franchises of all time, yet had never been featured on a PC, so Alienware worked with *Star Wars* to fill that void once and for all," said Robert Lusk, vice president of sales and marketing for Alienware ("Alienware …").

Other companies also joined in releasing *Star Wars* video games, like Tiger Games with its stand-alone *Star Wars Lightsaber Battle*. The game allows young gamers to wield a fourteen-inch sword and hone their lightsaber skills using infrared technology with a softball-shaped training droid connected to a television using audio/video jacks and positioned properly so that gamers can swing the saber and have their actions mimicked on screen. Another company followed suit with a low-cost alternative to expensive, high-end console systems, though with cheaper prices, graphics suffer.

JAKKS Pacific made its own *Revenge of the Sith* game package, released in April, that allowed gaming fans to plug a controller designed to look like Darth Vader into their televisions and play five original *Star Wars* games based on the final prequel. Three additional collector's controllers followed, with characters like R2-D2, Yoda, and General Grievous as design inspirations. The JAKKS Pacific games were a nice alternative to buying expensive consoles because gamers could just plug one of the controllers into a television and start playing. The five games included: Droid Invasion, Coruscant Attack, Grievous Onslaught, Gunship Battle, and Utapau Chase, giving gamers a variety of options and game types.

Showcased at *Star Wars* Celebration III in Indianapolis, Indiana, *Star Wars: Battlefront II* expanded upon the most popular game in the franchise's history. The sequel offered gamers new space combat, playable Jedi, new environments from *Revenge of the Sith*, and a new single-player campaign with an extensive story. Vice President of Global Marketing and Sales for LucasArts John Geoghegan said, "The original was a huge success for LucasArts and we plan to build on that success to make *Star Wars: Battlefront II* exceed what we did for the first game in every measurable way" ("LucasArts Joins ..."). The game was available for PlayStation 2, the Xbox, and the PC. When it launched with the *Revenge of the Sith* DVD, both products combined for a $210 million haul from consumers, though Lucasfilm would not break down which product accounted for how much of the total ("Combined Force ..."). Nonetheless, the company believed *Battlefront II* could beat its predecessor's impressive sales (Hettrick "'Star Wars' wins ...").

Reviews for *Battlefront II* were positive, though many game reviewers remarked how it serves more as an upgrade to the first title than a true sequel. Chris Chan of *New Straits Times* wrote, "All in all, *Star Wars: Battlefront II* is a tweaked version of *Battlefront*. It continues a successful yet stable *Star Wars* franchise and is basically an 'if it ain't broke, don't fix it' game." Victor Godinez of *The Dallas Morning News* gave the game a "B+" and called it "a really fun game" that "satisfies every *Star Wars* itch you might have." Mike Antonucci of the *San Jose Mercury News*, who had been impressed with the first *Battlefront* game, noticed a large disparity in graphical quality between the Xbox and PlayStation 2 versions of *Battlefront II*, however, calling the game "notably less [valuable] for PS2 owners." The game received some critical acclaim from The Academy of Science Fiction, Fantasy & Horror, though, winning a Saturn Award in 2006 for Best Science Fiction Video Game.

LucasArts released another real-time strategy game set in the *Star Wars* universe in February 2006, titled *Star Wars: Empire at War*. The game received generally positive reaction, with GameSpot giving it an 8.7 out of 10 and writing, "As a strategy game, *Empire at War* delivers a true *Star Wars* experience." IGN gave it a solid 7.6 out of 10, saying it "scores big in terms of style." Ted Morris, development director for Petroglyph Games, which teamed with LucasArts to bring *Empire at War* to gamers, said, "This is a dream job. The people I work with love being part of the *Star Wars* universe, especially now that it's coming to a crescendo. It makes me feel good that even with all the other titles, we're still stopping traffic with the hard-core gamers" (Hopkins "… gamer's dream"). No doubt years into the future, impressive *Star Wars* games will continue to give fans and gamers a way to interact with the galaxy far, far away.

Although the video game business was down for 2005, with console game sales falling 12 percent to $4.6 billion, *Star Wars* games dominated, proving wildly successful (Fritz "Ode …"). Four of the top five best-selling console games[2] based on Hollywood properties were *Star Wars* titles, also representing the only studio tie-in titles to break the top ten. *Star Wars: Battlefront II* led the way with 2.1 million copies sold, while *Battlefront* sold an additional million copies roughly (ibid.). The *Revenge of the Sith* official game sold 1.5 million units while the Eidos Entertainment *LEGO Star Wars* sold 1.7 million units. Though *Harry Potter and the Goblet of Fire* and *Batman Begins* were huge hits at the box office, their video games were not hits with consumers, proving that great box office results alone are not enough to sell games.

As Jim Ward had hoped, 2005 was a return to prominence for the company, which occupied two of the top three slots for best-selling video games of the year. Although *Madden NFL 2006* ranked first, *Star Wars: Battlefront II* and *Star Wars: Episode III—Revenge of the Sith* ranked second and third, respectively. Along with strong sales from a non–*Star Wars* game called *Mercenaries*, developed by Pandemic Studios, LucasArts increased its company sales rank from thirteenth in 2004 to eighth in 2005 (Holson "At LucasArts …").

Perhaps the greatest challenge lies in the years after the final *Star Wars* film for LucasArts, though. "We are not the *Star Wars* game company and Jim [Ward]

---

2. According to NPD Group data, which is the most comprehensive data available in a business that does not release figures as readily as others like theatrical box office revenue, for instance. NPD Group data does not include sales of PC games and sometimes leaves off a few smaller retailers (Fritz "Ode…").

knows what he has to do," Lucasfilm President Micheline Chau said (ibid.). Transitioning into creating additional original, successful franchises to go along with its *Star Wars* titles may prove challenging, but having prospered for more than two decades, LucasArts still has the force to succeed. Though LucasArts enjoyed great success with its product sales in 2005, many other companies also prospered with their merchandise for the final prequel and faced similar questions of how they will adapt to a world without new *Star Wars* movies.

"*Star Wars* is Forever":
Merchandise Sales

Before *Revenge of the Sith* came to theaters, the *Star Wars* franchise had earned more than $9 billion from merchandising sales, according to numerous industry estimates. The final prequel massively boosted the total, however, surpassing even the highest expectations for the *Star Wars* brand. Hasbro revived a slogan for its marketing that rang true as cash registers rang loudly across the nation throughout 2005 with consumers buying more merchandise from the franchise: *Star Wars* is Forever.

According to Jim Ward, senior vice president of marketing and distribution for Lucasfilm, half of all Americans owned at least one *Star Wars* video or product. Lucasfilm hoped to help the other deprived half of citizens find suitable products throughout 2005. "It feels like 1977 all over again. To see this level of success almost thirty years later confirms that *Star Wars* has become a staple in the toy aisles. When we say '*Star Wars* is forever,' we mean it," said Howard Roffman, president of Lucas Licensing. The pre-existing consumer base interested in merchandise for the saga, and the millions of moviegoers discovering the saga for the first time, helped make *Revenge of the Sith* one of the biggest merchandising successes in the history of cinema.

In 1999, *The Phantom Menace* became the most successfully merchandised film of all time, at least by pure dollars earned for its year of release, having generated $2 billion at retail for the year, surpassing the success of 1994's *The Lion King* at $1.5 billion (Tanaka). Three years later, *Attack of the Clones*, still a *Star Wars* juggernaut but suffering from some of the middle-of-the-trilogy doldrums that also led its box office gross to be less than the expected level for a film in the franchise, generated a still-awesome $1.2 billion at retail to go along with its worldwide box office gross nearing $650 million (M. Rose). As such, "We expected that sales based on *Episode III* would be somewhere in between those two figures, with a hope of reaching $1.6 billion at retail," Roffman said ("'Star Wars' Property …").

Merchandise for *Revenge of the Sith* came to retailers on April 2, about six weeks before the film's release. Lucasfilm had also allowed licensees to release their first waves of products several weeks in advance of the previous two prequels, giving fans an opportunity to delve into the films' characters and stories before the movies hit theaters. As is customary for *Star Wars* fans with any major event, many people lined up outside of stores nationwide to have the first look at the new merchandise. In New Jersey, where the toy retailer is based, nearly one hundred fans lined up outside of Toys "R" Us on Route 46 to purchase the new toys that went on sale at 12:01 a.m. (Spadora). In advance of the theatrical release of *Revenge of the Sith*, *Star Wars* merchandise was selling at a torrid pace around the world. In Tulsa, Oklahoma, Anne Largent of Game X-Change said, "Anything *Star Wars* has been flying off the shelves, whether it be old or current" (Riggs).

The tradition of opening stores at 12:01 a.m. to accommodate fan enthusiasm, as with many new trends in the film and merchandising industries, began with *The Phantom Menace* and has taken on the term "Midnight Madness," appropriate perhaps for all of the people spending hundreds of dollars on toys. "History has shown this is an event *Star Wars* fans look forward to. Fans mark this date on their calendars," said Kathleen Waugh, a spokeswoman for Toys "R" Us, which opened 316 of its stores at midnight for fans (Choi "'Star Wars' ..."). The biggest celebration occurred at the store in Times Square, where the retailer encouraged fans to come dressed as their favorite characters. The store gave away prizes for trivia contests and featured appearances by characters from marketing partners, like Darth Tater from Hasbro and mPIRE characters from M&M's *Star Wars* promotion.

Despite the precedent that *Star Wars* set in 1999, Toys "R" Us has never opened its stores at 12:01 a.m. for any other merchandise launch. The off-hour openings were an honor bestowed only upon *Star Wars*, as the world's preeminent toy franchise. "There's nothing comparable to the scale of the mania [in the toy world]. *Batman* merchandise doesn't come close, and neither does any other film," said Steveanne Auerback, a toy expert based in San Francisco (ibid.). Toy industry expert Jim Silver, publisher of *Toy Wishes* magazine, agreed. "There is no comparison. *Star Wars* is on an entirely different level," he said (Crawford).

Many media articles noted how the primary group in front of toy stores consisted of men in their twenties and thirties, sometimes older. Usually toys are associated with younger children, but *Star Wars* has achieved lasting success in the industry largely because of its strong base of adult collectors. "The kids see [a toy] and want it. But it's the collectors who are really the ones who are going to be standing in front of Toys 'R' Us," said Chris Byrne, an independent toy indus-try analyst (Sarkar). Because of the sheer volume of products released, only adult collectors with fat bank accounts could possibly hope to buy all or most of the products on sale in early April.

Wal-Mart also took advantage of the huge sales opportunity with about four hundred stores holding a "48 Hours of The Force" marathon complete with dec-orated tents outside participating stores, DJs playing *Star Wars* music, and photo opportunities with costumed characters from the saga. Many Wal-Mart stores boasted interactive toy and game demonstrations and free *Star Wars* prize give-aways. "We're anticipating a great deal of excitement at our stores for the April 2 launch and are celebrating the occasion with an action-packed *Star Wars* weekend for fans of all ages," said Scott McCall, vice president and divisional merchandise manager for the toy division of Wal-Mart stores ("Hasbro's New …"). Because many Wal-Mart stores are already open twenty-four hours daily, the chain did not have to have special midnight openings at its major locations.

Retail and specialty stores outside of North America also enjoyed strong busi-ness. At Forbidden Planet, a specialty sci-fi store in England, books sold at a tor-rid pace to fans eager to learn more about the final movie before it came to theaters. Louisa Ryrie, manager of the store in Cross Cheaping, Coventry, said in May 2005, "*Star Wars* has been by far the biggest thing for us this year. We've got lots of other toys and collectibles; *Batman*, *Sin City*, and so on. But *Star Wars* stomps on all of it" ("Star Wars conquers …"). She said that the store doubled its space devoted to *Star Wars* items and added, "I think this is possibly the biggest range of merchandising they have ever put out for a movie."

On Monday, July 18, Hasbro announced that its second quarter profits rose 56 percent on the strength of *Star Wars* merchandise sales (Lewis). Shares rose 51 cents, or 2.4 percent, to $21.99 on midday trading on the New York Stock Exchange. The company's total revenue climbed 10.8 percent, from $516.4 mil-lion to $572.4 million. The results significantly beat analysts' expectations of $542.4 million. A segment of analysts worried that Hasbro would be unable to meet store demand for *Star Wars* products, to which President and CEO Alfred J. Verrecchia said, "The pipeline is being filled now" (ibid.).

On the other side of the industry, Mattel, the perennial #1 toy company, dis-appointed investors with second quarter net profits falling almost $5 million from the previous year. Hasbro profits topped Mattel, $29.5 million to $18.9 million. *The Evening Standard* in London had a great headline for the announce-ment: "Mattel profit slumps as *Star Wars* beats Barbie." Although *Star Wars* has often dominated the boys' toy market, Barbie has traditionally enjoyed a comparatively stronger grip on the girls' toy market, which usually leads to the Barbie brand winning the market-share crown each year.

According to a report from the NPD Group in late October 2005, *Star Wars* toys had become the #1 best-selling toy property in the United States since the release of *Revenge of the Sith* in May ("'Star Wars' Property ..."). The franchise demonstrated such dominance that it commanded a 9.1 percent market share of all licensed and branded toy sales from May through July, 60 percent ahead of the nearest property. The *Star Wars* toy sales, ranking as the top selling boys' toy property for the year, helped fuel double-digit growth in categories like action figures, accessories, and building sets for 2005 compared to the prior year (ibid.).

Lucasfilm could not have been more impressed and pleased with the toy sales for *Revenge of the Sith*, which from the first weekend of availability had destroyed expectations. Howard Roffman said, "2005 is proving to be a watershed year for *Star Wars*. The film has clearly struck a cord with consumers around the world, our toy products have never been better, and retailers have out-done themselves with focused, impactful programs" (ibid.). Unlike in 1999, when despite great sales retailers had still overbought *Star Wars* toys from *The Phantom Menace*, sometimes stores could not meet demand for the final prequel. "The biggest problem we've faced has been keeping *Star Wars* toys in stock," Roffman said (ibid.).

Aside from the summer success that *Revenge of the Sith* enjoyed at the box office and with merchandise sales, retailers expected a strong fourth quarter, partially because of the November 1 DVD release of the prequel. "Retailers are telling us that they expect *Star Wars* to perform strongly throughout the all-important holiday season and well into 2006" ("'Star Wars' Property ..."). The outlook had changed greatly from 1999, when Hasbro enjoyed strong sales from *The Phantom Menace* but many retailers complained about unsold products sitting on their store shelves. "Our partnership with Lucasfilm has generated outstanding sales and allowed us to better meet the wants and needs of Target guests," said Target Vice President of Toys Keri Jones (ibid.).

Speaking of the $1.6 billion goal that Lucasfilm had set for *Revenge of the Sith* merchandise, Roffman said, "Based on sales to date and with the bulk of retail sales yet to come in the fourth quarter, we believe we're on track to substantially exceed that figure" (ibid.). For the fourth quarter in 2005, Hasbro profits rose 15 percent while Mattel's profits slipped 2 percent, another success for the #2 toy maker over its bitter rival (Jewell). The *Star Wars* toy company reported net earnings of $94.3 million. Sales of *Star Wars* toys and games exceeded company expectations, accounting for $494 million in 2005 revenue (ibid.).

Even eBay benefitted from the remarkable success of *Star Wars* toys. On the company's list of most popular toys for the holiday season in 2005, the *Star Wars Millennium Falcon* LEGO set ranked first, Master Replicas FX Lightsabers ranked ninth, and the *Star Wars* Clone Trooper Action Figure came in tenth ("Star Wars LEGO ..."). "With the final release in the *Star Wars* series, *Star Wars*–licensed merchandise has been an overwhelming success across the product spectrum both in retail and on eBay," said Jim Migdal, Senior Category Manager for eBay Toys & Hobbies (ibid.).

Star Wars succeeded at the box office and in toy stores nationwide, so nobody was too surprised when the franchise also boasted an extremely successful Halloween costume line for 2005. According to one survey conducted for The Macerich Company by August Partners, *Harry Potter* costumes held a 21 percent market share while *Star Wars* held second place at 18 percent, ahead of *Batman*'s 14 percent ("Shopping ..."). A Lucasfilm-Fox press release, though, called *Star Wars* "the most popular Halloween costume line in 2005" ("Combined Force ..."). For fans who prefer Christmas over Halloween, Kurt Adler offered a series of ornaments for sale. Over the years, Hallmark has offered a nice assortment of collectible ornaments for fans to use for decoration or keep unopened as collectibles.

Another area of success for the franchise was trading cards. Beckett Media, the leading authority on the trading card hobby for more than twenty years, proclaimed *Star Wars* cards by far the most popular movie tie-in trading cards in history. In twenty-eight years, more than 250 trading card sets based on the movies produced nearly ten thousand cards, sold across twenty countries. "Before *Star Wars*, trading cards for movies weren't big business," said Doug Kale, editor at Beckett Entertainment ("Star Wars is Top ..."). He added, "We based our list of top movie card franchises on several factors—overall sales, pricing on the secondary markets, total cards manufactured, numbers of countries in which the cards were distributed, and, of course, demand." *Star Trek* ranked second and *The Lord of the Rings* third. "By just about any measure, *Star Wars* is light years ahead of the competition," Kale said.

Star Wars books continued to sell well for Lucasfilm. Matthew Stover's well-received novelization of *Revenge of the Sith*[1] sold briskly to fans, making #2 on the *Wall Street Journal*'s best-seller list for April 14. DelRey/LucasBooks planned for a 500,000 copy first printing, but claimed to have printed 650,000 copies of the

---

1.   *Entertainment Weekly*'s Dalton Ross gave the book a "B+" and *Publishers Weekly* called it "the perfect companion to the blockbuster film."

book initially to meet demand (Italie). In all, publishers have printed more than 70 million copies of all total *Star Wars* books and spinoffs (Italie). At ninth on the best-sellers list was DK Publishing's *Star Wars: Revenge of the Sith: The Visual Dictionary* by James Luceno. For the same week, Stover's novelization also ranked second on *USA Today*'s list while the junior novelization of the story, by Patricia C. Wrede, ranked eighteenth. Additionally, *The Visual Dictionary* came in at twenty-third and the graphic novel for the film's story placed forty-seventh.

On the *Publishers Weekly* hardcover fiction list for the same week, the pre-quel's adult novelization ranked first while on the non-fiction/general list, *The Visual Dictionary* took seventh. Another entry, *The Making of Star Wars: Revenge of the Sith* by J. W. Rinzler (Del Rey/LucasBooks), also sold well, coming in at fif-teenth on the trade paperback list. In all, *Publishers Weekly* reported that fans had 2,792 pages of *Star Wars*–licensed books out in 2005 to read from seven different publishing houses. Sales for the titles proved strong, too. According to Betsy Mitchell, vice president of Del Rey Books, early sales of the final prequel novel-ization through about three weeks in April were up 10 percent over the *Attack of the Clones* novelization in a comparable period.

According to the International Digital Publishing Forum, which tracks e-book sales, Stover's novelization of *Revenge of the Sith* was the best-selling e-book title of 2005. The children's novelization of *Revenge of the Sith* by Scholastic sold 294,275 copies in 2005, ranking tenth for the year on the Children's Paperback Frontlist, according to *Publishers Weekly*. On the same list, the *Revenge of the Sith* movie storybook from Random House sold 212,707 copies, ranking twenty-fourth, and the scrapbook from Random House sold 158,151 copies, good for forty-sixth.

John Williams's final *Star Wars* score, as with the books related to *Revenge of the Sith*, sold well by any standard, but especially for a score. During its first week of release, the soundtrack sold 96,000 copies and ranked sixth on Billboard's album sales list ("'Sith' soundtrack …"). The final prequel's soundtrack was the third *Star Wars* score to premiere in the top ten of the Billboard 200, setting a record and breaking a tie with *Spider-Man* and *American Idol*, both of which had also landed two soundtracks in the top ten ("Star Wars: Episode III Revenge of the Sith Soundtrack …"). Five of the six *Star Wars* soundtracks at some point made the top ten of the Billboard list, with the only exception being *Return of the Jedi*.

Besides the strong DVD sales Lucasfilm enjoyed with the Original Trilogy and the prequels, the company earned more money on the saga when in October Spike TV acquired the rights to the six *Star Wars* movies for between $65 million and $70 million for a six-year exclusive window ("News Briefs"). The deal guaranteed Spike TV the television premiere of the final prequel, but the other two prequels also were slated to have their basic cable premieres on the network. Industry insiders considered the deal somewhat of a coup for the smaller network, which beat larger rivals like Fox to secure the rights. *Variety* called the deal "the biggest movie purchase in the net's 22-year history" (Martin and Dempsey). The trade paper had earlier estimated the saga would command about a $50 million deal, but bidding from the USA Network and the Sci Fi Channel drove up the price (ibid.).

Aside from strong sales, LEGO won an award for its *Revenge of the Sith* toys. At the Toy Industry Association's annual event to celebrate the top toys in the industry, held Saturday, February 11, 2006, at the Marriot Marquis in New York City, the group awarded LEGO with the Toy of the Year Award for Best Activity Toy. "We are thrilled that the industry recognized the creativity, imagination, and role play that LEGO *Star Wars* delivers to children and collectors of all ages," said Michael Moynihan, senior director of marketing for LEGO Systems ("LEGO Star Wars ..."). The Toy of the Year award is like the Best Picture Oscar of the toy industry. LEGO had collected eight such awards in various categories since 2000 (ibid.).

In early 2006, after the success of its *Revenge of the Sith* sets, LEGO extended its *Star Wars* license with Lucasfilm to 2011, guaranteeing the construction toy maker the opportunity to introduce toys based on the animated series under development at the time. Since LEGO started making *Star Wars* toys, it had generated more than $1 billion in worldwide retail sales ("Lego Extends ..."). "LEGO *Star Wars* has been a blockbuster success for us year after year, so we are thrilled to solidify our partnership with Lucasfilm through 2011," said Jay Bruns, director of global licensing for LEGO (ibid.). He added, "The evergreen appeal of *Star Wars* and its strong following among children and adult collectors fits perfectly with the LEGO community of builders and collectors."

After the resounding success of merchandise based on *Revenge of the Sith*, *Star Wars* had further ascended into the stratosphere of earnings. According to an article in *The Observer* by David Smith, even before the release of the last film, "*Star Wars* is richer than the large majority of African countries," a statistic found by comparing the total amount of money the franchise has earned to the Gross Domestic Product of African nations. The article continued, "It dwarfs the economies of the Republic of Congo, Niger, Chad, Swaziland, Malawi, Rwanda, the Central African Republic, Lesotho, Sierra Leone, Eritrea and Liberia put together." Over the decades, *Star Wars* has become an industry unto itself, the "gold standard," as toy industry analyst Sean McGowan said (Rabil).

By 2006, the saga's total had risen to $12 billion in merchandise revenue alone. *Revenge of the Sith* nearly doubled expectations, adding $3 billion to the saga's treasure trove and becoming the new most successfully merchandised film in the history of the world (Rabil). The three prequels, including *Attack of the Clones* and its relatively paltry $1.2 billion, achieved such a phenomenal level of sales that they will long remain the standard by which all other film merchandising campaigns must be judged. Along with more than $4.2 billion in box office ticket sales, the franchise revenue total stood at more than $16.2 billion in its nearly thirty years in existence.

"A Jedi Craves Not These Things": Awards

Despite the *Star Wars* saga coming to an end in film form, the movies have left enough of an impact on generations of fans to ensure their continued relevance many decades into the future. Not only was *Revenge of the Sith* able to tie together two trilogies and an entire story successfully, to the satisfaction of the vast majority of fans and critics, but it was able to do so well enough to garner the film a few awards as well as support from voters in numerous polls. While Oscar success eluded *Revenge of the Sith* as with the previous prequels, the final film still managed to gain attention in other arenas.

At the 32nd Annual People's Choice Awards, *Revenge of the Sith* won for Favorite Movie and Favorite Movie Drama, the highest honor at the awards ceremony. A market research company named Knowledge Networks names the nominees based on box office grosses, then fans online vote for their favorite choices in each category. The awards ceremony took place at the Shrine Auditorium in Los Angeles, where talk show host Craig Ferguson hosted the event. Lucas attended the event to thank fans, saying, "I'm not a favorite of the critics, but who listens to them? The audience rules" (M. Brown). The results confirmed box office receipts, but so did a few other awards.

Revenge of the Sith also won Movie of the Year from the 9th Annual Hollywood Film Festival, based upon online voting by moviegoers. The awards ceremony took place at the Beverly Hilton Hotel on Monday, October 24, 2005. With seventy thousand votes cast, *Star Wars* annihilated the competition, receiving nearly a third of the total ("George Lucas ..."). *Batman Begins* finished second in the voting with *War of the Worlds* at third. "We are very proud that the winner of this year's Hollywood Movie of the Year Awards is George Lucas's film, *Star Wars: Episode III—Revenge of the Sith*. Mr. Lucas is a creative genius, a visionary at its best," said Executive Director Carlos de Abreu, also the festival's founder (ibid.).

In the 11th Annual Moviefone Moviegoer Awards, *Revenge of the Sith* received nominations for Movie of the Year, Actor of the Year (Hayden Christensen), Biggest Badass (Ewan McGregor), and Vilest Villain (Ian McDiarmid and Christensen both received nominations). "For more than a decade, the Moviefone Moviegoer Awards have given real movie fans a chance to speak up and make their opinion count," said Erik Flannigan, vice president of programming and entertainment for Moviefone ("Harry Potter …"). The Moviefone awards proved a bit different from others online, however, as *Harry Potter and the Goblet of Fire*, a film not nearly as acclaimed or popular with most audiences or critics as *King Kong* or *Revenge of the Sith*, somehow won top honors. The final prequel left empty-handed, suggesting that Moviefone viewers are apparently more impressed with magic than with the Force.

The Academy of Science Fiction, Fantasy & Horror has an ongoing tradition of honoring movies in the genre with its Annual Saturn Awards, founded in 1972. The voting procedure incorporates the opinions of industry professionals, fans, and academics, splitting each voting committee (like acting or directing, for instance) into three equal groups, as closely as possible. The committee leaders for the groups help decide which films are to be nominated in each category, though lists are sent to the Board of Directors for final approval before ballots are sent to voters for choosing the winners. To ensure fairness, the votes are counted at an accounting firm or by an accountant ("The Academy …").

For the 32nd Annual Saturn Awards, *Revenge of the Sith* led all nominees, receiving a whopping ten nominations, including Best Science Fiction Film, Best Actor (Christensen), Best Actress (Portman), Best Supporting Actor (McDiarmid), Best Direction, Best Writing, Best Music, Best Costume Design (Trisha Biggar), Best Make-Up (Dave Elsey, Lou Elsey, and Nikki Gooley), and Best Special Effects (John Knoll, Roger Guyett, Rob Coleman, and Brian Gernand). The awards show took place on May 2, 2006, in Universal City.

Revenge of the Sith could not beat its competition in most fields at the Saturn Awards, but in the most important one, the film triumphed, taking home Best Science Fiction Film as well as Best Music for John Williams. The composer also managed a Grammy nomination for his score, along with another nomination in the instrumental composition category for the track "Anakin's Betrayal." Yet somehow, voters in the special effects field at the Saturn Awards were more impressed with *King Kong*'s huge, hairy ape than *Revenge of the Sith*'s diminutive, green Yoda, proving that sometimes, size does matter.

In the 4th Annual Visual Effects Society (VES) Awards, *Revenge of the Sith* received four nominations, including Outstanding Visual Effects in a Visual Effects Driven Motion Picture, Best Single Visual Effect of the Year (opening space battle over Coruscant), Outstanding Created Environment in a Live Action

Motion Picture, and Outstanding Models and Miniatures in a Motion Picture. Unfortunately, the prequel visual effects artists had to be satisfied with nominations as the movie took home no awards.

The three prequels, years ahead of the competition upon release, did not receive the critical consideration they deserved for visual effects, which is strange because the media gave the effects work plenty of attention. Given that *Revenge of the Sith* set a record for visual effects shots in a movie, and that ILM is the most technologically advanced special effects house in the industry, one has to wonder whether either an anti–*Star Wars* or anti-Lucas bias prevented the prequels from winning awards they deserved.

While *Revenge of the Sith* scored many nominations and a number of meaningful wins from more populist organizations, the original *Star Wars* film continued to demonstrate its power and influence in the twenty-first century, assuring the place of the franchise well into the future. In September 2005, the American Film Institute (AFI) named the score from *Star Wars: Episode IV—A New Hope* the greatest of all time, beating out films such as *Gone With the Wind* (#2), *Lawrence of Arabia* (#3), *Jaws* (#6), and other classics. John Williams was the most nominated composer on the top twenty-five list that the AFI compiled, with three scores.[1]

To create its list, the AFI distributed a ballot with 250 nominated movie scores to a jury of more than five hundred people, including composers, musicians, film artists (directors and screenwriters, for instance), critics, and film historians. The AFI asked voters to consider the creative impact, historical significance, and legacy of the scores in question ("Star Wars Tops ..."). The legacy consideration, or in other words how widely the film score is enjoyed apart from the movie, probably won the award for *A New Hope*, with its main theme arguably the most recognizable piece of film music ever written.

Aside from having the greatest musical score ever, *A New Hope* also had the greatest special effect ever, according to *SFX* magazine results published in early 2005 based upon fan voting. Respondents voted for the opening shot of the film as the greatest special effect in cinema history ("Force ..."). For a film nearing its thirtieth anniversary at the time, the vote was impressive. *A New Hope*'s opening shot triumphed over the climax of *King Kong* (1933) in second and the spider head from *The Thing* (1982) in third, as well as more recent film effects like bullet time in *The Matrix* (1999), the train fight in *Spider-Man 2* (2004), and Gollum from the *Lord of the Rings* films (2001–2003). Additionally, more than eight

---

1.   Besides *Star Wars* and *Jaws* (1975), *E.T.* (1982) also made the list at #14.

thousand voters from Amazon.co.uk and IMDb.com named R2-D2 the top robot ever, beating Bender from *Futurama* in second, Crew from *Mystery Science Theater* in third, and even C-3PO in fourth ("Star Wars' droid ...").

In another poll, conducted by Tesco.com in 2004, more than fourteen thousand U.K. film fans voted for the top men's and women's films of all time, with *Star Wars* being named the best men's film (Pio). The 1977 epic beat *The Great Escape* (1963), *The Godfather* (1972), *Scarface* (1983), and *Pulp Fiction* (1994) in the two through five slots, respectively. Tesco.com Marketing Director Dave Clements said, "*Star Wars* is without doubt the number one fellas' flick of all time" (Pio). In 2006, Tesco Pharmacy ran another movie-related poll, asking what film moviegoers most want to watch when ill. Again, *Star Wars* topped the list for men, while *Dirty Dancing* (1987) repeated for women ("Dirty ..."). Ironically, women's favorite film to watch while sick would make most men sick, leading to a necessary *Star Wars* viewing soon afterwards.

Chipmaker AMD took a poll in 2003 asking, "What is your favorite breakout performance?" In the online survey, with more than twenty thousand responses worldwide, Web surfers voted for their favorite breakout performances in three categories: sports, arts and entertainment, and science and technology ("More than ..."). Albert Einstein won for the science and technology category with his Theory of Relativity while Lance Armstrong won in the sports category for beating cancer and winning the Tour de France for the first of seven career victories in the ultimate event for cycling. *Star Wars* won top honors for the entertainment category, a noteworthy achievement considering the breadth of possible responses.

In 2005, George Lucas also received a number of awards and honors. ShoWest, the annual convention of theater owners in Las Vegas, presented him with a "galactic achievement award" on March 17 for his film work. Co-Manager of ShoWest Mitch Neuhauser said, "This unique award celebrates the enduring popularity of the *Star Wars* movies and the enormous impact and influence they have had on audiences and popular culture" ("'Star Wars' creator George ..."). He continued, "No other movie series has been so successful for so long, and no movie is more eagerly anticipated this year than *Revenge of the Sith*." Besides his award a few months later at the Cannes Film Festival, Lucas received another major honor in 2005.

In the ultimate tribute to his impact on the film industry, the American Film Institute (AFI) honored Lucas with its 33rd Life Achievement Award, presented on Thursday, June 9, 2005. The tribute included guests like Robert Duvall from Lucas's *THX 1138*, Carrie Fisher, Mark Hamill, Harrison Ford, and William

Shatner. While Duvall recalled stories of shaving his head for Lucas's film, Fisher and Hamill gave Lucas a good-natured ribbing about the merchandising his films inspired. Shatner performed a variation of "My Way" while a line of stormtroopers did a chorus line routine. He told Lucas, in a variation of the *Star Trek* slogan, "Live long. You've already prospered enough" (Germain "American ..."). Lucas's best friend and fellow filmmaker Steven Spielberg presented the award to him, saying, "You have many years ahead of you to create the dreams that we can't even imagine dreaming. You have done more for the collective unconscious of this planet than you will ever know" (ibid.). The AFI show aired on June 20 on the USA Network.

The AFI wanted to honor Lucas earlier, but the director refused, saying he was too young. "I said, 'You know, I'm too young. Look, I'm not ready yet.' Then they came back again, and I said, 'Look, wait until I'm over sixty. Then I'll do it.' As soon as I turned sixty, they called me" ("Lucas Finally ..."). Industry trade paper *Variety* featured a long article by Dale Pollock about Lucas's achievements and contributions to the film industry. Pollack wrote, "Lucas has achieved more financially, creatively and technologically than any other filmmaker in history. No other successful director has owned the copyright to the major work of his career, spanning almost 30 years and six films" ("Epoch ..."). From his pioneering visual effects work for the first *Star Wars* through his contributions with ILM and his push for digital cinema, Lucas "changed an entire industry," Pollack wrote.

Only about a month after Lucas received the AFI's Life Achievement Award, he enjoyed the honor of having all five previous *Star Wars* films before *Revenge of the Sith* showcased at the AFI Silver Theatre's Fourth of July Weekend program, taking place in Silver Springs, Maryland. Murray Horwitz, director of the AFI Silver Theatre, said, "George Lucas has not only changed filmmaking and the film industry, he has done so in multiple ways and on multiple levels" ("Lucas showcase ..."). The two-week showcase also featured *THX 1138*, the *Indiana Jones* trilogy, and *American Graffiti*.

One of the most frustrating and ridiculous oversights by an awards committee came with the Oscar nominations announcement, where *Revenge of the Sith* received only one nomination. Somehow, the Academy of Motion Picture Arts and Sciences (AMPAAS) did not feel that the final prequel, with the most visual effects shots ever put on film, deserved even a nomination for Best Visual Effects. Similarly, with its five hundred costumes and otherworldly designs, it still was not able to earn a nomination for Best Costume Design, which already was a terrible mistake on the Academy's part for *The Phantom Menace*, a film that boasted some of the most impressive costumes in cinema history. Despite the ground-breaking work that Skywalker Sound had done on the *Star Wars* films, with *Revenge of the Sith* no exception, the final prequel did not receive nominations for either Best Sound Effects or Best Sound Effects Editing. The sole nomination for *Revenge of the Sith* was for Best Make-Up, a nice honor but hardly sufficient for a film of such beautiful craft.

Despite the hype backlash, many negative fan reactions, and mixed critical reviews, many analysts still thought *The Phantom Menace* had a shot at winning a number of technical awards because it was an extremely sophisticated achievement technically, not only on a visual effects level but on every visual, auditory, and aesthetic level. Yet the first prequel failed to receive nominations in any key categories outside of sound and visual effects, which was still more acclaim than the better-reviewed final prequel enjoyed with the Academy. The total lack of a visual effects nomination was shocking, especially because the film was visually several years ahead of any work from the rest of the industry.

ILM made possible the advancements in effects technology that led to characters such as Gollum from *The Lord of the Rings* and King Kong in Peter Jackson's remake, yet ILM has reaped none of the rewards from the Academy. The company managed to create the three most advanced films in history from a technological perspective at the time of their respective releases, with the best special effects ever put to film, and come away with no Oscar awards and only two nominations. Finding an explanation for the snubbing of the prequels' visual effects is difficult if not impossible. One must conclude it comes from the media bias against the prequels, film industry bias against Lucas, and perhaps a backlash against the saga in general from voters eager to award other projects.

Martin A. Grove of *The Hollywood Reporter* thought *Revenge of the Sith* had an excellent shot at winning significant awards later in the year. In an article written in early June, "'Sith' success could extend to awards galaxy," Grove noted that "'Sith's' potential awards strength reflects not only the fact that it was well received by critics across the country who consider it the best in the series, but also that as the final episode in its series it could benefit on the awards front the same way 'The Lord of the Rings: The Return of the King' did in 2004." Unfortunately, Lucas had no such fortune with voters. Jackson became Hollywood's Golden Boy with the *Lord of the Rings* films, while Lucas remained its social pariah, withdrawn from Hollywood by choice but also exiled; necessary for his technical wizardry, but also distrusted for his powerful independence.

The failure to nominate *Revenge of the Sith* for a visual effects award, a category the film series practically invented, is an invitation not to take the Oscars seriously as a whole or for its opinions about the *Star Wars* franchise. The snub is nothing short of an outrage. If moviegoers exist who would pick *King Kong*'s effects over *Revenge of the Sith*, as they inevitably do, virtually nobody would agree the prequel did not at least deserve one of three nominations in the effects category. *The Chronicles of Narnia: The Lion, The Witch, and The Wardrobe* and *War of the Worlds* received nominations over *Star Wars*, the former being the biggest surprise as its effects were not particularly impressive, realistic, or original.

As a result of the politics and bias that have become part of the Oscar awards, the Academy has become obsolete and laughable. If no objectivity exists even in technical awards, where voters should attempt to review the field in question without bias about a film's complete artistic merits or its creator, nobody should care about the awards, which do not reflect reality either critically or publicly. The voters either knowingly voted against the film with the best visual effects out of spite, or they simply have no concept of what goes into special effects work and what constitutes impressive effects versus solid but not revolutionary work like *Narnia*.

The Academy's bias is easy to dismiss as a *Star Wars* fan because the opinions of critics and awards ceremonies have never greatly concerned fans of any franchise. Likewise, Lucas can dismiss the snubs easily because he profits massively and is free artistically. The bias, however, is disappointing for the talented people who made the prequels great artistic achievements. Many amazingly talented people, like Costume Designer Trisha Biggar and Visual Effects Supervisors John Knoll and Roger Guyett, deserved recognition for the years of their lives they put into the prequels.

While fans will always appreciate the efforts of Knoll, Guyett, and Biggar, as well as others who worked on the prequels, workers in their industries have let bias and politics influence their decisions to ignore their fellow artists' achievements, which is sad and disgraceful. The artists who devoted much of a decade to the *Star Wars* prequels, however, have the ultimate revenge coming. In fifty years, people will still be watching *Star Wars* and appreciating their work, while the movies that the Academy has honored over them will quickly fade with time. All but the best and most powerful films are doomed to obscurity.

Epilogue

The prequel trilogy provided an ideal set of movies with which to premiere many new technologies. It also offered the chance to establish trends and business patterns that have continued with other movies and are likely to remain well into the future, perhaps forever remaining part of the landscape of American movies. Before *The Phantom Menace* came to theaters, nobody saw midnight showings of movies because theaters never offered them. Today, every major blockbuster has midnight showings, with most teenagers probably taking them for granted, no longer remembering how the trend started. Before *A New Hope* came to theaters in 1977, movie theaters had no reason to clear the auditoriums following showings; *Star Wars* gave them one as fans saw it dozens of times (Jenkins 152–53).

Before *The Phantom Menace*, no major film had ever screened digitally for the public. One day, every movie will be seen digitally at every theater nationwide. Before *Attack of the Clones*, major productions did not use digital cameras for filming because nobody thought they could provide high enough quality for mainstream presentation, but Lucas and the Sony-Panavision partnership proved them wrong. Directors once only dreamed of all-digital, realistic, speaking characters in movies, but Lucas and Industrial Light & Magic made them a reality, leading to moviegoer favorites like Gollum in *The Lord of the Rings* and a fighting Yoda in the final two *Star Wars* prequels.

Steve Sailer wrote in late 2002 in a review of *Attack of the Clones* on DVD that the prequel trilogy "strikes me as misbegotten" and that prequels "appeal to the obsessive fan, not to the average moviegoer," going as far as to say that Lucas should "scrap Episode 3." Regardless, the entire prequel trilogy and especially *Revenge of the Sith* enjoyed immense success. Not only did the films introduce a new generation of fans to the saga, but they doubled the size of the *Star Wars* film story and added depth to the politics of the epic, explaining how unchecked power combined with intense fear of loss can lead to enough poor decisions to thrust someone into despair and a life of evil. The prequels added emotional depth to the Original Trilogy, making it a richer experience for fans and casual moviegoers alike. The proof is in the numbers, which demonstrate that almost everyone is glad Lucas did not take Sailer's advice.

Revenge of the Sith served as a uniting force for *Star Wars* fans. While the previous two prequels were immensely successful, and pleased most fans, they also created a chasm between younger fans and older fans, often leading to intense debates online. Any fans who still were not pleased with *Revenge of the Sith* were never going to enjoy the prequels anyway and are probably lost as fans. For everyone else, though, the final prequel either continued a tradition of excellence spread across nearly thirty years of filmmaking, or it redeemed the saga in glorious fashion. It won over many critics who seemed destined to dismiss the final movie as they had the last two prequels, if not *Return of the Jedi* as well, which has since become a classic.

Financially, *Revenge of the Sith* met high expectations and became the highest grossing movie of the year domestically. It also exceeded already high standards for merchandising sales, catapulting the franchise's total gross to more than $16.2 billion (roughly $12 billion in merchandising and $4.2 billion in ticket sales). In countries worldwide, it broke opening day and opening weekend records, shattering industry speed marks and bolstering weak box office frames in many markets around the globe.

Beyond succeeding critically and financially, the movie brought a satisfying sense of closure to its creator. "I feel very satisfied that I have accomplished what I set out to do with *Star Wars*. I was able to complete the entire saga and say this is what the whole story is about," Lucas said ("Closing …"). When asked whether the saga changed him, Lucas said, "I am not sure that it changed me very much other than the fact that I got a lot older, and I didn't realize it" (ibid.). *Star Wars* may not have changed its creator greatly, but it changed the world for many people, and for the film industry. "*Star Wars* is one of those cultural presences that will be experienced by people who watch Fox News and people who watch ESPN and people who watch Nickelodeon," said Robert Thompson, a professor of popular culture at Syracuse University (Kloer).

In the thirty years since the public first had its introduction to *Star Wars*, the franchise has become a formidable cultural force and a timeless mythology that has inspired and entertained generations of fans and moviegoers. In October 2005, a new exhibit called "*Star Wars*: Where Science Meets Imagination" had its world premiere at Boston's Museum of Science. The exhibit showcased the science behind the fiction in the space saga. Museum spokeswoman Carole McFall said, "*Star Wars* really ties into the museum's new vision of incorporating more technology and engineering. We're not talking about science fiction. There is real-world technology in the exhibit" (Kunzelman). The museum chose to host the *Star Wars* exhibit instead of a 3,000-square-foot exhibit celebrating the three hundredth anniversary of Founding Father Benjamin Franklin's birth (ibid.). The *Star Wars* exhibit, though, was designed to be educational, not just serve as a collection of props, costumes, and models.

In September 2006, Lucasfilm re-released the Original Trilogy on DVD, sending another 5 million copies to retailers initially (Ault "Fox Plots ..."). The new releases gave fans the opportunity to own the original theatrical releases of the classic films, without any alterations. Meanwhile, for the first time fans could buy the enhanced films individually. "As guardians, we have to look at the total allocation and see if it's in line with what the market absorbs," said Fox Executive Vice President of Marketing Peter Staddon of the number of copies shipped (ibid.). Retailers complained that they wanted more copies, but Fox has a reputation of being able to replenish inventories for sellers quickly.

Lucasfilm, no doubt, will release many more versions of the *Star Wars* movies in the future, though probably will wait to see which next-generation format wins, Blu-Ray or HD-DVD. Even prequel Producer Rick McCallum does not think Lucas will ever stop tinkering with the *Star Wars* movies, though any additional changes will likely come years after the release of *Revenge of the Sith* on DVD (Salas "ON DVD; ..."). With more storage capacity on future formats, perhaps fans will see more in-depth bonus offerings. "We shot about 800 hours of behind-the-scenes footage [for *Revenge of the Sith*], from the day we started prep to the day we finished, and we have about 3,200 hours for all three films," McCallum said (ibid.).

Mark Hamill, who many people cannot picture as anyone else but Luke Skywalker, still takes pride in the impact that his role had on generations of fans. "It's not so much from the industry ... but the nine-year-old kid who looks at you like a cross between Superman and Santa Claus. And you'd have to be a really, really hardened cynic not to be moved by that," he said (Hamill). When asked what he thought of the movies "finally ending," Hamill responded, "I've learned that the movies will never finally end. It just goes on and on and on and on" (ibid.). He continued, only half-jokingly, "I mean, it's going to be in 3D, then it's going to be smellivision, then it's going to be a ride in an amusement park, then they'll come to your house and perform it with puppets on your lawn."

While Lucasfilm is fully engaged in keeping *Star Wars* around for many decades into the future, and producing new content to please fans, Lucas claims to be done with the franchise, at least as far as having any major involvement in creative decisions. "You reach a point where you have to plan your life and I'm sort of at that point. I love *Star Wars*, but I'm not going to spend the rest of my life doing it," he said (Fulton "Leaving ..."). When questioned whether he would be able to leave the franchise for good, Lucas said, "I did it for sixteen years. I'm ready to do it for good" (Lawson).

Executives at Lucasfilm made sure fans knew that their favorite sci-fi franchise still had a future, though. Lucasfilm Licensing President Howard Roffman said, "The films may have ended, but the franchise hasn't. It has been around thirty years, and this isn't even the midpoint" (James "'Star Wars' ..."). When Roffman joined Lucasfilm, *Star Wars* had lost its merchandising viability, at least temporarily. Many companies would not pay any significant sum of money for licensing rights. One client told Roffman that *Star Wars* was dead, a message he passed on to Lucas, who told him, "It isn't dead. It's just hibernating" (ibid.). Roffman, after watching the *Star Wars* juggernaut return to prominence like a mythical phoenix rising from the ashes, said in a licensing speech, "I'm bullish on the future, as I know the awesome staying power of the brand" (ibid.).

Without a new movie in 2006, *Star Wars* merchandise sales remained strong. Merchandise from the saga still outsold merchandise from summer hits like *Cars*, *Pirates of the Caribbean: Dead Man's Chest*, and *Superman Returns* (Kang). In fact, *Star Wars* action figures were the top seller through the summer and the franchise ranked first in boys' toy sales, according to the NPD Group, a market-research firm (ibid.). Roffman said that *Star Wars* toys were outselling the nearest competitor, *Cars*, by a two-to-one margin. While the sales had dipped considerably for *Star Wars* merchandise between 2005 and 2006, interest still remained strong, with Lucasfilm intending to avoid a repeat of the *Star Wars* Dark Ages, the period that followed the Original Trilogy's release (ibid.).

To keep the *Star Wars* franchise strong, Lucasfilm must continue to develop new content in the form of new storylines, both with familiar characters and new ones. A major focus of the effort centers around the story between the two *Star Wars* trilogies, bridging the gap between the two halves of the saga. Lucas said, "The comic books and videos and novels are out there. [*Star Wars*] is sort of going to have a life of its own" (Lucas *Birmingham Post*). Lucasfilm's Head of Fan Relations Steve Sansweet concurred, saying, "We will keep *Star Wars* alive and well as long as there is an audience, which we think is an indefinite horizon" (Collura). The company had many plans for the future, including another fan gathering.

In May 2006, Lucasfilm announced plans for *Star Wars* Celebration IV, to take place in Los Angeles at the Los Angeles Convention Center, annexing the entire complex the following May. Lucasfilm extended the length of the event to five days, giving fans more opportunity to celebrate the thirtieth anniversary of the first film. "This is the first chance to celebrate all six movies in the saga—George Lucas's complete story—as well as the vibrant future of *Star Wars*," said Sansweet ("Star Wars Celebration IV ..."). Noting the interest in a fourth Celebration even while the third was still running, Sansweet assured fans that Celebration IV would be bigger and better than all of the previous attempts. To address complaints about the store, Lucasfilm announced it planned to keep the store open from the start of the Celebration through the end, twenty-four hours a day (ibid.).

In August 2004, Lucasfilm announced its plans to employ up to three hundred people at a high-tech animation studio in Singapore with the intention of creating animated work for television shows, feature films, and video games (McGirk). The move to create an animation studio in Singapore, Lucas said, was not a cost-saving decision but an aesthetic one. "I've been a big fan of Asian animation and illustration all my life. By having a base in Singapore, we can create a new style of animation that will blend East and West and offer something not seen before," Lucas announced (ibid.). Lucasfilm also appreciated Singapore's harsh stance on copyright laws, citing better protection than any other Asian country (ibid.). The Singapore government and investors from the city-state took one-quarter ownership of Lucasfilm Animation Singapore.

With an eye toward a future in television for the *Star Wars* franchise, Lucasfilm hired Joshua Katz as head of global marketing in August 2005. Katz had experience with many cable network rebranding campaigns, preparing Lucasfilm for a move into television production. "We have to stop being just a movie studio and have to move to being a television and movie studio," Katz said (Cohen and Hettrick). Acknowledging the continued importance of the *Star Wars* franchise to Lucasfilm, Katz said it is "at the heart of this company, and I can't envision a time when it isn't the central rod that keeps us going" (ibid.). Katz served as part of the launch team for Cartoon Network and was previously senior vice president of marketing at music television network VH1.

By the time *Star Wars* Celebration III gave fans a chance to meet one last time before the final *Star Wars* movie hit theaters, Lucas already had plans to continue the franchise on television with two series, one 3-D animated and one live-action. He announced his intentions formally at the Celebration. "I'll never let go of *Star Wars*," Lucas later told four thousand computer professionals at SIGGRAPH,[1] the computer graphics conference held at the Los Angeles Convention Center in 2005 (D. Cohen "Lucas ..."). Lucas explained his goal of producing the live-action television series cheaply, much like *The Young Indiana Jones Chronicles*,

---

1.   SIGGRAPH is short for Special Interest Group for Computer Graphics.

where a number of prequel crew members had worked previously. "Television is an easier medium to work in (than film).... It's more fun, there's less pressure and it's a great medium to experiment in," he said (ibid.). Lucas wanted the live-action series to focus on the period between the two *Star Wars* trilogies.

On October 26, 2005, Lucasfilm Animation Singapore finally opened formally. "We're very excited about the opening of a new studio," Lucas said ("Lucasfilm Animation ..."). "Our first series—a TV adventure titled *Clone Wars*, based on the time between *Attack of the Clones* and *Revenge of the Sith*—is already in active development and we hope to see it on the air in 2007," he continued. Lucasfilm opened the animation studio with the intention of it doing more than just *Star Wars* work, however. In the future, the studio will serve as a headquarters for animating both television shows and feature films, starting a new era in the Lucasfilm empire.

On March 17, 2005, at ShoWest in Las Vegas, Lucas had unveiled his plans for re-releasing the *Star Wars* movies in 3-D once a sufficient number of theaters convert to digital projection. The conversion process of turning 2-D images into 3-D footage is now possible with a remarkable level of success, thanks to a company called In-Three that converted a few clips from the *Star Wars* films for Lucasfilm. At ShoWest, where theater exhibitors and film industry executives gather every year for meetings and presentations about the state of the film exhibition industry, people in attendance had the opportunity to see the speeder chase from *Attack of the Clones* in 3-D and the entire first reel of *A New Hope* in 3-D.

Lucas mentioned that many companies had attempted to make demos for him showing 3-D versions of the films over the past two decades, but none of them met his standards until In-Three's conversion, which relies on digital projection technology to work (Kleiman). Lucas expressed his interest in converting all of the six *Star Wars* movies to 3-D with the goal of releasing them starting in several years at a rate of one per year until they all come to theaters. Also at the convention, fellow filmmaker James Cameron expressed his intent to shoot entire movies in 3-D for commercial distribution, one of which, *Battle Angel*, he had already announced as a future project.

Although *Star Wars* fans no doubt want to see the saga's movies in 3-D primarily for the thrill of a new experience, Lucas's motivations probably come from his persistent desire to use his movies to push technology forward. From the early innovations in both special effects and sound with *A New Hope* to the computer graphics work pioneered in the prequels, the *Star Wars* movies have always been technological showcases for cutting-edge developments in the film industry and in film presentation technology. As such, Lucas hoped that the prospect of play-ing the *Star Wars* movies in 3-D would convince many theaters to adopt digital projection sooner.

Fortunately for supporters of digital technology, James Cameron announced his intentions to make films using digital 3-D camera equipment, as he had already done with several documentaries, *Ghosts of the Abyss* (2003) and *Aliens of the Deep* (2005). In June, he announced a second planned project, known as *Project 880* at the time, that he planned to shoot before *Battle Angel* ("Lights …"). Cameron said he hoped to have at least one thousand 3-D digital projectors in major theaters before the release of his first 3-D movie (ibid.). Between Cameron and Lucas, a formidable financial duo, one would think the-ater chains would have solid financial reasons for wanting to upgrade their equip-ment.

In late June 2005, Lucasfilm celebrated its move, along with the majority of its staff, to the new Letterman Digital Arts Center in San Francisco, near the Golden Gate Bridge at the Presidio National Park. A bronze Yoda statue greets visitors at the entrance to the front door, sitting atop a tiled fountain (Stone). The complex includes four buildings with more than six hundred miles of cable connecting them to one another, the largest high-performance data network in the industry (ibid.). Every desktop included fiber optic cable access for the artist stationed there. Previously, Lucasfilm's primary operations were headquartered at Sky-walker Ranch in Marin County, California; the company continues to maintain Skywalker Ranch, despite the move. In all, about fifteen hundred employees moved to the new Lucasfilm headquarters, with a total of twenty-five hundred workers planned for the future.

The new digital arts and entertainment center, at $350 million, is one of the most sophisticated of its kind in the world. It houses all of Lucasfilm's primary departments in one location, including ILM, Lucas Licensing, LucasArts, and Lucas's corporate offices. The complex boasts tight security, easy collaboration between Lucasfilm's departments, and an ideal setting on twenty-three acres of land with two theaters, one three-hundred-seat auditorium and another sixty-five-seat auditorium built for film editors to use for reviewing work.

With the creative artists and Lucasfilm departments connected both physically and digitally, Lucasfilm hoped for greater artistic collaboration and efficiency at the 850,000-square-foot complex. Senior Visual Effects Supervisor Dennis Muren said, "The creation of the campus and the technology inside means that fewer and fewer obstacles are in the way of the creative process" (Norton "'Star Wars' creator …"). Lucas, however, intended to spend just a few hours each month at the new complex. "In terms of being a corporate executive, I'm pretty much tired. I'm going to focus on making movies," he said (ibid.). Lucas has worked hard to ensure that his companies can function without his constant attention, freeing up his time to delve into creative filmmaking endeavors again. "What I am doing is so I don't need to be a visionary," Lucas said, allowing the company to function without "some genius at the head" of it (Holson "At Lucasfilm …").

While Lucas has expressed much frustration at the slowness of the industry to adopt digital technology, especially with theaters upgrading to digital projection, he remains optimistic about the state of the industry and the future of technology. "The real leap has been made. Digital cinema is here. It's not like we're going to reinvent the wheel. It's been reinvented," he said (D. Cohen "Lucas …"). Lucas envisions being remembered more for his storytelling than what he contributed to the industry technologically, though. "I'll be remembered as a filmmaker. The technological problems that I solved will be forgotten by then, but hopefully some of the stories I told will still be relevant. I'm hoping that *Star Wars* doesn't become too dated, because I think its themes are timeless," he said (Lucas *Wired*).

Aside from his *Star Wars* legacy, Lucas has donated generously to USC's School of Cinematic Arts,[2] assuring that future generations of filmmakers have the technology and means to succeed. School Dean Elizabeth Daley said of Lucas, "This school would not be the same without George," noting his position as a role model, leader, and passionate advocate for film and film school (Goldman). "Our school is seventy-five years old, but in those early days, attending film school did not get the respect it gets today. That is largely due to George—he has provided that leadership," Daley said (ibid.). She continued, "Our school is very much the house that George built."

In September 2006, Lucas donated a whopping $175 million to USC, $75 million for new educational buildings and renovations of existing ones and $100 million to be used as endowment for the school. The donation was the largest in USC's history. "I'm very fortunate to be in a position to combine my two passions [education and filmmaking] and to be able to help USC continue molding the futures of the moviemakers of tomorrow," Lucas said (Zollinger). While his films have inspired thousands of people to pursue careers ranging from filmmaking and animating to aeronautics and engineering, his generous donations to

---

2.   Formerly called the School of Cinema-Television.

USC have helped grow and maintain the nation's oldest and arguably most prestigious film school.

Although the *Star Wars* film franchise may have ended with *Revenge of the Sith*, the greater franchise will continue in many forms, from video games to novels to television shows, well into the future. Hasbro used a phrase in its marketing that is truer today than ever before: "*Star Wars* is Forever." The final prequel is not the end of *Star Wars*, nor the beginning of the end, though perhaps it is the end of the beginning. In 2005, after weaving together numerous plot threads, delighting fans, impressing critics, and ending a thirty-year period of his life devoted to the most ambitious film project ever undertaken, at last, Lucas had his revenge.

Special Thanks To:

My father for his support of my writing.

Matt Busch for his helpful interview commentary.

Steve Kunert at Oregon State University for his stylistic and grammatical advice.

Jonathan Shelton Lawrence for his support and encouragement.

The iUniverse editorial staff for their support.

Mark Newbold for his support of my writing career and most of all his friendship.

Lou Tambone for his continued support of my work.

All of the fans who provided interview commentary for the book and greatly enriched its pages.

All of the people who read my first book and helped it gain exposure.

Bibliography

"$115,000,000 Day One Worldwide Sales for Star Wars; Star Wars Dominates Global Retail as Consumers Snap up DVD and Games at Light Speed." *Business Wire* 22 Sep. 2004. Accessed: 1 Aug. 2006. Available: http://www.highbeam.com.

"2005 U.S. Piracy Fact Sheet." Motion Picture Association of America. Accessed: 2 Jan. 2007. Available: http://www.mpaa.org/USPiracyFactSheet.pdf.

"48th annual Grammy nominations list—part 2." *Variety* 8 Dec. 2005. Accessed: 19 Dec. 2005. Available: http://www.variety.com.

"60 Minutes." *60 Minutes* 13 Mar. 2005. CBS. Transcript available: http://www.highbeam.com.

"8 Charged in Illegal Release of 'Star Wars'." *AP Online* 28 Sep. 2005. Accessed: 19 Jun. 2006. Available: http://www.highbeam.com.

"A Closer Look at a Mashing Success: Darth Tater." *The Official Star Wars Web Site* 23 Feb. 2005. Accessed: 15 Jun. 2006. Available: http://www.starwars.com.

"A Darker Side/Last 'Star Wars' May Get A PG-13 Rating." *The Cincinnati Post* 11 Mar. 2005. Accessed: 14 Jun. 2006. Available: http://www.highbeam.com.

"A Tale of Three Trilogies?" *Cinefantastique* Vol. 37, No. 3 Jun. 2005: 34–35.

"About LIFE Magazine." *LIFE.* Accessed: 29 Nov. 2006. Available: http://www.life.com/about.

Adams, Neale. "All day and all (Jedi) night … Empire, it had to be, hosts Star Wars-athon but are the fans from another planet?" *The Evening Standard* 16 May 2005. Accessed: 9 Jun. 2006. Available: http://www.highbeam.com.

Ahrens, Frank. "Final 'Star Wars' Caps Moneymaking Empire." *The Washington Post* 14 May 2005. Accessed: 2 Jun. 2006. Available: http://www.highbeam.com.

"AIS taps into Star Wars theme for refill cards." *Bangkok Post* 26 Mar. 2005. Accessed: 15 Jun. 2006. Available: http://www.highbeam.com.

Alexander, Derek. "Pirates Taking the Sith; Counterfeiters cash in." *Daily Record* 30 May 2005. Accessed: 27 Jun. 2005. Available: http://www.highbeam.com.

"Alias-Maya Helps Power Digital Characters and Key Scenes in Star Wars: Episode III—Revenge of the Sith." *Business Wire* 24 May 2005. Accessed: 15 Jun. 2006. Available: http://www.highbeam.com.

"Alienware Creates Star Wars PC." *Wireless News* 2 May 2005. Accessed: 2 Jun. 2006. Available: http://www.highbeam.com.

"All Eyes On August." *The Official Star Wars Web Site* 11 Mar. 2004. Accessed: 17 Jun. 2006. Available: http://www.starwars.com.

"All Too Queasy: Virgin Airlines' Unique Collectibles." *The Official Star Wars Web Site* 14 Jun. 2005. Accessed: 17 Jun. 2006. Available: http://www.starwars.com.

"Always in Motion are these TV Guide Covers." *The Official Star Wars Web Site* 26 Apr. 2005. Accessed: 17 Jun. 2006. Available: http://www.starwars.com.

"Americans Prefer Watching Movies at Home." *Yahoo! Movies* 16 Jun. 2005. Accessed: 16 Jun. 2005. Available: http://movies.yahoo.com.

"An Introduction to Episode III; *Revenge* Fantasies." *The Official Star Wars Web Site* 18 May 2005. Accessed: 15 Jun. 2006. Available: http://www.starwars.com.

"Analysis: Dove Foundation questions appropriateness of Burger King's promotion of 'Revenge of the Sith' on its Kids Meals." *Day to Day* 24 May 2005. NPR. Transcript available: http://www.highbeam.com.

"Animal Planet Travels to a Whole New Galaxy with Animal Icons: Star Wars Creatures." *PR Newswire* 2 May 2005. Accessed: 3 Jun. 2006. Available: http://www.highbeam.com.

Antonucci, Mike. "'Star Wars' video game gives fans interactive preview of new film." Rev. of *Star Wars: Episode III—Revenge of the Sith* (video game). *San Jose Mercury News* 10 May 2005. Accessed: 7 Jun. 2006. Available: http://www.highbeam.com.

"AOL Movies and Moviefone.com to Offer Online Premiere of Star Wars: Episode III Revenge of the Sith Teaser Trailer." *Business Wire* 26 Oct. 2004. Accessed: 18 Jun. 2006. Available: http://www.highbeam.com.

"April 2 Launches *Star Wars* Promotions." *The Official Star Wars Web Site* 4 Mar. 2005. Accessed: 17 Jun. 2006. Available: http://www.starwars.com.

Armitage, Alex. "News Corp.'s 'Star Wars' Leads Advance Ticket Sales on Internet." *Bloomberg* 27 May 2005. Accessed: 27 May 2005. Available: http://www.bloomberg.com.

Arnold, Gary. "The last 'Star'; 'Sith' puts end to 'Wars'." Rev. of *Star Wars: Episode III—Revenge of the Sith. The Washington Times* 18 May 2005. Accessed: 14 Jun. 2006. Available: http://www.highbeam.com.

Ascenzi, Joseph. "'Star Wars' Brings New Hope to U.S. Toy Vendors." *The Business Press* 20 May 2002. Accessed: 9 Aug. 2006. Available: http://www.highbeam.com.

"Aspyr Media, Inc. Ships Star Wars Battlefront For Macintosh." *Business Wire* 19 Jul. 2005. Accessed: 7 Jun. 2006. Available: http://www.highbeam.com.

"Attack of the Cartoons; 'Star Wars' Series Fills Void Between Movies." *The Washington Post* 6 Nov. 2003. Accessed: 18 Jun. 2006. Available: http://www.highbeam.com.

Ault, Susanne. "Batman avoids Sith street." *Video Business* 1 Aug. 2005. Accessed: 15 Jun. 2006. Available: http://www.videobusiness.com.

———. "Fox Plots 5 Million *Star Wars*." *Video Business Online* 11 Aug 2006. Accessed: 25 Aug. 2006. Available: http://www.videobusiness.com.

————. "Fox skimps on Star Wars: avoids heavy returns." *Video Business* 26 Sep. 2005. Accessed: 19 Jun. 2006. Available: http://www.videobusiness.com.

————. "*Sith* Promos Target Mass Merchants." *Video Business* 7 Oct. 2005. Accessed: 25 Aug. 2006. Available: http://www.videobusiness.com.

————. "Starry *Sith* Debut." *Video Business* 4 Nov. 2005. Accessed: 6 Nov. 2005. Available: http://www.videobusiness.com.

————. "Wal-Mart Offers Exclusive *Sith* Disc." *Video Business* 26 Sep. 2005. Accessed: 25 Aug. 2006. Available: http://www.videobusiness.com.

Australian Government. "The Office of Film & Literature Classification." Accessed: 29 Nov. 2006. Available: http://www.oflc.gov.au.

"Auteur Is Born." *The Wall Street Journal* 20 May 2005: W11.

Bacon, Richard. "Bacon at the Movies: Revenge is Sweet." Rev. of *Star Wars: Episode III—Revenge of the Sith*. *The People* 15 May 2005. Accessed: 15 Jun. 2006. Available: http://www.highbeam.com.

Bakay, Nick. "A tale of two empires." *ESPN.com Page 2*. Accessed: 29 May 2005. Available: http://www.espn.com.

Beckerman, Jim. "A brilliant finish for 'Star Wars'." Rev. of *Star Wars: Episode III—Revenge of the Sith*. *The Record* 18 May 2005. Accessed: 3 Jun. 2006. Available: http://www.highbeam.com.

"Behind Hip Hop Yoda: Making a DVD Easter Egg." *The Official Star Wars Web Site* 10 Nov. 2005. Accessed: 15 Jun. 2006. Available: http://www.starwars.com.

Bentley, Rick. "'Star Wars' fan pursues his dream; The Valley's own Elvis Trooper makes a cameo on the DVD of a special-edition board game." *The Fresno Bee* 26 Apr. 2005. Accessed: 2 Jun. 2006. Available: http://www.highbeam.com.

————. "Toon in to the Force: The 'Star Wars' mythology returns via animated shorts." *The Fresno Bee* 6 Nov. 2003. Accessed: 18 Jun. 2006. Available: http://www.highbeam.com.

Bernard, Jami. Rev. of *Star Wars: Episode III—Revenge of the Sith. New York Daily News* 16 May 2005. Accessed: 7 Jun. 2006. Available: http://www.highbeam.com.

"Bettors Believe 'Star Wars: Episode III' Will Set Box Office Records." *PR Newswire* 17 May 2005. Accessed: 15 Jun. 2006. Available: http://www.highbeam.com.

Bhatnagar, Parija. "Hasbro's hyping 'Star Wars'." *CNN Money* 28 Mar. 2005. Accessed: 28 Mar. 2005. Available: http://money.cnn.com.

"Big Numbers: Ep III Animation." *The Official Star Wars Web Site* 18 Aug. 2005. Accessed: 17 Jun. 2006. Available: http://www.starwars.com.

Biggar, Trisha. Interview with Nickelodeon Magazine. *Nickelodeon Magazine* May 2005: 62.

"BioWare Delivers Hit Titles on PC and Console; Neverwinter Nights: Shadows of Undrentide and Star Wars: Knights of the Old Republic storm up the charts in back-to-back months." *PR Newswire* 25 Aug. 2003. Accessed: 19 Jun. 2006. Available: http://www.highbeam.com.

Blake, Larry. "Star Wars Episode II: Attack of the Clones." *Mix* 1 Jun. 2002. Accessed: 9 Aug. 2006. Available: http://www.highbeam.com.

Blank, Wayne. "What Does The '666' Mean?" *The Daily Bible Study* 21 Oct. 2002. Accessed: 15 Jun. 2005. Available: http://www.keyway.ca/htm2002/20021021.htm.

"Blockbuster Offers Star Wars Entertainment That Is Out of This Galaxy; Survey Findings, Exclusive Offerings and Midnight Events—All Part of the Star Wars Celebration at Blockbuster." *PR Newswire* 28 Apr. 2005. Accessed: 3 Jun. 2006. Available: http://www.highbeam.com.

"Blog All About It." *The Official Star Wars Web Site* 17 May 2005. Accessed: 17 Jun. 2006. Available: http://www.starwars.com.

Bodeen, Christopher. "Latest 'Star Wars' film gets quiet opening in China." *AP Worldstream* 19 May 2005. Accessed: 9 Jun. 2006. Available: http://www.highbeam.com.

Boland, Michaela. "B.O. decline afflicts Oz disc sales." *Variety* 27 Feb. 2006. Accessed: 18 Jun. 2006. Available: http://www.variety.com.

———. "Fox's 'Sith' secures B.O. crown in Oz." *Variety* 18 Aug. 2005. Accessed: 23 Aug. 2005. Available: http://www.variety.com.

Boland, Michaela et al. "Territories tell the tale (Overseas box office totals for 2005 a mixed bag)." *Variety* 8 Jan. 2006. Accessed: 9 Jan. 2006. Available: http://www.variety.com.

Bond, Jeff. "Force-ful: John Williams returns with an impressive Revenge of the Sith." Rev. of *Star Wars: Episode III—Revenge of the Sith* (soundtrack). *Cinefantastique* Vol. 37, No. 3 Jun. 2005: 56.

Booth, William. "Episode III: Attack Of the Media Droids." *The Washington Post* 7 May 2005. Accessed: 3 Jun. 2006. Available: http://www.highbeam.com.

Bowles, Scott. "Generation flap." *USA Today* 13 May 2005: 1E–2E.

———. "In 'Sith,' Vader's tale sets more ominous tone." *USA Today* 5 May 2005: 1D.

"Box Office Performance for 20th Century Fox Movies in 2004." *The Numbers.* Accessed: 11 Dec. 2006. Available: http://www.the-numbers.com.

"Box Office Performance for 20th Century Fox Movies in 2005." *The Numbers.* Accessed: 11 Dec. 2006. Available: http://www.the-numbers.com.

"Braving the Prequel Path." *The Official Star Wars Web Site* 4 Aug. 2005. Accessed: 17 Jun. 2006. Available: http://www.starwars.com.

"Brenden Theatres Boosts Box Office Sales With Award-Winning 'Star Wars' Promotion." *PR Newswire* 15 Mar. 2006. Accessed: 19 Jun. 2006. Available: http://www.highbeam.com.

Bresnan, Conor. "Around the World Roundup: 'Revenge' Reigns Again, 'Sin City' Creeps In." *Box Office Mojo* 7 Jun. 2005. Accessed: 22 Aug. 2006. Available: http://www.boxofficemojo.com.

————. "Around the World Roundup: 'Sith' Builds Overseas Empire." *Box Office Mojo* 23 May 2005. Accessed: 25 May 2005. Available: http:// www.boxofficemojo.com.

————. "Around the World Roundup: 'Sith's' Empire Declines But Still Huge." *Box Office Mojo* 2 Jun. 2005. Accessed: 22 Aug. 2006. Available: http:// www.boxofficemojo.com.

Breznican, Anthony. "Lucasfilm Unveils New 'Star Wars' Title." *AP Online* 24 Jul. 2004. Accessed: 18 Jun. 2006. Available: http://www.highbeam.com.

————. "'Star Wars' DVD Set to Debut in September." *AP Online* 11 Feb. 2004. Accessed: 18 Jun. 2006. Available: http://www.highbeam.com.

————. "'Star Wars' fan has 'Revelations'." *USA Today* 12 May 2005: 3D.

Bridget, Byrne. "'Sith' Goes Forth, And Comes In First." *The Washington Post* 23 May 2005. Accessed: 27 May 2005. Available: http://www. washingtonpost.com.

Britton, Bonnie. "'Star Wars' Lands in Indy." *The Indianapolis Star* 21 Apr. 2005: A1, A9.

Brown, Maressa. "People catch 'Star'." *Variety* 11 Jan. 2006. Accessed: 13 Jan. 2006. Available: http://www.variety.com.

Brown, Rich. Rev. of *Star Wars Galaxies: An Empire Divided* (video game). *PC Magazine* (online). Accessed: 1 Aug. 2006. Available: http:// www.pcmag.com.

Buchanan, Levi. "'Lego Star Wars' bridges generations." Rev. of *LEGO Star Wars* (video game). *Chicago Tribune* 6 Apr. 2005. Accessed: 9 Jun. 2006. Available: http://www.highbeam.com.

————. "'Republic Commando' takes gritty look at 'Star Wars' universe." Rev. of *Star Wars: Republic Commando* (video game). *Chicago Tribune* 2 Mar. 2005. Accessed: 9 Jun. 2006. Available: http://www.highbeam.com.

————. "The Force is with Cingular cell phones." *Chicago Tribune* 18 May 2005. Accessed: 28 Jun. 2005. Available: http://www.highbeam.com.

Burton, Bonnie. "Listening for the Story: Inside the DVD Commentary." *The Official Star Wars Web Site* 27 Sep. 2005. Accessed: 15 Jun. 2006. Available: http://www.starwars.com.

Busch, Matt. E-mail to the author. 9 Aug. 2006.

Butler, Grant. "'Star Wars' Index." *The Oregonian* 18 May 2005.

Butt, Riazat. "Star Wars fans turn out in force for final instalment." *The Guardian* 17 May 2005. Accessed: 17 May 2005. Available: http://film. guardian.co.uk.

Butts, Steve. Rev. of *Star Wars: Empire at War* (video game). *IGN*. Accessed: 30 Nov. 2006. Available: http://pc.ign.com.

"California Lottery Promotes New Star Wars Scratchers With Licensed Collectible Coins." *PR Newswire* 10 May 2005. Accessed: 14 Jun. 2006. Available: http://www.highbeam.com.

"California man pleads guilty to pirating 'Star Wars' film." *AP Worldstream* 14 Dec. 2005. Accessed: 19 Jun. 2006. Available: http://www.highbeam.com.

"Carmike Cinemas, Inc. Completes Acquisition of GKC Theatres, Refinances Credit Facilities and Announces Results for Second Quarter of 2005." *Arrive Net* 9 Aug. 2005. Accessed: 13 Aug. 2005. Available: http:// press.arrivenet.com.

Caro, Mark. "New 'Star Wars' film inadvertently has political overtones." *Chicago Tribune* 19 May 2005. Accessed: 7 Jun. 2006. Available: http:// www.highbeam.com.

"Cartoon Network and Lucasfilm Announce Star Wars Animated Shorts; 20 Animated 'Clone Wars' Serial Shorts to Appear on Cartoon Network in 2003–2004." *Business Wire* 20 Feb. 2003. Accessed: 18 Jun. 2006. Available: http://www.highbeam.com.

Castaneda, Antonio. "Between bombs and incoming shells, tanning and 'Star Wars' offer soldiers respite from war." *AP Worldstream* 11 Jun. 2005. Accessed: 15 Jun. 2006. Available: http://www.highbeam.com.

Caterinicchia, Dan. "'Star Wars' novelist keeps the Force at heart." *AP Worldstream* 10 Jun. 2005. Accessed: 2 Jun. 2006. Available: http://www.highbeam.com.

"Caught on the Cam: Bradley Alexander." *The Official Star Wars Web Site* 17 Mar. 2004. Accessed: 17 Jun. 2006. Available: http://www.starwars.com.

"Celebration III Set for Indy." *The Official Star Wars Web Site* 23 Jan. 2004. Accessed: 17 Jun. 2006. Available: http://www.starwars.com.

"Celebration III Shopping Spree!" *The Official Star Wars Web Site* 6 Apr. 2005. Accessed: 15 Jun. 2006. Available: http://www.starwars.com.

Cella, Matthew. "'Star Wars' fans camp at theater; Devotees await third prequel's May 19 opening." *The Washington Times* 10 May 2005. Accessed: 15 Jun. 2006. Available: http://www.highbeam.com.

Chan, Chris. "Tweaked version of Battlefront." Rev. of *Star Wars: Battlefront II* (video game). *New Straits Times* 15 Dec. 2005. Accessed: 1 Aug. 2006. Available: http://www.highbeam.com.

Chapa, Sergio. "Illegal Star Wars DVDs are hot items in border markets." *Brownsville Herald* 22 May 2005. Accessed: 14 Jun. 2006. Available: http://www.highbeam.com.

"'Charlotte's' Web of Ep III DVD Intrigue." *The Official Star Wars Web Site* 2 Nov. 2005. Accessed: 15 Jun. 2006. Available: http://www.starwars.com.

"Chinese SF fans seeking for 'Star Wars'." *Xinhua News Agency* 26 May 2006. Accessed: 19 Jun. 2006. Available: http://www.highbeam.com.

Choi, Candice. "Experts see lukewarm outlook for 'Star Wars' collectibles' value." *Los Angeles Daily News* 12 Apr. 2005. Accessed: 7 Jun. 2006. Available: http://www.highbeam.com.

―――. "'Star Wars' Toys Coming Out in Force." *Los Angeles Daily News* 1 Apr. 2005. Accessed: 7 Jun. 2006. Available: http://www.highbeam.com.

"Chris Neil: Coaching Vader; Impressive Performances." *The Official Star Wars Web Site* 5 Jul. 2005. Accessed: 15 Jun. 2006. Available: http://www.starwars.com.

Christensen, Hayden. Interview with Bruno Lester. *The Evening Standard* 11 Apr. 2005. Accessed: 2 Jun. 2006. Available: http://www.highbeam.com.

———. Interview with RJ Smith. "The Empire's New Clothes." *GQ* May 2005: 188–201.

Christensen, Hayden et al. "The Many Faces of Vader." *Rolling Stone* 2 Jun. 2005: 48.

Chung, Philip W. "She Takes it Off, 'Star Wars' Takes Her Out." *Asian Week* 18 May 2005. Accessed: 15 Jun. 2006. Available: http://www.highbeam.com.

"*Cinefex* Trilogy Set to Hyperspace Members." *The Official Star Wars Web Site* 16 Feb. 2006. Accessed: 15 Jun. 2006. Available: http://www.starwars.com.

"Cingular Gives Star Wars Fans Content Worth Celebrating." *PR Newswire* 19 Apr. 2005. Accessed: 2 Jun. 2006. Available: http://www.highbeam.com.

"Clearview Cinemas' Legendary Ziegfeld Theatre Rolls Out Red Carpet for Opening Night of 'Star Wars: Episode III—Revenge of the Sith.'" *PR Newsfire* 16 May 2005. Accessed: 27 Jun. 2005. Available: http://www.highbeam.com.

"*Clone Wars* Micro-Series Wins Emmy Award." *The Official Star Wars Web Site* 13 Sep. 2004. Accessed: 16 Aug. 2006. Available: http://www.starwars.com.

"*Clone Wars* Q & A." *The Official Star Wars Web Site* 20 Feb. 2004. Accessed: 17 Aug. 2006. Available: http://www.starwars.com.

"*Clone Wars* Volume 2 Wins Emmy Award." *The Official Star Wars Web Site* 19 Sep. 2005. Accessed: 16 Aug. 2006. Available: http://www.starwars.com.

"*Clone Wars* Volume 2 Wins Juried Emmy Award." *The Official Star Wars Web Site* 18 Aug. 2005. Accessed: 16 Aug. 2006. Available: http://www.starwars.com.

"Closing the circle of 'Star Wars'." *CNN.com* 19 May 2005. Accessed: 19 May 2005. Available: http://www.cnn.com.

Cloud, John. "How *Star Wars* Saved My Life." *Time* 9 May 2005: 64.

Cohen, David S. "Lucas touts tube moves." *Variety* 1 Aug. 2005. Accessed: 2 Aug. 2005. Available: http://www.variety.com.

————. "The Darth side of Lucas' politics." *Variety* 8 Oct. 2006. Accessed: 11 Dec. 2006. Available: http://www.variety.com.

Cohen, David S. and Ben Fritz. "More bucks for F/X bangs." *Variety* 4 Sep. 2005. Accessed: 15 Nov. 2005. Available: http://www.variety.com.

Cohen, David S. and Scott Hettrick. "Lucasfilm taps marketer." *Variety* 9 Aug. 2005. Accessed: 13 Aug. 2005. Available: http://www.variety.com.

Cohen, Peter. "First-person shooter; Star Wars: Battlefront." Rev. of *Star Wars: Battlefront* (video game). *Macworld* 1 Jul. 2005. Accessed: 7 Jun. 2006. Available: http://www.highbeam.com.

————. "Macworld's 2005 Game Hall of Fame." *Macworld* 1 Jan. 2006. Accessed: 1 Aug. 2006. Available: http://www.highbeam.com.

Colayco, Bob. Rev. of *Star Wars: Empire at War* (video game). *Game Spot* 16 Feb. 2005. Accessed: 30 Nov. 2006. Available: http://www.gamespot.com.

Colford, Paul D. "Companies line up to market 'Star Wars' products." *New York Daily News* 2 Apr. 2005. Accessed: 7 Jun. 2006. Available: http://www.highbeam.com.

Collier, Joe Guy. "Driving force is with them: Fans modify cars in spirit of 'Star Wars'." *Detroit Free Press* 26 May 2005. Accessed: 15 Jun. 2006. Available: http://www.highbeam.com.

Collura, Scott. "Lucasfilm: TV is Next for *Star Wars*." *Now Playing Magazine* 21 Mar. 2005. Accessed: 1 Dec. 2006. Available: http://www.nowplayingmag.com.

"Combined Force of 'Revenge of the Sith' DVD Debut and 'Star Wars Battlefront II' Video game Generates Worldwide First-Week Sales of $210 million." *Business Wire* 8 Nov. 2005. Accessed: 19 Jun. 2006. Available: http://www.highbeam.com.

Conlin, Shaun. "'Star Wars' Shoot-'Em-Up." Rev. of *Star Wars: Republic Commando* (video game). *The Palm Beach Post* 4 Mar. 2005. Accessed: 9 Jun. 2006. Available: http://www.highbeam.com.

Coolidge, Alexander. "'Star Wars' Newest Stars." *The Cincinnati Post* 1 Apr. 2005. Accessed: 9 Jun. 2006. Available: http://www.highbeam.com.

Coonan, Clifford. "China B.O. could jump 30%." *Variety* 20 Nov. 2005. Accessed: 19 Dec. 2005. Available: http://www.variety.com.

———. "Dark Side at work among China pirates." *Variety* 23 May 2005. Accessed: 23 Sep. 2005. Available: http://www.variety.com.

———. "'Fire' charms China." *Variety* 30 Nov. 2005. Accessed: 19 Dec. 2005. Available: http://www.variety.com.

———. "U.S. prods China on piracy enforcement." *Variety* 27 Oct. 2005. Accessed: 15 Nov. 2005. Available: http://www.variety.com.

Corliss, Richard. "Dark Side Rising." *Time* 9 May 2005: 52–57.

Corliss, Richard and Jess Cagle. "Dark Victory." *Time* 29 Apr. 2002: 56–68.

Cornwell, Rupert. "The Real Star Wars: Genesis of a new arms race." *The Independent* 30 May 2005. Accessed: 14 Jun. 2006. Available: http://www.highbeam.com.

Cowing, Emma. "Which one's Darth Vader again..?" *The Scotsman* 19 May 2005. Accessed: 21 May 2005. Available: http://www.scotsman.com.

Coyle, Jake. "As 'Star Wars' release approaches, George Lucas appears on 'The O.C.'" *AP Worldstream* 11 May 2005. Accessed: 14 Jun. 2006. Available: http://www.highbeam.com.

———. "Star Wars: A galaxy all its own." *AP Worldstream* 13 May 2005. Accessed: 3 Jun. 2006. Available: http://www.highbeam.com.

Crawford, Krysten. "The 'Star Wars' blitzkrieg." *CNN Money* 13 May 2005. Accessed: 15 May 2005. Available: http://money.cnn.com.

"Critical Effect." *Cinefantastique* Vol. 37, No. 3 Jun. 2005: 26.

"CTIA Showcase: Cingular Offering 'Star Wars' Content Suite." *Wireless News* 14 Mar. 2005. Accessed: 3 Jun. 2006. Available: http://www. highbeam.com.

Culley, Maureen. "The man in black, has Ewan gone over to the Dark Side? McGregor upsets fans with fleeting visit to Star Wars opening." *The Daily Mail* 17 May 2005. Accessed: 9 Jun. 2006. Available: http://www. highbeam.com.

Curnutte Jr., Rick. "Very brief thoughts on 'Sith'." Rev. of *Star Wars: Episode III—Revenge of the Sith. The Film Journal Blog* 20 May 2005. Accessed: 21 May 2005. Available: http://www.thefilmjournal.blogspot.com.

D'Alessandro, Anthony. "Waging 'Wars' on foreign soil." *Variety* 8 Jun. 2005. Accessed: 9 Jun. 2005. Available: http://www.variety.com.

D'Angelo, Mike. "Attacking the clones: who's responsible for big-budget Hollywood dreck? This critic blames you (and this magazine) and calls for drastic action." *Esquire* 1 May 2005. Accessed: 27 Jun. 2005. Available: http://www.highbeam.com.

Dale, David. "The Lucas strikes back." *The Sydney Morning Herald* (online) 19 Jul. 2005. Accessed: 24 Jul. 2006. Available: http://www.smh.com.au.

———. "What sank the Sith?" *The Sydney Morning Herald* (online) 12 Jul. 2005. Accessed: 24 Jul. 2006. Available: http://www.smh.com.au.

"Darth Vader and M&M's Brand Candies Dare New Yorkers to go to the 'Dark Side'." *PR Newswire* 29 Mar. 2005. Accessed: 9 Jun. 2006. Available: http://www.highbeam.com.

Davies, Mike. "Our critic's verdict: Dark side of Star Wars finally makes this one of the best." Rev. of *Star Wars: Episode III—Revenge of the Sith. Birmingham Post* 14 May 2005. Accessed: 14 Jun. 2006. Available: http:// www.highbeam.com.

Davis, Jon. "It takes deep pockets to preview 'Sith'." *Daily Herald* 13 May 2005. Accessed: 27 Jun. 2005. Available: http://www.highbeam.com.

Deahl, Rachel. "Top e-Books point to Widening Audience." *Publishers Weekly* 4 Jan. 2006. Accessed: 13 Dec. 2006. Available: http://www. publishersweekly.com.

Dedrick, Jay. "Send in the 'Clones'; Marketing Force Lands with New Space Epic from George Lucas." *Rocky Mountain News* 11 May 2002. Accessed: 9 Aug. 2006. Available: http://www.highbeam.com.

Denerstein, Robert. "Cease-fire 'Star Wars' Goes Out with a Bang in 'Revenge'." Rev. of *Star Wars: Episode III—Revenge of the Sith. Rocky Mountain News* 19 May 2005. Accessed: 7 Jun. 2006. Available: http://www. highbeam.com.

Devlin, Desmond. "The Untold History of MAD Magazine." *DC Comics.* Accessed: 29 Nov. 2006. Available: http://www.dccomics.com/mad/ ?action=about.

"Did AOTC meet your expectations?" *TheForce.net.* Accessed: 25 Jun. 2005. Available: http://www.theforce.net.

DiOrio, Carl. "'Clones' shows digital heft." *Variety* 24 Jun. 2002. Accessed: 9 Aug. 2006. Available: http://www.variety.com.

———. "Embrace the Dark Side." *Video Business Online* 27 May 2005. Accessed: 9 Jun. 2005. Available: http://www.videobusiness.com.

———. "Imax clips 'Clones' chatter." *Variety* 25 Nov. 2002. Accessed: 9 Aug. 2006. Available: http://www.variety.com.

"Direct from Sydney: Colin Fletcher; From the Fishbowl." *The Official Star Wars Web Site* 23 Apr. 2004. Accessed: 17 Jun. 2006. Available: http:// www.starwars.com.

"Dirty Dancing is Ultimate Movie Medicine." *Contact Music* 13 Jan. 2006. Accessed: 17 Jan. 2006. Available: http://www.contactmusic.com.

"Discovery takes flight with 'Star Wars' fare." *Multichannel News* 9 May 2005. Accessed: 9 Jun. 2006. Available: http://www.highbeam.com.

Dizon, Kristin. "One last, long campout for 'the Star Wars guy'." *Seattle Post-Intelligencer* 15 Jan. 2005. Accessed: 2 Sep. 2006. Available: http://www.seattlepi.nwsource.com.

"DLP Cinema Projection a Digital Force for 'Star Wars: Episode III—Revenge of the Sith' During Production, Post and Exhibition." *PR Newswire* 12 May 2005. Accessed: 15 Jun. 2006. Available: http://www.highbeam.com.

Dobnik, Verena. "'Star Wars' Draws Global Fans for Charity." *AP Online* 1 May 2005. Accessed: 15 Jun. 2006. Available: http://www.highbeam.com.

Dobuzinskis, Alex. "Revenge of the law falls on 'Star Wars' film pirates." *Los Angeles Daily News* 26 Jan. 2006. Accessed: 19 Jun. 2006. Available: http://www.highbeam.com.

"Does final 'Star Wars' mean the death of the superfan?" *The Hollywood Reporter* 28 May 2005. Accessed: 27 May 2005. Available: http://www.hollywoodreporter.com.

"Does 'Star Wars' Have Political Message?" *The O'Reilly Factor* 18 May 2005. Fox News Network. Transcript available: http://www.highbeam.com.

"Doing *Star Wars* the Burger King Way." *The Official Star Wars Web Site* 20 May 2005. Accessed: 17 Jun. 2006. Available: http://www.starwars.com.

Doland, Angela. "From 'Star Wars' to tiny independent films, Cannes had something for all tastes." *AP Worldstream* 22 May 2005. Accessed: 15 Jun. 2006. Available: http://www.highbeam.com.

"Dolby Digital Cinema Debuts in Japan with the Release of Star Wars: Episode III—Revenge of the Sith." *Business Wire* 23 Jun. 2005. Accessed: 27 Jun. 2005. Available: http://www.highbeam.com.

"Dolby Launches Dolby Digital Cinema in Theatres Worldwide with Star Wars Episode III: Revenge of the Sith." *Business Wire* 23 May 2005. Accessed: 27 Jun. 2005. Available: http://www.highbeam.com.

"Domestic Grosses #1–100." *Box Office Mojo*. Accessed: 29 Nov. 2006. Available: http://www.boxofficemojo.com.

"Donald Trump Celebrates *Star Wars* with Special *Apprentice* Nov 10 on NBC." *The Official Star Wars Web Site* 3 Nov. 2005. Accessed: 15 Jun. 2006. Available: http://www.starwars.com.

Donovan, Derek. "Revenge of the stuff: Toys and gear in 'Star Wars' orbit shift into hyperdrive." *The Kansas City Star* 10 May 2005. Accessed: 7 Jun. 2006. Available: http://www.highbeam.com.

Duncan, Jody. "Love & War." *Cinefex* Jul. 2002: 60–119.

———. "Toward a New Hope." *Cinefex* Jul. 2005: 66–93.

Duong, Senh. "Critical Consensus: 'Star Wars' Prequels Actually Better Reviewed Than Originals." *Rotten Tomatoes* 19 May 2005. Accessed: 9 Jun. 2005. Available: http://www.rottentomatoes.com.

"EB Games Celebrates 'Star Wars Episode III: Revenge of the Sith' at Special Live Event at Regal Cinema Waterford Lakes in Orlando, Fl." *Business Wire* 20 May 2005. Accessed: 26 Jun. 2005. Available: http://www.highbeam.com.

Ebert, Roger. Rev. of *Star Wars: Episode III—Revenge of the Sith. Chicago Sun-Times* 19 May 2005. Accessed: 19 Jul. 2006. Available: http://rogerebert.suntimes.com.

"Eidos and Giant Announce LEGO Star Wars: The Video Game Now Available in North America; Two of the World's Most Beloved Entertainment Names Come Together to Deliver a Unique Take on Star Wars Gaming." *PR Newswire* 6 Apr. 2005. Accessed: 3 Jun. 2006. Available: http://www.highbeam.com.

"Eidos Announces Force-Wielding Promotional Campaign for LEGO Star Wars: The Video Game in North America." *PR Newswire* 11 May 2005. Accessed: 2 Jun. 2006. Available: http://www.highbeam.com.

"Eidos Brings 'The Force' to the Nintendo Gamecube With LEGO Star Wars: The Video Game." *PR Newswire* 25 Oct. 2005. Accessed: 19 Jun. 2006. Available: http://www.highbeam.com.

Eigelbach, Kevin. "Like it They Do; Faithful Turn Out for Final 'Star Wars'." *The Cincinnati Post* 19 May 2005. Accessed: 7 Jun. 2006. Available: http://www.highbeam.com.

"Eight charged on allegations of Star Wars: Episode III piracy." *Xinhua News Agency* 27 Sep. 2005. Accessed: 19 Jun. 2006. Available: http://www.highbeam.com.

"Emmy Award-Winning, Animated Star Wars Action-Adventure Clone Wars Debuts on iTunes Beginning May 25." *Business Wire* 25 May 2006. Accessed: 19 Jun. 2006. Available: http://www.highbeam.com.

"Episode II on International Newstands." *The Official Star Wars Web Site* 11 Apr. 2002. Accessed: 14 Sep. 2006. Available: http://www.starwars.com.

"Episode III Animatics Experimentation." *The Official Star Wars Web Site* 28 Mar. 2003. Accessed: 17 Jun. 2006. Available: http://www.starwars.com.

"Episode III Easter Egg Hunt." *The Official Star Wars Web Site* 26 May 2005. Accessed: 15 Jun. 2006. Available: http://www.starwars.com.

"Episode III: It's a Wrap." *The Official Star Wars Web Site* 17 Sep. 2003. Accessed: 17 Jun. 2006. Available: http://www.starwars.com.

"Episode III Magazine Covers: Smits and Special Effects." *The Official Star Wars Web Site* 25 May 2005. Accessed: 26 Jul. 2006. Available: http://www.starwars.com.

"Episode III Magazine Roundup." *The Official Star Wars Web Site* 20 May 2005. Accessed: 26 Jul. 2006. Available: http://www.starwars.com.

"Episode III Magazines: *MAD*, *Martial*, *Cosmo*." *The Official Star Wars Web Site* 10 Jun. 2005. Accessed: 15 Jun. 2006. Available: http://www.starwars.com.

"Episode III: Picking Up the Pace." *The Official Star Wars Web Site* 25 Jun. 2004. Accessed: 17 Jun. 2006. Available: http://www.starwars.com.

"Episode III Release Dates." *The Official Star Wars Web Site* 28 Jan. 2005. Accessed: 15 Jun. 2006. Available: http://www.starwars.com.

"Episode III Teaser Poster Revealed." *The Official Star Wars Web Site* 28 Oct. 2004. Accessed: 15 Jun. 2006. Available: http://www.starwars.com.

"Episode III Trailer: Online, On Screens and On TV." *The Official Star Wars Web Site* 28 Feb. 2005. Accessed: 15 Jun. 2006. Available: http://www.starwars.com.

"Episode III: You Pick the Droid Color." *The Official Star Wars Web Site* 31 Jul. 2003. Accessed: 5 Sep. 2006. Available: http://www.starwars.com.

Evatt, Robert. "Theaters brace for 'Star Wars'." *Tulsa World* 18 May 2005. Accessed: 15 Jun. 2006. Available: http://www.highbeam.com.

"Even 'Star Wars' tainted by culture wars." *The Wichita Eagle* 22 May 2005. Accessed: 15 Jun. 2006. Available: http://www.highbeam.com.

"Eyes Only Communique." *Geek Squad.* Accessed: 30 Nov. 2006. Available: http://www.geeksquad.com/content/absentee/work.html.

Faiz, Ahmad. "'Star Wars Galaxies' bug-filled yet popular." Rev. of *Star Wars Galaxies: An Empire Divided* (video game). *New Straits Times* 11 Sep. 2003. Accessed: 1 Aug. 2006. Available: http://www.highbeam.com.

————. "Star Wars saga comes to an end." Rev. of *Star Wars: Episode III—Revenge of the Sith. New Straits Times* 19 May 2005. Accessed: 9 Jun. 2006. Available: http://www.highbeam.com.

"Fans Share the Spotlight at Celebration III." *The Official Star Wars Web Site* 7 Apr. 2005. Accessed: 17 Jun. 2006. Available: http://www.starwars.com.

"FAQ." *Liningup.net.* Accessed 30 Nov. 2006. Available: http://www.liningup.net/faq.

Fasig, Lisa Biank. "Hasbro Strikes New Star Wars Deal." *Providence Journal* 31 Jan. 2003. Accessed: 19 Jun. 2006. Available: http://www.highbeam.com.

"Feature-Packed DVD of 'Star Wars: Episode III Revenge of the Sith' Brings Unparalleled Depth and Excitement to the Biggest Movie of the Year." *Business Wire* 26 Sep. 2005. Accessed: 19 Jun. 2006. Available: http://www.highbeam.com.

"Fed: Star Wars to remain M rated." *AAP General News* 16 May 2005. Accessed: 9 Jun. 2006. Available: http://www.highbeam.com.

Feran, Tom. "Latest 'Star Wars' Touches Political Nerves." *The Post-Standard* 29 May 2005. Accessed: 15 Jun. 2006. Available: http://www.highbeam.com.

Fienberg, Daniel. "'Star Wars: Episode III' rediscovers the force of original trilogy." Rev. of *Star Wars: Episode III—Revenge of the Sith. Zap2It.com* via Knight-Ridder/Tribune News Service 18 May 2005. Accessed: 14 Jun. 2006. Available: http://www.highbeam.com.

"Film fan's tribute to Star Wars." *Coventry Evening Telegraph* 12 May 2005. Accessed: 15 Jun. 2006. Available: http://www.highbeam.com.

"Final 'Star Wars' debuts at Cannes." *CNN.com* 15 May 2005. Accessed: 15 May 2005. Available: http://www.cnn.com.

"Final 'Star Wars' film leaked to Web." *CNN.com* 19 May 2005. Accessed: 19 May 2005. Available: http://www.cnn.com.

"Final Star Wars Movie is Fandango's Fastest Seller." *PR Newswire* 19 May 2005. Accessed: 19 May 2005. Available: http://www.prnewswire.com.

Finney, Daniel. "Cartoon Network's 3-minute shorts join 'Star Wars' galaxy." *Knight Ridder Tribune* 6 Nov. 2003. Accessed: 18 Jun. 2006. Available: http://www.highbeam.com.

"Force is still with Star Wars." *Daily Post* 10 Jan. 2005. Accessed: 15 Jun. 2006. Available: http://www.highbeam.com.

Franklin, Mary. *Star Wars Celebration III Program Guide.*

Frater, Patrick. "'Sith' tunnels promo on subway walls." *Variety* 22 Jun. 2005. Accessed: 24 Jun. 2005. Available: http://www.variety.com.

"Free Collectible Star Wars Magazine Expected to Disappear From Theater Within First 24 Hours." *PR Newswire* 18 May 2005. Accessed: 7 Jun. 2006. Available: http://www.highbeam.com.

Frisch, Gary. Rev. of *Star Wars: Episode III—Revenge of the Sith*. *Video Business* 24 Oct. 2005. Accessed: 6 Nov. 2005. Available: http://www.videobusiness.com.

"Frito-Lay Launches 'Darth Vader Dark' and 'Yoda Green' Colored Cheetos." *The Official Star Wars Web Site* 8 Apr. 2005. Accessed: 15 Jun. 2006. Available: http://www.starwars.com.

Fritz, Ben. "Ode to joysticks." *Variety* 17 Jan. 2006. Accessed: 18 Jun. 2006. Available: http://www.variety.com.

———. "Studios do a digital dance." *Variety* 27 Jul. 2005. Accessed: 27 Jul. 2005. Available: http://www.variety.com.

———. "WB, Fox share year's bounty." *Variety* 3 Jan. 2006. Accessed: 13 Jan. 2006. Available: http://www.variety.com.

Fritz, Ben and Gabriel Snyder. "End of summer bummer." *Variety* 5 Sep. 2005. Accessed: 6 Sep. 2005. Available: http://www.variety.com.

Fuentez, Tania. "Star Wars Fans Happy With Last 'Episode'." *AP Online* 19 May 2005. Accessed: 20 May 2005. Available: http://www.ap.org.

Fulton, Rick. "I've got the last word on Star Wars; C-3PO star Anthony Daniels not only had the opening line in the first movie in 1977 but reveals he's landed the final line too." *Daily Record* 17 Mar. 2005. Accessed: 2 Jun. 2006. Available: http://www.highbeam.com.

———. "Leaving the Dark Side; Star Wars creator George Lucas tells why Revenge of the Sith is his last space odyssey." *Daily Record* 19 May 2005. Accessed: 4 Jun. 2006. Available: http://www.highbeam.com.

Fuson, Brian. "'Revenge of the Sith' midnight shows reap about $17 million." *The Hollywood Reporter* 20 May 2005. Accessed: 20 May 2005. Available: http://www.hollywoodreporter.com.

"GameFly Announces Top 20 Game Rentals for 2003; 'Star Wars: Knights of the Old Republic' from LucasArts Ranks #1 Rental Overall." *Business Wire* 13 Jan. 2004. Accessed: 19 Jun. 2006. Available: http://www.highbeam.com.

"Games: PS2, Xbox, PSP, PC—The Star Wars Constellation." Rev. of *Star Wars: Battlefront II* (video game). *San Jose Mercury News* 28 Oct 2005. Accessed: 1 Aug. 2006. Available: http://www.highbeam.com.

Gardner, Amy. "New 'Star Wars' movie isn't kid stuff." *The News & Observer* 19 May 2005. Accessed: 7 Jun. 2006. Available: http://www.highbeam.com.

Gaudiosi, John. Rev. of *Star Wars: Battlefront* (video game). *Video Store* 19 Sep. 2004. Accessed: 1 Aug. 2006. Available: http://www.highbeam.com.

———. "Star Wars flies onto DVD." *Post* 1 Nov. 2001. Accessed: 8 Feb. 2007. Available: http://www.highbeam.com.

Gensler, Howard. "Brad and Angelina rutting in the jungle?" *Philadelphia Daily News* 5 May 2005. Accessed: 2 Sep. 2006. Available: http://www.highbeam.com.

Gentile, Gary. "'Star Wars' Breaks Single-Day Sales Mark." *AP Online* 22 May 2005. Accessed: 15 Jun. 2006. Available: http://www.highbeam.com.

———. "'Star Wars' Fails to Stem Box Office Slump." *AP Online* 23 May 2005. Accessed: 9 Jun. 2006. Available: http://www.highbeam.com.

"George Lucas' 'Star Wars: Episode III—Revenge of the Sith' Wins Hollywood Movie of the Year Award." *PR Newswire* 19 Oct. 2005. Accessed: 19 Jun. 2006. Available: http://www.highbeam.com.

"George Lucas to Attend Celebration III!" *The Official Star Wars Web Site* 5 Apr. 2005. Accessed: 15 Jun. 2006. Available: http://www.starwars.com.

Germain, David. "American Film Institute honors 'Star Wars' creator Lucas as cinema's galactic explorer." *AP Worldstream* 10 Jun. 2005. Accessed: 15 Jun. 2006. Available: http://www.highbeam.com.

———. "Cannes premiere of 'Star Wars' raises questions of U.S. imperialism." *AP Worldstream* 15 May 2005. Accessed: 15 Jun. 2006. Available: http://www.highbeam.com.

———. "Last 'Star Wars' Movie Said Not for Kids." *AP Online* 4 May 2005. Accessed: 15 Jun. 2006. Available: http://www.highbeam.com.

————. "Lucas Glad to Leave Star Wars Behind." *AP Online* 12 May 2005. Accessed: 7 Jun. 2006. Available: http://www.highbeam.com.

————. "'Star Wars' mastermind Lucas sets stage for Vader's ascent." *AP Worldstream* 17 Mar. 2005. Accessed: 9 Jun. 2006. Available: http://www.highbeam.com.

————. "'Star Wars' retains U.S. box-office force with $70 million weekend; 'Madagascar' in 2nd." *AP Worldstream* 30 May 2005. Accessed: 9 Jun. 2006. Available: http://www.highbeam.com.

————. "'Star Wars' Tidbits From Cannes Festival." *AP Online* 16 May 2005. Accessed: 3 Jun. 2006. Available: http://www.highbeam.com.

————. "'Star Wars' Trilogy Debuts on DVD." *AP Online* 15 Sep. 2004. Accessed: 18 Jun. 2006. Available: http://www.highbeam.com.

Gernand, Brian. Interview with starwars.com. "World-Building: An Interview with Brian Gernand." *The Official Star Wars Web Site* 17 Dec. 2004. Accessed: 15 Jun. 2006. Available: http://www.starwars.com.

Getlen, Larry. "'Star Wars' premiere costs fan plenty." *Bankrate.com* 20 May 2005. Accessed: 9 Jun. 2005. Available: http://www.bankrate.com.

"Giant Pez dispensers commemorate Star Wars movie." *Professional Candy Buyer* 1 May 2005. Accessed: 15 Jun. 2006. Available: http://www.highbeam.com.

Gillespie, Eleanor Ringel. "'Star Wars' saga regains luster with 'Revenge of the Sith'." Rev. of *Star Wars: Episode III—Revenge of the Sith. The Atlanta Journal-Constitution*. Accessed: 19 Jul. 2006. Available: http://www.accessatlanta.com.

Giovis, Jaclyn. "Dayton Ohio-area retailers await excitement over Star Wars DVD release." *Dayton Daily News* 20 Sep. 2004. Accessed: 18 Jun. 2006. Available: http://www.highbeam.com.

Gire, Dann. "'Sith' zapped with PG-13 rating." *Daily Herald* 9 Apr. 2005. Accessed: 27 Jun. 2005. Available: http://www.highbeam.com.

———. "'Star Wars' leads box office race." *Daily Herald* 2 Sep. 2005. Accessed: 19 Jun. 2006. Available: http://www.highbeam.com.

"Global Wireless Entertainment Announces New Star Wars Vinyl Skins for Cellfan.com." *Business Wire* 27 Feb. 2006. Accessed: 19 Jun. 2006. Available: http://www.highbeam.com.

"Go on Safari with 'Animal Icons: *Star Wars* Creatures.'" *The Official Star Wars Web Site* 29 Apr. 2005. Accessed: 26 Jul. 2006. Available: http://www. starwars.com.

Godinez, Victor. "Attack of the Cutes: 'Star Wars' meets Lego." Rev. of *LEGO Star Wars* (video game). *The Dallas Morning News* 21 Jun. 2005. Accessed: 7 Jun. 2006. Available: http://www.highbeam.com.

———. "Electronic adventures: 'Star Wars' title was the best game of 2003." *The Dallas Morning News* 30 Dec. 2003. Accessed: 19 Jun. 2006. Available: http://www.highbeam.com.

———. "Reviews of 'Donkey Kong Country 3' and 'Star Wars Battlefront II'." *The Dallas Morning News* 8 Nov. 2005. Accessed: 1 Aug. 2006. Available: http://www.highbeam.com.

Gohman, Dave. Personal interview. 14 Dec. 2006.

Golden Joystick Awards. Accessed: 12 Dec. 2006. Available: http://www. goldenjoystick.com.

Goldman, Michael. "The house that George built." *Variety* 8 Jun. 2005. Accessed: 9 Jun. 2005. Available: http://www.variety.com.

"Good Charlotte Plays TRL's *Star Wars* Special." *The Official Star Wars Web Site* 3 May 2005. Accessed: 17 Jun. 2006. Available: http://www.starwars.com.

Goodale, Gloria. "Why the Force is still with him; George Lucas's influence on pop culture broadens with the final 'Star Wars'." *The Christian Science Monitor* 13 May 2005. Accessed: 7 Jun. 2006. Available: http://www. highbeam.com.

————. "Will 'Star Wars' reverse declining cinema attendance?" *The Christian Science Monitor* 19 May 2005. Accessed: 15 Jun. 2006. Available: http://www.highbeam.com.

Gordon, Kevin. Personal interview. 18 Dec. 2006.

Gowen, Bill. "Williams' work on epic 'Star Wars' scores well-deserving of praise." Rev. of *Star Wars: Episode III—Revenge of the Sith* (score). *Daily Herald* 27 May 2005. Accessed: 3 Jun. 2006. Available: http://www.highbeam.com.

"Grab your light-sabre and let Star Wars begin." Rev. of *Star Wars: Episode III—Revenge of the Sith* (video game). *Coventry Evening Telegraph* 7 May 2005. Accessed: 14 Jun. 2006. Available: http://www.highbeam.com.

Gray, Brandon. "Final 'Star Wars' is Box Office 'Revenge'." *Box Office Mojo* 23 May 2005. Accessed: 11 Dec. 2006. Available: http://www.boxofficemojo.com.

————. "'King' of the World: $250M in 5 Days." *Box Office Mojo* 22 Dec. 2003. Accessed: 11 Dec. 2006. Available: http://www.boxofficemojo.com.

————. "'Sith' Destroys Single Day Record." *Box Office Mojo* 20 May 2005. Accessed: 20 May 2005. Available: http://www.boxofficemojo.com.

Gross, Max. "Star Wars Saga Unfolds on Small Screen—As a Cartoon." *Forward Newspaper* 27 May 2005. Accessed: 3 Jun. 2006. Available: http://www.highbeam.com.

Grove, Martin. "'Sith' success could extend to awards galaxy." *The Hollywood Reporter* 3 Jun. 2005. Accessed: 3 Jun. 2005. Available: http://www.hollywoodreporter.com.

Grover, Ronald. "The Force behind *Star Wars*." *BusinessWeek Online* 4 May 2005. Accessed: 4 May 2005. Available: http://www.businessweek.com.

Groves, Don. "'Star Wars' a force for fewer Oz licensees." *Variety* 6 May 2002. Accessed: 9 Aug. 2006. Available: http://www.variety.com.

Guggenmos, Neil. Personal interview. 18 Dec. 2006.

"Guide to Fan Club Fun at Celebration III." *The Official Star Wars Web Site* 11 Feb. 2005. Accessed: 15 Jun. 2006. Available: http://www.starwars.com.

Haeck, Corwin. "'I'm Having The Time Of My Life Out Here'." *KOMO TV* 5 Jan. 2005. Accessed: 5 Jan. 2005. Available: http://www.komotv.com.

Hafetz, David. "Fan dance." *Variety* 8 Jun. 2005. Accessed: 9 Jun. 2005. Available: http://www.variety.com.

Halbfinger, David M. "'Star Wars' on Track for Record Opening." *The New York Times* 18 May 2005. Accessed: 19 May 2005. Available: http://www.nytimes.com.

Hamill, Mark. "Q&A: Mark Hamill reminisces on 'Star Wars'." *AP Worldstream* 13 May 2005. Accessed: 14 Jun. 2006. Available: http://www.highbeam.com.

"Harry Potter, Star Wars and Wedding Crashers Receive the Most Nominations in the Eleventh Annual Moviefone Moviegoer Awards." *Business Wire* 26 Jan. 2006. Accessed: 19 Jun. 2006. Available: http://www.highbeam.com.

"Hasbro, Inc. Announces the Promotion of Brian Goldner To Chief Operating Officer." *Hasbro* 17 Jan. 2006. Accessed: 5 Dec. 2006. Available: http://www.hasbro.com.

"Hasbro Brings Final Chapter in Legendary Saga to Life with New Star Wars: Episode III Revenge of the Sith Toys and Games." *Business Wire* 15 Feb. 2005. Accessed: 26 Jun. 2005. Available: http://www.highbeam.com.

"Hasbro Gets Star Wars License Extension." *AP Online* 31 Jan. 2003. Accessed: 18 Jun. 2006. Available: http://www.highbeam.com.

"Hasbro's New Star Wars Toys and Games to Hit Store Shelves on April 2." *Wireless News* 28 Mar. 2005. Accessed: 2 Jun. 2006. Available: http://www.highbeam.com.

Hatton, Lois. "'Star Wars' heroes slay stereotypes." *USA Today* 1 Jul. 2005: 13A.

"Hayden and Nat in *Teen People* and *Seventeen*." *The Official Star Wars Web Site* 5 May 2005. Accessed: 17 Jun. 2006. Available: http://www.starwars.com.

"Hayden Christensen Live from Italy." *The Official Star Wars Web Site* 12 Apr. 2005. Accessed: 15 Jun. 2006. Available: http://www.starwars.com.

Hayes, Dade. "If You Had Rented a DVD You'd Be Home Now: Can Revenge of the Sith halt a serious slump at the box office? Or are the movies as doomed as Darth Vader?" *Entertainment Weekly* 13 May 2005. Accessed: 26 Jun. 2005. Available: http://www.highbeam.com.

Henkel, Guido. Rev. of *Star Wars: Episode III—Revenge of the Sith*. *DVD Review*. Accessed: 25 Aug. 2006. Available: http://www.dvdreview.com.

Herbst, Peter. "The Sith Hits the Fans." *Premiere* May 2005: 14.

Hernandez, Greg. "Box office fails to recover from erratic year." *Los Angeles Daily News* 6 Jan. 2006. Accessed: 10 Aug. 2006. Available: http://www.azcentral.com.

———. "IMAX Makes Giant Leap; Big Pictures Push Firm Into Profit." *Los Angeles Daily News* 28 Feb. 2003. Accessed: 9 Aug. 2006. Available: http://www.highbeam.com.

———. "Online movie ticket sales are galactic with 'Sith'." *Los Angeles Daily News* 24 May 2005. Accessed: 27 Jun. 2005. Available: http://www.highbeam.com.

———. "'Sith' is summer box-office star, makes Fox industry leader." *Los Angeles Daily News* 26 Aug. 2005. Accessed: 19 Jun. 2006. Available: http://www.highbeam.com.

———. "'Sith' Marches Beyond 'Clones'; Film Passes Gross in Less Than 3 Weeks." *Los Angeles Daily News* 9 Jun. 2005. Accessed: 23 Jun. 2005. Available: http://www.highbeam.com.

———. "'Sith' Set to Lord Over Box Office." *Los Angeles Daily News* 20 May 2005. Accessed: 27 Jun. 2005. Available: http://www.highbeam.com.

———. "'Sith' Soars in Lackluster Year; In Six Days, Lucas' Latest Has Outgrossed All Other Films Released in 2005." *Los Angeles Daily News* 26 May 2005. Accessed: 27 Jun. 2005. Available: http://www.highbeam.com.

———. "'Star Wars' Blasts Competition at People's Choice Awards." *Los Angeles Daily News* 11 Jan. 2006. Accessed: 19 Jun. 2006. Available: http://www.highbeam.com.

———. "The Force is Strong With This One; 'Revenge of the Sith' Expected to Fire Up Summer Box Office." *Los Angeles Daily News* 18 May 2005. Accessed: 26 Jun. 2005. Available: http://www.highbeam.com.

"Heroic Costumes." *The Official Star Wars Web Site* 4 Sep. 2003. Accessed: 15 Jun. 2006. Available: http://www.starwars.com.

Heron, Robert. "Experiencing the new Star Wars, Digitally." *Extreme Tech* 13 May 2005. Accessed: 21 May 2005. Available: http://www.extremetech.com.

Hettrick, Scott. "'Apprentice' links to 'Sith'." *Variety* 6 Nov. 2005. Accessed: 18 Jun. 2006. Available: http://www.variety.com.

———. "Of Darth, Donald & Arnold." *Video Business* 4 Nov. 2005. Accessed: 6 Nov. 2005. Available: http://www.videobusiness.com.

———. "'Revenge' served globally." *Variety* 26 Jul. 2005. Accessed: 10 Nov. 2005. Available: http://www.variety.com.

———. "Spending on DVDs up 10%." *Variety* 29 Dec. 2005. Accessed: 31 Dec. 2005. Available: http://www.variety.com.

———. "'Star Wars' wins consumer battle." *Variety* 8 Nov. 2005. Accessed: 10 Nov. 2005. Available: http://www.variety.com.

———. "The force is with DVD Sept. 21: original Star Wars trilogy finally arrives." *Video Business* 16 Feb. 2004. Accessed: 18 Jun. 2006. Available: http://www.highbeam.com.

Hiatt, Rick. "Star Wars on the Campus." *The Cincinnati Post* 20 May 2005. Accessed: 15 Jun. 2006. Available: http://www.highbeam.com.

Hidalgo, Pablo. "Did Palpatine Throw the Fight?" *The Official Star Wars Web Site* 23 Jun. 2005. Accessed: 17 Jun. 2006. Available: http://www.starwars.com.

————. "Episode III Set Diary: Blue Guards & Tall Pilots." *The Official Star Wars Web Site* 24 Jun. 2003. Accessed: 17 Jun. 2006. Available: http://www.starwars.com.

————. "Episode III Set Diary: Bring Me the Head of Yoda." *The Official Star Wars Web Site* 1 Jul. 2003. Accessed: 17 Jun. 2006. Available: http://www.starwars.com.

————. "Episode III Set Diary: Concentrated Action." *The Official Star Wars Web Site* 2 Sep. 2003. Accessed: 15 Jun. 2006. Available: http://www.starwars.com.

————. "Episode III Set Diary: Dueling for the First Day." *The Official Star Wars Web Site* 27 May 2003. Accessed: 17 Jun. 2006. Available: http://www.starwars.com.

————. "Episode III Set Diary: Lights, Camera, Testing." *The Official Star Wars Web Site* 25 Jun. 2003. Accessed: 15 Jun. 2006. Available: http://www.starwars.com.

————. "Episode III Set Diary: Matching Moves & Making Faces." *The Official Star Wars Web Site* 17 Jul. 2003. Accessed: 17 Jun. 2006. Available: http://www.starwars.com.

————. "Episode III Set Diary: Quick Turnarounds." *The Official Star Wars Web Site* 14 Jul. 2003. Accessed: 17 Jun. 2006. Available: http://www.starwars.com.

————. "Episode III Set Diary: Return of the Wookie." *The Official Star Wars Web Site* 29 Jul. 2004. Accessed: 18 Jun. 2006. Available: http://www.starwars.com.

————. "Episode III Set Diary: The Best Starpilot in the Galaxy." *The Official Star Wars Web Site* 11 Aug. 2003. Accessed: 18 Jun. 2006. Available: http://www.starwars.com.

————. "Jump to Hyperspace, Jump to Sydney." *The Official Star Wars Web Site* 7 Aug. 2003. Accessed: 17 Jun. 2006. Available: http://www.starwars.com.

"Hiding in the Open." *The Official Star Wars Web Site* 24 Nov. 2004. Accessed: 15 Jun. 2006. Available: http://www.starwars.com.

Higgins, Bill. "'Star' lights for charity." *Variety* 17 May 2005. Accessed: 14 Jun. 2006. Available: http://www.variety.com.

Hinckley, David. "Moviegoers out in Force for $158M 'Sith' opening." *New York Daily News* 23 May 2005. Accessed: 27 Jun. 2005. Available: http://www.highbeam.com.

Hollinger, Hy. "'Sith' kicks off big in 48 int'l territories." *The Hollywood Reporter* 20 May 2005. Accessed: 20 May 2005. Available: http://www.hollywoodreporter.com.

Holson, Laura M. "At LucasArts, quest to be No. 1 is no game." *International Herald Tribune* 18 Apr. 2006. Accessed: 1 Aug. 2006. Available: http://www.highbeam.com.

————. "Is There Life After 'Star Wars' for Lucasfilm?" *The Wall Street Journal* 1 May 2005, Section 3: 1, 6.

Honeycutt, Kirk. Rev. of *Star Wars: Episode III—Revenge of the Sith*. *The Hollywood Reporter* 6 May 2005. Accessed: 19 Jul. 2006. Available: http://www.hollywoodreporter.com.

Hopewell, John. "Spanish B.O. takes dramatic dive." *Variety* 5 Jan. 2006. Accessed: 18 Jun. 2006. Available: http://www.variety.com.

Hopkins, Brent. "'Star Wars' a gamer's dream." *Los Angeles Daily News* 20 May 2005. Accessed: 3 Jun. 2006. Available: http://www.highbeam.com.

————. "'Star Wars' to Appear on Giant Imax Screens." *Los Angeles Daily News* 10 Sep. 2002. Accessed: 9 Aug. 2006. Available: http://www.highbeam.com.

Horn, John and Chris Lee. "Jockeying for 'Sith' spot." *The Record* 20 May 2005. Accessed: 27 Jun. 2005. Available: http://www.highbeam.com.

Horwitz, Jane. "The Family Filmgoer." *The Washington Post* 20 May 2005. Accessed: 20 Jul. 2006. Available: http://www.highbeam.com.

"Hotter than Hell." *The Official Star Wars Web Site* 2 Feb. 2006. Accessed: 15 Jun. 2006. Available: http://www.starwars.com.

"How Movies are Rated." *Motion Picture Association of America.* Accessed: 29 Nov. 2006. Available: http://www.mpaa.org.

"HowStuffWorks' Stuffo.com Kicks Off Star Wars Week With a Look Back at the Life and Times of Tatooine's Favorite Son, Darth Vader." *PR Newswire* 16 May 2005. Accessed: 7 Jun. 2006. Available: http://www.highbeam.com.

Humphries, Stephen. "How to do the Star Wars trilogy in 58 minutes; When Ross finished performing, his elbow and kneepads scuffed and clothes drenched in sweat, 3,000 fans stood up and cheered like braying Wookies." *The Christian Science Monitor* 1 Jun. 2005. Accessed: 7 Jun. 2006. Available: http://www.highbeam.com.

Hunter, Stephen. "'Sith': The Promise Fulfilled." Rev. of *Star Wars: Episode III—Revenge of the Sith. The Washington Post* 18 May 2005. Accessed: 19 Jul. 2006. Available: http://www.washingtonpost.com.

Ibrahim, Jeanine. "George Lucas appears at 'Star Wars' convention." *AP Worldstream* 23 Apr. 2005. Accessed: 7 Jun. 2006. Available: http://www.highbeam.com.

Idelson, Karen. "Hollywood calling." *Variety* 25 Sep. 2005. Accessed: 2 Oct. 2005. Available: http://www.variety.com.

———. "Timeless toys: 'Star Wars' keeps the focus on fun as its audience ages and film series ends." *Variety* 21 Jun. 2005. Accessed: 4 Jun. 2006. Available: http://www.highbeam.com.

"IDG Entertainment to Publish Star Wars Insider; Will Team with Lucasfilm for Best Fan Club Package Ever." *Business Wire* 4 May 2004. Accessed: 18 Jun. 2006. Available: http://www.highbeam.com.

"IGDA Announces Winners of 2004 Game Developers Choice Awards; Star Wars: Knights of the Old Republic Takes Game of the Year." *PR Newswire* 25 Mar. 2004. Accessed: 19 Jun. 2006. Available: http://www.highbeam.com.

"IGN Announces Best of 2003; LucasArts' 'Star Wars: Knights of the Old Republic' Wins Overall Game of the Year." *Business Wire* 16 Jan. 2004. Accessed: 19 Jun. 2006. Available: http://www.highbeam.com.

"IGT Acquires Licensing Rights to Develop Star Wars Gaming Machine." *PR Newswire* 17 Jul. 2003. Accessed: 18 Jun. 2006. Available: http://www.highbeam.com.

"ILM Visual Effects Wizards at Celebration III." *The Official Star Wars Web Site* 30 Mar. 2005. Accessed: 15 Jun. 2006. Available: http://www.starwars.com.

IMAX. "IMAX: The Ultimate Movie Experience." Web site. Accessed: 30 Nov. 2006. Available: http://www.imax.com.

"Inside the DVD: *Revenge of the Sith*." *The Official Star Wars Web Site* 6 Oct. 2005. Accessed: 15 Jun. 2006. Available: http://www.starwars.com.

"Intec Introduces Its Lineup of 'Star Wars' Branded Controllers; Embedded Video Game Technologies Arm Players with the Ultimate Fighting Tools!" *Business Wire* 22 Feb. 2005. Accessed: 14 Jun. 2006. Available: http://www.highbeam.com.

"International Coverage of Episode III." *The Official Star Wars Web Site* 11 Mar. 2005. Accessed: 15 Jun. 2006. Available: http://www.starwars.com.

"International Episode III Titles." *The Official Star Wars Web Site* 1 Apr. 2005. Accessed: 15 Jun. 2006. Available: http://www.starwars.com.

Irvine, Martha. "'Star Wars Kid' Becomes Internet Star." *AP Online* 21 Aug. 2003. Accessed: 18 Jun. 2006. Available: http://www.highbeam.com.

Italie, Hillel. "Fantasy Writer Gets a Touch of 'Star Wars'." *AP Online* 31 Mar. 2005. Accessed: 7 Jun. 2006. Available: http://www.highbeam.com.

"It's revenge of the Dolph Lundgren." *The Evening Standard* 23 May 2005. Accessed: 28 Jun. 2005. Available: http://www.highbeam.com.

Jackson, Patrick Thaddeus. "The Politics of *Star Wars*." *Progressive Commons* 22 May 2005. Accessed: 17 Jul. 2006. Available: http://www.progressivecommons.org.

Jacobsen, Farin. "'Sith' pulls 'Star Wars' films together." Rev. of *Star Wars: Episode III—Revenge of the Sith. The Fresno Bee* 29 May 2005. Accessed: 14 Jun. 2006. Available: http://www.highbeam.com.

Jacobson, Harlan. "'Revenge' will be sweet at Cannes." *USA Today* 8 May 2005. Accessed: 9 May 2005. Available: http://www.usatoday.com.

"JAKKS Pacific's Star Wars: Revenge of the Sith TV Games Title Hits Shelves; Now Gamers Can Play as a Jedi Knight in Five Original Games." *PR Newswire* 7 Apr. 2005. Accessed: 2 Jun. 2006. Available: http:// www.highbeam.com.

James, Alison. "France: Blooming 'Flowers' keeps distrib Bac in the game." *Variety* 30 Oct. 2005. Accessed: 15 Nov. 2005. Available: http:// www.variety.com.

———. "Gaul box office down 10% in 2005." *Variety* 5 Jan. 2006. Accessed: 18 Jun. 2006. Available: http://www.variety.com.

———. "'Star Wars' brand stays hot." *Variety* 18 Oct. 2005. Accessed: 15 Nov. 2005. Available: http://www.variety.com.

"Jedi fever strikes online as Star Wars film premieres in the UK." *M2 Presswire* 17 May 2005. Accessed: 3 Jun. 2006. Available: http://www.highbeam.com.

Jenkins, Garry. *Empire Building: The Remarkable Real Life Story of Star Wars.* New Jersey: Carol Publishing Group, 1997.

Jenkinson, Peter. "Testing: May the force be with you; Peter Jenkinson fights the dark side to reveal the latest Star Wars gadgets." *Daily Post* 19 May 2005. Accessed: 14 Jun. 2006. Available: http://www.highbeam.com.

Jensen, Jeff. "Plan of Attack." *Entertainment Weekly* 17 May 2002: 26–35.

———. "What A Long Strange Trip It's Been." *Entertainment Weekly* 20 May 2005: 22–30.

Jewell, Mark. "Star Wars boosts Hasbro." *Inland Valley Daily Bulletin* 7 Feb. 2006. Accessed: 19 Jun. 2006. Available: http://www.highbeam.com.

Johannes, Amy. "Burger King Under Fire For Star Wars Premiums." *Promo* 26 May 2005. Accessed: 20 Jul. 2006. Available: http://www.highbeam.com.

————. "Star Wars Premiums, Sweeps Invade Burger King." *Promo* 11 May 2005. Accessed: 7 Jun. 2006. Available: http://www.highbeam.com.

Johnson, Paul H. Rev. of *Star Wars: Episode III—Revenge of the Sith* (video game). *The Record* 4 Jun. 2005. Accessed: 27 Jun. 2005. Available: http://www.highbeam.com.

————. Rev. of *Star Wars: Knights of the Old Republic II* (video game). *The Record* 12 Feb. 2005. Accessed: 14 Jun. 2006. Available: http://www.highbeam.com.

"Join the Force and Collect All 12 Star Wars Scratchers from the California State Lottery." *Business Wire* 4 Apr. 2005. Accessed: 7 Jun. 2006. Available: http://www.highbeam.com.

Kaminski, Michael. Personal interview. 14 Dec. 2006.

Kang, Stephanie. "A New Way to Use the Force." *The Wall Street Journal* 22 Aug. 2006. Accessed: 22 Aug. 2006. Available: http://www.wsj.com.

Kapalka, Jeff. "Using The Force and Having a Ball." Rev. of *Star Wars: Battlefront* (video game). *The Post-Standard* 3 Oct. 2004. Accessed: 1 Aug. 2006. Available: http://www.highbeam.com.

Kaplan, Simone. "Star Wars preorder campaign blasts off: extensive extras help build momentum." *Video Business* 12 Apr. 2004. Accessed: 18 Jun. 2006. Available: http://www.highbeam.com.

"Kashyyyk Revisited." *The Official Star Wars Web Site* 5 Aug. 2004. Accessed: 15 Jun. 2006. Available: http://www.starwars.com.

Keaten, Jamey. "Around the world, excitement mounts for last installment in 'Star Wars' series." *AP Worldstream* 16 May 2005. Accessed: 9 Jun. 2006. Available: http://www.highbeam.com.

————. "Star Wars Fans Flock to Paris." *AP Online* 15 May 2005. Accessed: 7 Jun. 2006. Available: http://www.highbeam.com.

Kee, Lorraine and Joe Holleman. "'Revenge of the Sith' Too Dark for Kids? Movie Tie-Ins Targeting Kids Make it Harder for Parents to Say No." *St. Louis Post-Dispatch* 15 May 2005. Accessed: 26 Jun. 2005. Available: http://www.highbeam.com.

Kelley, Jeffrey. "'Star Wars' fans plan to call in sick for a dose." *Richmond Times-Dispatch* 19 May 2005. Accessed: 15 Jun. 2006. Available: http://www.highbeam.com.

"Kellogg Company Celebrates Star Wars: Episode III Revenge of the Sith By 'Fueling the Force'." *PR Newswire* 12 May 2005. Accessed: 2 Jun. 2006. Available: http://www.highbeam.com.

Kent, Steven. Rev. of *Star Wars Galaxies: An Empire Divided* (video game). *Seattle Post-Intelligencer* 8 Jul. 2003. Accessed: 1 Aug. 2006. Available: http://www.highbeam.com.

Key, Philip. "Star Wars is a dark force to reckon with." Rev. of *Star Wars: Episode III—Revenge of the Sith. Daily Post* 20 May 2005. Accessed: 14 Jun. 2006. Available: http://www.highbeam.com.

Kleiman, Joseph L. "Five Major Filmmakers Support TI's Digital 3D Cinema." *World Enteractive* 17 Mar. 2005. Accessed: 28 Dec. 2006. Available: http://www.jackthompsonmedia.com.

Kloer, Phil. "Unifying Force." *Atlanta Journal and Constitution* 17 May 2005: A1, A4.

Koehler, Robert. "Fox fire." *Variety* 28 Aug. 2005. Accessed: 6 Sep. 2005. Available: http://www.variety.com.

Koltnow, Barry. "Hayden Christensen enjoys being a bad guy in 'Revenge of the Sith'." *The Orange County Register* 20 May 2005. Accessed: 27 Jun. 2005. Available: http://www.highbeam.com.

Kovalcin, Diane. Personal interview. 15 Dec. 2006.

Kunkle, Brian. Personal interview. 12 Dec. 2006.

Kunzelman, Michael. "Boston museum picks Star Wars over Benjamin Franklin exhibit." *AP Worldstream* 20 May 2005. Accessed: 15 Jun. 2006. Available: http://www.highbeam.com.

"Lady in the Water (2006)." *Rotten Tomatoes*. Accessed: 25 Nov. 2006. Available: http://www.rottentomatoes.com/m/lady_in_the_water.

Laidman, Dan. "'Star Wars' deal pays off for collectibles firm." *Contra Costa Times* 21 May 2005. Accessed: 3 Jun. 2006. Available: http://www.highbeam.com.

Lamberson, Carolyn. "Why 'Star Wars' geeks get bad rap." *The Register-Guard* 13 May 2005. Accessed: 14 Jun. 2006. Available: http://www.highbeam.com.

"Last Chance for BK *Star Wars* Lenticular Cards." *The Official Star Wars Web Site* 7 Dec. 2005. Accessed: 17 Jun. 2006. Available: http://www.starwars.com.

"Last Chance for Charity Screenings." *The Official Star Wars Web Site* 2 May 2005. Accessed: 15 Jun. 2006. Available: http://www.starwars.com.

"Latest 'Star Wars' Movie Leaked Onto Web, Blog Reports." *Information Week* 20 May 2005. Accessed: 26 Jun. 2005. Available: http://www.highbeam.com.

Lawson, Terry. "George Lucas, emperor of 'Star Wars' universe, finishes his story." *Detroit Free Press* 9 May 2005. Accessed: 9 Jun. 2006. Available: http://www.highbeam.com.

"Layers of Sound." *The Official Star Wars Web Site* 2 Mar. 2006. Accessed: 15 Jun. 2006. Available: http://www.starwars.com.

"Lego Extends Star Wars Franchise License Pact with Lucasfilm." *Wireless News* 19 Feb. 2006. Accessed: 19 Jun. 2006. Available: http://www.highbeam.com.

"Lego Star Wars credited for top sales at SCi Entertainment." *Birmingham Post* 24 Jan. 2006. Accessed: 19 Jun. 2006. Available: http://www.highbeam.com.

"LEGO Star Wars Named Best Activity Toy of the Year." *Business Wire* 12 Feb. 2006. Accessed: 19 Jun. 2006. Available: http://www.highbeam.com.

"Leicester Square." *Wikipedia.org.* Accessed: 30 Nov. 2006. Available: http://en.wikipedia.org/wiki/Leicester_Square.

Leopold, Todd. "'Instinct 2' named worst movie of the year." *CNN.com* 25 Feb. 2007. Accessed: 25 Feb. 2007. Available: http://www.cnn.com.

Levy, Shawn. "His Destiny Fulfilled." Rev. of *Star Wars: Episode III—Revenge of the Sith. The Oregonian* 18 May 2005: A1, A13.

Lewis, Richard C. "Hasbro Q2 Profit Up on 'Star Wars' Sales." *AP Online* 18 Jul. 2005. Accessed: 15 Jun. 2006. Available: http://www.highbeam.com.

"*LIFE* Magazine Explores *Star Wars* Costumes." *The Official Star Wars Web Site* 5 Apr. 2005. Accessed: 26 Jul. 2006. Available: http://www.starwars.com.

"Life Size Origami made during Star Wars Celebration III." *Star Wars Origami.* Accessed: 30 Nov. 2006. Available: http://starwarsorigami.com/lifesize/Lifesize.htm.

"Lights, Camera, Cameron!" *Yahoo! Movies* 14 Jun. 2005. Accessed: 14 Jun. 2005. Available: http://movies.yahoo.com.

"Lists of Best-Selling Books." *AP Online* 14 Apr. 2005. Accessed: 28 Jun. 2005. Available: http://www.highbeam.com.

Lively, Tarron. "'Star Wars' fans near end of line; Faithful out in force to wrap an epic tradition." *The Washington Times* 18 May 2005. Accessed: 3 Jun. 2006. Available: http://www.highbeam.com.

Long, Sam. Personal interview. 13 Dec. 2006.

Longino, Bob. "'Star Wars: Episode III—Revenge of the Sith': 'Sith' debut brings in a universe of greenbacks." *The Atlanta Journal and Constitution* 20 May 2005. Accessed: 26 Jun. 2005. Available: http://www.highbeam.com.

Lowman, Rob. "Life Without 'Star Wars'." *Los Angeles Daily News* 15 May 2005. Accssed: 7 Jun. 2006. Available: http://www.highbeam.com.

Lowry, Brian. "That elusive 'Sith' sense: long, long relationship with Lucas' 'Star Wars' saga nears its far, faraway end." *Variety* 16 Mar. 2005. Accessed: 27 Jun. 2005. Available: http://www.variety.com.

"Lucas Finally Decides to Get AFI's Honor." *Yahoo! Movies* 9 Jun. 2005. Accessed: 9 Jun. 2006. Available: http://www.yahoo.com.

Lucas, George. Interview with Matthew d'Ancona. "The Emperor strikes back." *The Sunday Telegraph* 22 May 2005. Accessed: 21 Jun. 2005. Available: http://www.highbeam.com.

———. Interview with Gavin Edwards. "The Cult of Darth Vader." *Rolling Stone* 2 Jun. 2005: 42–46.

———. Interview with Alison Jones. "Culture: Sith Sense." *The Birmingham Post* 19 May 2005. Accessed: 26 Jun. 2005. Available: http://www.highbeam.com.

———. Interview with Steve Silberman. "George Lucas on *Star Wars, Fahrenheit 9/11*, and his own legacy." *Wired* May 2005, Issue 13.05: 134–43.

———. Interview with *Time*. "A Look Back in Wonder." *Time* 9 May 2005: 61–62.

Lucas, Katie. "The father of the force." *CosmoGirl!* Jun./Jul. 2005: 94–95.

"Lucas Makes Cameo in 'Revenge of the Sith'." *AP Online* 17 May 2005. Accessed: 27 Jun. 2005. Available: http://www.highbeam.com.

"Lucas Promises to Return to Australia for *Episode III*." *ShowBizData* 8 Nov. 2000. Accessed: 8 Nov. 2000. Available: http://www.showbizdata.com.

"Lucas showcase screens 'Star Wars,' 'Indiana Jones' films." *Zap2It.com* via Knight-Ridder/Tribune News Service 21 Jun. 2005. Accessed: 15 Jun. 2006. Available: http://www.highbeam.com.

"LucasArts Celebrates Star Wars Galaxies: An Empire Divided One Year Anniversary!" *Business Wire* 28 Jun. 2004. Accessed: 18 Jun. 2006. Available: http://www.highbeam.com.

"LucasArts History." *LucasArts.* Accessed: 29 Nov. 2006. Available: http://www.lucasarts.com.

"LucasArts Joins the Celebration with the Announcement of Star Wars Battlefront II." *Business Wire* 21 Apr. 2005. Accessed: 2 Jun. 2006. Available: http://www.highbeam.com.

"Lucasfilm Animation Singapore Officially Opens." *The Official Star Wars Web Site* 26 Oct. 2005. Accessed: 17 Jun. 2006. Available: http://www.starwars.com.

"Lucasfilm Archive Exhibit at Celebration III." *The Official Star Wars Web Site* 7 Apr. 2005. Accessed: 15 Jun. 2006. Available: http://www.starwars.com.

"Lucasfilm Ltd. Uses Dolby Digital Surround EX to Enhance Audio Experience for Star Wars Episode III: Revenge of the Sith; Dolby's Latest Sound Format Creates Optimum Surround Sound in Theatres Worldwide." *Business Wire* 23 May 2005. Accessed: 27 Jun. 2005. Available: http://www.highbeam.com.

"Lucasfilm to launch paid 'Star Wars' Web site." *Zap2It.com* via Knight-Ridder/Tribune News Service 30 May 2003. Accessed: 18 Jun. 2006. Available: http://www.highbeam.com.

Lund, Mike. "Fan's log: Star Wars queue." *BBC News* 23 May 2005. Accessed: 2 Aug. 2006. Available: http://news.bbc.co.uk.

Lunsford, Ja'Rena. "'Star Wars Episode III Revenge of the Sith's Ticket Wars." *Daily Oklahoman* 18 May 2005. Accessed: 9 Jun. 2006. Available: http://www.highbeam.com.

"Lycos Announces Web Users Are Seeing Stars, Catapulting Star Wars 3 to the New Number One Search Term." *PR Newswire* 24 May 2005. Accessed: 2 Jun. 2006. Available: http://www.highbeam.com.

Lyttle, John. "How Darth helped me find my dark side; He plays the arch villain in the Star Wars finale … and it was the perfect chance to rebel." *The Evening Standard* 11 May 2005. Accessed: 15 Jun. 2006. Available: http://www.highbeam.com.

"M & M's move to the dark side (of chocolate) for coming Star Wars Episode III promotion." *Confectioner* 1 Feb. 2005. Accessed: 2 Jun. 2006. Available: http://www.highbeam.com.

"Magazine Covers From Around the World." *The Official Star Wars Web Site* 11 Apr. 2005. Accessed: 26 Jul. 2006. Available: http://www.starwars.com.

Mallas, Steven. "Foxy Marketing: 'Star Wars' Meets 'The O.C.'" *The Motley Fool* 10 Mar. 2005. Accessed: 14 Jun. 2006. Available: http://www.fool.com.

Mallory, Michael. "A Little on the Dark Side." *Make Up Artist* Jun./Jul. 2005: 48–60.

"Mark of the Beast." *Countdown to Armageddon.* Accessed: 14 Jun. 2005. Available: http://www.countdown.org/armageddon/mark_of_beast.htm.

Martin, Denise and John Dempsey. "Spike's 'Star' wattage." *Variety* 18 Oct. 2005. Accessed: 15 Nov. 2005. Available: http://www.variety.com.

Martin, Paul. "As a boy I had only one dream … to pull on Darth Vader's evil mask and move to the dark side; Star Wars Hayden Christensen on his Sith Sense." *The Mirror* 10 May 2005. Accessed: 15 Jun. 2006. Available: http://www.highbeam.com.

Maryles, Daisy. "A Shining Star." *Publishers Weekly* 11 Apr. 2005. Accessed: 13 Dec. 2006. Available: http://www.publishersweekly.com.

"Mattel profit slumps as Star Wars beats Barbie." *The Evening Standard* 19 Jul. 2005. Accessed: 15 Jun. 2006. Available: http://www.highbeam.com.

"May the Facts Be With You." *The Daily Mail* 14 May 2005. Accessed: 3 Jun. 2006. Available: http://www.highbeam.com.

"'May the Fandango Be With You': Advance Tickets for Star Wars: Episode III—Revenge of the Sith Now Available on Fandango.com More Than A Month Before the Film's May 19 Opening." *PR Newswire* 15 Apr. 2005. Accessed: 15 Jun. 2006. Available: http://www.highbeam.com.

"May the Fourth Be With Episode III Moviegoers This Weekend." *The Official Star Wars Web Site* 29 Jul. 2005. Accessed: 15 Jun. 2006. Available: http://www.starwars.com.

Maynard, John. "Wookie! 'Star Wars' Trilogy Set for Sept. DVD Release." *The Washington Post* 10 Feb. 2004. Accessed: 18 Jun. 2006. Available: http://www.highbeam.com.

McCallum, Rick. Interview with Joseph Kleiman. *World Enteractive* 3 May 2005. Accessed: 28 Dec. 2006. Available: http://www.jackthompsonmedia.com.

McCarthy, Sean L. "'Sith' seats hard to come by." *The Boston Herald* 18 May 2005. Accessed: 27 Jun. 2005. Available: http://www.highbeam.com.

McCarthy, Todd. Rev. of *Star Wars: Episode III—Revenge of the Sith. Variety* 5 May 2005. Accessed: 19 Jul. 2006. Available: http://www.variety.com.

McDiarmid, Ian. Interview with Anwar Brett. *BBC Movies.* Accessed: 19 Jun. 2005. Available: http://www.bbc.co.uk.

McGirk, Jan. "'Star Wars' creator Lucas opens studio in Singapore." *The Independent* 7 Aug. 2004. Accessed: 18 Jun. 2006. Available: http://www.highbeam.com.

McGorry, Ken. "Lucasfilm declares war." *Post* 1 Jun. 2002. Accessed: 9 Aug. 2006. Available: http://www.highbeam.com.

McGregor, Ewan. Interview with Scott Raab. "Me and Obi-Wan at the Zoo." *Esquire* Jun. 2005: 92–97.

McIver, Brian. "Star Wars 3: The Empire gets it right." *Daily Record* 12 Mar. 2005. Accessed: 7 Jun. 2006. Available: http://www.highbeam.com.

McManis, Sam. "Famous critics have a voice, but it's in the chorus." *The News Tribune* 29 May 2005. Accessed: 29 May 2005. Available: http://www.thenewstribune.com.

McNary, Dave and Ian Mohr. "'Batman' begins to seduce o'seas auds." *Variety* 26 Jun. 2005. Accessed: 26 Jun. 2005. Available: http://www.variety.com.

McNary, Dave. "'Batman' flexes o'seas muscle." *Variety* 19 Jun. 2005. Accessed: 20 Jun. 2005. Available: http://www.variety.com.

———. "'Batman' flying high o'seas in 2nd frame." *Variety* 26 Jun. 2005. Accessed: 26 Jun. 2005. Available: http://www.variety.com.

———. "'Charlie' an o'seas sweetie." *Variety* 31 Jul. 2005. Accessed: 1 Aug. 2005. Available: http://www.variety.com.

———. "'Chocolate' eating up sweet o'seas success." *Variety* 7 Aug. 2005. Accessed: 8 Aug. 2005. Available: http://www.variety.com.

———. "'Fantastic' fends off fauna, winning o'seas." *Variety* 24 Jul. 2005. Accessed: 26 Jul. 2005. Available: http://www.variety.com.

———. "Force is with 'Sith' across globe." *Variety* 29 May 2005. Accessed: 2 Jun. 2005. Available: http://www.variety.com.

———. "H'w'd finds world isn't flat." *Variety* 27 Nov. 2005. Accessed: 19 Dec. 2005. Available: http://www.variety.com.

———. "'Island,' 'Charlie' keep WB atop o'seas." *Variety* 21 Aug. 2005. Accessed: 23 Aug. 2005. Available: http://www.variety.com.

———. "Japan's high on 'Sith'." *Variety* 28 Jun. 2005. Accessed: 29 Jun. 2005. Available: http://www.variety.com.

———. "O'seas auds on 'War' path." *Variety* 10 Jul. 2005. Accessed: 11 Jul. 2005. Available: http://www.variety.com.

———. "O'seas auds put 'Island' on the map." *Variety* 28 Aug. 2005. Accessed: 28 Aug. 2005. Available: http://www.variety.com.

———. "O'seas B.O. goes for a little dip." *Variety* 3 Jan. 2006. Accessed: 18 Jun. 2006. Available: http://www.variety.com.

———. "'Sith' still strong in its o'seas orbits." *Variety* 5 Jun. 2005. Accessed: 6 Jun. 2005. Available: http://www.variety.com.

———. "'Sith' takes revenge on o'seas competish." *Variety* 12 Jun. 2005. Accessed: 15 Jun. 2005. Available: http://www.variety.com.

———. "'Sith' voted movie of year." *Variety* 18 Oct. 2005. Accessed: 15 Nov. 2005. Available: http://www.variety.com.

———. "'Sith' wages war against o'seas competish." *Variety* 5 Jun. 2005. Accessed: 5 Jun. 2005. Available: http://www.variety.com.

———. "'Smith' slows 'Sith' advance o'seas." *Variety* 12 Jun. 2005. Accessed: 13 Jun. 2005. Available: http://www.variety.com.

———. "'Star Wars' hits int'l zenith." *Variety* 22 May 2005. Accessed: 23 May 2005. Available: http://www.variety.com.

———. "'The Island' proves an o'seas survivor." *Variety* 14 Aug. 2005. Accessed: 14 Aug. 2005. Available: http://www.variety.com.

———. "'Wars' strikes again in o'seas soph sesh." *Variety* 30 May 2005. Accessed: 30 May 2005. Available: http://www.variety.com.

Meitner, Sarah Hale. "Slurpees' galaxy expands with nod to 'Star Wars'." *The Orlando Sentinel* 2 Mar. 2005. Accessed: 15 Jun. 2006. Available: http://www.highbeam.com.

Melago, Carrie. "New York police seize 1,000 pirated copies of 'Star Wars III'." *New York Daily News* 20 May 2005. Accessed: 15 Jun. 2006. Available: http://www.highbeam.com.

Meller, Henry. "My drinking was out of control, says McGregor; Star Wars actor admits he's going sober after booze got the better of him." *The Daily Mail* 5 Jul. 2005. Accessed: 15 Jun. 2006. Available: http://www.highbeam.com.

"Mental Roy." *3D World* Jul. 2005: 28.

"Microsoft Security Glossary." *Microsoft* 29 Oct. 2002. Accessed: 28 Dec. 2006. Available: http://www.microsoft.com.

Millar, John. "May the force really be with my hero Sir Alex; Star Wars actor Hayden on his move to the red side." *Sunday Mail* 8 May 2005. Accessed: 9 Jun. 2006. Available: http://www.highbeam.com.

"Millimeter April 2005." *Digital Content Producer.* Accessed: 29 Nov. 2006. Available: http://www.digitalcontentproducer.com.

Mitchell, Betsy. Interview by Dick Donahue. "Three Answers: Betsy Mitchell." *Publishers Weekly* 25 Apr. 2005. Accessed: 13 Dec. 2006. Available: http://www.publishersweekly.com.

Modine, Austin. "Sky's limit in tech advances." *Variety* 8 Jun. 2005. Accessed: 9 Jun. 2005. Available: http://www.variety.com.

Mohr, Ian. "'Sith' sticks overseas." *Variety* 11 Jul. 2005. Accessed: 12 Jul. 2005. Available: http://www.variety.com.

———. "U.K. grosses drop in wake of attacks." *Variety* 17 Jul. 2005. Accessed: 17 Jul. 2005. Available: http://www.variety.com.

Montgomery, Jenny. "'Star Wars' Fans Flock to Indy Convention." Accessed: 3 Jun. 2006. Available: http://www.highbeam.com.

Moore, Oliver. "'Star Wars' Kid named most-seen clip on Net." *Globe and Mail* 28 Nov. 2006. Accessed: 18 Dec. 2006. Available: http://www.theglobeandmail.com.

Moran, Jonathon. "Fed: Reviewers give latest Star Wars flick thumbs up." *AAP General News* 12 May 2005. Accessed: 3 Jun. 2006. Available: http://www.highbeam.com.

"More Episode III Cover Stories." *The Official Star Wars Web Site* 9 May 2005. Accessed: 26 Jul. 2006. Available: http://www.starwars.com.

"More International Coverage for Episode III." *The Official Star Wars Web Site* 27 Apr. 2005. Accessed: 15 Jun. 2006. Available: http://www.starwars.com.

"More International Magazine Covers." *The Official Star Wars Web Site* 1 May 2002. Accessed: 14 Sep. 2006. Available: http://www.starwars.com.

"More International Magazines." *The Official Star Wars Web Site* 19 Apr. 2002. Accessed: 14 Sep. 2006. Available: http://www.starwars.com.

"More International Mags Cover Episode III." *The Official Star Wars Web Site* 11 May 2005. Accessed: 26 Jul. 2006. Available: http://www.starwars.com.

"More 'Star Wars' Fun to Enter Disney's Galaxy With Two More Weekends Added to Disney-MGM Studios Event." *PR Newswire* 8 Jun. 2005. Accessed: 3 Jun. 2006. Available: http://www.highbeam.com.

"More than 20,000 worldwide answer, 'What is your favorite breakout performance?' in AMD's online survey; Montana resident wins grand prize; Lance Armstrong, 'Star Wars' and 'Theory of Relativity' selected best breakout performances." *M2 Presswire* 17 Apr. 2003. Accessed: 19 Jun. 2006. Available: http://www.highbeam.com.

Motion Picture Association of America. "2005 US Movie Attendance Study." Accessed: 8 Dec. 2006. Available: http://www.mpaa.org.

"MovieTickets.com Sells Nearly 10% of Projected Weekend Box Office for Star Wars Episode III: Revenge of the Sith." *PR Newswire* 22 May 2005. Accessed: 7 Jun. 2006. Available: http://www.highbeam.com.

"MovieTickets.com Unveils Its New Web Site as Star Wars Episode III: Revenge of the Sith Breaks All Advance Ticket Sales Records." *PR Newswire* 18 May 2005. Accessed: 27 Jun. 2005. Available: http://www.highbeam.com.

"MTV Winner Gets a Prize of a Lifetime." *The Official Star Wars Web Site* 1 Jun. 2005. Accessed: 17 Jun. 2006. Available: http://www.starwars.com.

Munk, Simon. "By George, They've Got It; Move over, George Lucas, there are now armies of filmmakers releasing their own Star Wars films on the web." *The Daily Mail* 23 Jan. 2005. Accessed: 2 Jun. 2006. Available: http://www.highbeam.com.

Musgrove, Mike. "Sadness in 'Star Wars' World." *The Washington Post* 2 Feb. 2006. Accessed: 19 Jun. 2006. Available: http://www.highbeam.com.

"NBA and *Star Wars* Go One-on-One." *The Official Star Wars Web Site* 25 Apr. 2005. Accessed: 17 Jun. 2006. Available: http://www.starwars.com.

Nesbitt, Sara. "Demand for Star Wars Tie-In Merchandise Lower Than for Previous Film." *The Gazette* 25 Apr. 2002. Accessed: 9 Aug. 2006. Available: http://www.highbeam.com.

Netherby, Jennifer. "Fox Releases *Sith* on DVD Only." *Video Business* 26 Aug. 2005. Accessed: 25 Aug. 2006. Available: http://www.videobusiness.com.

Netherby, Jennifer and Susanne Ault. "Thin Shipments Worry Retailers." *Video Business* 4 Nov. 2005. Accessed: 6 Nov. 2005. Available: http://www.videobusiness.com.

"New Round of SportsCenter Commercials Debut on ESPN Networks." *PR Newswire* 18 Nov. 2004. Accessed: 19 Jun. 2006. Available: http://www.highbeam.com.

"New 'Star Wars' movie wows French audiences before worldwide release." *Agence France Presse English* 18 May 2005. Accessed: 28 Jun. 2005. Available: http://www.highbeam.com.

Newbold, Mark. Personal interview. 18 Dec. 2006.

Newman, Bruce. "'Star Wars' maintains sway over popular imagination." *San Jose Mercury News* 15 May 2005. Accessed: 3 Jun. 2006. Available: http://www.highbeam.com.

"News Briefs." *Television Week* 24 Oct. 2005. Accessed: 19 Jun. 2006. Available: http://www.highbeam.com.

"Newsweek: Marketing Pitch for Next Star Wars Sequel, 'Attack of the Clones,' Promises 'Darker Feel, Closer to the Original Saga' With 'No Silly Characters or Kids'; Last Movie 'Did Not Live Up to Expectations;' Director Lucas 'is Now Much Smarter About What He Should Do and Should Not Do,' Says One Associate." *PR Newswire* 21 Apr. 2002. Accessed: 8 Aug. 2006. Available: http://www.highbeam.com.

"Night of Star Wars is sell-out." *Coventry Evening Telegraph* 26 Apr. 2005. Accessed: 14 Jun. 2006. Available: http://www.highbeam.com.

Norton, Justin M. "'Star Wars' creator opens new headquarters in California." *AP Worldstream* 26 Jun. 2005. Accessed: 15 Jun. 2006. Available: http://www.highbeam.com.

———. "'Star Wars' Fans Turn Out for Premieres." *Associated Press* 13 May 2005. Accessed: 3 Jun. 2006. Available: http://www.highbeam.com.

"Now that you've seen AOTC, where does it rate in the saga?" *TheForce.net.* Accessed: 25 Jun. 2005. Available: http://www.theforce.net.

O'Sullivan, Charlotte. "Revenge is darker, disturbing and light years ahead of the others." Rev. of *Star Wars: Episode III—Revenge of the Sith. The Evening Standard* 9 May 2005. Accessed: 15 Jun. 2006. Available: http://www.highbeam.com.

"Obi-Wan is here and the force is with him." *USA Today* 1 Jan. 2005. Accessed: 7 Jun. 2006. Available: http://www.highbeam.com.

"On DVD for the First Time Sept. 21: 'Star Wars Trilogy' Brings New Excitement, Insight and Adventure to the Most Highly Anticipated DVD in History." *Business Wire* 20 Apr. 2004. Accessed: 18 Jun. 2006. Available: http://www.highbeam.com.

"On the Level." *The Official Star Wars Web Site* 22 Dec. 2004. Accessed: 15 Jun. 2006. Available: http://www.starwars.com.

"Online Ticket Sales Reach Galactic Heights." *ShowBizData* 2 Jun. 2005. Accessed: 2 Jun. 2005. Available: http://www.showbizdata.com.

"Orange Launches *Star Wars* Mobile Box Set." *The Official Star Wars Web Site* 29 Mar. 2005. Accessed: 17 Jun. 2006. Available: http://www.starwars.com.

Ordower, Garrett. "Traffic jam a return to reality for midnight 'Star Wars' fans." *Daily Herald* 20 May 2005. Accessed: 15 Jun. 2006. Available: http://www.highbeam.com.

Osegueda, Mike and Anthony Witrado. "This game is pretty cool if you're a 'Star Wars' fan." Rev. of *Star Wars: Episode III—Revenge of the Sith* (video game). *The Fresno Bee* 20 May 2005. Accessed: 7 Jun. 2006. Available: http://www.highbeam.com.

Osterman, Rachel. "Fanatics willing to miss work to wait in line, catch latest 'Star Wars'." *The Sacramento Bee* 19 May 2005. Accessed: 7 Jun. 2006. Available: http://www.highbeam.com.

"Out in Force for Star Wars game." *The Evening Standard* 5 May 2005. Accessed: 14 Jun. 2006. Available: http://www.highbeam.com.

"Outdoor Provides International Impact." *The Official Star Wars Web Site* 10 Jun. 2005. Accessed: 17 Jun. 2006. Available: http://www.starwars.com.

Page, Clarence. "Should We Call Him 'Darth Bush'?" *The Southern Illinoisan* 29 May 2005. Accessed: 17 Jul. 2006. Available: http://www.southernillinoisan.com.

Pandya, Gitesh. "Star Wars Episode III Opening Day Update." *Box Office Guru* 20 May 2005. Accessed: 20 May 2005. Available: http://www.boxofficeguru.com.

———. "Weekend Box Office (June 3–5, 2005)." *Box Office Guru* 6 Jun. 2005. Accessed: 10 Aug. 2006. Available: http://www.boxofficeguru.com.

———. "Weekend Box Office—June 7–9." *Box Office Guru* 10 Jun. 2002. Accessed: 9 Aug. 2006. Available: http://www.boxofficeguru.com.

———. "Weekend Box Office (June 10–12, 2005)." *Box Office Guru* 13 Jun. 2005. Accessed: 10 Aug. 2006. Available: http://www.boxofficeguru.com.

———. "Weekend Box Office—June 14–16." *Box Office Guru* 17 Jun. 2002. Accessed: 9 Aug. 2006. Available: http://www.boxofficeguru.com.

———. "Weekend Box Office (June 17–19, 2005)." *Box Office Guru* 20 Jun. 2005. Accessed: 10 Aug. 2006. Available: http://www.boxofficeguru.com.

———. "Weekend Box Office—May 17–19." *Box Office Guru* 20 May 2002. Accessed: 9 Aug. 2006. Available: http://www.boxofficeguru.com.

———. "Weekend Box Office—May 24–27." *Box Office Guru* 28 May 2002. Accessed: 9 Aug. 2006. Available: http://www.boxofficeguru.com.

———. "Weekend Box Office (May 28–31, 2004)." *Box Office Guru* Jun. 1 2004. Accessed: 30 Nov. 2006. Available: http://www.boxofficeguru.com.

———. "Weekend Box Office—May 31–Jun 2." *Box Office Guru* 3 Jun. 2002. Accessed: 9 Aug. 2006. Available: http://www.boxofficeguru.com.

Paynter, Susan. "Seattle sidewalks no longer safe for silliness." *Seattle Post-Intelligencer* 2 Feb. 2005. Accessed: 2 Sep. 2006. Available: http://seattlepi.nwsource.com.

———. "'Star Wars' Fan is a Throwback to Seattle's Oddball Days." *Seattle Post-Intelligencer* 24 Jan. 2005. Accessed: 15 Jun. 2006. Available: http://seattlepi.nwsource.com.

———. "The Force of the Law is Against 'Star Wars' Squatter." *Seattle Post-Intelligencer* 26 Jan. 2005. Accessed: 15 Jun. 2006. Available: http://seattlepi.nwsource.com.

Pearson, Mike. "'Star Wars' Force Remains With 'Sith'." *Denver Rock Mountain News* 4 Nov. 2005. Accessed: 19 Jun. 2006. Available: http://www.highbeam.com.

Pellerito, Linda. Personal interview. 19 Dec. 2006.

"People Who Mattered 2005." *Time* 26 Dec. 2005. Accessed: 25 Jul. 2006. Available: http://www.highbeam.com.

"Pepsi Turns to the Force and the Dark Side for Star Wars: Episode III Revenge of the Sith Promotions; Star Wars' Beloved Yoda Leads Pepsi Online Sweepstakes With More than $1 Million in Prizes up for Grabs." *PR Newswire* 24 Mar. 2005. Accessed: 3 Jun. 2006. Available: http://www.highbeam.com.

Petrakis, John. "Space opera finale." Rev. of *Star Wars: Episode III—Revenge of the Sith. The Christian Century* 14 Jun. 2005. Accessed: 14 Jun. 2006. Available: http://www.highbeam.com.

Pfanner, Eric. "A new force to promote 'Star Wars'." *International Herald Tribune* 30 May 2005. Accessed: 9 Jun. 2006. Available: http://www.highbeam.com.

"PG-13 'Revenge of the Sith' is the darkest 'Star Wars' episode yet." *New York Daily News* 5 May 2005. Accessed: 7 Jun. 2006. Available: http://www.highbeam.com.

Pinkerton, James. "Star Wars, It Turns Out, Includes Political Allegory." *The Cincinnati Post* 25 May 2005. Accessed: 9 Jun. 2006. Available: http://www.highbeam.com.

"PinnacleSports.com Announces Odds on Success of 'Star Wars: Episode III'." *PR Newswire* 12 May 2005. Accessed: 7 Jun. 2006. Available: http://www.highbeam.com.

Pio, Emenike. "Star Wars voted top men's film of all time." *The Mirror* 12 Apr. 2004. Accessed: 18 Jun. 2006. Available: http://www.highbeam.com.

Podhoretz, John. "Captivating, Says John Podhoretz." *New York Post* 18 May 1999. Accessed: 15 Jul. 2006. Available: http://www.nypost.com.

———. "Jedi Warmongers." *National Review Online* 13 May 2005. Accessed: 15 Jul. 2006. Available: http://www.nationalreview.com.

———. "Naboo, Dooku, and a mission to the Wookies." Rev. of *Star Wars: Episode III—Revenge of the Sith. The Weekly Standard* 23 May 2005, Volume 010, Issue 34. Accessed: 17 Jul. 2006. Available: http://www.weeklystandard.com.

———. "Since George Lucas is Using Darth Vader to Sell M&Ms …" *National Review Online* 17 May 2005. Accessed: 17 Jul. 2006. Available: http://www.nationalreview.com.

Pollock, Dale. "Epoch filmmaker; In the film biz, there's Before George and After George." *Variety* 8 Jun. 2005. Accessed: 9 Jun. 2005. Available: http://www.variety.com.

Pols, Mary F. "Lucas' pre-emptive strike before 'Attack of the Clones'." *Contra Costa Times* 10 May 2002. Accessed: 9 Aug. 2006. Available: http://www.highbeam.com.

Porter, Martin. "'All that is necessary for the triumph of evil is that good men do nothing' (or words to that effect): A study of a Web quotation." Accessed: 29 Nov. 2006. Available: http://www.tartarus.org/~martin/essays/burkequote.html.

Portman, Natalie. Interview with David Edwards. *The Mirror* 16 May 2005. Accessed: 14 Jun. 2006. Available: http://www.highbeam.com.

Powell, Cody. Personal interview. 12 Dec. 2006.

"Profile: How the 'Star Wars' series has changed director George Lucas." *Morning Edition* 18 May 2005. NPR. Transcript available: http://www.highbeam.com.

"Profile: People skipping work and school to see newest installment of 'Star Wars'." *All Things Considered* 19 May 2005. NPR. Transcript available: http://www.highbeam.com.

"Profile: Theme music for 'Star Wars' movies." *Weekend Edition—Sunday* 22 May 2005. NPR. Transcript available: http://www.highbeam.com.

"Proxy Statement For Extraordinary General Meeting of Shareholders." *Corgi International* 17 Nov. 2006. Accessed: 8 Jan. 2007. Available: http://www.sec.gov.

Puig, Claudia. "A galaxy of 'Sith' reviews, some ga-ga, some so-so." *USA Today* 19 May 2005. Accessed: 21 May 2005. Available: http://www.usatoday.com.

———. "The stars finally align in 'Revenge of the Sith'." Rev. of *Star Wars: Episode III—Revenge of the Sith. USA Today* 15 May 2005. Accessed: 20 Jul. 2006. Available: http://www.usatoday.com.

Quinn, Michelle. "Latest 'Star Wars' is a PG-13 dilemma." *San Jose Mercury News* 20 May 2005. Accessed: 14 Jun. 2006. Available: http://www.highbeam.com.

Rabil, Sarah. "Merchandise Sales in Midst of a Slump: Movie stuff in need of a jump." *The Charlotte Observer* 9 Jun. 2006. Accessed: 13 Dec. 2006. Available: http://www.highbeam.com.

Rahner, Mark. "The Force is with Lucas in his 'Star Wars' finale." Rev. of *Star Wars: Episode III—Revenge of the Sith. The Seattle Times* 18 May 2005. Accessed: 20 Jul. 2006. Available: http://seattlepi.nwsource.com.

"Ready, Sith, Go: Episode III Games from JAKKS Pacific." *The Official Star Wars Web Site* 28 Feb. 2005. Accessed: 15 Jun. 2006. Available: http://www.starwars.com.

"Renowned Card Stacker To Build Famous Star Wars Cityscape Using Only Star Wars Trading Cards and 'The Force'." *Business Wire* 20 Apr. 2005. Accessed: 4 Jun. 2006. Available: http://www.highbeam.com.

"Report: Two injured by makeshift 'Star Wars' light sabers." *AP Worldstream* 24 May 2005. Accessed: 15 Jun. 2006. Available: http://www.highbeam.com.

"*Revenge* DVD Retailer Exclusives." *The Official Star Wars Web Site* 31 Oct. 2005. Accessed: 15 Jun. 2006. Available: http://www.starwars.com.

"Revenge Is Sweet: Final Star Wars Movie Breaks Fandango Records." *PR Newswire* 22 May 2005. Accessed: 15 Jun. 2006. Available: http://www.highbeam.com.

"Revenge of the MPAA." *ShowBizData* 26 May 2005. Accessed: 26 May 2005. Available: http://www.showbizdata.com.

"'Revenge of the Sith' New Star Wars Movie." *United Press International* 25 Jul. 2004. Accessed: 18 Jun. 2006. Available: http://www.highbeam.com.

"*Revenge of the Sith* Wins Two DVD Awards." *The Official Star Wars Web Site* 10 Aug. 2006. Accessed: 14 Aug. 2006. Available: http://www.starwars.com.

"*Revenge* Returns to Burger King." *The Official Star Wars Web Site* 8 Sep. 2005. Accessed: 15 Jun. 2006. Available: http://www.starwars.com.

Rich, Joshua. "The Next Dimension." *Entertainment Weekly* 1 Apr. 2005: 8–9.

Rickey, Carrie. "Debate brews about cultural impact of 'Star Wars'." *The Philadelphia Inquirer* 13 May 2005. Accessed: 7 Jun. 2006. Available: http://www.highbeam.com.

Riggs, Angel. "'Star Wars' prequel moves merchandise." *Tulsa World* 19 May 2005. Accessed: 2 Jun. 2006. Available: http://www.highbeam.com.

Riley, Mike. "A Special Guide to DRM and Software Activation Tools: Protect Data, Enforce Licenses." *Dr. Dobb's Portal* 17 Jan. 2006. Accessed: 30 Nov. 2006. Available: http://www.ddj.com.

Rinzler, J. W. *The Making of Star Wars: Revenge of the Sith*. New York: Random House, 2005.

Roback, Diane. "Potter Leads the Pack." *Publishers Weekly* 27 Mar. 2006. Accessed: 13 Dec. 2006. Available: http://www.publishersweekly.com.

Roberts, Lynde. Personal interview. 14 Dec. 2006.

Robertson, Barbara. "Inside Episode III: Star Wars." *3D World* Jul. 2005: 30–39.

Robertson, Cameron. "Ewan in attack on Star Wars." *The Mirror* 23 Feb. 2005. Accessed: 14 Jun. 2006. Available: http://www.highbeam.com.

———. "Oldman quits Star Wars film." *The Mirror* 14 Sep. 2004. Accessed: 19 Jun. 2006. Available: http://www.highbeam.com.

Robey, Tim. "Galactic epic creaks to its climax." Rev. of *Star Wars: Episode III—Revenge of the Sith. Telegraph* 20 May 2005. Accessed: 13 Jul. 2006. Available: http://www.highbeam.com.

Rock, Carol. "Kids' Charity To Be Helped By the World of the 'Wars'; Fans Wait at Grauman's, As Tradition Dictates, For 'Sith'." *Los Angeles Daily News* 2 May 2005. Accessed: 27 Jun. 2005. Available: http://www.highbeam.com.

"Rocketing ticket sales turn Star Wars III into hit." *Xinhua News Agency* 23 May 2005. Accessed: 15 Jun. 2006. Available: http://www.highbeam.com.

Rose, Jason. Personal interview. 12 Dec. 2006.

Rose, Marla Matzer. "Toy Wars: Summer Movie Tie-ins Anything but Child's Play to Studios." *The Columbus Dispatch* 30 May 2006. Accessed: 19 Jun. 2006. Available: http://www.highbeam.com.

Ross, Dalton. "Hot Off the Presses." Rev. of *Star Wars: Episode III—Revenge of the Sith* (book). *Entertainment Weekly* 8 Apr. 2005. Accessed: 26 Jun. 2005. Available: http://www.highbeam.com.

Roston, Tom. "Holy Sith! It's the Last Star Wars!" *Premiere* May 2005: 52–60, 121–22.

Rubio, Kevin. Interview with DarkHorse.com. "Kevin Rubio on the Return of Tag and Bink." *DarkHorse.com* 30 Mar. 2006. Accessed: 27 Dec. 2006. Available: http://www.darkhorse.com.

Ryan, Joal. "'Sith' Happens at 2005 Box Office." *Yahoo! News* 3 Jan. 2006. Accessed: 4 Jan. 2006. Available: http://news.yahoo.com.

Ryckman, Lisa. "PG-13 Violence Takes." *Denver Rocky Mountain News* 19 May 2005. Accessed: 20 Jul. 2006. Available: http://www.highbeam.com.

Sabin, Jim. "'Star Wars' helps boy through tough times." *The Lima News* 23 Dec. 2005. Accessed: 1 Aug. 2006. Available: http://www.highbeam.com.

Salas, Randy A. "New Force on DVD; A 4-disc set of the original 'Star Wars' trilogy takes us to a long time ago, in a galaxy far, far away." *Star Tribune* 21 Sep. 2004. Accessed: 18 Jun. 2006. Available: http://www.highbeam.com.

———. "ON DVD; FX, from Mars to 'Star Wars'; 'The War of the Worlds' and 'Sith' DVDs show how special effects have changed over the decades." *Star Tribune* 30 Oct. 2005. Accessed: 19 Jun. 2006. Available: http://www.highbeam.com.

———. "'Revenge' is Sweet with Bonus DVD." Rev. of *Star Wars: Episode III—Revenge of the Sith* (soundtrack). *Star Tribune* 10 May 2005. Accessed: 28 Jun. 2005. Available: http://www.highbeam.com.

Sanchez, Robert. "Fans out in force; Line forms early for seats at midnight showing of 'Star Wars'." *Daily Herald* 19 May 2005. Accessed: 14 Jun. 2006. Available: http://www.highbeam.com.

Sarkar, Pia. "'Star Wars' action will be at toy stores this morning." *San Francisco Chronicle* 2 Apr. 2005. Accessed: 2 Apr. 2005. Available: http://www.sfgate.com.

Schaefer, Stephen. "Back in black; Actor turns back time as evil emperor in 'Star Wars' finale." *The Boston Herald* 16 May 2005. Accessed: 15 Jun. 2006. Available: http://www.highbeam.com.

———. "Darth lucky; Hayden Christensen thanks 'Star Wars' for changing his life." *The Boston Herald* 15 May 2005. Accessed: 14 Jun. 2006. Available: http://www.highbeam.com.

———. "The gospel according to Lucas; The creator of Vader says it's time to move beyond 'Star Wars'." *The Boston Herald* 19 May 2005. Accessed: 14 Jun. 2006. Available: http://www.highbeam.com.

Schorow, Stephanie. "Lightsabers, camera, action! 'Star Wars' fan films show creators' devotion to series." *The Boston Herald* 12 May 2005. Accessed: 2 Jun. 2006. Available: http://www.highbeam.com.

Schwankert, Steven. "A 'Mission' to China." *Variety* 17 Nov. 2005. Accessed: 19 Dec. 2005. Available: http://www.variety.com.

"*Sci Fi* Magazine Welcomes Back Vader." *The Official Star Wars Web Site* 7 Apr. 2005. Accessed: 26 Jul. 2006. Available: http://www.starwars.com.

Scott, A. O. "Some Surprises in That Galaxy Far, Far Away." Rev. of *Star Wars: Episode III—Revenge of the Sith. New York Times* 16 May 2005. Accessed: 17 Jul. 2006. Available: http://www.nytimes.com.

"See *Revenge* This Father's Day Weekend, Get a Free Poster!" *The Official Star Wars Web Site* 15 Jun. 2005. Accessed: 15 Jun. 2006. Available: http://www.starwars.com.

"Seeing Through Vader's Eyes." *The Official Star Wars Web Site* 13 Oct. 2005. Accessed: 15 Jun. 2006. Available: http://www.starwars.com.

"Series B.O. to soar with 'Sith'." *Variety* 23 May 2005. Accessed: 27 Jun. 2005. Available: http://www.variety.com.

Shargel, Raphael. "Conflicting concepts of evil." *The New Leader* May/Jun. 2005. Accessed: 15 Jun. 2006. Available: http://www.highbeam.com.

Sheffield, Rob. "Behind the Mask." *Rolling Stone* 2 Jun. 2005: 52.

"Shopping in America Survey: Halloween No Spook to Consumer Spending." *Business Wire* 27 Sep. 2005. Accessed: 19 Jun. 2006. Available: http://www.highbeam.com.

Shuster, Fred. "Some 'Star Wars' Fans Reject Lucas' Escort Offer." *Los Angeles Daily News* 13 May 2005. Accessed: 9 Jun. 2006. Available: http://www.highbeam.com.

———. "'Star Wars' Fans May Be Lining Up in Vain." *Los Angeles Daily News* 7 Apr. 2005. Accessed: 7 Jun. 2006. Available: http://www.highbeam.com.

Siemaszko, Corky. "The fear may be with you in final 'Star Wars' sequel." *New York Daily News* 11 Mar. 2005. Accessed: 15 Jun. 2006. Available: http://www.highbeam.com.

Silver, Marc. "Ask Us (fans of Star Wars make their own films to show on the net)." *U.S. News & World Report* 23 May 2005. Accessed: 14 Jun. 2006. Available: http://www.highbeam.com.

Singh, Anita. "Celebrity Watch: Star Wars the film marathon." *Daily Post* 20 Apr. 2005. Accessed: 28 Jun. 2005. Available: http://www.highbeam.com.

Singh, Rob. "Final force is with us; Last episode of Star Wars gets multiple premieres across the US." *The Evening Standard* 13 May 2005. Accessed: 28 Jun. 2005. Available: http://www.highbeam.com.

"'Sith' earns $108.5 million in first U.S. weekend." *The Hollywood Reporter* 23 May 2005. Accessed: 23 May 2005. Available: http://www.hollywoodreporter.com.

"*Sith* Earns Four VES Nominations." *The Official Star Wars Web Site* 10 Jan. 2006. Accessed: 15 Jun. 2006. Available: http://www.starwars.com.

"Sith Happens: Force is With Star Wars Online Advertising as Fans Await Star Wars Opening." *PR Newswire* 19 May 2005. Accessed: 2 Jun. 2006. Available: http://www.highbeam.com.

"'Sith' Hits $200 Million." *Yahoo! Movies* 27 May 2005. Accessed: 27 May 2005. Available: http://movies.yahoo.com.

"'Sith' Rampage goes on, crosses 145.5 million." *24x7 Updates* 24 May 2005. Accessed: 6 Jun. 2005. Available: http://www.24x7updates.com.

"'Sith' soundtrack soars." *Zap2It.com* via Knight-Ridder/Tribune News Service 12 May 2005. Accessed: 27 Jun. 2005. Available: http://www.highbeam.com.

Slagle, Matt. "Star Wars video games through the ages." *AP Worldstream* 13 May 2005. Accessed: 2 Jun. 2006. Available: http://www.highbeam.com.

Smith, Amber. "Not All Kids Mature Enough to Handle Darker 'Star Wars'." *The Post-Standard* 16 May 2005. Accessed: 14 Jun. 2006. Available: http://www.highbeam.com.

Smith, Bec. "'Madagascar,' 'Worlds' earn $61 mil o'seas for UIP." *The Hollywood Reporter* 18 Jul. 2005. Accessed: 18 Jul. 2005. Available: http://www.hollywoodreporter.com.

Smith, David. "Star Wars—the empire strikes gold." *The Observer* 15 May 2005. Accessed: 15 May 2005. Available: http://observer.guardian.co.uk.

Smith, Eric. "'Clone' clips: the Force is with them." *Multichannel News* 27 Oct. 2003. Accessed: 18 Jun. 2006. Available: http://www.highbeam.com.

Smith, Kevin. "Darth & Me." *Rolling Stone* 2 Jun. 2005: 50.

Smith, Kyle. "'Til Darth Do Us Part." *The New York Post* 17 May 2005. Accessed: 17 May 2005. Available: http://www.nypost.com.

"Snow Patrol's Sith Obsession." *The Official Star Wars Web Site* 24 Feb. 2006. Accessed: 15 Jun. 2006. Available: http://www.starwars.com.

Snyder, Gabriel. "A force to be reckoned with." *Variety* 17 May 2005. Accessed: 17 May 2005. Available: http://www.variety.com.

———. "B.O. doesn't meet halfway." *Variety* 20 Jun. 2005. Accessed: 20 Jun. 2005. Available: http://www.variety.com.

———. "'Batman' in the black." *Variety* 19 Jun. 2005. Accessed: 20 Jun. 2005. Available: http://www.variety.com.

———. "Inside Move: Fanatics laying it on the line." *Variety* 5 Apr. 2005. Accessed: 2 Sep. 2006. Available: http://www.variety.com.

———. "'Sith' is already a star." *Variety* 19 May 2005. Accessed: 19 May 2005. Available: http://www.variety.com.

———. "'Sith' smackdown." *Variety* 26 May 2005. Accessed: 27 May 2005. Available: http://www.variety.com.

———. "Summer pix get muddled in middle." *Variety* 21 Aug. 2005. Accessed: 23 Aug. 2005. Available: http://www.variety.com.

———. "The 'Sith' hits the fans." *Variety* 22 May 2005. Accessed: 23 May 2005. Available: http://www.variety.com.

———. "Who's on top?" *Variety* 25 Dec. 2005. Accessed: 31 Dec. 2005. Available: http://www.variety.com.

Soriano, César G. "Lucas rules fans' empire." *USA Today* 25 Apr. 2005: 1D–2D.

"Souvenir Magazine for *Revenge of the Sith*." *The Official Star Wars Web Site* 1 Feb. 2005. Accessed: 15 Jun. 2006. Available: http://www.starwars.com.

Spadora, Brian. "'Star Wars' still force for kids at heart." *The Record* 3 Apr. 2005. Accessed: 7 Jun. 2006. Available: http://www.highbeam.com.

"Special Announcement: Episode III Title." *The Official Star Wars Web Site* 24 Jul. 2004. Accessed: 15 Jun. 2006. Available: http://www.starwars.com.

"Sportsbook.com offers odds on Star Wars Episode III: Revenge of the Sith." *PR Newswire* 12 May 2005. Accessed: 27 Jun. 2005. Available: http://www.highbeam.com.

"SpudTrooper Joins Ranks with Darth Tater." *The Official Star Wars Web Site* 10 Jun. 2005. Accessed: 17 Jun. 2006. Available: http://www.starwars.com.

Stanley, T. L. "Can 'Sith' Restore Balance to Summer?" *Advertising Age* 23 May 2005. Accessed: 27 Jun. 2005. Available: http://www.highbeam.com.

———. "Tie-in partners tiptoe into PG-13 rated films; Marketers break taboo, linking carefully with edgier, more racy flicks." *Advertising Age* 25 Jul. 2005. Accessed: 20 Jul. 2006. Available: http://www.highbeam.com.

"Star Wars 3 in On-Line Confrontation." *United Press International* 3 Feb. 2004. Accessed: 18 Jun. 2006. Available: http://www.highbeam.com.

"Star Wars blasts past its rivals." *The Daily Mail* 23 May 2005. Accessed: 15 Jun. 2006. Available: http://www.highbeam.com.

"'Star Wars' by the numbers." *Publishers Weekly* 23 May 2005. Accessed: 13 Dec. 2006. Available: http://www.publishersweekly.com.

"'Star Wars' cartoons fill in story." *The Cincinnati Post* 6 Nov. 2003. Accessed: 18 Jun. 2006. Available: http://www.highbeam.com.

"Star Wars Celebration III Logo Revealed." *The Official Star Wars Web Site* 7 Apr. 2004. Accessed: 17 Jun. 2006. Available: http://www.starwars.com.

"Star Wars Celebration IV in Los Angeles to Mark 30th Anniversary of Saga." *Business Wire* 26 May 2006. Accessed: 19 Jun. 2006. Available: http://www.highbeam.com.

"Star Wars Collectibles from Japan." *The Official Star Wars Web Site* 7 Apr. 2005. Accessed: 15 Jun. 2006. Available: http://www.starwars.com.

"*Star Wars* Collectors' Show at Celebration III." *The Official Star Wars Web Site* 13 Dec. 2004. Accessed: 15 Jun. 2006. Available: http://www.starwars.com.

"Star Wars conquers all on store shelves." *Coventry Evening Telegraph* 26 May 2005. Accessed: 3 Jun. 2006. Available: http://www.highbeam.com.

"'Star Wars' creator George Lucas receives 'galactic achievement award'." *AP Worldstream* 9 Mar. 2005. Accessed: 15 Jun. 2006. Available: http://www.highbeam.com.

"'Star Wars' creator hopes special effects production site will make San Francisco a film capital." *AP Worldstream* 9 Feb. 2003. Accessed: 19 Jun. 2006. Available: http://www.highbeam.com.

"'Star Wars' day 1: A record $50M." *Reuters* 20 May 2005. Accessed: 20 May 2005. Available: http://www.cnn.com.

"Star Wars director praises Australian film crews." *AAP General News* 16 May 2005. Accessed: 14 Jun. 2006. Available: http://www.highbeam.com.

"Star Wars' droid R2D2 is world's favourite robot." *Western Mail* 26 Jul. 2004. Accessed: 18 Jun. 2006. Available: http://www.highbeam.com.

"Star Wars DVD Box Set Wins Big at DVDX Awards." *The Official Star Wars Web Site* 10 Feb. 2005. Accessed: 15 Jun. 2006. Available: http://www.starwars.com.

"Star Wars DVD Rockets to Top." *The Mirror* 22 Sep. 2004. Accessed: 19 Jun. 2006. Available: http://www.highbeam.com.

"*Star Wars: Episode 3* To Be 'Very, Very, Very Dark,' Says Lucas." *ShowBizData* 10 Aug. 1999. Accessed: 10 Aug. 1999. Available: http://www.showbizdata.com.

"'Star Wars: Episode II Attack of the Clones' Coming to IMAX Theatres This Holiday Season For A Limited Release; Digitally Re-mastered From Its Digital Source Using IMAX DMR Technology." *PR Newswire* 9 Aug. 2002. Accessed: 9 Aug. 2006. Available: http://www.highbeam.com.

"Star Wars: Episode III—Revenge of the Sith (2005)." *Yahoo! Movies.* Accessed: 20 May 2005. Available: http://movies.yahoo.com.

"Star Wars: Episode III Revenge of the Sith Soundtrack Makes History as the Third Star Wars Soundtrack to Debut in the Top 10 on Billboard's Top 200 Album Chart." *PR Newswire* 11 May 2005. Accessed: 26 Jun. 2005. Available: http://www.highbeam.com.

"Star Wars: Episode III Teaser Trailer." *The Official Star Wars Web Site* 28 Oct. 2004. Accessed: 15 Jun. 2006. Available: http://www.starwars.com.

"Star Wars Episode III—XBOX." *Game Rankings.* Accessed: 30 Nov. 2006. Available: http://www.gamerankings.com.

"'Star Wars' fan already in line for 'Episode III'." *Zap2It.com* via Knight-Ridder/ Tribune News Service 9 Jan. 2005. Accessed: 15 Jun. 2006. Available: http://www.highbeam.com.

"'Star Wars' fans embrace the Dark Side of obsession." *Yahoo! News* 16 May 2005. Accessed: 17 May 2005. Available: http://news.yahoo.com.

"'Star Wars' fans miss Solo turn." *USA Today* 24 May 2005: 1D.

"Star Wars Frenzy May Sap Corporate Bandwidth." *Business Wire* 20 May 2005. Accessed: 14 Jun. 2006. Available: http://www.highbeam.com.

"Star Wars Galaxies: An Empire Divided Surpasses 275,000 Registered Players." *Business Wire* 27 Aug. 2003. Accessed: 18 Jun. 2006. Available: http:// www.highbeam.com.

"'Star Wars' grosses $16.5 million from midnight showings." *AP Worldstream* 20 May 2005. Accessed: 14 Jun. 2006. Available: http://www.highbeam.com.

"Star Wars 'honour' for rockers Ash." *Coventry Evening Telegraph* 16 Apr. 2005. Accessed: 15 Jun. 2006. Available: http://www.highbeam.com.

"Star Wars Is Top Choice of Collectors." *PR Newswire* 16 May 2005. Accessed: 3 Jun. 2006. Available: http://www.highbeam.com.

"Star Wars: Knights of the Old Republic is a major success on the Xbox; BioWare's current hit wins yet another award." *PR Newswire* 1 Dec. 2003. Accessed: 19 Jun. 2006. Available: http://www.highbeam.com.

"Star Wars: Knights of the Old Republic Named GameSpy 2003 Game of the Year; Gamers' Choice Awards Voted By Readers to be Revealed Christmas Eve." *Business Wire* 23 Dec. 2003. Accessed: 18 Jun. 2006. Available: http://www.highbeam.com.

"Star Wars: KOTOR II—PC." *Game Rankings*. Accessed: 30 Nov. 2006. Available: http://www.gamerankings.com.

"'Star Wars' Leads to Piracy." *The Online Reporter* 6 Sep. 2004. Accessed: 19 Jun. 2006. Available: http://www.highbeam.com.

"Star Wars leaked on to internet." *Daily Record* 20 May 2005. Accessed: 15 Jun. 2006. Available: http://www.highbeam.com.

"Star Wars LEGO Sets and Thomas the Tank Engine Top eBay's 2005 Hot new Toys List." *Business Wire* 3 Nov 2005. Accessed: 19 Jun. 2006. Available: http://www.highbeam.com.

"Star Wars M&M's make debut in advance of film." *MMR* 13 Jun. 2005. Accessed: 7 Jun. 2006. Available: http://www.highbeam.com.

"*Star Wars Magazine* #57 in the UK." *The Official Star Wars Web Site* 6 May 2005. Accessed: 15 Jun. 2006. Available: http://www.starwars.com.

"Star Wars mania for film premiere." *Daily Post* 17 May 2005. Accessed: 7 Jun. 2006. Available: http://www.highbeam.com.

"'Star Wars' Movie Hits DVD on Nov. 1." *AP Online* 26 Jul. 2005. Accessed: 9 Jun. 2006. Available: http://www.highbeam.com.

"'Star Wars' Property Dominates the U.S. Toy Business; Toys from a Galaxy Far, Far Away Take the No. 1 Spot." *Business Wire* 27 Oct. 2005. Accessed: 19 Jun. 2006. Available: http://www.highbeam.com.

"*Star Wars* Racing is Here." *The Official Star Wars Web Site* 4 Apr. 2005. Accessed: 15 Jun. 2006. Available: http://www.starwars.com.

"Star Wars Republic Commando—PC." *Game Rankings.* Accessed: 30 Nov. 2006. Available: http://www.gamerankings.com.

"Star Wars: Revenge of the Sith Breaks MovieTickets.com Sales Marks." *Wireless News* 20 May 2005. Accessed: 26 Jun. 2005. Available: http://www.highbeam.com.

"Star Wars: Revenge of the Sith Selling up to 10 Tickets Per Second on MovieTickets.com." *PR Newswire* 20 May 2005. Accessed: 15 Jun. 2006. Available: http://www.highbeam.com.

"'Star Wars Revenge of the Sith' Sustains Record Buzz Among Fans, Reports Intelliseek's BlogPulse.com." *PR Newswire* 16 May 2005. Accessed: 15 Jun. 2006. Available: http://www.highbeam.com.

"Star Wars sale mania." *Daily Record* 2 Apr. 2004. Accessed: 18 Jun. 2006. Available: http://www.highbeam.com.

"Star Wars Shopping: These Are the Products You're Looking For …" *The Official Star Wars Web Site* 7 Aug. 2003. Accessed: 17 Jun. 2006. Available: http://www.starwars.com.

"'Star Wars' Spoof is a Film Even Weird Al Could Like." *The News & Record* 23 Jun. 2005. Accessed: 9 Jun. 2006. Available: http://www.highbeam.com.

"*Star Wars* Tests The Digital Cinema Supply Chain." *Information Week* 19 May 2005. Accessed: 26 Jun. 2005. Available: http://www.highbeam.com.

"*Star Wars:* The Best of 2005." *The Official Star Wars Web Site* 23 Dec. 2005. Accessed: 15 Jun. 2006. Available: http://www.starwars.com.

"Star Wars too strong for young." *Daily Post* 12 Mar. 2005. Accessed: 14 Jun. 2006. Available: http://www.highbeam.com.

"Star Wars Tops AFI's List of 25 Greatest Film Scores of All Time." *PR Newswire* 24 Sep. 2005. Accessed: 19 Jun. 2006. Available: http://www.highbeam.com.

"'Star Wars' Trailer to Premiere March 10." *AP Online* 1 Mar. 2005. Accessed: 15 Jun. 2006. Available: http://www.highbeam.com.

"*Star Wars* Trilogy DVD Details." *The Official Star Wars Web Site* 20 Apr. 2004. Accessed: 17 Jun. 2006. Available: http://www.starwars.com.

"Star Wars voted top for effects." *BBC News* 9 Jan. 2005. Accessed: 29 Nov. 2006. Available: http://news.bbc.co.uk.

"*Star Wars* Weekends 2005 Guest List." *The Official Star Wars Web Site* 29 Apr. 2005. Accessed: 15 Jun. 2006. Available: http://www.starwars.com.

"'Star Wars Weekends' Returns to Disney's Galaxy." *Columbia Times* 26 May 2004. Accessed: 18 Jun. 2006. Available: http://www.highbeam.com.

"starwars.com @ Celebration III." *The Official Star Wars Web Site* 28 Apr. 2005. Accessed: 17 Jun. 2006. Available: http://www.starwars.com.

"starwars.com at Celebration III; Behind *The Art of Revenge*." *The Official Star Wars Web Site* 19 Apr. 2005. Accessed: 17 Jun. 2006. Available: http://www.starwars.com.

"starwars.com at Celebration III; Effects Secrets from John Knoll." *The Official Star Wars Web Site* 19 Apr. 2005. Accessed: 17 Jun. 2006. Available: http://www.starwars.com.

"starwars.com at Celebration III; General Rumblings: Matthew Wood on Grievous and Sound." *The Official Star Wars Web Site* 19 Apr. 2005. Accessed: 17 Jun. 2006. Available: http://www.starwars.com.

"starwars.com at Celebration III; Let the Celebration Begin: Report from Opening Ceremonies." *The Official Star Wars Web Site* 19 Apr. 2005. Accessed: 17 Jun. 2006. Available: http://www.starwars.com.

"starwars.com at Celebration III; Makeup Masters: Dave & Lou Elsey." *The Official Star Wars Web Site* 19 Apr. 2005. Accessed: 17 Jun. 2006. Available: http://www.starwars.com.

"starwars.com at Celebration III; Master Behind the Action: Nick Gillard." *The Official Star Wars Web Site* 19 Apr. 2005. Accessed: 17 Jun. 2006. Available: http://www.starwars.com.

"starwars.com at Celebration III; Meet the *Star Wars* Fan Film Winners." *The Official Star Wars Web Site* 19 Apr. 2005. Accessed: 17 Jun. 2006. Available: http://www.starwars.com.

"starwars.com at Celebration III; Previsionary: Dan Gregoire." *The Official Star Wars Web Site* 19 Apr. 2005. Accessed: 17 Jun. 2006. Available: http://www.starwars.com.

"starwars.com at Celebration III; Rick McCallum's Spectacular Spectacular." *The Official Star Wars Web Site* 19 Apr. 2005. Accessed: 17 Jun. 2006. Available: http://www.starwars.com.

"starwars.com at Celebration III; *Star Wars* Next Top Model: Celebration III Costume Pageant." *The Official Star Wars Web Site* 19 Apr. 2005. Accessed: 17 Jun. 2006. Available: http://www.starwars.com.

"starwars.com at Celebration III; Thank the Maker: George Lucas." *The Official Star Wars Web Site* 19 Apr. 2005. Accessed: 17 Jun. 2006. Available: http://www.starwars.com.

Stone, Brad. "Darth Vader's New Offices; What happens to Lucasfilm now that 'Star Wars' is over? The company has big plans, soon to move into spectacular $350 million digs." *Newsweek* 27 Jun. 2005. Accessed: 14 Jun. 2006. Available: http://www.highbeam.com.

Story, Richard. Personal interview. 13 Dec. 2006.

Stover, Matt. Interview with starwars.com. "Inside Del Rey's Episode III Library." *The Official Star Wars Web Site* 30 Mar. 2005. Accessed: 15 Jun. 2006. Available: http://www.starwars.com.

Suciu, Peter. "Games: The Force is Strong." *Newsweek* 20 Oct. 2003. Accessed: 19 Jun. 2006. Available: http://www.highbeam.com.

"Summer bust leaves Hollywood worried." *Associated Press* 5 Sep. 2005. Accessed: 6 Sep. 2005. Available: http://www.cnn.com.

"Superfans Face Life After 'Star Wars'." *Yahoo! Movies* 27 May 2005. Accessed: 27 May 2005. Available: http://movies.yahoo.com.

"Sydney Fans: Get Your DVD Early!" *The Official Star Wars Web Site* 24 Oct. 2005. Accessed: 15 Jun. 2006. Available: http://www.starwars.com.

Szadkowski, Joseph. "Blasting through 'Star Wars' battles." Revs. of *Star Wars: Battlefront* and *Star Wars Trilogy: Apprentice of the Force* (video games). *The Washington Times* 21 Oct. 2004. Accessed: 1 Aug. 2006. Available: http://www.highbeam.com.

———. "Desktops set Lucas plan; A 'Star Wars' force for storyboards." *The Washington Times* 20 May 2005. Accessed: 10 Jun. 2006. Available: http://www.highbeam.com.

———. "Fans are the real stars at 'Star Wars' fun fest." *The Washington Times* 30 Apr. 2005. Accessed: 3 Jun. 2006. Available: http://www.highbeam.com.

———. "'Star Wars'–inspired creativity on display." *The Washington Times* 5 May 2005. Accessed: 7 Jun. 2006. Available: http://www.highbeam.com.

———. "Star Wars players fight for supremacy." *The Washington Times* 28 Apr. 2005. Accessed: 7 Jun. 2006. Available: http://www.highbeam.com.

Szymanski, Mike. "Lucas names third 'Star Wars'." *Zap2It.com* via Knight-Ridder/Tribune News Service 26 Jul. 2004. Accessed: 18 Jun. 2006. Available: http://www.highbeam.com.

———. "Portman readies for re-shoots of third 'Star Wars'." *Zap2It.com* via Knight-Ridder/Tribune News Service 20 Jul. 2004. Accessed: 18 Jun. 2006. Available: http://www.highbeam.com.

———. "'Star Wars' trilogy DVD filled with extras co-funded by A&E." *Zap2It.com* via Knight-Ridder/Tribune News Service 10 Sep. 2004. Accessed: 18 Jun. 2006. Available: http://www.highbeam.com.

Tabach-Bank, Lauren. "The 25 Hottest Stars Under 25." *Teen People* Jul. 2005: 120–21.

"Take a Breather: Read and Hear *Empire's* Latest." *The Official Star Wars Web Site* 28 Apr. 2005. Accessed: 26 Jul. 2006. Available: http://www.starwars.com.

Tambone, Lou. Personal interview. 18 Dec. 2006.

Tanaka, Wendy. "May the Sales Force be with you." *The Philadelphia Inquirer* 15 May 2005. Accessed: 2 Jun. 2006. Available: http://www.highbeam.com.

"Target is the Galactic Destination for Star Wars: Episode III Revenge of the Sith Licensed Products; Exclusive Merchandise for Star Wars Fans on Sale April 2." *PR Newswire* 29 Mar. 2005. Accessed: 27 Jun. 2005. Available: http://www.highbeam.com.

"Ten Charities Selected for Episode III Benefit Premieres on May 12." *The Official Star Wars Web Site* 16 Nov. 2004. Accessed: 15 Jun. 2006. Available: http://www.starwars.com.

"Ten Saturn Nominations for *Sith*." *The Official Star Wars Web Site* 17 Feb. 2006. Accessed: 15 Jun. 2006. Available: http://www.starwars.com.

"Texas Instruments Announces Worldwide Lineup of 94 DLP Cinema-Enabled Digital Screens to Show Star Wars: Episode II Attack of the Clones." *PR Newswire* 15 May 2002. Accessed: 9 Aug. 2006. Available: http://www.highbeam.com.

"Thank you, George a Million Times Over! Fans Get the Chance to Thank Star Wars Creator as Saga Comes to an End." *PR Newswire* 25 Apr. 2005. Accessed: 3 Jun. 2006. Available: http://www.highbeam.com.

The Academy of Science Fiction Fantasy & Horror Films. Accessed: 29 Nov. 2006. Available: http://www.saturnawards.org.

"The *Clone Wars* Micro-Series Continues!" *The Official Star Wars Web Site* 8 Jun. 2004. Accessed: 15 Aug. 2006. Available: http://www.starwars.com.

"The dark side of Star Wars." *Recycling Today* 1 Jul. 2005. Accessed: 7 Jun. 2006. Available: http://www.highbeam.com.

"The Evolution of Environments." *The Official Star Wars Web Site* 29 Sep. 2005. Accessed: 15 Jun. 2006. Available: http://www.starwars.com.

"The Force is strong with Nokia as Star Wars: Episode II Attack of the Clones arrives." *M2 Presswire* 12 Mar. 2002. Accessed: 8 Aug. 2006. Available: http://www.highbeam.com.

"The Force is Strong With Sith." *PR Newswire* 6 May 2005. Accessed: 7 May 2005. Available: http://biz.yahoo.com.

"The force is with fans of 'Star Wars'." *The Boston Herald* 17 Sep. 2004. Accessed: 18 Jun. 2006. Available: http://www.highbeam.com.

"The Grand Experiment." *The Official Star Wars Web Site* 16 Feb. 2006. Accessed: 15 Jun. 2006. Available: http://www.starwars.com.

"The Highly-Awaited, Final Installment of Star Wars Heats Up Premiere's May Issue." *PR Newswire* 12 Apr. 2005. Accessed: 15 Jun. 2006. Available: http://www.highbeam.com.

"The Hyperspace Horizon." *The Official Star Wars Web Site* 29 Apr. 2004. Accessed: 17 Jun. 2006. Available: http://www.starwars.com.

"The Life of a Set." *The Official Star Wars Web Site* 14 Oct. 2004. Accessed: 17 Jun. 2006. Available: http://www.starwars.com.

"The Most-Requested DVD Ever is Finally Available in September When the Star Wars Trilogy Comes to DVD for the First Time." *DVD News* 10 Feb. 2004. Accessed: 18 Jun. 2006. Available: http://www.highbeam.com.

"The New Face of Evil." *The Official Star Wars Web Site* 15 Mar. 2004. Accessed: 17 Jun. 2006. Available: http://www.starwars.com.

"'The O.C.' Creator Talks About Lucas Cameo." *The Official Star Wars Web Site* 11 May 2005. Accessed: 17 Jun. 2006. Available: http://www.starwars.com.

"The Official *Star Wars* Fan Club is Back Home at Lucasfilm—and Better than Ever." *The Official Star Wars Web Site* 28 Apr. 2004. Accessed: 17 Jun. 2006. Available: http://www.starwars.com.

"The Ultimate Star Wars Celebration Rocks the Galaxy Nov. 1 With Simultaneous Debuts of Revenge of the Sith DVD and Star Wars Battlefront II Game." *PR Newswire* 26 Jul. 2005. Accessed: 18 Jun. 2006. Available: http://www.highbeam.com.

"The Voice of Grievous." *The Official Star Wars Web Site* 3 Feb. 2005. Accessed: 17 Jun. 2006. Available: http://www.starwars.com.

Thomas, Archie. "'Star Wars Kid' suits up vs. stolen clip." *Variety* 15 Sep. 2003. Accessed: 18 Jun. 2006. Available: http://www.variety.com.

Thomas, Ceri. "Before Hope Comes Darkness." *Total Film* Apr. 2005: 52–59.

Thomson, Desson. "'Star Wars': Darth Lite." Rev. of *Star Wars: Episode III—Revenge of the Sith. The Washington Post* 20 May 2005. Accessed: 7 Jun. 2006. Available: http://www.highbeam.com.

"THQ Wireless Joins Forces With Lucasfilm to Develop First Ever Star Wars Multiplayer Mobile Game, Available Exclusively on Cingular Wireless." *PR Newswire* 27 Sep. 2005. Accessed: 19 Jun. 2006. Available: http://www.highbeam.com.

Tillson, Tamsen. "'Revenge' of Quebec exhibbers." *Variety* 19 May 2005. Accessed: 19 May 2005. Available: http://www.variety.com.

Tobias, Suzanne Perez. "'Sith' a little intense for little ones. But parents with young kids are accompanying them to the PG-13 'Star Wars: Episode III—Revenge of the Sith." *The Wichita Eagle* 20 May 2005. Accessed: 20 Jul. 2006. Available: http://www.highbeam.com.

Tommasini, Anthony. "John Williams's surprising score for 'Sith'." Rev. of *Star Wars: Episode III—Revenge of the Sith* (score). *International Herald Tribune* 25 May 2005. Accessed: 27 Jun. 2005. Available: http://www.highbeam.com.

Tong, Eugene. "'Star Wars' fans feel the force a month early." *Chicago Sun-Times* 13 Apr. 2002. Accessed: 2 Sep. 2006. Available: http://www.findarticles.com.

Tookey, Chris. "Not out of this world; With Star Wars fever about to sweep Britain, the Mail gets a sneak preview of the latest epic." Rev. of *Star Wars: Episode III—Revenge of the Sith. The Daily Mail* 9 May 2005. Accessed: 14 Jun. 2006. Available: http://www.highbeam.com.

"Top DVD sellers: week ended June 5, 2005." *Video Business* 13 Jun. 2005. Accessed: 25 Jun. 2005. Available: http://www.highbeam.com.

"Top DVD sellers: week ended May 8, 2005." *Video Business* 16 May 2005. Accessed: 25 Jun. 2005. Available: http://www.highbeam.com.

"Top DVD sellers: week ended May 22, 2005." *Video Business* 30 May 2005. Accessed: 25 Jun. 2005. Available: http://www.highbeam.com.

"Top Rentals: For Week Ended 11/06/05." *Video Business Online*. Accessed: 10 Nov. 2005. Available: http://www.videobusiness.com.

Toto, Christian. "'Sith' for sale? Product tie-ins roll off the line with film." *The Washington Times* 13 May 2005. Accessed: 27 Jun. 2005. Available: http://www.highbeam.com.

"Toys 'R' Us Stores to Open at 12:01 AM .on April 2 to Celebrate the Arrival of Star Wars: Episode III Revenge of the Sith Toy Collection." *PR Newswire* 28 Mar. 2005. Accessed: 26 Jun. 2005. Available: http://www.highbeam.com.

Travers, Peter. "Clone Wars." *Rolling Stone* 2 Jun. 2005: 87–88.

Triplett, Ward. "The power of the Force: Seeing 'Star Wars' everywhere, we are." *The Kansas City Star* 6 May 2005. Accessed: 2 Jun. 2006. Available: http://www.highbeam.com.

Tweiten, Jeff. "Waiting for Star Wars." Blog. Accessed: 30 Nov. 2006. Available: http://waitingforstarwars.blogspot.com.

"Two obsessions combined; Aspyr Media Inc. plans to release Lego Star Wars Mac version." *Macworld* 1 Aug. 2005. Accessed: 15 Jun. 2006. Available: http://www.highbeam.com.

"UK Plans Ultimate *Star Wars* Celebration Day for Episode III Premiere." *The Official Star Wars Web Site* 19 Apr. 2005. Accessed: 15 Jun. 2006. Available: http://www.starwars.com.

"U.S. shuts down network that leaked 'Star Wars'." *Yahoo! Movies* 25 May 2005. Accessed: 25 May 2005. Available: http://movies.yahoo.com.

Vadeboncoeur, Joan E. "Sounding Out Ben Burtt Jr.; CNY Native Played Off-Screen Role in All 6 'Star Wars' Films." *The Post-Standard* 26 May 2005. Accessed: 7 Jun. 2006. Available: http://www.highbeam.com.

"Vader Chokes Up Lex Luthor: Episode III Celebrity Reviews." *The Official Star Wars Web Site* 19 May 2005. Accessed: 15 Jun. 2006. Available: http://www.starwars.com.

Vancheri, Barbara. "'Star Wars' Top Film in a Down Season." *The Cincinnati Post* 8 Sep. 2005. Accessed: 19 Jun. 2006. Available: http://www.highbeam.com.

Verniere, James. "Lucas gets his 'Revenge'; 'Star Wars' returns to glory with 'Episode III'." Rev. of *Star Wars: Episode III—Revenge of the Sith. The Boston Herald* 14 May 2005. Accessed: 3 Jun. 2006. Available: http://www.highbeam.com.

"Video of the Week: 'Attack of the Clones'." *United Press International* 11 Nov. 2002. Accessed: 8 Sep. 2006. Available: http://www.highbeam.com.

Vincent, Mal. "Advance ticket sales show 'Star Wars' is still a force." *The Virginian Pilot* 30 Apr. 2005. Accessed: 14 Jun. 2006. Available: http://www.highbeam.com.

"Visions of Vader." *The Official Star Wars Web Site* 12 May 2005. Accessed: 17 Jun. 2006. Available: http://www.starwars.com.

"Visual Effects Society Announces 4th Annual VES Awards Winners." *Visual Effects Society* 16 Feb. 2006. Accessed: 29 Nov. 2006. Available: http://www.visualeffectssociety.com.

Vivarelli, Nick. "Italians find 'Sith' a summer snooze." *Variety* 26 Jun. 2005. Accessed: 27 Jun. 2005. Available: http://www.variety.com.

Vogel, Ed. "Nevada gaming regulators approve slot machines with 'Star Wars' theme." *Las Vegas Review-Journal* 27 Aug. 2004. Accessed: 18 Jun. 2006. Available: http://www.highbeam.com.

"Wal-Mart's Your Headquarters for Star Wars: Episode III Revenge of the Sith—Featuring Exclusive Merchandise and '48 Hours of the Force' Ultimate Star Wars Party." *PR Newswire* 30 Mar. 2005. Accessed: 27 Jun. 2005. Available: http://www.highbeam.com.

"'War' brings life to o'seas gate." *The Hollywood Reporter* 5 Jul. 2005. Accessed: 5 Jul. 2005. Available: http://www.hollywoodreporter.com.

Waugh, Rob. "Charge of the Light Brigade." *The Daily Mail* 8 May 2005. Accessed: 26 Jun. 2005. Available: http://www.highbeam.com.

———. "Lego Star Wars: the Force is strong with this one." Rev. of *LEGO Star Wars* (video game). *The Evening Standard* 11 Apr. 2005. Accessed: 7 Jun. 2006. Available: http://www.highbeam.com.

———. "Space Oddity; Think you're a devoted Star Wars fan? Rob Waugh meets the world's number one collector." *The Daily Mail* 8 May 2005. Accessed: 2 Jun. 2006. Available: http://www.highbeam.com.

———. "The Billion Dollar Man." *The Daily Mail* 8 May 2005. Accessed: 3 Jun. 2006. Available: http://www.highbeam.com.

Wellner, Allison Stein. "Reel Appeal." *The Chronicle of Philanthropy* 6 Apr. 2006. Accessed: 5 Sep. 2006. Available: http://www.philanthropy.com.

Wells, Tish. "A 'Star Wars' fan film is born." *Knight Ridder Washington Bureau* 17 Mar. 2005. Accessed: 3 Jun. 2006. Available: http://www.highbeam.com.

———. "No films draw fan filmmakers like 'Star Wars'." *Knight Ridder Washington Bureau* 17 Mar. 2005. Accessed: 4 Jun. 2006. Available: http://www.highbeam.com.

———. "'Star Wars Revelations' a sophisticated fan film." *Knight Ridder Washington Bureau* 13 Apr. 2005. Accessed: 7 Jun. 2006. Available: http://www.highbeam.com.

Welych, Maria T. "Eager to See 'Star Wars'? Check Out This Parody." *The Post-Standard* 11 May 2005. Accessed: 15 Jun. 2006. Available: http://www.highbeam.com.

"What did you think of AOTC?" *TheForce.net.* Accessed: 25 Jun. 2005. Available: http://www.theforce.net.

"What Do President Bush, Lindsay Lohan and Star Wars Have in Common? They Topped Ask Jeeves Search Categories in 2005." *PR Newswire* 22 Dec. 2005. Accessed: 19 Jun. 2006. Available: http://www.highbeam.com.

"What is the title of Episode III?" *TheForce.net.* Accessed: 29 Nov. 2006. Available: http://www.theforce.net.

"What's your Star Wars IQ?" *Entertainment Weekly* 1 Apr. 2005: 30–33, 35.

"Where do you rank Episode II among the *Star Wars* films?" *The Official Star Wars Web Site* 22 May 2002. Accessed: 25 Jun. 2005. Available: http://www.starwars.com.

White, Kathy. "'Star Wars Flu' May Strike IT Productivity." *Publish* 19 May 2005. Accessed: 21 May 2005. Available: http://www.publish.com.

———. "Star Wars Remains Ahead of the Digital Curve." *Publish* 17 May 2005. Accessed: 17 May 2005. Available: http://www.publish.com.

Williams, David E. "The Circle is Now Complete." *Cinefantastique* Vol. 37, No. 3 Jun. 2005: 20–22, 70.

Williams, John. Interview with Martin Steinberg. "Q&A: 'Star Wars' composer John Williams." *AP Worldstream* 13 May 2005. Accessed: 15 Jun. 2006. Available: http://www.highbeam.com.

Wilmington, Michael. Rev. of *Star Wars: Episode III—Revenge of the Sith. Chicago Tribune* 16 May 2005. Accessed: 15 Jun. 2006. Available: http://www.highbeam.com.

Wilson, Johanna D. "Experts, parents weigh in on PG-13-rated movie 'Episode III—Revenge of the Sith'." *The Sun News* 18 May 2005. Accessed: 20 Jul. 2006. Available: http://www.highbeam.com.

Wiltshire, Jo and Mike Goodridge. "Return of the Jedis; Star Wars was labour of love for Samuel L. Jackson, but fellow Jedi knight Ewan McGregor wanted to be in the films for a very different reason: his children." *The Daily Mail* 8 May 2005. Accessed: 7 Jun. 2006. Available: http://www.highbeam.com.

"Win Admiration … and a Pinball Game By Seeing *Revenge* This Weekend." *The Official Star Wars Web Site* 8 Jun. 2005. Accessed: 15 Jun. 2006. Available: http://www.starwars.com.

Windolf, Jim. "Star Wars: The Last Battle." *Vanity Fair* Feb. 2005: 108–21, 166–67.

Wolf, Jessica. "'Star Wars Trilogy' DVD details unveiled." *Video Store Magazine* 12 Sep. 2004. Accessed: 18 Jun. 2006. Available: http://www.highbeam.com.

Wood, Matthew. Interview with CelebrityCloseups.com. "'Star Wars Celebration III' Matthew Wood Interview Video." Accessed: 30 Nov. 2006. Available: http://www.celebritycloseups.com/videos/CelebrationIII/SWC3-MW.htm.

———. Interview with starwars.com. "Online Chat: Matthew Wood." *Star Wars Insider* Jan./Feb. 2006: 80–81.

"World of Warcraft Surpasses Five Million Customers Worldwide." *Blizzard Entertainment* 19 Dec. 2005. Accessed: 1 Aug. 2006. Available: http://www.blizzard.com.

Yalonen, Din. "You are either for or against Star Wars." Rev. of *Star Wars: Episode III—Revenge of the Sith. Catholic New Times* 19 Jun. 2005. Accessed: 9 Jun. 2006. Available: http://www.highbeam.com.

Yancey, Kitty Bean. "Puke skywalkers can rest queasy on Virgin Atlantic." *USA Today* 3 Jun. 2005: 1D.

Yeldell, Cynthia. "Last 'Star Wars' installment poised to keep registers beeping more than R2-D2." *The Knoxville News-Sentinel* 18 May 2005. Accessed: 7 Jun. 2006. Available: http://www.highbeam.com.

"Yoda: Recycle You Must, or the Dark Side You Invite; Earth911.Org's Top Five Ways to Recycle & Reuse Star Wars Souvenirs." *Business Wire* 17 May 2005. Accessed: 7 Jun. 2006. Available: http://www.highbeam.com.

Youngs, Ian. "Fan frenzy for Star Wars finale." *BBC News* 17 May 2005. Accessed: 24 May 2005. Available: http://news.bbc.co.uk.

Zisko, Allison. "Star Wars Presents New Opportunity for Kurt Adler." *Home Furnishing Network Newspaper* 3 Oct. 2005. Accessed: 19 Jun. 2006. Available: http://www.highbeam.com.

Zolkos, Rodd. "Will Sith's revenge be insurance claims?" *Business Insurance* 23 May 2005. Accessed: 26 Jun. 2005. Available: http://www.highbeam.com.

Zollinger, John. "Lucasfilm Donates $175 Million to USC." *USC Today* 20 Sep. 2006. Accessed: 1 Dec. 2006. Available: http://www.usc.edu.

Index

978-0-595-87533-7
0-595-87533-5

Printed in the United States
83961LV00006B/10/A